Chester Bowles—New Dealer in the Cold War

CHESTER BOWLES
New Dealer in the
Cold War

Howard B. Schaffer

An Institute for the Study
of Diplomacy Book

HARVARD UNIVERSITY PRESS
Cambridge, Massachusetts
London, England
1993

This book is printed on recycled and acid-free paper, and its
binding materials have been chosen for strength and durability.

Library of Congress Cataloging-in-Publication Data
Schaffer, Howard B.
Chester Bowles : new dealer in the Cold War /
Howard B. Schaffer.
p. cm.
"An Institute for the Study of Diplomacy book."
Includes bibliographical references (p.   ) and index.
ISBN 0-674-11390-X (acid-free paper)
1. Bowles, Chester, 1901–1986.
2. Ambassadors—United States—Biography.
3. Ambassadors—India—Biography.
4. United States—Foreign relations—1945–1990.
5. United States—Foreign relations—India.
6. India—Foreign relations—United States.
I. Georgetown University.
Institute for the Study of Diplomacy.
II. Title.
E748.B73S33 1993
327.2'092—dc20   93-12224
CIP

For Tezi, Mike, and Kim

Preface

I was United States ambassador in Bangladesh when Chester Bowles died in Connecticut in May 1986 at the age of eighty-five. The event brought back to me memories of the years in the 1960s when I had worked with him in the embassy in India and the State Department. I wondered at the time what kind of judgment history would eventually pass on this unusual and controversial man who had tried so hard to leave his mark on it.

When I returned to Washington, I was surprised to find how little had been written about him. He had set down autobiographical accounts in books of his own, but aside from unpublished oral histories prepared by those who knew him well, other assessments had mostly been brief narratives prompted by the many turning points in his crowded life. There had been no serious, systematic effort to consider his role in foreign affairs or in other aspects of public life.

An assignment by the State Department to the Center for the Study of Foreign Affairs at the Foreign Service Institute in 1989 gave me an opportunity to undertake this study of Bowles's foreign policy role, made more relevant by the momentous world events which have taken place in the years since his death. I was able to complete it with the generous support of the Institute for the Study of Diplomacy at Georgetown University. The book focuses largely on the period from 1951 to 1969, from the time Bowles became Harry Truman's ambassador to India to his retirement from public life.

Fascinating as his earlier careers in advertising, wartime administration, and politics often were, I have looked at them mainly for what they disclose about his ideas on foreign affairs and his capacity to become a major influence in the making of foreign policy when, at age fifty, he first made it his principal concern. I have dealt in a similarly limited way with his activities in domestic politics in the 1950s and 1960s.

In discussing the private Bowles I have tried to present the flavor of his personality, his values, and the way he operated, paying special heed again to how these influenced his foreign policy role. I have left it to others to develop convincing psychological explanations about how he got to be the complex person he became.

My principal sources have been Bowles's own writings. These were voluminous. He wrote a long account of his years in public life; published two major books and several shorter ones on foreign policy; and prepared countless magazine articles, speeches, and lectures. He was also an energetic private correspondent and a prolific drafter of memoranda both as a government official and as a private citizen. From time to time he kept a diary. Much of this material, expertly catalogued, is in the Bowles Papers collection at the Yale University Library. The collection also includes valuable oral histories prepared by Bowles and people who had worked with him in his various incarnations.

Other useful material by and about Bowles is available in the presidential libraries and in the collected papers of some of his associates. The *Foreign Relations of the United States* volumes on South Asia proved a vital source for his views and activities during his first assignment as ambassador to India. The material covering the longer period of his second tenure in New Delhi has not been published, but I was successful in obtaining under the Freedom of Information Act many new, relevant documents to supplement those declassified earlier. Although they do not provide as complete a record as I would like of Bowles's efforts and accomplishments in India in the 1960s, they offer a sound basis for analyses and judgments.

I have also benefited from interviews with many of those who dealt with Bowles on foreign policy issues, including former Secretary of State Dean Rusk, former Secretary of Agriculture Orville Freeman, George Ball, Lucius D. Battle, McGeorge Bundy, Henry Byroade, Abram Chayes, Clark Clifford, Phillip Coombs, Everett Drumwright, J. William Fulbright, John Kenneth Galbraith, Selig Harrison, John Hubbard, Thomas Hughes, Pat Durand Jacobson, U. Alexis Johnson, Jean Joyce, Robert W. Komer, Samuel Lewis, Edward Logue, Inder Malhotra, Dilip Mukherjee, George C. McGhee, Jagat Singh Mehta, Brij Kumar Nehru, Paul H. Nitze, James Reston, Walt W. Rostow, Arthur M. Schlesinger, Jr., David Schneider, Phillips Talbot, James C. Thomson, Jr., and the late Carol Laise Bunker and T. Eliot Weil. Sally

Bowles was also most generous in sharing with me her recollections of her father. Sessions with old friends who served with me in New Delhi during Bowles's second assignment there proved especially valuable.

As one would expect, the assessments of Bowles by those I interviewed varied greatly. But for most of them, he was as arresting a figure as he was for me, and I found them willing and pleased to stretch their memories back twenty-five years and more to give me their recollections.

Many people have been generous with their time in helping me shape this book. I'm particularly grateful to Margery Boichel Thompson, director of publications at the Institute for the Study of Diplomacy at Georgetown University, for her invaluable editing and resourceful efforts in arranging for the book to be published. Jean Joyce was tremendously helpful in bringing to bear both her many recollections of Chester Bowles and her great skill with a blue pencil. The staffs at the presidential libraries and at the Yale University Library provided valuable assistance. I wish to cite especially the contributions of David Humphrey at the LBJ Library, Dwight Standberg at the Eisenhower Library, and William Massa at Yale. I would also like to thank my Georgetown student and friend James Rutter for helping me get started on the work. I am grateful to Katherine Bruner for her expert indexing.

Many of those who were acquainted with Bowles's work were kind enough to read through all or a part of the text and offer me their comments. They include Lucius Battle, Douglas Bennet, Jr., David Blee, Sally Bowles, Richard Celeste, Stephen P. Cohen, Carleton and Jane Coon, Robert Goheen, Brandon Grove, Jr., Fred Hill, Thomas Hughes, Abid Hussain, John P. Lewis, Samuel Lewis, Charles Lindblom, David Schneider, Herbert Spivack, James Thomson, Jr., Thomas Thornton, Nicholas Veliotes, Michael Vlahos, and Howard Wriggins. Unusual as it may be in the preface of a book of this sort, I also want to tip my hat to the Baltimore Orioles, especially Brady Anderson, Chris Hoiles, and Mike Mussina. Their unexpectedly fine performance in the 1992 season kept my adrenalin flowing just as the book was coming to completion.

Finally, I need to acknowledge the devoted support of my family. My uncle, Jerome Bruner, provided valuable psychological insights into Bowles's personality as well as warm encouragement as I sought to join him among the family's authors. My mother, Minnie Schaffer, and my mother-in-law, Teresita Sparre Currie, herself a biographer, were also most supportive. My two sons, Mike and Kim, were valiant in putting up with more talk about Bowles around the family dinner table than they probably relished. But my most heartfelt tribute must go to my wife, Ambassador Teresita Currie Schaffer. It may be trite to say so, but I truly believe that without her I could never have written this book.

Contents

Illustrations

Following p. 112. Illustrations are courtesy of Chester Bowles Papers, Manuscripts and Archives, Yale University Library, unless otherwise indicated.

Chester Bowles—New Dealer in the Cold War

Introduction: An Idealistic Vision of America's National Purpose

WHEN President Harry S. Truman offered to make him ambassador to Jawaharlal Nehru's India in the spring of 1951, Chester Bowles was already a prominent figure in American public life. Just turned fifty, he had made a small fortune in the advertising business in New York during the Depression years, then gone on to Washington to play an effective and highly visible role as wartime head of the Office of Price Administration. These early successes paved the way for his entry into postwar elective politics. An ardent New Dealer despite his family's longtime allegiance to the Republican party, he became the Democratic governor of Connecticut in 1948 in a closely contested race. His national standing as a thoughtful, outspoken liberal and his performance in Hartford made him appear, in the late 1940s, eminently eligible to become Truman's successor in the White House. But, to his dismay, the voters of his state put his political ambitions on temporary hold by rejecting his bid for reelection, despite his accomplishments in enacting far-reaching reforms during his two-year term. He was angling for something important to do in government operations overseas when the call came from the president.

Few who knew Bowles would have predicted that Truman's offer would be a crucial turning point in his life. He had taken considerable interest in international affairs both before and after the war and had briefly held several foreign policy positions, but he had focused his major attention much more on domestic matters. In 1951, the smart money would have bet that Bowles would bring to the embassy in New Delhi the same creativity, energy, and enthusiasm that had won him fortune in Manhattan, fame and respect in Washington, and political power in Connecticut, but that after two years or so in India foreign policy would again move back to second place on his professional agenda. The ambassadorship would no doubt look good on his résumé as he returned to the domestic political battlefields; it would certainly not mark the beginning of two decades focused on international affairs.

To his friends' surprise, and very possibly his own, it did. In the 1950s and 1960s, at home and abroad, Bowles was one of the leading liberal lights on the American foreign policy scene. When Dwight D. Eisenhower's 1952 election victory brought Bowles's impressive performance in New Delhi to an early end, he returned to Connecticut and became a chief Democratic party spokesman and adviser on international affairs. He spoke and wrote extensively on foreign policy issues. As a freshman congressman at the end of the decade, he played a highly active role on the House Foreign Affairs Committee and served as foreign policy adviser to Senator John F. Kennedy during his campaign for the Democratic presidential nomination. Disappointed when Kennedy did not make him secretary of state, he accepted the second slot in the department under Dean Rusk. His relations with Kennedy and Rusk became increasingly difficult, and after less than a year he was dismissed and kicked upstairs to become the president's special representative and adviser on Asian, African, and Latin American affairs. In 1963, a decade after he had completed his first ambassadorial assignment, Bowles returned to India for what proved to be a six-year stint. He left New Delhi in 1969, following the return to power of the Republicans under Richard M. Nixon, and retired from public life.

▾   ▾   ▾

Bowles was a remarkable man, important and interesting in his own right. But his significance in foreign affairs goes beyond his immediate, often limited, achievements. His career provides broad insights into the objectives of U.S. foreign policy and the way it is made. It has particular contemporary relevance as the United States debates its role in a world suddenly made less threatening, yet more challenging, by the end of the Cold War. The part Bowles played at the height of the Cold War as the standard bearer of idealism and liberal interventionism raises in particular this fundamental issue: is there a higher American purpose beyond immediate national interests, and, if there is, how should the United States pursue it?

Bowles had been a young admirer of the universalist tenets of Woodrow Wilson, and perhaps more than any major figure of his time he believed that U.S. foreign policy should be guided by American values and principles. For him, these were the liberal political, economic, and social ideals he had imbibed during the New Deal and sought to put into practice when he took the job of price administrator and later governor of Connecticut. He was convinced that these ideals—"the continuing American revolution"—could inspire and move leaders and peoples everywhere, whatever their countries' historical experience and current circumstances. The United States should promote these principles worldwide, he contended, not by the exercise of military power but by supporting the forces of political democracy, economic progress, and social justice abroad, and by setting exemplary standards in its practices at home. He called for "a good America, a strong America [as] a vehicle for the betterment of life in all corners of the world" and "an instrument in the creation of a truly world society."[1]

These views set him apart from most other foreign policy practitioners and commentators of the time. Many of them considered him the ultimate unreconstructed, out-of-date liberal, a woolly-minded New Dealer beyond his intellectual depth in an America confronted by the harsh challenges of the Cold War. They also regarded him, more accurately, as an outsider, drawn neither from the foreign policy establishment of lawyers, bankers, and academics who moved in and out of government during the 1950s and 1960s nor from the foreign affairs community itself, the Foreign Service officers and career civil servants who permanently staffed the State Department and other foreign policymaking organizations.

Bowles agreed with these much-praised "wise men" that the "free world" faced dangerous challenges from Moscow and Peking and that the United States needed to take the lead in containing Communist power. He devised his foreign policy constructs in a Cold War context and considered them not only morally just and in accord with America's historic purpose but also effective containment strategy. He took issue, however, with many of the containment policies adopted by successive administrations, a disagreement most notable in his view of the role of the military. A realist as well as an idealist, Bowles was not, as his detractors sometimes alleged, unmindful of the need for powerful armed forces. In his view, the United States had to be prepared to respond credibly and flexibly to the threat of aggression from Communist powers. Nor was he in any way "soft on Communism," another charge leveled against him. But he resented and resisted the militarization of foreign policy that had begun in 1950 in the Truman administration. He believed that effective use of military force had narrow limits. He did not want U.S. foreign policies to ignore the power of the gun, but to stress also the power of the ideas that had made America a distinct society, "a city set upon a hill" with a message for the world.

Nowhere, in Bowles's view, were such policies more needed than in the Third World, the vast belt of poor, often politically fragile countries of Asia, Africa, and Latin America. Differing again with many members of the largely Eurocentric foreign policy establishment of his time, he maintained that the fate of the globe would turn on what happened in this Third World. Though he acknowledged that a firm commitment to the security of Western Europe had to be the bedrock of U.S. foreign policy, the Third World became the focus of his attention and his creative energies. His fundamental, long-held position was that the United States needed to stress "positive" policies that would identify it with the aspirations of Third World leaders and peoples, not "negative" ones such as military measures designed simply to thwart Communist threats.

A major element in Bowles's approach was his insistence that Washington recognize the potency of nationalism and accept the preferences of many Third World governments, such as Nehru's, for independent, nonaligned foreign policies. He was confident that the appeal of nationalism could counteract both external Communist challenges to Third World countries and the more menacing danger he found in the seductive attractiveness of Communism to their illiterate, poverty-stricken masses. For years he argued that the United States should mobilize Asian nationalism against the threat of Chinese Communist expansionism in Southeast Asia and elsewhere, not by drawing Asian countries into the Western security system but by encouraging and providing behind-the-scenes support for an indigenous Asian Monroe Doctrine led by India. As he looked for more effective ways to contain Communist China, a country that both fascinated and frightened him, he also explored approaches that could moderate the behavior of the Peking regime and reduce its ties to the Soviet Union. Like so many of Bowles's initiatives, these endeavors often brought him into sharp conflict with powerful contemporaries more ideologically rigid or less politically courageous than he was.

Economic assistance to the developing world was another major item on Bowles's "positive" foreign policy agenda. He believed that extensive, carefully programmed aid linked to precepts assuring its proper use, preferably in a democratic setting, could be an important Cold War tool. His emphasis in the immediate postwar years and long afterwards on the importance of foreign aid helped give it the centrality to U.S. policy toward the Third World it has had since the mid-1950s. But unlike many of his contemporaries, Bowles also saw foreign aid as a moral obligation that reflected the historic spirit and revolutionary principles of America. It represented for him the most rewarding and tangible aspect of America's postwar international role, the opportunity to export American wealth, experience, and values to help the world's poor help themselves to achieve better lives under free institutions. He believed such aid could foster a global New Deal that would bring about a just society for the common man, whose cause he championed at home and abroad.

▾　　　▾　　　▾

Bowles's ideas, ably set forth in a host of books, magazine articles, memoranda, speeches, and private correspondence, made him as unique and arresting a figure in his foreign policy years as he had been earlier in his life. He had great strengths: his enthusiastic and indefatigable energy, his creativity and skill as a wordsmith, his long-sighted approach to the great changes coursing through the mid-twentieth century world, and his ability to inspire younger people with his realistic idealism and devotion to public service. But he also suffered from glaring weaknesses: an inability to master the game of bureaucratic politics and to relate to his peers, a cultural insensitivity which led him to underestimate seriously the obstacles to the kinds of social and economic change he wanted the developing countries to undertake, a reputation as a visionary unwilling or unable to deal with immediate pressing problems, and an overidentification with the Third World in general and India in particular that reduced his credibility and effectiveness.

His influence and standing waxed and waned, leading him to private moments both of great hope and of bitter despair. He was enormously successful in his first assignment to India, where his role in winning greater understanding for U.S. policies and fostering the newly established economic assistance program contributed to a decided improvement in bilateral relations at a time when these had become badly frayed. As a leading Democratic foreign affairs spokesman later in the 1950s, he effectively propagated his liberal interventionist approach to foreign policy both within the party and outside. His failure to become a strong voice within the Kennedy administration and to persuade it to place less emphasis on military power was a terrible disappointment to him, especially since he had viewed the 1960 election, which brought Kennedy to power, as an opportunity for a historic breakthrough in America's approach to international affairs.

His long second ambassadorship to India in the 1960s was less productive than his first. He played a major part in the effort to bring about the reforms in food and agricultural policy that led to the Green Revolution. But he was frustrated in his determined campaign to develop a closer U.S.-Indian security relationship as a cornerstone of U.S. containment policy in Asia, and in his last years in New Delhi he saw India slip downward on the Johnson administration's foreign policy agenda, which was increasingly dominated by Vietnam. Highly skeptical of military solutions to political problems and concerned about the United States playing a colonialist role in Southeast Asia, he used his New Delhi perch, as he had his earlier ones in Washington, to try to influence U.S. policy in Indochina, with scant success.

Bowles was ambitious both for himself and for his country. He thought he might become president, and for years set his sights on being appointed secretary of state. Despite his frustrating setbacks, he never flagged in his persistent efforts to promote the fundamental changes he believed necessary for the preservation of American security and the flowering of American ideals in the postcolonial Cold War world. He would no doubt have seen in the outcome of the Cold War the triumph of these ideals and the vindication of his belief that they represented universal aspirations. He would today be in the forefront of those urging the United States to employ its resources, depleted as these have become, to sustain and strengthen free political institutions and more liberal and equitable economies in the former Communist world, much as he had called on it to do in Asia, Africa, and Latin America in the 1950s and 1960s.

The United States and the rest of the world are vastly different now from what they were then. The specific battles Bowles fought have long since ended, and the players and stakes have changed. As Dean Rusk observed, "Only the historians can determine who was right and who was wrong."[2] For the first time in forty-five years the United States faces an international system not dominated by a single crucial contest. In consequence, Americans are reexamining many of the larger foreign policy issues that Bowles's career highlighted. In this new context, there is surprising resonance in the story of this New Dealer who came to political maturity in the last decade of relative U.S. isolation and went on to promote, in the Cold War era, a distinctively American view of the world and an idealistic vision of America's national purpose.

1

Manhattan, Washington, and Hartford

LIKE many of the men who took part in foreign policymaking in the postwar decades, Chester Bowles came from a prominent, well-to-do Eastern establishment family of distinguished Yankee stock. The first Bowles to come over from England sailed into Boston harbor on a skiff called the *Hopewell* in 1632. The subsequent history of New England is studded with his ancestors and relatives. He was proud of them, despite the rock-ribbed Federalist or Republican views many of them held, and made a point of mentioning them from time to time in the historical analogies he cited to spice his writings and lectures on foreign affairs.

He reserved his greatest admiration for his grandfather, Samuel Bowles, the famous and outspoken editor of the Springfield (Massachusetts) *Republican,* who had made that small-town paper one of the most influential and widely circulated dailies in mid-nineteenth century America. The autocratic elder Bowles, a political as well as journalistic power in his day, played a major role in establishing the Republican party in the 1850s and was a strong supporter of Abraham Lincoln. Family legend has it that he also had a romantic connection with Emily Dickinson of nearby Amherst. Chester, who was born in Springfield in 1901, eighteen years after Samuel died, seems to have idolized the memory of his deceased grandfather and held him up as a model of political and social independence and courage he would do well to emulate. He especially loved to recall his grandfather's harsh condemnation of New York's corrupt Tweed Ring of Tammany Hall; so vitriolic were the *Republican*'s attacks that on a visit to Manhattan Samuel Bowles had been seized and jailed by city officials on the Tammany payroll. "My grandfather," Chester wrote, "was a man with strong views which he never hesitated to express."[1] The description would have been equally apt for Samuel Bowles's grandson.

Chester—Chet, as he would be called throughout his life—was the third child in the family and was considerably younger than his sister and brother. Their father, Charles Allen Bowles, who was forty-four when Chet was born, was in the paper manufacturing business; the *Republican* remained in the family but was run by other relatives. Chet remembered his father as a dyed-in-the-wool New England conservative: "[He] always felt that the less government you had the better and that government had no useful purpose except to put out fires and collect taxes to be utilized for such purposes as the police department."[2] Chet's mother, Nellie Harris Bowles, came from a Vermont manufacturing family. She had turned forty by the time of Chet's birth and is said to have protected him as the baby in the family. Like her husband, she was a deeply committed conservative Republican.

Chet lived a comfortable upper middle class life in Springfield. He attended the Springfield public schools and two Connecticut boarding schools, Choate at Wallingford and Roxbury in Cheshire. It was at Choate that he first met Adlai Stevenson, one year his senior.

Like many others in his family, Chet went on to Yale. His father had attended the university with the Class of 1883 and his brother, Charles Allen, Jr., had graduated with the Class of 1913. Bowles entered in 1921, and by what he recalled was an academic accident enrolled in the Sheffield Scientific School (as had his father and brother) rather than in the more prestigious liberal arts college. His life as an undergraduate there offered no clues about his future. He joined the Book and Snake fraternity and enjoyed the thriving social life available to well-to-do "preppies" at Ivy League colleges. He took the general scientific course, enrolled in a few liberal arts classes as well, and was an indifferent student, happy no doubt to get by with the "Cs" which were the mark of a gentleman in those days of raccoon coats and hip flasks.

Most of his intellectual interests and almost all of his intellectual attainments came later in his life. It was only in his late twenties and thirties, during his years in New York, that he undertook to read history, political science, and economics seriously and systematically, becoming, for all his Yale background, a self-educated man. By his own amused confession, his most noteworthy achievement in his college years seems to have been his election as captain of the Yale golf team and president of the Intercollegiate Golf Association.[3]

Bowles graduated in 1924 and remained a loyal Yale alumnus in later years. He met and spoke with student and faculty groups and used the university as a resource in his public life. As governor of

Connecticut, he served as an ex-officio trustee and later became an associate fellow. Many of the bright young people who surrounded him during his career had Yale backgrounds. He recruited some of these directly from the campus, especially the law school. In 1941 he had been discussing with University President Charles Seymour the possibility of returning to Yale in a senior administrative position—his title would have been chancellor—when Pearl Harbor intervened. Appropriately, his papers are lodged at the Yale library, and the memorial service following his death in 1986 was held at the university chapel.

▾   ▾   ▾

In his class yearbook, Bowles said that he intended to take up insurance or manufacturing.[4] He did neither, but returned instead to Springfield and the family newspaper, where he worked for about a year. He recalled that his interest in restoring the *Republican* to the prestige, integrity, and liberal orientation it had had under his grandfather and uncle was thwarted by his cousin Sherman Bowles, who tightly controlled the paper. (In the 1950s, after Sherman's death, he had an opportunity to buy the *Republican* but passed it up.)

He eventually drifted to New York, but his hope of entering big city journalism was upset by a major newspaper merger, which put dozens of experienced newsmen out of work just as he began looking for a job. Yale contacts helped him find a position in advertising, where he spent four years mostly writing copy for a major agency before breaking loose, in 1929, to found the firm of Benton & Bowles with William Benton, another Yale alumnus. The careers of that oddly matched couple—the short, egotistical, domineering Benton and the lanky, much more modest Bowles—remained intertwined long after they had sold their interests in the firm and separately entered public life.

Bowles was immensely successful in advertising. He brought to it the great capacity for fresh ideas—and an unswerving conviction that they were right—that was so much in evidence in his later career in foreign affairs. Among the many concepts he and Benton pioneered was the use by ad agencies of consumer surveys, later a standard practice. Bowles himself sometimes went from door to door querying housewives about their preferences to get a better understanding of the market. These polling ventures gave him some eye-opening impressions of America in the Depression years and had an important impact on his political thinking. He was also unusual in trying to get agency clients to improve their products and cut prices; the lower one-third of Americans were living in a separate economic world from that of the upper two-thirds, he maintained, and if businesses wanted to expand their markets they would have to set their prices low enough to enable that bottom third to buy. Clients such as Maxwell House Coffee and Columbia Records took his advice, to their benefit.[5]

While Benton and a third partner, Atherton Hobler, primarily serviced Benton & Bowles's fast-growing list of clients, Bowles headed the creative end of the business. His most outstanding contribution came in the fairly new field of radio advertising, where he developed the concept of packaging hour-long weekly programs with regular formats, casts, and sponsors. He not only provided the basic ideas for such top-ranking shows as the Maxwell House Showboat and the Palmolive Beauty Box Theater, but also saw to their scripts and production in the greatest detail. The programs were the first to create an image in the mind of the listener: so convincing was Bowles's imaginary *Showboat* moving along the Mississippi that people literally flocked to the Memphis dock to see it come in—and were disappointed when it all turned out to be make-believe. In these shows, effective plugs were so skillfully concealed in an atmosphere that fitted the product that the average listener hardly knew he was being sold. The novelty of the productions and their success in attracting large audiences and sharply boosting sponsors' sales made Bowles a major figure in the "golden age of radio" of the 1930s.

Benton & Bowles was noted on Madison Avenue for its ability to attract creative young people to its ranks. This was mostly Bowles's doing. A comment his associate James Rogers made about the way Bowles operated in his advertising days is interesting as a foretaste of his gift for leading and inspiring people when he entered public life:

> Chet stimulated people to look at things in a different way. . . . His standards for the presentation of any ideas were very, very high. . . . He was not a hard person to work for, in the sense that he was always very reasonable with everyone, but he wouldn't stand for sloppy work and was, I think, an excellent trainer. . . . He had a great talent for bringing people along, for sort of turning them inside out. He would encourage them not to worry if their ideas seemed a little screwy at the beginning, but he could stimulate them to try something new and different and not worry if it didn't sound like the standard way of doing things. . . . He was encouraging and supportive and the result was that a high percentage of the people who worked for him were devoted to him, and therefore were the more anxious to do things as he wanted them done.[6]

By the mid-1930s, Benton & Bowles had come to dominate radio entertainment; of the four shows with the largest audiences it produced three. Its billings shot up to make it the nation's sixth largest advertising agency. Bowles's personal income also rose meteorically. He had been lured into advertising in 1925 by an offer of $25 a week. By the mid-1930s, he was making $250,000 a year, an impressive sum in those hard times. The success of the agency was particularly remarkable because it came in the worst of the Depression. The two young partners had organized the agency on $5,000 of borrowed capital in July 1929, three months before the Wall Street crash. Bowles believed that the distress of the Depression actually helped the firm. The management of most corporations, under pressure from falling sales and profits, was in a mood for change, and firing their advertising agencies and taking on new ones was one way of proving to directors and share-holders that they were on the job.

In later years, when conservative critics blasted him as an impractical liberal do-gooder, Bowles would point out that far more than many of them he had been successful in the business world and had met large payrolls in the worst of times. But he was generally reluctant to talk about his experience in advertising. He wrote later that he thought the reason for his reticence was his having mixed feelings about those years in Manhattan. From his early twenties he had thought about a career in public service. A long-standing legend has it that he had promised himself that once he made a million dollars he would sell his share of the business. This was also said of Benton and is probably apocryphal in both cases. What Bowles *was* determined to do was to leave adver-tising for public life by the time he was thirty-five. Benton's own departure in 1936 and the problems this caused the firm ruled out his meeting that deadline, and he continued in active management of Benton & Bowles until early 1942, when he was forty. He later con-cluded that he would have been happier and more effective if he had not delayed and had gone into public service immediately after gradu-ating from Yale.[7]

His attitude in later years was that Madison Avenue had been an important episode in his life, but it was over. He did not welcome efforts to recall his business background once he entered public life. When his Connecticut supporters wanted him to organize a business-men's committee to back his candidacy as a fellow businessman, he turned them down. As a senior State Department official, he confided to associates that he was embarrassed by the continuing use of his name in Benton & Bowles, which remained a leading advertising firm under its new management. He was ambivalent about the money he had accumulated in his advertising days. While he recognized that it had assured him greater independence and had paved the way for the careers that opened for him later, he did not want to identify himself with the rich and seemed almost ashamed of his prosperity. His attitude toward wealth was reflected in a distaste for ostentation and conspicuous consumption that was particularly evident in later years in the style he adopted as ambassador to India.

Bowles brought from Madison Avenue to his later careers the experience of running a large operation and some firm ideas about effective management practices. His background in advertising also made him a highly skilled publicist and promoter. Few in public life during his best years there could rival his talent and energy as a salesman of ideas. His use of the media in innovative and imaginative ways, his lifelong interest in polling techniques, and an ability to write in brief declarative sentences which avoided what he called twenty-five-dollar words were other important legacies of his advertising days.

The advertising background also left marks not universally applauded. One was his practice as ambassador of loading the policy options he presented to Washington in ways that favored the one he preferred. "If there's one thing I learned in the advertising business," he told a New Delhi embassy officer, "it was to make people think they have a choice but not give them one."[8] A more serious failing was his proclivity to be highly repetitive, especially when he was arguing for something important to him, as often happened. To derisive critics at the State Department and elsewhere in the 1950s and 1960s, he sometimes seemed to be marketing foreign policy as if it were a breakfast cereal or a dentifrice.

Bowles was one of the few major figures in foreign affairs who came from the advertising business. The only other with a substantial ad agency background was his partner Benton, who had preceded him into public life and served during Truman's first term as assistant secretary of state for public affairs. In later years, Bowles's detractors would sometimes sniff at his Madison Avenue origins, which they regarded as considerably less impressive than the experience in law and banking they themselves brought to the conduct of foreign policy. Typically, Dean Acheson was the most acerbic on this score. Writing to Yale Law School Dean Eugene Rostow about Bowles (and Benton) in 1958, Truman's secretary of state reflected that "time spent in the advertising business seems to create a permanent deformity, like the Chinese habit of footbinding."[9]

▾   ▾   ▾

In 1925 Bowles married Julia (Judy) Fisk of Springfield. An attractive and vivacious debutante, she and Chet became well-known figures on the New York social scene. They had two children, Chester, Jr. (Chessie), and Barbara, before they were divorced in 1932. On a vacation cruise the following year Bowles renewed his acquaintance with Dorothy Stebbins, a friend of Judy's from their Vassar days. "Steb," who had been raised in Newton, Massachusetts, had done postgraduate studies in social work at Smith College and was then traveling director of the national Junior League. They were married the next winter in Newton.

A warm, outgoing woman of great humanity, broad social and artistic interests, and keen political sense, Steb Bowles was a remarkable person both in her own right and as an influence and help to Bowles throughout their married life. They were thoroughly devoted to one another. For all his contacts and friends at home and abroad, Chet was fundamentally a lonely, somewhat shy man, and Steb was able to give him the companionship and love he needed. She also brought into his life a gaiety and fun which helped leaven his earnestness. In a career marked by dizzying successes and embittering disappointments, she was the constant he needed to get him through.

The Bowleses were very much a team. Chet drew Steb into all of his important decisions, and on those few occasions when he did not take her advice he often rued his mistake later. India offered a woman of her interests and temperament a special opportunity to play a highly visible role in his efforts. She was able during his two assignments there to reach out well beyond the upper-crust, Westernized circle of Indians that surrounds senior diplomats to win admirers for herself, fresh contacts for Bowles, and friends for the United States.

Bowles had three children by his second marriage: Cynthia, Sally, and Sam. The children, then of school age, accompanied their parents to India in 1951. They figure prominently in the book Bowles wrote about those years, *Ambassador's Report*. Cynthia herself authored a book about her Indian experiences, *At Home in India*.

▾   ▾   ▾

Although he personally prospered, Bowles was profoundly affected by the Depression. Before then, his interest in liberal social and political causes had been limited. As a high school student, he had come under the influence of his father's older sister, Mrs. Ruth Standish Baldwin, and remained close to her long into his adult life. A friend of Norman Thomas, she was a mild socialist and a pacifist. Her husband had founded the National Urban League, a welfare organization for black Americans. Bowles, who later served on the Urban League board, proudly recalled that Mrs. Baldwin had resigned as a Smith College trustee when the visiting black educator Booker T. Washington was not permitted to eat in the campus dining room.

Mrs. Baldwin's views on politics, foreign affairs, and civil rights differed sharply from the rigidly orthodox Republicanism of the Bowles household. But in college and in his earlier years in Manhattan, her influence was not much in evidence. Bowles seemed more concerned in those days with his golf game (he had a handicap of three and competed for the national amateur championship) than he was with the lot of the underdog.

The Depression changed this and convinced Bowles that radical changes in America's philosophy of economics and government were essential. His growing concerns about social issues may have helped bring about his estrangement from Judy and his dissatisfaction with the society life she continued to relish. Unlike Judy, Steb shared these concerns, and many of Bowles's old friends are convinced that his marriage to her in 1934 was crucial in confirming him in the beliefs he held as the liberal activist he remained for the rest of his life. In an interview years later, Bowles spoke of Steb's "extraordinary social conscience and great awareness of all that was going on" in the Depression years, saying that she was the most important influence in determining his course at that time.[10]

Bowles became an outspoken New Dealer. Like other "traitors to his class," he also became a great admirer of FDR. In his case, the admiration extended not only to Roosevelt's economic and social programs, but to his management techniques as well. Disagreeing with many critics, he considered the president an effective administrator whose unorthodox approach helped overcome the inflexibility of old-line agencies and hardened bureaucrats. He sought to follow Roosevelt's lead—often to the consternation of those affected by his management practices—when he later held senior government positions.

▾   ▾   ▾

America's entry into the Second World War provided an opportunity for Bowles to pursue his interest in public service. A bad ear ruled out active duty in the navy, and soon after Pearl Harbor he left Benton & Bowles to set up a statewide tire rationing system at the request of the governor of Connecticut. (He had been associated with the state since

1936, when he bought a house in Old Saybrook and began to spend weekends there.) A few months later he became Connecticut district director of the newly established federal Office of Price Administration. He was soon recognized as one of the most outstanding of the state directors and in July 1943 was called to OPA national headquarters.

When Bowles came to Washington, OPA was in deep political and administrative difficulties. Its first administrator had been Leon Henderson, a brilliant New Deal economist whom FDR had reportedly chosen because he was "the toughest bastard in town." Henderson's initiatives, aimed at establishing a legal basis for economic controls, had triggered bitter opposition from congressmen and from business, labor, and farm interests eager to make money after the lean years of the Depression. He was ultimately successful in these efforts and in recruiting to top agency positions a group of gifted lawyers and economists such as David Ginsburg (general counsel) and John Kenneth Galbraith (deputy administrator for price), two men with whom Bowles became close in later years. But Henderson was unable to win the support and understanding OPA needed from the public, Congress, and economic interest groups. He became the target of every conceivable pressure group and was widely disliked on Capitol Hill. Sick, battered, and tired, he resigned under pressure in December 1942.[11]

The appointment as Henderson's successor of Prentiss Brown, a recently defeated liberal Democratic senator from Michigan who had strongly supported controls, was designed to improve the deteriorating relations between OPA and the Hill. Brown's efforts to placate Congress with the promise of a more flexible policy on controls were not successful in satisfying opponents of OPA there. He too was soon beleaguered. Intramural battling over policy between New Deal economists and conservative businessmen working in senior OPA positions led to a spate of resignations. Galbraith quit under fire and a few weeks later his rival for influence, agency Public Relations Director Lou Maxon—an anti-New Deal advertising executive Brown had brought to Washington—also left the agency. In a sharply worded statement that made headlines, Maxon let loose against impractical, leftist professors and theorists who, in his words, were trying to "force radical and dangerous concepts on the public under the excuse of wartime needs." OPA's young lawyers had bound the agency in red tape Houdini himself couldn't untangle, he charged.[12]

Following Maxon's exit in the summer of 1943, Brown turned to Bowles, whom he asked to become general manager and deputy head of the agency. An expert yachtsman, Bowles was sailing at that time off Cape Cod on a rare vacation in his seventy-two foot schooner *Nordlys,* and it took the Coast Guard days to track him down. When he reached Washington he told Brown that no sensible person would seek the general manager's job, but accepted it nonetheless. OPA by then was at a low point; it seemed ready either to fall apart or to be torn apart by angry businessmen, confused housewives, and a furious Congress. Brown was rumored to be on his way out, and indeed he resigned in October. Early in November Bowles was confirmed by the Senate as the new OPA administrator.

It was said at the time that optimists gave Bowles six weeks to keep the agency afloat. He rose to the occasion, immediately undertaking a sweeping reorganization of the agency. He quickly moved to simplify regulations and, as he later did in Connecticut with great success, to decentralize responsibility. These new management practices were highly effective in strengthening OPA and holding the line against inflation.

Characteristically, Bowles was able to identify talent (this time in the business world) and persuade those he had spotted to join OPA. He worked out a successful modus operandi among the businessmen, lawyers, and economists on his staff and proved a tough scrapper against such bureaucratic adversaries as Interior Secretary Harold Ickes, the Old Curmudgeon whom FDR had made wartime petroleum administrator. Much more adept than his predecessors had been in dealing with Congress, Bowles treated members with a respect and urbanity they appreciated and wooed them with special services, setting up an office on Capitol Hill where they could readily register their gripes and establishing a facility to answer their constituents' complaints about OPA practices. Congressmen welcomed his candor and the confessions of agency shortcomings he interspersed with his appeals for support. His advertising background helped: he was the first head of a civilian federal agency to use easy-to-understand charts in presentations to congressional committees. Aware that he would be accused of employing Madison Avenue techniques, Bowles saw to it that the charts looked quite rough-and-ready, to avoid charges that he was being unduly slick. The practice was soon widely copied.

Bowles also drew more broadly on his publicist's skills. Convinced, as he always was, that reasonable explanations of policies would evoke constructive public responses, he used a regular weekly radio program, magazine articles, and a spate of press releases to describe the objectives of OPA programs, detail the problems the agency faced, and win support. As he had in Connecticut, where he had recruited a mix of school teachers, businessmen, labor leaders, farmers, doctors, clergy-men, and other representative citizens to staff local rationing boards, he succeeded in involving the public as much as possible in OPA operations. He saw this, correctly, as a way to develop greater confidence in an organization whose work—especially rationing—was inherently unpopular. He also brought about greater business partici-pation in OPA by establishing a plethora of advisory committees for controlled and rationed products. This technique reduced business opposition and suspicion and helped Bowles develop a much better relationship with the business community than his predecessors had achieved.

OPA was remarkably effective in containing inflationary pressures. From the time FDR issued his "hold the line" order in April 1943, directing that no further price increases be allowed save under excep-tional circumstances, to the spring of 1946, the consumer price index rose only 3.4 percent. Wholesale industrial price figures went up 4.8 percent. Even allowing for a deterioration of quality, this was vastly better than the experience of the First World War, when the cost of living had risen 108 percent and industrial prices had skyrocketed 165 percent. This impressive record was achieved despite increasing pres-sure to allow price rises or even to abandon controls altogether fol-lowing the end of the war in August 1945.[13]

The postwar call for scrapping controls was led by Senator Robert Taft of Ohio. Over the previous years, the powerful Republican con-servative had emerged as one of the most bitter critics of OPA and of Bowles personally. Bowles fought back hard. He and others had been unsuccessful in earlier efforts to win administration support for a program to reduce the pressure of accumulated purchasing power through higher taxes, compulsory savings, or a combination of the two. Fearful in 1946 that these pent-up dollars could trigger an infla-tionary spiral similar to the one that caused economic havoc at the end of the First World War, he urged that controls be kept until postwar production could absorb the excess cash. This situation led to a series of increasingly bitter and hard-fought battles within the administration and on the Hill.

Bowles's last months in Washington were a time of frustration and setbacks for him. In January 1946 his effort to hold down steel prices was challenged by John Snyder, who had recently become director of War Mobilization and Reconversion. When President Truman backed Snyder, Bowles felt he had no choice but to resign. He did not leave Washington, however. Instead, he was persuaded to accept the leadership of the Office of Economic Stabilization, a newly revived super-agency with the power to set policies on all programs relating to the control of rents, prices, production, and wages, but which lacked operational responsibilities. He remained there from February until June, fighting the good fight to hold down inflation against an angry chorus of charges that he wanted to continue controls to perpetuate his own power and impose socialism on the country. When, in June 1946, Congress gutted the Price Control Act, he recommended that Truman veto the legislation and again resigned. Truman accepted the resignation, which Bowles had submitted to remove himself as a factor in the climactic debate on the future of controls. The president also followed his advice in rejecting the legislation, but the vetoed bill was replaced by one not much better, which Truman then accepted. As Bowles had foreseen, prices soon shot upward.[14]

By the time he left Washington to return to Connecticut after this setback, Bowles's name had long since become a household word. More than any other civilian agency, OPA had affected the life of every American. His recognition by the public as its sympathetic and coura-geous chief was heightened by his frequent radio broadcasts and ex-tensive travel. For all the criticism and bad jokes leveled against OPA and the occasional blunders that helped spark them, the agency was generally regarded as effective and fair in its efforts to curb inflation, assure the equitable sharing of wartime burdens, and stem profiteering. Bowles rightly received a good deal of the credit, and was seen as an able administrator and a personable advocate.

Time, rarely a fan of New Deal Democrats, put it well in reporting easy congressional approval of the extension of OPA in March 1945. The turnabout in attitudes, the magazine found, "is partly due to belated recognition by civilians of the fact that wartime price control is necessary. But it is chiefly a tribute to Chester Bowles, who is often described in Washington, a town of masterminds, as a man of ordinary intellect who knows how to talk to the public and to Congressmen, i.e., other men of ordinary intellect."[15]

Aside from the favorable national exposure OPA leadership pro-vided, Bowles's experience in wartime Washington also gave him an intimate familiarity with congressional and bureaucratic corridors of power and useful associations throughout the country. These ranged from Roosevelt and Truman down to the tens of thousands of employ-ees and unpaid volunteers who staffed the OPA operation. They in-cluded important leaders of farm organizations and labor unions. These contacts were a major asset in Bowles's later political incarnation, but he also accumulated liabilities. Powerful conservative Republicans such as Taft and his Senate colleagues Kenneth Wherry and Homer Capehart never forgave Bowles for his alleged sins at OPA and OES, and they and others in the right wing of the GOP remained his staunch political enemies for years afterwards.

▾   ▾   ▾

Bowles's Washington experience both whetted his interest in politics and improved his prospects for political success. He had known Eleanor Roosevelt socially when he was still in advertising, and it was her suggestion in 1938 that he run for office that first led him to think about the possibility. His subsequent interest in becoming a candidate at some point was supported by Connecticut Democratic leader Frank Maloney. In 1943, when Roosevelt chose Bowles to head OPA, Maloney extracted from FDR an agreement to release him the following year in time to run for the U.S. Senate. When Bowles's preoccupation with the OPA congressional budget request in early 1944 ruled out a bid, Maloney then suggested that he run instead for governor; the announcement of a gubernatorial candidacy could be made later than that of a bid for the Senate.[16]

Bowles wrote to Roosevelt in late June 1944 about his interest in the governorship, leaving it to FDR to decide whether he should run or stay on at OPA. "I am told," he said, "that I could probably win the nomination, and with strong labor support and a good knowledge of the state, I assume that I would have a 50–50 chance of being elected."[17] Roosevelt opted for Bowles to continue as price administrator. In a letter addressed to "Dear Chester" a few days later, the president wrote: "I would not want to stand in the way of your seeking the nomination for Governor if that is your ambition, but I am satisfied that you can perform an even greater service in the national field."[18]

Bowles did seek the Democratic gubernatorial nomination in 1946, after quitting OES, but miscalculated the strength of local political leaders, especially the emerging power of John Bailey, soon to be state and later national chairman of the Democratic party, and lost out to Wilbert Snow. He turned down the party's consolation prize offer of the candidacy for the U.S. Senate. Explaining his decision later, he recalled that "[1946] was clearly a Republican year, and after five hard years in OPA I was dead tired."[19] His prediction of GOP gains proved correct. The Republicans won a landslide victory in Connecticut that fall, reflecting their successes throughout the country. They easily took the governorship, the Senate seat, and all six House seats. Snow received only 42.6 percent of the major party vote and Joseph Tone, running for senator, 42.0 per cent. Bowles, too, would almost certainly have been defeated in the Democratic debacle.

Two years later, with John Bailey's support and important financial backing from CIO labor unions, he launched a successful bid for the governorship. In a hard-fought campaign in which he made imaginative and energetic use of radio and drew on favorable popular recollections of his OPA efforts, he eked out a narrow (2,225-vote) margin over Governor James Shannon.[20] It was a notable upset, almost on a par with Harry Truman's unexpected victory over New York Governor Thomas E. Dewey the same year. (Interestingly, Truman ran slightly behind Bowles in Connecticut and lost the state.)

Others who reached high or higher office in the landmark 1948 election included Senator Lyndon Johnson of Texas, Senator Hubert Humphrey of Minnesota, Governor Adlai Stevenson and Senator Paul Douglas of Illinois, and Governor G. Mennen Williams of Michigan. All of them had come to political maturity under the powerful influence of Franklin Roosevelt and sought in office to adapt New Deal principles to the rapidly changing postwar setting. Bowles developed important political and personal friendships with fellow members of this "class of 1948," several of whom figured significantly in his career. He and Humphrey had been politically associated in the launching in 1947 of the liberal lobby, Americans for Democratic Action, though Bowles soon distanced himself from the organization.[21]

Bowles had given a good indication of what he thought needed to be done in postwar America while he was still in Washington. He made major contributions to two important speeches Roosevelt gave in 1944, one outlining an "economic bill of rights," the other calling for a liberal, full-employment program to create sixty million jobs when the war was won. He spelled out his ideas more comprehensively in his first book, *Tomorrow without Fear,* published in 1946.[22] It was written for a general audience in an easy and popular style conveying Bowles's warm concern for people and his optimistic conviction that their lot can be improved. His main argument was that the enormous productive capacity the United States had demonstrated in wartime could be put to work in the postwar years to abolish poverty and to assure every citizen the right to economic, social, and political justice.

Adopting a Keynesian approach, Bowles blamed insufficient purchasing power and improper income distribution for the failures of the past. He disparaged those who argued that as a "mature economy" the United States could no longer count on expansion. He foresaw a

$200 billion postwar economy, twice the 1940 level, brought about by intelligent government policies designed to redistribute and expand income. These included maximizing free competition, raising minimum wages, extending social security, reforming the tax structure, guaranteeing farm income, and encouraging home building. Government spending should rise and fall as needed to assure full production and employment. The long-term goal was a steady expansion in which all classes would benefit and none experience the deprivation and fear of economic disaster that had haunted the country in the past.

At the state house in Hartford, Bowles demonstrated his confidence that government could play a constructive role in improving the lives of ordinary citizens. He later recalled his conviction that unless state administrations were improved, the load on the federal government would become overwhelming. "This may seem strange coming from a liberal," he told an interviewer, "but I have always felt strongly that you want the minimum government necessary to do a good job. And if the states are competent and responsible and ready to talk about something more than states' rights but also about state responsibilities, . . . this process [of looking to Washington] could be greatly changed."[23]

Like many other states in the early postwar years, Connecticut faced serious problems. Housing was in short supply for the growing families of returned veterans. The educational system did not match the needs of an expanding population aspiring to better schooling. Medical facilities were outdated. The machinery of state government was antiquated. The outgoing Republican state administration had done little to address these problems.

As he had promised in his campaign, Bowles quickly developed an ambitious agenda to improve Connecticut's housing, education, and medical care. He successfully pushed through the legislature an unorthodox but fiscally sound program which financed the construction of some 14,000 housing units for rent or purchase by low-income and low-middle-income families during his two-year tenure as governor. The legislature adopted his proposal for a major bond issue to help local communities finance a school-building program on a "pay as you use" basis, a big breakthrough. He was also able to obtain additional funds for the construction of new facilities at the University of Connecticut and state teachers' colleges, and to develop emergency training programs to remedy the shortage of qualified teachers. These improvements in housing and education were brought about without raising taxes or resorting to a budget deficit. But he was less successful in promoting change in the medical field. Despite his resourceful campaign to win the support of the state's medical profession, his programs for insurance against catastrophic illness and the establishment of a second medical school in the state were blocked by entrenched interests.

These major forces in what his longtime associate Thomas Hughes called the highly structured, ethnic, controlled, and corrupt world of Connecticut politics were also instrumental in defeating Bowles's efforts to bring about a massive overhaul of the state's inefficient administrative structure and a thoroughgoing reform of its heavily rural-biased political bodies.[24] To limit the opposition he anticipated to his proposals for such far-reaching changes, Bowles appointed a five-man commission of distinguished businessmen and saw to it that four of them were Republicans. This strategy of cultivating bipartisan support failed. Almost all of the changes the commission proposed with Bowles's backing were stymied by the large Republican majority in the lower house of the State Assembly, where a rotten-borough constituency system assured perpetual GOP preponderance. The lower house refused to accept constitutional changes that would have made the state legislature reflect more accurately the composition of the Connecticut electorate and would have eliminated other long-standing inequities and inefficiencies. The lower house also frustrated proposals to reduce the number of state departments and agencies from 202 to 17, moves that threatened a wide range of vested interests in the legislature, the state bureaucracy, and elsewhere. This part of Bowles's political agenda could only be enacted in the mid-1950s, when Abraham Ribicoff led the Democrats back to power in Hartford.

Although his legislative accomplishments were fewer than Bowles had hoped, he was confident that he would be able to win reelection in 1950 and overcome opposition to his programs in a second term. (Under a newly approved constitutional provision, governors' terms beginning in 1951 were to be for four years rather than two.) The 1950 race also had an importance for him well beyond Connecticut politics. Even before he won the governorship in 1948, he had been considered a potential contender for the White House. Though he apparently had not turned to those closest to him to think through a strategy for getting there, nor made any explicit plans to develop his candidacy, there is little doubt that he entertained the possibility of becoming president at some point. Victory in 1950 and the enactment of a strong liberal agenda during his second term would strengthen his claim to the Democratic presidential nomination, if not in 1952, when Truman was expected to run for reelection, then later.[25]

To Bowles's chagrin and bitter disappointment, he was beaten by Representative John Davis Lodge by a narrow 17,000-vote margin, despite a labor union–led effort that brought a heavy turnout of potential Democratic supporters to the polls. Analysts cited a variety of political considerations which might have contributed to his defeat. Some of these incalculables related to his alienating the special interest groups, ranging from doctors and dentists who felt threatened by his proposed medical programs (and had been encouraged to oppose them by the American Medical Association) to fishermen and hunters resentful of his insistence on higher user fees. Also noted were his refusal to play the political game by time-honored rules (that is, making deals with the Republican legislature as other Democratic governors had done) and his alleged failure to build a regular Democratic party machine through patronage. His selection of bright young staffers, some of them experts recruited from outside the state, was said to have offended Democratic leaders.[26] Some observers also believed that he had lost popular support by calling five special sessions of the state legislature, made necessary in Bowles's view by the refusal of the Republicans to enact his proposals during the brief period fixed by law for the legislature's biennial session. His personal shyness and his reputed ambition for higher office were also mentioned as working against him.

Bowles blamed his defeat on a different set of factors. He believed that he had tried to do too much too soon. He also cited his failure to respond adequately to a Republican smear campaign accusing him of such alleged political sins as support for the recognition of Communist China and "creeping socialism." Because he had not recognized his vulnerability to Lodge's charges, he had become overconfident and had consequently failed to campaign hard enough. The tentative move of Communist Chinese troops across the Yalu River into North Korea just before the election—and the implications this had for the Connecticut national guardsmen who had been called up for active duty in the Korean War—had also hurt him, he concluded.

He left Hartford at the end of 1950, his ambitious agenda only partly completed, again a private citizen. Like so many other Americans in the turbulent war and postwar years, he had come a long way over the previous decade. In 1940 he had been a prominent and creative figure in the Madison Avenue advertising world who had flirted with the idea of entering public service and elective politics. By 1950 he had become a major liberal Democratic party leader and state governor, whose effective work as head of critical wartime federal government agencies was still well remembered throughout the country. Though he had remained faithful to his New Deal convictions over those years, he had sharply revised his views of how they related to America's role in the world, as the next chapter will detail. In putting a temporary hold on his political career by voting him out of office in the gubernatorial election, the voters of Connecticut had set the stage for other far-reaching changes that marked the next decade in Bowles's unpredictable and improbable career.

2

From America Firster to Liberal Interventionist

BOWLES faced an uncertain future after his defeat. The *New York Times* summed up his situation in a report from its Hartford correspondent: "In many quarters it was believed that he would be named to a position with the United Nations or in the Truman administration. Others felt that he would try again in Connecticut four years from now. Others thought he was through."[1] Discussing his options in *Promises to Keep,* the account of his years in public life he wrote in the early 1970s, Bowles recalled that, following the 1950 election, President Truman, Presidential Special Counsel Clark Clifford, and others had suggested that he return to Washington, but he had been more inclined to seek a position overseas.[2]

▼   ▼   ▼

Bowles's interest in international affairs had first found serious, if brief, expression in 1925, when on leaving the *Republican* he sought a career in the Foreign Service. He later credited the move to his admiration for Woodrow Wilson, which his aunt Ruth Baldwin had nurtured over the objections of Bowles's father, a bitter critic of the liberal Democratic president. After several interviews arranged by a politically powerful family friend, he was then offered a position at the U.S. consulate general in Shanghai, but his father's sudden illness ruled out his taking the job. He mused later that had he gone to China at the time, he would almost certainly have become a charter member of the Old China Hands Club and been victimized by Senator Joseph McCarthy in the early 1950s. (Years later, when one of those who did become a charter member heard Bowles as under secretary of state tell a conference of American diplomats that they should get out from behind their desks and spend more time following peasants plowing their furrows, he commented, "My God, that was what we were doing in China, and look what we got out of it."[3])

Bowles paid scant attention to international affairs before the outbreak of the Second World War in Europe in September 1939. Many who are aware of his postwar record as a liberal interventionist, outspoken in his conviction that the United States should actively seek to make the world a better place, find it both astonishing and ironic that his initial role was one of staunch opposition to U.S. involvement in the war before Pearl Harbor brought the United States into battle.

Even more surprising to those who know him only in his later incarnation is his association with the America First Committee. When the AFC was organized in September 1940 to lead opposition to intervention, Bowles became a member of its national committee and played an influential role in its New York chapter.[4] With other AFC leaders, he fought hard against the passage of the Lend Lease Act, the repeal of key provisions of the Neutrality Act, and other measures that the Roosevelt administration sponsored to help the hard-pressed British following the fall of France. Like his America First colleagues and others in the noninterventionist camp, he believed it was more important for the United States to keep out of war than to assure a British victory over the Axis powers.

As Wayne Cole has pointed out, the forces which motivated opposition to intervention were many and complex. American nationalism, distrust of Europeans in general and the British in particular, the special appeal of noninterventionism to German and other ethnic groups, and, for a small minority, pro-Nazi and anti-Semitic views, all came into play. Conservatives feared that intervention might result in the destruction of American capitalism and democracy, liberals that it might lead to the loss of the social and economic progress recently achieved under the New Deal. Opposition to intervention was especially strong in the Midwest, but it also had important followings in most other parts of the country outside the Southern states.[5]

Like many liberal opponents of intervention, Bowles believed that America's foremost national responsibility lay in fulfilling the promises of the New Deal. If the country went to war, this priority would be sidetracked and later lost sight of in postwar bitterness and disillusion. He was convinced that it was not in the American anticolonial tradition to subsidize and protect Western European empires in Asia and Africa, which the United States would necessarily do if it entered the war. The effect America's participation would have on its future view of the world also troubled him; intervention was "bound to produce a new isolationism, more disastrous to world peace than the isolationism which followed the [first world] war."[6] Apparently he was no longer an admirer of his childhood hero Woodrow Wilson: "In 1917 we were sold a crusade [and] entered it with high idealism and an abysmal lack of understanding of the complicated forces with which we were dealing. . . . If America goes to war in 1942," he forecast shortly before Pearl Harbor, "we shall again be disillusioned at the peace table, and retire into our shell."[7]

Although the AFC leadership had tried hard to recruit liberals and Democrats into the organization, most members of its executive and national committees represented various shades of conservatism on domestic political and economic issues, and Republicans predominated among those with party affiliations. AFC leaders who shared Bowles's New Deal views were in a decided minority. The *New Republic* probably reflected a widely held opinion among liberal Democrats when it asserted that "the America First Committee was established at such a pre-election [of 1940] moment that it gave the impression of having been organized not so much to oppose Roosevelt's foreign policy as to oppose Roosevelt on the basis of his foreign policy."[8]

Not surprisingly under those circumstances, Bowles was troubled by the anomaly of his supporting everything Roosevelt stood for except his foreign policy.[9] He had been a Connecticut delegate to the Democratic convention in Chicago that summer, and his fidelity to FDR's domestic program led him to support the president's bid for a third term in November 1940. Bowles told an interviewer that Republican candidate Wendell Willkie's opposition to the Tennessee Valley Authority and his negative position on labor had helped keep him in the FDR camp.[10] (TVA was a Bowles favorite. In his foreign policy years he often cited it as a model for regional development projects in the Third World.) But despite his allegiance and the importance he gave to the completion of the New Deal program, his liberal commitment seems to have come under some strain. In May 1940, when the isolationist and conservative Senator Robert Taft was making a bid for the Republican nomination, Bowles wrote him that "our only hope [of avoiding stumbling into the war] lies in the election of a person like yourself for the Presidency who really believes that at any cost America must remain on her own side of the ocean."[11] (This message of support did not prevent the two men from becoming bitter antagonists during Bowles's OPA days and afterwards.) And later, in July 1941, he spoke of the conservative Colonel Charles A. Lindbergh, the AFC's most charismatic leader, as a logical spokesman for a new party in a postwar redrawing of political lines.[12]

He also became painfully aware that his noninterventionist activism could hurt his business. Though this did not lead him to abandon or curtail his AFC activities, it made him reluctant to take on fresh ones. Writing to fellow liberal Sidney Hertzberg to turn down a role in a proposed committee of New Deal noninterventionists, he reported that "several of our clients feel very emphatic against the stand that I have taken. . . . Advertising," he complained, "is one helluva business—you can never call your soul your own. And whether you like it or not you are usually more or less owned by the clients for whom you work."[13] He put his dilemma in the context of the mood among liberals in early 1941. People had become intolerant and fanatic over the intervention issue and traditionally liberal groups opposed to the war were not willing to speak out. He wondered whether it was "because they are afraid of criticizing Roosevelt to whom they owe so much on other scores."[14] His personal situation grew worse over the year. "It is rather tough mental and emotional sledding these days in the usual circles we all travel around New York," he wrote in late October to his former partner William Benton, who was also involved with the AFC.[15]

Like other AFC leaders drawn from the Republican and Democratic political mainstream, Bowles was concerned about the danger of the committee's infiltration by unsavory elements, particularly pro-Nazis and anti-Semites. He strongly endorsed the AFC Chicago chapter's request to the FBI for a complete examination of its donors and members, and urged that all chapters be asked by the committee to follow suit. Despite his admiration for Lindbergh, and his continuing conviction that the colonel was "one of the truly great citizens of this age," he took the AFC executive committee to task for failing to recognize that a highly publicized speech Lindbergh made in Des Moines in September 1941 could be read as anti-Semitic and needed to be dealt with as such.[16]

Although Bowles saw Lindbergh and other AFC leaders playing a role in a postwar political party or movement to combat the threats of Communism and fascism—an outline for the future that he admitted was still hazy in his thinking—he did not believe the committee should try to establish itself as a political party in 1941. It was too diverse; members agreed on little more than the importance of keeping America out of the war. As he wrote to AFC Executive Secretary R. Douglas Stuart: "You would have a rather hopeless time in getting them to agree on such subjects as deficit spending, labor relations, monopolies, social security, etc." The committee's interest in politics should be "confined purely to a question of the war," essentially as a single-issue pressure group.[17] He envisaged America First effectively using its political strength in this way to influence the outcome of the 1942 congressional elections.

Bowles consistently drew a distinction between noninterventionists such as himself and isolationists, a theme he spelled out in "What's Wrong with the Isolationists," an article he wrote for the December 1941 issue of *Common Sense* magazine. He scoffed at the isolationist belief that "we can afford to ignore the world and build our civilization behind a barricade of armaments." He was equally critical of internationalists who held that "we can establish world democracy with the sword." His goal was a more equitable and prosperous postwar world: "To make the world even reasonably safe for democracy we must attempt, in every practical way, to alleviate suffering and economic maladjustment wherever they may exist." But he diluted this foretaste of the later Bowles with an important caveat, warning that "this does not mean that we should turn away from our staggering problems at home in an endless attempt to cure poverty in China." He called rather "for a far greater awareness of the problems of other countries, the effect of our tariffs on the economies of other lands, the hatreds and the bitter nationalism that grow out of lack of raw materials."[18] Discussing the article with Stuart, he noted: "Our present position illustrates that neutrality laws and even a strong determination to stay out of war will not necessarily keep us out once the drums start beating and the British begin to call for help. Thus our only hope, over a period of time, of staying out of war is to do all we can to see that major wars do not occur. That calls for world cooperation in time of peace, a more sensible attitude towards tariffs, etc."[19]

He became a strong advocate of a negotiated peace. In the first half of 1941, before the Germans attacked the Soviet Union, he thought it unlikely that Britain could get through the year with or without American aid. "England herself would be better off if she took a negotiated peace this year rather than to face the certain destruction which would be involved in a long war that she would most likely lose in the end," he wrote in April.[20] When, in October, Nazi forces were thrusting toward Moscow, he thought that Britain, seeing ahead the possibility of a Soviet defeat, might make peace in return for German restoration of the Western democracies.[21]

On the eve of Pearl Harbor, Bowles developed his own plan for a compromise settlement. In another illustration of his willingness to embrace strange political bedfellows in the noninterventionist cause, he sent the plan to Herbert Hoover as a draft outline for a speech he urged the Republican former president to make before Christmas.

Hoover's stature and long experience in world affairs, he said, made him "much the most logical spokesman for the expression of some reasonable peace proposal."[22]

Bowles's premise was that the war had stalemated. The British were safe from defeat, so that "the major objective of American foreign policy for the last two years has been achieved." The retreat of the Soviet army had made Germany relatively invulnerable on the Continent. In these circumstances, he proposed a settlement in which Germany would restore the political independence of the occupied Western European countries in return for German political and economic domination of Central and Eastern Europe. He called for the United States to guarantee Western European boundaries for ten years and form a "protective alliance" with Britain for that purpose. He also suggested efforts to begin a disarmament program and to bring about a better distribution of natural resources. In a flight of fancy, he said Hitler, Mussolini, and Churchill should agree to step aside or at least to keep completely out of the peace negotiations.

Bowles told Hoover that he would be personally sorry to see America guarantee any boundary lines in Europe or form an alliance with Britain. But that was the price to pay for peace. The Anglo-American military alliance, he thought, "might readily develop into the machinery for far broader international cooperation, with other nations joining the group, and with the military provisions dropping gradually into the background." He hoped that "once the war has been stopped and the propaganda turned off, the trend [in America] may swing rapidly away from dabbling too extensively in international power politics." In a prompt, brief reply Hoover said he felt the time had not yet come when such a presentation would be of use, though it might before winter was over. He thanked Bowles for providing what he called "an able summary for such an address."[23]

Bowles had written to Hoover on November 28 and the former president had responded the following day. When the Japanese attack on Pearl Harbor a little more than a week later led the AFC to dissolve itself, Bowles had no regrets about the noninterventionist position he had taken. In a letter to General Robert E. Wood, who had been AFC chairman, he asserted that Roosevelt had led the country into an unrealistic policy that could have but one result. "I am as confident as I have ever been in my life that the future will prove the rightness of the [AFC's] policies," he declared.[24]

Despite these bold December 1941 words, Bowles preferred in later years to forget his America First role. In the brief paragraphs he gave to his pre-Pearl Harbor stand against intervention in *Promises to Keep*, he made no mention of his AFC membership. It does not appear in the autobiographic sketches he prepared from time to time nor did he ever cite it in the Senate hearings on his confirmation for the high offices he later held. Although he was ordinarily meticulous in preserving his extensive correspondence, the letters he exchanged with other America First and noninterventionist figures in 1940 and 1941 are missing from his files. His reticence resembled that of many other AFC leaders. Like them, he found the America First connection an embarrassment which could damage him politically. It is worth noting that as late as 1960, when he was eager to become John F. Kennedy's secretary of state, Jewish groups attacked Bowles for his AFC role.[25]

America's participation in the Second World War had different consequences for the country and the world than those Bowles had forecast. In the war and postwar years his view of America's international role fundamentally changed. But at least a few of the concepts that shaped his thinking before Pearl Harbor were reflected in his later approach to foreign policy. Throughout his career he maintained an aloofness from European affairs that contrasted sharply with the attraction they had for other postwar foreign policymakers with similar Eastern establishment backgrounds. While he accepted the importance for U.S. security of a strong and prosperous Western Europe, he never gave to this aspect of foreign policy the powerful emotional commitment and detailed involvement many of his contemporaries did. His opposition to European colonialism and U.S. support for it, a major element in his thinking in the postwar decolonization period, can also be traced to his earlier views. So can the conviction he frequently expressed in his later career about the limits to the effective use of military force as a means of resolving political disputes.

In an interesting assessment, James Thomson, a close associate of Bowles's who was raised in a missionary family, contended that the sharp contrast between Bowles's prewar noninterventionism and his later zeal for promoting American ideals worldwide, beginning at home, can be interpreted in the context of his missionary-like approach to foreign policy:

> [Bowles's] concern in the 1930s when he was a non-interventionist, the "America First" period, was to keep the beacon alight here while the world went into darkness. And in American missionism, there have always been two kinds of forces in contention—one is the kind that says let's build the new Jerusalem at home, "a city built upon a hill" that all the world may see it and emulate it, and the other being to export what

we have, to bring it to the neglected and blighted peoples of the world. Bowles in the 30's, I think, was much more in the first tradition, avoiding the export of benevolence, at least finding Europe too done-in by its own tragic history, so that we should not tangle there. Bowles, with his eyes opened by India, first of all becomes a major proponent of the export of American benevolence to serve and save mankind.[26]

▾   ▾   ▾

In August 1945 Secretary of State James Byrnes offered Bowles a senior management position in the State Department. He turned it down because he did not feel he could leave OPA during the reconversion period. Soon afterwards, however, he became at least peripherally involved in foreign policy. In November 1945, as price administrator, he urged Truman to send the largest possible shipments of food overseas, not only for humanitarian reasons but also because the food "will serve to increase the general respect for our country in world affairs and to win for us the friendship and gratitude of many peoples." He assured the president that opinion polls indicated that the move, which "would offer dramatic testimony to the fact that America feels deeply her responsibilities as a world power," would be acceptable to the American people if the need for the required sacrifices were clearly outlined to them.[27] The letter foreshadowed his frequent contention in the 1950s and 1960s that foreign assistance was far more acceptable to the public than many political leaders thought it was.

His involvement in foreign affairs deepened between 1946 and 1948, when he was between full-time jobs. In 1946 he served as a delegate to the first session of the United Nations Educational, Scientific, and Cultural Organization (UNESCO) in Paris, and the following year became part-time special assistant for administrative affairs for U.N. Secretary General Trygve Lie and international chairman of the U.N. Appeal for Children. He traveled to Europe in 1948 to promote the Appeal and met a number of major leaders. That trip and other exposure to international problems in those years were important in shaping the way Bowles viewed foreign policy issues.

His emerging conviction that economic assistance was vital for Third World development and some of his ideas on the most effective ways to use aid in pursuit of U.S. international objectives date from that time. In 1948 he first came into contact with Dr. Y. C. James Yen, a Chinese development expert who had served as a senior official in Chiang Kai-shek's government before it was driven off the mainland. Yen's approach stressed social reconstruction in the countryside through basic adult literacy campaigns, cooperatives, preventive health measures, and local self-government. In the 1930s he had developed programs which had improved the lot of peasants in South China. At Supreme Court Justice William O. Douglas's suggestion, Yen had passed his ideas to Bowles, giving him his first insights into the importance of a rural political base for economic growth in a developing nation. These ideas helped establish the framework for the detailed program of economic assistance and development Bowles promoted when he reached India.[28]

Perhaps the most important among the themes emerging in this 1947–48 period that became major elements in his later approach to foreign policy was Bowles's conviction that the United States needed to ally itself with forces of economic and social change. In a memorandum he sent to Secretary of State George Marshall in March 1948, soon after returning from his European trip, he warned against "the danger of positioning ourselves as the great reactionary power in a revolutionary world." This constituted "a far greater threat to American security than the atomic bomb. . . . The only practical answer," he told Marshall, "lies in an *economic* and *social* as well as political offensive designed to identify ourselves in all parts of the world with revolutionary reforms."[29]

Bowles's belief in the importance of U.S. support for reformist forces led him to question the way the plan for European recovery, which carried the secretary's name, was being implemented. Like other liberal Democrats, he had supported the Marshall Plan, but he had become concerned that the United States had not been tough enough in insisting that European recipients of assistance make changes in their economic, social, and political structures and policies. Critical of what he believed was undue U.S. identification with unpopular right-wing governments and political groups, he called for more forceful interventions to bring about reform in Italy and Greece. He advocated the economic isolation of the Franco dictatorship in Spain and wanted the United States to offer generous assistance to any reformist democratic government that replaced it.

But Bowles's main focus, in his memorandum to Marshall and elsewhere, was on the Middle East, Asia, and Latin America. This foreshadowed the central interest the Third World came to have for him in the 1950s and 1960s. He urged the secretary to consider developing Tennessee Valley Authority–like programs for the Tigris, Euphrates, and Jordan river basins. He wanted the United States to propose to the 1948 Pan-American Conference a bold approach to reform and development in Latin America. "If we took up the case of the oppressed people of all the South American countries in ringing terms and offered our tangible help, under specific conditions, in improving their living standards," he told Marshall, "we would capture the imagination of people not only in South America but throughout the world." He called for similarly ambitious programs and policies in India and, "once a moderate middle-of-the-road government is established," in China, where the civil war was then reaching a climax. Such an approach would be "the deepest survival insurance that we can possibly buy."

In public speeches and articles, Bowles raised many of these and similar ideas that he would later stress. Addressing a gathering at Freedom House in New York in January 1947, he urged the allocation of 2 percent of U.S. national income for economic and technical assistance abroad.[30] At a May 1947 convention in Chicago, he spoke of the need for a revolution in world agriculture through expanded inputs and land reform, and a strengthened United Nations to help bring this about.[31] In an April 1948 *New York Times Magazine* piece titled "We Need a Program *For* as Well as *Against*," he warned that "if we choose to think in terms of Governments instead of people, and to base our decisions on strategic concepts rather than moral and humanitarian principles, we may stumble into catastrophe." America could only exercise effective world leadership by identifying itself with the hungry and oppressed in their struggle for economic security. It must convince them "that we stand wholeheartedly for long overdue economic and social reforms, and that with our help they can achieve higher living standards and political freedom, too." He wanted a strong stand against European colonial vestiges in Asia to be an important element in the U.S. approach.[32]

Bowles's conviction that the postwar United States had adopted an unduly negative approach to foreign policy in its stress on military preparedness and security and needed to understand and identify itself with rising popular hopes and aspirations for a better life was perhaps best reflected in a letter he sent Dean Acheson on Acheson's appointment as secretary of state in January 1949:

My argument [with conservatives on foreign policy] is not over the question of whether or not we should be firm with Russia. I assume that goes without saying. The issue . . . is whether firmness itself is enough. I am sure that you would agree most emphatically that it is not. We badly need . . . to establish a liberal viewpoint in the handling of foreign affairs which will bring us closer to the needs and fears of people everywhere. There has always been unrest and there always will be until we begin to solve some of the basic human economic and social problems. The point is that now our Soviet friends are in a position to crystallize unrest where it occurs through the Communist Party. . . . There is only one way to stop it and that is to really go to work on the basic difficulties which make people fearful and insecure.[33]

▾   ▾   ▾

After his term as governor, during which domestic issues had again dominated his agenda, Bowles began to focus his foreign affairs concerns even more on the Third World, especially on Asia. The rise of the People's Republic of China had convinced him that efforts to contain Communism would be increasingly waged in the developing Asian nations rather than in Europe, where the success of the Marshall Plan and the establishment of the North Atlantic Treaty Organization had stabilized the political division between the Eastern and Western power blocs. His search for a foreign policymaking position reflected this increasing Asian orientation.

As governor, Bowles had named William Benton to a vacant seat in the U.S. Senate in 1949. (It was a controversial appointment which later proved to have been a major political mistake.)[34] Benton had been elected in 1950 to fill the two remaining years of his Senate seat at the same time that Bowles lost the governorship. As a senator and former State Department official, close friend, political associate, and former business partner, Benton was someone to whom he naturally turned in his quest for a foreign policy job.

The correspondence between them suggests that considerations of political strategy as well as concern for foreign policy prompted Bowles to look overseas for a postelection job. In one letter, Bowles recalled that he, Benton, and other Bowles associates had concluded that an overseas job would demonstrate that he had the full support of the Truman administration, including the president, and this would be reassuring to him and his Connecticut supporters. It would also remove him from "all the pulling and hauling of Connecticut politics" and enable him to keep more or less aloof from the difficulties his old conservative enemies would cause for him if he were to go to Washington instead. It would give him valuable experience, particularly in the field in which, he said, he had been intently interested, "the development of practical programs designed to raise the living standards in the East."[35]

Bowles was anxious to get a job quickly. He was apparently confident that he stood in good stead with the president, who knew him well from their association during Truman's first year in the White House. Although he had later damaged his standing with Truman by taking the lead in an unsuccessful effort mounted by some liberals in the party to dump him and make Eisenhower the Democratic nominee in 1948, he eventually swung behind the president, and the two men had campaigned together in Connecticut as they both headed for upset victories.[36] By 1950, he could be reasonably sure that, as Clark Clifford has recalled, Truman had forgiven him for his brief political apostasy.[37]

Like many office seekers, particularly those angling for diplomatic assignments, Bowles felt frustrated by the slow pace of the appointment process. An early nomination had seemed in the cards when Truman asked him in December to go to the Philippines as ambassador, but word of the offer leaked and the idea was shelved.[38] Economic Cooperation Administrator William Foster talked to him about becoming a roving director for economic assistance in Southeast Asia and India. But as Bowles reported later, that possibility quickly faded "when Senator Robert Taft made it clear to the Truman administration that he was in no mood to forget our conflicts during OPA days and would strongly oppose my appointment."[39]

This setback was a big disappointment to him. He wrote to Truman in February 1951 that he was convinced that a bold program carefully adapted to the peculiar problems of the Near East, South Asia, and Southeast Asia could be "as dramatically effective as the Marshall Plan. . . . It would demonstrate to those friendly nations which have questioned our policy in the U.N. that we are determined to supplement our armament program with a continuing, positive effort to build a peaceful world."[40] He reacted badly to speculative reports that he was being given the brush-off and feared that there was some truth in them. "It all adds up to a distinctly unpleasant and undignified situation which has been definitely hurtful," he complained.[41]

Though the political advantages of an early appointment were gone, he continued his efforts and sought political allies. Benton was among them, as was Averell Harriman, then director of the Mutual Security Agency. Benton reported that Harriman had talked to Truman about a Bowles appointment, and that he and Harriman had also talked to Secretary Acheson. "I think we have a commitment," Benton reassured Bowles.[42] Things were being worked on, the senator noted, and Bowles shouldn't press for the job. The correspondence must have a dreary familiarity to generations of job seekers.

The efforts of Bowles and his allies finally bore fruit. He learned in early May that four major ambassadorial posts, in the Soviet Union, Japan, West Germany, and India, were to be filled within the next four months. Loy Henderson, the career diplomat who was ambassador in New Delhi, was to be shifted to Iran. Bowles had earlier mentioned his interest in India to Acheson, but at that point the job was not expected to come open.[43] He now confided to Harriman that it was his first choice.[44] The posting, he had told Benton the month before, would meet his requirement that an assignment "should be a position of top importance not only in the inner circles of the State Department but in the public mind."[45]

Bowles later recalled that in a meeting with Truman, the president suggested two or three ambassadorships to him. When he had shown no interest in them, Truman had asked him if there were not some country to which he would like to go. "To my own surprise," he recorded in *Promises to Keep*, "I found myself answering 'India'."[46] He remembered that the president phoned him a few days later to ask him if he really wanted to go, and that he accepted after consultation with his family. Curiously, he stated in this account that the Indian assignment had not occurred to him at first because an ambassador was already assigned there. The passage of time, twenty years, between the event and the writing of his book, may account for this apparent contradiction with his message to Harriman, sent in early May before the Truman interview.

Bowles's recollection of Truman's reaction to the preference he expressed for an Indian assignment provides an interesting insight into the problems he and others similarly convinced of the importance of India to U.S. national interests faced in seeking stronger bilateral ties with New Delhi. The president, Bowles remembered, was appalled at the thought of anyone wanting to go there. According to Bowles, Truman said, "Well, I thought India was pretty jammed with poor people and cows wandering around the streets, witch doctors and people sitting on hot coals and bathing in the Ganges, and so on, but I did not realize that anybody thought it was important." In a subsequent meeting as he was preparing to depart, he discussed with the president the 1949 visit of Indian Prime Minister Nehru to the United States, an encounter which had been a disappointment to both sides. "The first thing you've got to do," he recalled Truman instructing him, "is to find out if Nehru is a Communist. He sat right on that chair and he talked just like a Communist."[47]

Similar distortions, usually less colorfully expressed, in American perceptions of India have continued to handicap efforts to strengthen

U.S.-Indian relations over the subsequent forty years despite efforts by Bowles and others to correct them. As one American specialist has said in comparing views in the United States of China and India, "When competing against a hidden or inaccessible China, India's flaws seemed all too evident. . . . People knew enough about [India] to dislike it, but not enough to appreciate it."[48]

Recounting later the views he had held in early 1951, Bowles wrote that he "had come to see India as the political and economic key to a free and stable Asia."[49] Though this assessment quickly became an article of faith once he was named ambassador, there is no evidence for this recollected belief in the primacy of India in his writings or speeches up to that time. Confidants who were with him in those days recall that before his appointment he really had not thought much about India.[50] The Indian assignment was more a welcomed target of opportunity for him than the maturing of a long-held interest.

But whatever the extent of Bowles's attention to India before he was assigned there, he was obviously delighted with the appointment and convinced that it was just right for him. He was highly enthusiastic in letters to well-wishers who congratulated him on the posting. He told Eleanor Roosevelt that "the Indian assignment is a tremendously important one, and there is at least a fair chance that we can accomplish something out there with earnest effort and with the help of an improved and expanded staff."[51] "India," he wrote foreign affairs author Vera Micheles Dean, "is at least as important as any other country in the world today outside the Soviet Union itself. And if India is lost we shall surely be driven back into the 'citadel' which Herbert Hoover and Robert Taft are continually urging on us."[52] "We have learned some hard lessons in China during the last four years," he stressed to Senator Estes Kefauver of Tennessee, "and we must take every step to make sure these mistakes are not repeated in India because the loss of India would be a real disaster."[53]

Bowles's prominence in American public life, his reputation as a liberal, and his advocacy of greater U.S. assistance to the Asian countries assured a warm reception in India to his nomination. Unlike his two predecessors, he could claim a relationship with the Washington political power structure and potential clout there for his recommendations on U.S.-Indian relations. The Indians welcomed this. The appointment of a politically important and sympathetic public figure impressed them, and Bowles's subsequent performance as a supporter of Indian causes who apparently had a direct line to the White House impressed them even more.

This would later have an important impact on the standards Indians set for his successors. Perhaps more than people in other countries, Indians came to see the U.S. ambassador as a friend and advocate, able and eager to represent their viewpoint in high Washington places through strong personal and political ties. They were encouraged to take this view by an awareness that some American ambassadors, Bowles among them, believed that such sympathetic and supportive advocacy was at least part of their job. Some in Washington even insisted that this Indian standard ruled out the assignment of a career diplomat to New Delhi. Bowles's successor, George V. Allen, was a Foreign Service officer. But in the quarter century between Allen's departure in 1955 and the appointment of Harry Barnes in 1981, all U.S. ambassadors were political appointees with claims to importance in American public life.

Reaction to the appointment of American ambassadors is almost always more subdued in the United States than it is in the country of assignment. Although word of the Bowles appointment and the simultaneous shift of his predecessor to Iran got front-page coverage in the *New York Times,* it appears to have excited little interest elsewhere in the country, except in Connecticut and the Senate and among Bowles's friends. In his own state, even papers that had frequently criticized his performance as governor warmly endorsed his nomination.[54] The Senate was another story. There, Old Guard Republicans waged a spirited fight to block confirmation.

This opposition first emerged in the five-member panel the Senate Foreign Relations Committee had set up to consider the nomination. Its two Republicans, Owen Brewster of Maine and H. Alexander Smith of New Jersey, expressed concern over Bowles's lack of diplomatic experience and fear that as ambassador he would try to win unacceptably large economic assistance funds for India. They were particularly upset by Bowles's statement expressing the hope that the Foreign Relations Committee would do everything it could in allocating assistance money to assure that India got as much as possible; they alleged (though Bowles denied this) that he had spoken of annual aid levels of $250 million, at that time an extraordinarily high figure. The administration sought to counter their charges by despatching Assistant Secretary of State George McGhee to testify in Bowles's support. McGhee assured the senators that, like other ambassadors, Bowles would be responsible for the execution of policies, not their formulation, and that he would not be in charge of the administration of the economic assistance program in India. Unmollified, the Republican members voted against the nomination, which passed by a straight party vote, three to two.[55]

After the full committee had given its assent to the nomination in a voice vote, Senator Taft took the lead in forcing a fight on the Senate floor. Taft was vitriolic in his opposition. "I cannot think of anyone who is less qualified to be Ambassador to India than Chester Bowles," he declared. Citing Bowles's performance at OPA, the Ohio Republican angrily inveighed against his "general philosophy of spending and of a general, planned economy." Bowles's preference for spending money made his assignment to India particularly dangerous because the Indians' "whole view is that we should give them the world." Bourke Hickenlooper of Iowa chimed in with a nasty allusion to Bowles's advertising days. Truman, he complained, wanted to send a Fuller Brush Man rather than a diplomat to a sick area of the world. H. Alexander Smith argued that the Republican minority ought to have been consulted before the nomination was made. The vote which followed the angry debate was again along party lines. Bowles got the backing of all but one of the Democrats. Five Republicans, mostly Eastern liberals, also supported him. The final tally was forty-three to thirty-three in favor of the nomination.[56]

Senator Margaret Chase Smith of Maine was one of Bowles's Republican backers. In a postmortem in her newspaper column, she succinctly summed up the opposition line.

Strangely enough, many of those opposing the confirmation were the very persons who had been so vigorously calling for the appointment of more successful businessmen instead of "tea drinking" State Department career men as ambassadors. I took these complaints at face value and in good faith and voted for the confirmation for the appointee who was a proved, successful businessman. When this was pointed out to those who had opposed confirmation, they replied that the appointee had not had enough foreign service experience for the job and that he would consequently be a failure at it.[57]

Bowles wrote to Senator George Aiken of Vermont, another Republican supporter, that he was "frankly disappointed by the conflict over [the] nomination." He supposed it was "the kind of thing one has to get used to in public life."[58] But the wrangle did not affect his enthusiasm for the job and his determined effort to prepare himself for it. He was particularly concerned about economic assistance, as his confirmation hearing testimony attests. "We simply must find a pattern of economic development for the underdeveloped areas that is acceptable to the peoples of these countries and will win the support of our own people and our Congress," he wrote Nelson Rockefeller, then the chairman of the International Development Advisory Board, the planning unit for the Point Four program.[59] He took advantage of the delays in the appointment process to develop a network of bureaucratic support for aid.

He also focused on staffing the mission. With an eye for talent that would become well known in the State Department, he wrote to *Saturday Review* Editor Norman Cousins about the possibility of Dillon Ripley becoming cultural attaché, and sought unsuccessfully to inveigle Kingman Brewster to New Delhi from his teaching post at the Harvard Law School.[60] (Bowles knew what he was doing. Ripley, then an assistant professor of ornithology at Yale with great knowledge of Indian birds, was later appointed director of the Smithsonian Institution. Brewster became president of Yale and was President Jimmy Carter's ambassador to Great Britain.) He also tried to entice people who had already reached the top of their professions, such as former TVA Administrator David Lilienthal. He recruited three talented associates who had worked with him in Connecticut: Edward Logue became Bowles's special assistant, Jean Joyce was named editor of the embassy publication *American Reporter,* and Bernard Loshbough, who had been director of the state housing program, got the job of deputy chief of the economic assistance mission.

As he went about his preparations for New Delhi, Bowles appears to have found Foggy Bottom a more congenial place than he had anticipated. He told Hubert Humphrey, "I have been working with the State Department pretty intensively ever since my name was sent in and I have been very favorably impressed with the degree of flexibility which I have found there. They seem earnestly anxious to get different points of view. I have been encouraged to talk frankly and to go out there with an open mind."[61] The department's Office of South Asian Affairs, which under Donald Kennedy's direction had quickly established a good relationship with Bowles in Washington, became a useful ally in explaining and supporting many of his recommendations and advising him of the lay of the land in the executive branch and on Capitol Hill after he reached India. He also benefited greatly by the presence in Washington of Philip Coombs, a professional economist he had brought from Amherst College to Hartford as his economic adviser in 1949. Coombs was serving on the Material Policy Commission in the executive office of the president, and from that vantage point was able to act as his personal Washington liaison, especially on economic assistance matters.

After winning the harsh confirmation battle, Bowles lost no time in getting sworn in as the third United States ambassador to India. The Senate had voted October 9; the swearing-in ceremony was held October 11. He flew off to India soon afterwards with Steb and their three children. After a stop in Bombay, where they spent the night in the old-fashioned imperial splendor of the Taj Mahal hotel overlooking the Gateway to India, they boarded the old B-29 the embassy had sent down to fetch them. On October 20 they arrived in New Delhi to begin what would prove for Bowles, to use one of his favorite words, a watershed in his life.

3

A Connecticut Yankee in
Mr. Nehru's Court

BOWLES brought a new and distinctive style to the American embassy in New Delhi. His informality and candor struck the right note with many Indians, including Prime Minister Nehru. His sympathetic friendship for India allowed him to function almost as an unofficial adviser, especially on economic development issues. His gift for words—volubility to his critics—helped make him an outstanding practitioner of what later came to be called public diplomacy. He tried to imbue his staff with the sense of mission that colored his own approach to India, and to adopt operational practices geared to improving the mutual understanding on which better relations could be built.

He plunged quickly and energetically into his new job, bringing to it all the enthusiasm for ideas, experiences, and people that both his admirers and his critics had noted from his earliest days in the advertising business. He was soon constantly on the move, putting in long hours in his New Delhi rounds and on journeys across India to areas far off the track beaten by other senior diplomats. Old photographs at the embassy show him as a big, solid, almost hulking figure, usually dressed in a loosely fitting bush shirt and comfortable slacks. A full head of cropped dark hair framed a long-jawed face just beginning to take on the weather-beaten character of his later years.

Recalling Bowles in those days, people speak of a warm and outgoing man of physical stamina and intellectual vigor, caught up in an exciting new enterprise. Wherever he was, he would constantly raise fresh ideas, almost all of them on serious matters. They came out of the side of his mouth, the result of a boyhood mastoidectomy that had also deafened one ear, and gave an engaging, mock-conspiratorial edge to his speaking manner. Surprisingly, for a politician, he had little small talk. Above all, Bowles conveyed the sense of a man in a hurry to achieve important goals—Mark Twain's Connecticut Yankee come to hustle Rudyard Kipling's unchanging East.

▾　　　▾　　　▾

New Delhi in 1951 was an exciting place for a diplomat. The majestic but rather sedate and ingrown garden city the British had laid out as their imperial headquarters in the 1920s was quickly changing into the bustling, cosmopolitan capital of a free nation. Newcomers from all over India mingled with hordes of refugees who had fled from Pakistan. Together they easily outnumbered preindependence Delhiwallahs, whose ranks in the twin cities of Old and New Delhi had been depleted by the flight of many members of the once sizable and prominent Muslim community. Foreign diplomats, based in the port cities for all but the final years of the British *raj,* had set up scores of embassies through which they could deal with the leaders of the world's largest newly independent state. India's aspirations to play a major role in international diplomacy gave their assignments greater salience. The deference with which the diplomats and other foreigners were treated by the Indians made their assignments more attractive and compensated for long, hot, dusty summers, drenching monsoon rains, and a shortage of good housing.

Ambassadors were particularly well placed to make a mark. In the early 1950s and for decades afterwards those who represented major powers in New Delhi enjoyed both a visibility and a potential for influence far greater than their successors do today. They were in effect *ex officio* members of the Indian power structure, and became well-known figures far beyond the diplomatic circle. Their activities and views were well reported in the press, whose pages, even front pages, were easily available to them when they wanted to make copy.

Bowles flourished in this environment and quickly won recognition. His readiness to flout conventional diplomatic behavior was widely chronicled and seems for the most part to have been well received. His bicycling in the streets of New Delhi, the enrollment of his children in an Indian school (unprecedented for Western diplomatic offspring), the warmth with which he and his family treated their household staff, their indefatigable travels in the Indian countryside, their interest in learning Hindi, and their decision to move to a smaller house all won favorable public attention. In a country where legend plays an important role, Bowles quickly came close to becoming one in his own time.

▾　　　▾　　　▾

When Bowles presented his credentials on November 1, 1951, to Rajendra Prasad, the country's first president, India had been free for a little over four years. They had been years of both tumult and accomplishment. The new nation had been born in the turmoil of the sudden and unanticipated division of the British Indian empire into two separate and bitterly antagonistic dominions—secular, largely Hindu India and Islamic Pakistan. The partition had left in its wake hundreds of thousands of dead and millions of refugees. The massive dislocation it caused in both countries further complicated the enormous tasks of political, economic, and social reconstruction they faced as new nations. Making matters worse was the unresolved dispute between them over the border state of Kashmir, which had erupted into over a year of warfare before the United Nations negotiated an uneasy truce in January 1949. In the summer before Bowles reached India, relations between the two hostile neighbors had again deteriorated to the point where another round of fighting seemed imminent.

In face of its great problems, India had made remarkable progress in developing and strengthening the political institutions it needed to fulfill the ambitious goals its leaders had set for the country. In little over two years its Constituent Assembly had adopted an elaborate and sophisticated constitution making India a republic and affirming the democratic and secular heritage of the independence movement. Five hundred and more princely states had been integrated into the country's political, economic, and administrative fabric. Scattered Communist efforts at insurrection and subversion had been forcibly suppressed. Although much more needed to be done, not least in dealing with the country's volatile ethnic and linguistic divisions and the deep-rooted problem of untouchability, a particularly ugly and wasteful aspect of the pervasive Hindu caste system, India's large measure of domestic stability contrasted favorably with the record of other newly independent Asian and African states in the postwar decolonization period.

The Indian National Congress continued to dominate the political scene. Under the leadership of Mahatma Gandhi and Jawaharlal Nehru, Congress had spearheaded India's struggle for freedom. With independence attained, it transformed itself from a national movement to a firmly rooted political party and held power in New Delhi and almost all state and local governments. The party was led by experienced men devoted to popular government and broad-based economic progress. Its organization reached down to the hundreds of thousands of villages where the mass of Indians lived.

By 1951, after the assassination of Gandhi and the death of conservative Deputy Prime Minister Sardar Vallabhbhai Patel, Nehru held undisputed sway over both government and party. A lively and energetic sixty-two when Bowles arrived in India, he made all the key decisions—and many of the less important ones—on domestic political, economic, and social issues. Minister of external affairs as well as head of government, he was also the architect of Indian foreign policy. Despite his enormous authority, or perhaps because of it, he was careful to nurture India's newly established democratic institutions.

Parliamentary and state assembly elections were scheduled for early 1952 and preparations for them enveloped the political scene in the first months of Bowles's assignment. The role of the Congress party in the struggle against the British, the unrivaled strength of its grass-roots organization, and the great popularity of Nehru as its leader made it an odds-on favorite to win at the polls against a badly splintered opposition. But because the elections would be the first since Indian independence and the first under full adult franchise, there was an air of uncertainty about the outcome. The preoccupation of Nehru and other leaders with electioneering, and their reluctance to come to potentially unpopular decisions before the results were in, complicated Bowles's efforts to make headway with the Indian government during his initial months in New Delhi.

The efforts of the Indian political leadership to develop stable institutions had been greatly helped by the country's strong and experienced civil service. Its senior Indian members, who by the time of independence enjoyed positions of major responsibility, easily transferred their allegiance to the new government, which gladly accepted their services. Their ranks included such outstanding men as Minister of Finance C. D. Deshmukh and Girja Shankar Bajpai, the secretary general in the ministry of external affairs, both later Bowles's close friends and confidants.

This civil service, impressive as it was, still focused on law and order and revenue collection, as it had in imperial British days. The notion of the civil administration as a force in economic development did not easily catch hold. Nehru and his colleagues believed that rapid, widely shared economic and social progress was crucially important if the independence of India was to have real meaning for its 350 million people. The prime minister in particular was convinced that government had a major role to play in improving the lives of the impoverished Indian masses.

In 1951, this role was only beginning to take shape. Its centerpiece was the First Five Year Plan. A modest effort to initiate economic planning in a democratic setting, the plan was designed to raise India's pitifully low living standards, reduce its glaring economic inequalities, and prepare the way for more rapid future development. It was not so much a plan in the accepted meaning of the term as an amalgam of projects prepared earlier which it integrated into a rational framework. Although the time frame of the plan was April 1, 1951, to March 31, 1956, the document was still in draft outline form when Bowles arrived in India, six months after the scheduled takeoff date.[1]

As finally revised, the plan provided for an outlay of about five billion dollars by Indian federal and state governments. The planners anticipated that this would increase India's annual national income of $18 billion (a little more than $50 per capita) by about 11 percent. This might be higher, they believed, if community development and other projects designed to stimulate local initiative succeeded in evoking popular effort on a large scale. About a fifth of the increase in national income was to be added to investment and capital formation, setting the stage for faster growth in subsequent plan periods.

The major focus of the plan was on raising agricultural production, then the mainstay of seven out of ten Indians. Some 40 percent of projected expenditures was earmarked for agriculture and related sectors such as irrigation and community development. This figure also included a large share of the substantial outlay for power generation. Indian determination to reach self-sufficiency in food grains, the goal set in the plan, had been heightened by the droughts of 1950 and 1951, which had severely reduced harvests in large parts of the country and had forced the government to seek massive grain imports on an emergency basis. Industrial and mineral production received a much smaller share (less than 8 percent) in the expectation that once basic food grain shortages were overcome, greater funding could be made available in later plans. This in fact happened in the Second Five Year Plan (1956–61), which featured massive government investment in heavy industry.

Under Nehru's direction, India had adopted an activist foreign policy. The prime minister stressed independence as the cardinal point in India's approach. Even before freedom from Britain had been finally won, he had as leader of the interim government pledged that as far as possible India would "keep away from the power politics of groups, aligned against one another."[2] These, he argued, "have led in the past to world wars and . . . may again lead to disasters on an even vaster scale." India needed to judge each issue on the basis of its ideals and self-interest. "I do not think that anything could be more injurious to us from any point of view—certainly from an idealistic and highly

moral point of view, but equally so from the point of view of oppor-
tunism and national interest in the narrowest sense of that word—than
for us . . . to try to align ourselves with this power or that and become
its camp followers in the hope that some crumbs might fall from their
table," he told the Constituent Assembly in 1948.[3] India's commitment
to nonalignment was heightened by its recognition that, as the strongest
power in its region, it did not need outside support and would benefit
if its smaller neighbors also steered clear of linkups with power blocs.
Efforts to limit the role of major powers in South Asia have been a
key feature of Indian foreign policy ever since.

Nehru's approach also stressed amicable resolution of disputes and
support for the resurgence of an independent Asia in which India would
play a leading role. He was a dedicated foe of the colonialism and
racism the country had so recently suffered. "We believe that peace
and freedom are indivisible and the denial of freedom anywhere must
endanger freedom everywhere and lead to conflict and war," he had
told the nation in 1946. "We are particularly interested in the emancipation of colonial and dependent countries and peoples, and in the
recognition in theory and practice of equal opportunities for all races."[4]
He had devoted major effort to the struggle of the Indonesians for
independence from the Dutch and to the battle of the nonwhite majority in South Africa against discrimination. He placed great emphasis
on the quest for peace. As he told his biographer Michael Brecher,
"Apart from our desire for peace [itself] . . . is our feeling that peace
is absolutely essential for our progress and our growth. And if there
is war, big or small, it comes in the way of that [economic] growth
which is for us the primary factor."[5]

The Cold War confrontation between the two blocs had begun to
dominate the international scene just as India won its freedom. It
offered the Indians the opportunity—Nehru would see it as an obligation—to play a major diplomatic role far greater than their limited
economic and military power would otherwise have permitted. While
denying any interest in establishing a "third force" of nonaligned
countries under its leadership, India in fact played a guiding role among
them and used its influence to expand what it termed an area of peace
comprising countries that followed nonaligned policies similar to its
own. At the United Nations and other forums, India's articulate and
energetic diplomats involved themselves in many issues unconnected
with its immediate national interests and played a key part in developing the Asian-African bloc of nations. Nehru got great satisfaction
(as well as political benefit at home) from the prominent role he played
on the international stage.

In pursuing this independent foreign policy, the Indian approach differed sharply from that of the United States. Indians rejected the American view that international communism was the principal threat to world peace. The Nehru government had no interest in being drawn into the struggle between the West and the Communist world, a point the prime minister had made clear during his 1949 visit to the United States. Outside the ranks of the Communist party, this position won widespread support among politically literate Indians and helped independent India achieve the unity of purpose it needed in its infant years.

India's experience, its geographic setting, and its perceived political imperatives led it to question the U.S. conviction that the Cold War was a necessary if unsought struggle to deter Communist designs for world domination. In the immediate postwar years, Indian attention had been focused on the final struggle against British imperialism, not on Soviet encroachments in Eastern and Central Europe. Although it had put down a Communist uprising at home and continued to combat domestic Communists politically, the Indian government was more concerned with what it regarded as the continuing menace of colonialism than it was by prospects of further Communist gains at the expense of the "free world." In assessing U.S. policy, the Indians were also disturbed by evidence of U.S. support for Western colonial forces in Indochina. They considered Washington's Cold War strategy a dangerous approach that could lead to a third world war. They promoted instead efforts to reconcile differences between the rival blocs.

While it followed a fundamentally independent and nonaligned approach to international issues, in actual practice India was until 1950 more closely linked to the West than it was to the Communist bloc. It had chosen to remain within the British Commonwealth. Indian trade, financial ties, and cultural associations were largely with the West. The Indian armed forces looked almost exclusively to the British for military hardware and technical assistance. Moreover, the Nehru government was regularly castigated by Moscow in Stalin's time as a stooge of the West. Despite India's early recognition of the Chinese People's Republic and strong Indian support for its claim to China's seat in the United Nations, these Soviet denunciations were echoed by the Communist Chinese after they attained power in 1949.

The outbreak of the Korean War in June 1950 led to a shift in Indian positions toward a more anti-Western attitude within a continuing framework of nonalignment. At the United Nations, India initially joined with the overwhelming majority of members in condemning North Korean aggression against the Republic of Korea and calling for an international effort to repel the attack. But Nehru's interest in firmly opposing North Korea's action was soon overshadowed by his deter-mination to bring an end to the conflict, which he feared would develop into a major war, and a concern that in supporting collective resistance he was unduly aligning India with the West. Troubled by American linking of the Korean War with the fate of Taiwan and with what he regarded as a colonialist struggle against the Communist insurgency in Indochina, issues on which India and the United States had sharply differing views, the prime minister launched an effort to restore peace to the Korean peninsula. Subsequent Indian positions included a re-newed call to grant U.N. membership to the Chinese Communists in order to help bring about a settlement; opposition to U.N. troops crossing into North Korea (which the Chinese had warned the Indian ambassador in Peking would lead them to respond with force); and an active, ultimately unsuccessful effort to defeat a widely supported reso-lution condemning aggression by the People's Republic when it did intervene in November 1950. This last Indian initiative had particularly infuriated Washington, which regarded the move as encouraging Com-munist intransigence and prolonging the war.

U.S.-Indian relations were also damaged by India's refusal to take part in the 1951 San Francisco conference, convened to sign the peace treaty the United States had negotiated with Tokyo on behalf of most of the powers allied against Japan in World War II. Like its stand on a Korean settlement, India's decision not to participate was connected with its strong support for Chinese Communist claims to international recognition and its belief that an end to Peking's diplomatic isolation would be beneficial to world peace, positions the United States actively opposed. (Neither Communist China nor the Republic of China on Taiwan had been invited.) India's refusal to go to San Francisco also reflected among other considerations a concern that the treaty would keep Japan within the U.S. security orbit—for Nehru, interested in expanding the nonaligned area of peace, an unwelcome development—and a reluctance to take part in an American-arranged settlement opposed by the Soviet Union. The Indians later signed a separate treaty with Japan.

Closer to home, India's worry about the West was increased by what it perceived as American and British support for Pakistan in the con-tinuing United Nations effort to resolve the Kashmir dispute. New Delhi contrasted the Anglo-American position with Soviet neutrality on the issue, beneficial to India as the status quo power.

Ironically, the 1951 U.S. wheat loan to India probably also worsened

Indian attitudes toward the United States. Sponsored by the Truman administration as the severe impact of the 1950–51 drought became evident and promoted vigorously by senior administration spokesmen on both humanitarian and political grounds, the proposed two-million-ton shipment quickly ran into heavy weather on Capitol Hill. Some congressmen faulted it because of its easy terms (in its initial version it was to have been an outright grant); others objected because of India's foreign policy record, especially its attitude toward the Korean War and the Japanese Peace Treaty. The proposal was eventually enacted as a loan, though not before congressional debate and foot-dragging had generated enough ill will within India to undercut the favorable political impact such generous U.S. action might otherwise have created there.

Differences between the United States and India were heightened by their flawed perceptions of one another. Although contacts between the two dated back to the age of the clipper ship and had expanded during the Second World War, when FDR had taken a sympathetic though equivocal view of India's quest for independence, they still remained limited.[6] Americans and Indians were largely ignorant of one another's history and culture. Their views of each other were often shaped by national stereotypes.[7] For many Indians, the United States was crassly materialistic, prone to violence, and prejudiced against the colored races. For many Americans, India was a backward land of maharajas and untouchables, a nation of dubious spirituality that hypocritically promoted policies of peace and neutralism in distant places while not scrupling to use force in its own backyard.

The preachy and moralistic attitudes of many Americans and Indians and their unfortunate ability to rub one another the wrong way worsened the situation. The low priority the United States gave to South Asia, Washington's tendency to defer to the British in dealing with the region, and the unfamiliarity of most senior American foreign policymakers with the area also discouraged better understanding. American dismay and disappointment with the Indians were heightened by a feeling that a practicing democracy ought to adopt a more pro-Western line, or at least avoid bending so far toward the Communist bloc.

▾   ▾   ▾

Nine months before Bowles's arrival, National Security Council document 98/1 formally spelled out U.S. policy toward South Asia.[8] The paper was written in a Cold War context and reflected the Truman administration's concern about the future of Asia following the "loss of China," the Communist invasions of South Korea and Tibet, and the heightened confrontation in Indochina.[9] Marking the end of what the historian H.W. Brands has called the laissez-faire period in U.S.-Indian relations, it went farther than earlier policy statements in stressing the importance of the South Asian region in the struggle against Communism and the need for greater urgency and risk-taking in pursuing U.S. objectives there.[10] Thirteen months earlier, NSC 48/1 had concluded that "it would be unwise for us to regard South Asia, more particularly India, as the bulwark against the extension of Communist control in Asia."[11] NSC 98/1, by contrast, found that India's fall to Communism "would mean that for all practical purposes all of Asia would have been lost . . ., a serious threat to the security position of the United States." It was therefore important that South Asia's "political strategic manpower and resource potential be marshalled on the side of the United States."[12]

In this new framework, NSC 98/1 called for friendly U.S. relations with the region's countries, the strengthening of their individual and collective efforts to resist Communist imperialism in Asia, their association with the United States and other like-minded countries in opposition to Communism, and the development of South Asian attitudes that "would assist the United States and its allies to obtain the facilities desired in time of peace or required in the event of war." U.S. economic assistance, about to be programmed in the region on a regular basis under the Point Four program, was aimed among other objectives at "improving the Western orientation of India." In line with its essentially negative anti-Communist thrust, the document made no specific mention of any humanitarian need to relieve poverty or any U.S. political interest in strengthening democratic institutions. It was highly conditional in dealing with the possibility of an American security presence in the area: the United States was to seek such military rights in South Asia as it determined to be essential and provide military supplies to the countries in the region if those could be spared from higher priority areas. It was similarly imprecise in its finding that "if a desire for a regional association of non-communist countries exists, [the United States should] be sympathetic and consider to what extent [it] should encourage or associate itself with the movement."

Bowles's discussions and correspondence before leaving the United States made it clear that he would try to build a stronger U.S.-Indian relationship to reflect the importance he believed India had in the achievement of central U.S. foreign policy objectives. Strongly concurring with NSC 98/1 that the loss of India to Communism would expose the rest of "free Asia" to the danger of a Communist takeover, he quickly advanced fresh ideas about the role India could play in the Cold War confrontation between the two power blocs and the policies the United States should adopt to bring this about.

He spelled out these ideas most fully in a long memorandum he sent Acheson in early December, some six weeks after he had taken charge as ambassador.[13] Although he included a wide variety of findings and observations about subjects ranging from Indian attitudes toward the United States ("I have talked to scores of peasants and working people, and I have yet to see anyone whose face did not light up when he heard I was from America") to the need for better propaganda techniques ("Any attempt to force our own [Cold War] analysis upon [the Indians] by blunt accusations is doomed to failure"), three themes stand out: the importance Bowles attached to the role of Communist China in the U.S.-Indian equation; his call for a more substantial economic assistance program; and his hope that with proper treatment by the United States, India under Nehru might eventually be brought to a more pro-Western position.

China. Bowles used his message to Acheson to advance the idea that the comparative economic performances of India and Communist China had major significance for the United States.[14] He contended that should the Chinese Communists succeed and the Nehru government fail in efforts to improve the lot of their people, India's democratic society could rapidly disintegrate, with grave consequences elsewhere in Asia. In a variety of forms, many of them propagated by Bowles himself, this India versus China concept caught hold during the 1950s and became a major rationale for the greatly expanded program of U.S. economic assistance to India later in the decade. But Bowles claimed that Sino-Indian economic competition could work the other way too. India's success, he contended, "sooner or later . . . might have a substantial effect on China," as well as reassuring the Indians of the practical benefits of a democratic approach. "If cultural delegations can come to India to describe the gains of Communist China, cultural groups can also go to China to describe to the Chinese people how India is creating a better life for its people. If democratic India succeeds, the present India-China relationship which now offers such a potential threat to the West, may eventually work to our advantage."

China's relationship with the Soviet Union figured significantly in Bowles's analysis. Going well beyond his role as American ambassador to India into an area which was not his direct concern, he labeled "dangerously defeatist" the assumption of a permanent Sino-Soviet partnership and urged that even though the odds were against such changes, modification of China's current ties with the Soviet Union and the gradual easing of China into a more independent position should become a major long-term U.S. objective. India feared China's close relationship with the Soviet Union about as much as the United States did, he asserted, and it could help pry apart the two Communist giants. In his view, this made it even more important for Washington to develop stronger ties with New Delhi.

Economic Assistance. Before he was confirmed as ambassador, Bowles had let it be known that he favored an economic assistance program for India substantially larger than the one the administration was proposing for the 1952 Fiscal Year ($54 million was eventually appropriated). At his Senate confirmation hearing he had been sharply questioned about his reported call for $250 million annually over a four-year period, but denied ever specifying that price tag. In his memorandum to Acheson he made a strong plea for stepped-up aid to support the Indian Five Year Plan. The success or failure of the plan might be "a decisive factor in determining whether or not Communism takes over this part of the world," he contended. Indeed, developments in India could have even more far-reaching implications. Lenin had said, Bowles erroneously advised the secretary, that "the road to Paris and Western Europe may lie through Peking and Calcutta."[15] He called for an annual $300 million U.S. contribution over the life of the plan, but acknowledged that such aid would not alone ensure its success; economic progress would also require tough Indian government policy choices. He specifically mentioned the importance of vigorous movement on land reform programs.

India's Foreign Policy Posture. Bowles saw the wooing of India as a long-term operation. Agreeing with most other foreign policy analysts of the time, he held that aggressive action to win India to the side of the West would fail. But he was more hopeful than many others about future prospects. "We will make much faster progress," he asserted, "if we let India know that much as we disagree with her [nonaligned policies] we respect her desire to remain aloof for the present, and that our only wish is to help her to help herself (without strings) and to maintain her independence." Such a policy "will create far better feeling towards America [in India] and eventually may enable us to draw her to our side," perhaps moving her "in several stages—from her present cool neutralism, to benevolent neutralism, to the kind of association which we deeply desire." In the meantime, he concluded, "we must be patient, respectful, and above all we must accept India as the foremost Asian nation."

These ideas figured prominently in Bowles's approach to India throughout his first ambassadorship and long afterwards.

▾   ▾   ▾

Not surprisingly—for someone with his background in advertising and politics—Bowles gave considerable attention to public relations. He moved quickly to cultivate the press, and his willingness to meet with journalists for frank exchanges went well beyond the diplomatic norms of the time. His technique was to stress points of agreement between India and America, acknowledge differences candidly, explain U.S. policies in terms relevant to Indian experience and objectives, and admit American mistakes and shortcomings. He used the same approach with other audiences, particularly students, a group he always enjoyed meeting.

This approach appealed to the Indians. As *New Republic* India correspondent Krishnalal Shridharani reported, they found Bowles informal, shrewd, lucid, and fluent,

> a man who speaks like an Indian politician, "almost like Prime Minister Nehru," touching on all subjects, sometimes thinking aloud, often getting engrossed in philosophy and history. . . . But it is the ability to present America's story without neglecting the Indian angles that really counts. For instance, Mr. Bowles imparts to whomever he meets America's preoccupation with aggressive Communism. At the same time, he is not disappointed when Indians do not show the same intensity and the same concern about the problem. . . . He is quite able and willing to grant that India's preoccupation with imperialism and her distrust of foreign influences are psychologically quite sound, given her past experience, although they may not be factually sound.[16]

Bowles tried to ensure that United States Information Service (USIS) programs mirrored his own techniques. He had not been happy with USIS when he arrived. He complained to Benton that "it is not particularly good and in one sense dangerously lacking in judgment. A mistake in advertising or in public relations simply means that you fail to make the sale. In government information work a mistake can destroy all the good which has been built up laboriously over a period of months."[17]

He was particularly concerned with the way USIS had dealt with

Communism, a central theme in the information program. The best way to do that, he thought, was to show that America's interest in India was motivated by more than opposition to Communism. "Above all," he recalled, "our keynote had to be our desire to see India succeed in its efforts to build a strong and happy democracy for its own sake and not because the Communists opposed it."[18]

He soon replaced the USIS mission chief and embarked on an ambitious campaign to strengthen the USIS operation. This included opening new libraries in regional centers, making American paperbacks available at minimal cost, improving the quality of the Voice of America transmissions by broadcasting from Ceylon (Sri Lanka), expanding student grants, and encouraging visits to India by distinguished American educators and public figures. He also widened the distribution, and gave greater emphasis to the quality, of the fortnightly USIS magazine *American Reporter*, which was issued in fourteen regional languages. One particularly interesting and unorthodox aspect of the program was the use of films produced by USIS in India and articles in the *American Reporter* to highlight for the Indians what they were themselves accomplishing through the Five Year Plan. Bowles believed that this cheerleading effort would help instill a greater sense of self-confidence in the Indians and encourage further progress.

He insisted that the whole mission staff join in the campaign, which he led, to improve mutual understanding and bilateral ties. When Bowles arrived, the staff comprised about 150 Americans (and many more Indians) stationed at the embassy, the consulates general in Bombay, Calcutta, and Madras, and USIS cultural centers in several state capitals. During his tenure it expanded rapidly as economic assistance specialists came to man the new aid programs. Their assignment radically changed what had been the predominantly "diplomatic" character of the mission under his two predecessors.

Dissatisfied with the traditional ways they operated, Bowles encouraged embassy staffers to get out of New Delhi more often, study Hindi, and rely less in their reporting to Washington on the gossip of the diplomatic circuit and the columns of English language dailies. He wanted them to become exposed to what he saw as an emerging new India. In doing so they would offer Indians an opportunity to learn from them about the United States.

To further this effort to broaden contacts, he introduced the practice of celebrating the American national day at a large outdoor gathering on George Washington's Birthday, when the cool weather of a North Indian February ensured a pleasant setting. This replaced the conventional July Fourth observance, a small gathering of diplomats and senior Indian officials necessarily held indoors because of the heat and monsoon rains. (Forty years later the embassy in New Delhi and many other U.S. South Asian diplomatic posts continue to follow Bowles's lead.) His letter to Wesleyan University professor Stephen Bailey about the party gives the flavor of his approach:

> We had a large celebration on the Embassy grounds for about 2500 people. In addition to the regular diplomatic and top level Indian Government guests we asked members of the House of the People [lower house of the Indian Parliament], professors, teachers, social workers, and a great variety of other people, including foreign and Indian employees of all the embassies in town. It was the kind of a party which in the past has been given only by the communists (either Russian or Chinese). The rest of us, not only in Delhi but, I am afraid, in many other parts of the world, are inclined to invite only the top level diplomatic and government circles. From the comments we have already received the party was a great success in demonstrating to our Indian friends that we like them and that we like to be with them. It also gave us an opportunity to remind the Indian people that our country, too, was born in revolution and that we have that in common.[19]

Bowles's strongly held views about how to go about improving relations caused problems between him and some of the staffers he had inherited. In an otherwise highly favorable account of his first weeks in India, the *New York Times* reported that "his informality . . . has even appeared to disconcert some U.S. career Foreign Service officers who have been brought up in an atmosphere of austere diplomatic punctilio that is apparently foreign to the former Connecticut Governor."[20] These officers thought that in some of his practices, such as putting his children into an Indian school, Bowles was going too far in trying to make himself popular. They believed that many important Indians felt the same way.

But Foreign Service officers usually adjust reasonably quickly to the personal style of their new masters. Although Bowles's techniques were very different from those of the dignified and aloof career diplomat he succeeded, the staff at New Delhi soon came to live with the changes, whatever private misgivings they may have had. Steb Bowles played a helpful role in encouraging them to accept a less formal style than they were accustomed to. Though some resisted, and looked down their noses at newly arrived economic assistance agency families, many of them county agents and their wives who had never heard of calling cards, let alone which corner of the card was to be folded over when paying courtesy calls, Bowles seems to have been reasonably satisfied with the way this aspect of embassy life worked out.

There were more far-reaching problems, however. Some were related to policy. Not all of the staff were prepared to accept easily Bowles's highly positive view of the possibilities for improved relations with Nehru's India. In the opinion of one senior officer, the ambassador was mistaken in ignoring Nehru's anti-American bias. The officer recalled that, to Bowles, "Nehru was a great guy; everything he did was fine." Differences over China policy were another bone of contention. Bowles's impatience with those who disagreed with him on such fundamentals of policy, and his tendency to ignore them if they persisted in raising errant views, compounded the problem. "He didn't have much use for Foreign Service officers if they had their own opinions," the same officer remembered.[21]

Staff changes, some of them reflecting normal rotation, others prompted by Bowles, led to a more compatible professional relationship between the ambassador and his staff as his assignment progressed. But he was still dissatisfied at the end of his tenure, particularly with his political officers. "There are some good people on the Political Section staff," he wrote in early March 1953 to George V. Allen, who had been named to succeed him as ambassador, "but with the exception of [one officer], most of them do not know the country as well as they should. I have tried to insist on an average of 25 percent travel time for everyone, and this has helped." Political reporting remained inadequate, he told Allen. "We should do a great deal more digging, and I think it is particularly important to develop a closer understanding of the state governments and state leaders."[22]

Bowles was himself a great traveler: he told Donald Kennedy in December 1952 that he had covered 41,000 miles in his fourteen months in India.[23] He made good public relations use of his trips: glossies can still be found in embassy files depicting him lending a hand with a shovel on a road-building project or talking to a photogenic peasant about crops. He came to know leaders and ordinary people throughout the country. The reports he sent to the State Department of his meetings with them and other aspects of his journeys accented the changes taking place in India.

His focus was always on economic and social progress and how the United States could help India achieve it in a democratic framework. Traditional India had little appeal to him. He loved to visit new hydroelectric dams, not temples and palaces. It is a telling commentary on his interests and priorities that as he crisscrossed India seeking out evidence of development and modernization, he never found time to stop in Benares, the city sacred to Hindus on the banks of the Ganges and the epitome of the poor, conservative, backward land he wanted so impatiently to see changed.

▾   ▾   ▾

The high priest of this new India was Jawaharlal Nehru. During Bowles's first assignment, the prime minister further consolidated his virtually uncontested power by leading the Congress party to election victory. His influence in world affairs, which reached a zenith in the years immediately following Bowles's departure, was already enormous, a remarkable achievement in light of India's limited economic and military standing. The effectiveness of ambassadors to India depended critically on the rapport they were able to establish with Nehru and their ability to influence him.

Many who dealt with the prime minister in the 1950s were convinced he had a dislike for Americans as a people that helped fuel the suspicions he frequently entertained about Washington's policies and motives. Some attributed this bias to the influence of British socialism, others to the prime minister's upper-class English education. Nehru told David Lilienthal, who was his house guest in New Delhi a few months before Bowles became ambassador, that Americans were regimented by public opinion and lacked perception of things outside themselves: "So when differences arise between us, you can't see what Asia has in mind because of this lack of ability to imbibe anything outside yourselves, because you are so full of yourselves."[24] Escott Reid, the Canadian high commissioner in India during much of the 1950s, found that "when [Nehru] likes an individual American he says he is unrepresentative of the United States."[25]

Bowles's success in developing with Nehru a personal and professional relationship as candid in tone as it was broad in scope was especially noteworthy against this background. The two men met often during Bowles's first assignment, maintained their close ties through correspondence and visits for the next ten years, and resumed their regular contacts when Bowles came back to New Delhi as ambassador in 1963, ten months before Nehru died. Probably exaggerating somewhat, Bowles recalled sessions as frequent as two, three, or even four times a week, lasting anywhere from twenty minutes to three hours. "Nehru almost took me as a partner," he told an interviewer in discussing the patterns of his first ambassadorship.[26]

Not surprisingly, other ambassadors were envious. A conversation with Nehru, if he was in the right humor, was worth a dozen talks with lesser Indian government lights and made the diplomat look good at home. "Almost every Embassy in New Delhi used to come to us to find out what Nehru was thinking," Bowles recounted.

Like many foreigners and Indians who knew Nehru in his heyday, Bowles was fascinated by the prime minister. He wrote lengthy assessments of Nehru's character and views in both *Ambassador's Report* and *Promises to Keep*. As do many of the official messages, personal letters, and interviews in which he discussed Nehru, they reflect a sentiment approaching hero worship and a strong proclivity to apologize for the prime minister's shortcomings and the many opinions he had which were distasteful to Americans. Bowles's observations also tend to be disappointingly superficial, especially when contrasted with the sophisticated analyses of High Commissioner Reid and some of the prime minister's biographers.

Bowles found that "no one can put Nehru in a nutshell," and that he was "many-sided, complex, full of conflicting enthusiasms, and burdened by many sorrows." "The most important, most attractive, and in many ways the most puzzling character on the Asian scene," the prime minister was also the most articulate man Bowles had ever conversed with. Taking issue with the more common view, Bowles maintained that Nehru was not anti-American and that he had many American friends and liked most Americans he met. He acknowledged, however, that "Nehru looked upon Americans in general as an upper class Englishman might look on them—generous, well meaning, but clumsy and brash."[27]

Those familiar with the relationship agree that Nehru thought highly of this unusual American ambassador. Although the prime minister has left behind no available assessment of Bowles, it seems reasonable to conclude that he was gratified by the ambassador's strong support for India and the emphasis he gave to Asia. Nehru probably saw Bowles as an envoy who would report his views sympathetically and could be influenced into accepting them.

Some of their interests and attitudes blended well, strengthening the relationship. Both were conceptualizers who enjoyed sketching out ideas in speculative, rambling, yet highly articulate ways. They were both students of their countries' histories and frequently brought historical analogy into their analyses of foreign and domestic policy. They approached issues with a blend of realism and idealism. Nehru probably valued Bowles's earnestness, remarkable good will and frankness, and lack of pretension. Bowles's obvious admiration for Nehru also seems likely to have figured in the warm regard of the prime minister, who liked flattery and praise when they were offered in good taste.

Bowles and Nehru discussed a broad range of topics. Bowles found that "except on two or three particularly charged subjects, I have never known anyone in public life who seemed more willing to listen objectively and to change his mind when the facts or logic called for it."[28] One of these charged subjects was Kashmir: the prime minister's views were too colored by an emotional attachment to the disputed state for easy dialogue.

Concepts of economic development figured significantly in their talks. Land reform was particularly high on Bowles's agenda. He considered more equitable land distribution and tenure a crucial element for Third World economic and political progress. Although his views did not represent official U.S. government policy, which favored land reform in principle but did not give it the urgency he did, he pushed Nehru and others hard on the issue. He soon came to be troubled by the way the prime minister dealt with it. The problem was not Nehru's good intentions—he had called for reform as early as 1931—but his lack of political will when confronted by vested interests in the Congress party that considered land reform a threat to their own political, economic, and social positions.[29]

In his discussions with the prime minister, Bowles repeatedly stressed the need for urgent action. He brought American land reform experts Wolf Ladejinsky and Kenneth Parsons to India and arranged for them to meet with Nehru. He called to Nehru's attention the inadequacy of reform measures already taken. He was startled by the prime minister's lack of information about the absence of progress in implementing land reform programs. To Bowles, this indicated the extent to which Nehru was influenced and misled by the increasingly conservative views of some of his cabinet colleagues.[30] Discussing allegations that Nehru had dictatorial tendencies, Bowles reported to Washington that "the danger lies not in arbitrary action but . . . rather [in] his unwillingness, while praising China's land reform, actually to press the states to take action here; his failure to set up an administration with clear cut emergency powers; and his love of talk and give and take" in Parliament.[31]

Although he kept trying to move Nehru, he made little progress. In the impressions of the prime minister which he prepared for the Nehru Library oral history collection in 1971, he called the failure to bring about adequate land reform measures Nehru's greatest mistake. "If Nehru had put through land reform, which he could have done in 1951–53 when he was so powerful, I think he could have provided a

much more solid political base for Indian democracy," Bowles concluded.[32]

Personal relations were important for the prime minister, and to have
as American ambassador a liberal, sympathetic, Asia-oriented admirer
able to talk to him on a wave length he appreciated helped give him
a better understanding of U.S. policies and, on occasion, led him to
accept these. But Nehru's influence on Bowles was much more decisive,
especially on foreign policy issues.

The asymmetry of the relationship is not surprising. Although
Bowles came to India with some decided ideas about foreign affairs,
he was in 1951 still very much an impressionable novice in the field.
He was naturally susceptible to the views of the experienced and
articulate prime minister, particularly since these so often fitted well
with his own liberal and idealistic approach to the international scene
in general and to Asia and India in particular. Bowles was never blindly
uncritical of the prime minister, and he recognized Nehru's failings and
the narrowness of some of his policies. But the power of Nehru's ideas
on a wide variety of issues—China was the most evident example—had
a profound impact on Bowles at the time and continued to influence
his thinking long after he left New Delhi.

Bowles's admiration for Nehru was not shared by many in Washington, and the "great neutral's" approach to the world found little
favor among senior American officials. They found him arrogant and
overbearing, ponderous and evasive, a man with a chip on his shoulder
regarding America and Americans. The efforts of Bowles to win for
the prime minister a more sympathetic audience were largely unsuccessful. The dissatisfaction with the attitudes Nehru struck during his
disappointing 1949 visit lingered on. As increased Cold War pressures
in 1950 and afterwards made India more important to U.S. interests,
the policies the prime minister adopted toward East Asian issues and
the Kashmir problem heightened the negative feelings he aroused
within the Truman administration and elsewhere in the country.
Acheson acknowledged that Nehru was a force to be contended with:
"He was so important to India and India's survival so important to all
of us, that if he did not exist—as Voltaire said of God—he would have
to be invented."[33] But the secretary also found Nehru one of the most
difficult men he had ever dealt with and was deeply suspicious of his
ideas. Though others in the upper echelons of the State Department
could not match Acheson's cutting and scholarly eloquence, many of
them held similar views and thought Bowles naive and gullible in
believing otherwise.

4

Spotlighting Economic
Assistance

THE economic assistance program was by far the single most important focus for Bowles's attention, imagination, and enthusiasm during his first New Delhi assignment. It was the cornerstone of his agenda for bettering U.S.-Indian relations and helping India strengthen its commitment to democracy in the face of what he and many others considered a serious Communist challenge. Perhaps even more important, the aid program represented what for Bowles was the most exciting and rewarding aspect of America's postwar international role—the export of its wealth, skill, and values to help the disadvantaged of the world help themselves achieve better, more productive lives in a democratic setting. It was a tangible reflection abroad of the liberal precepts he championed at home, an opportunity to work with the Indians to develop programs that would have a direct positive impact on ordinary people—for him the ultimate purpose of policy, foreign and domestic.

Bowles believed that U.S. financial and technical support could play a crucial role in providing additional resources to achieve the objectives of India's First Five Year Plan. He generally accepted the plan, though in an early message to Assistant Secretary of State George McGhee, who shared his views on the importance of high levels of assistance to the Indians, he described it as "fuzzy" on many essential points.[1] Aid also offered the United States—and Bowles personally—the opportunity to influence the Indian government in its choice of economic policies and programs. For Bowles, this meant pressing for an approach that would move India toward a liberal, socially conscious private enterprise system in which the foreign exchange savings achieved by self-sufficiency in foodgrains could, over time, finance rapid industrial growth. He was confident that with extensive domestic economic reforms (especially in land tenure and tax policy), adequate incentives to producers, generous assistance from the United States, and a modicum of foreign private investment, India could be well on its way to developing such a system within only a few years.

▾   ▾   ▾

Before he left Washington, Bowles had made clear his determination to play a major part in both formulating and implementing the aid program. Once in India, he monitored the aid staff as closely as he could short of interfering in its day-to-day operations. He used aid mission Deputy Director Bernard Loshbough, his former Connecticut associate, to keep him fully informed about aid activities and ensure that these were in line with his own thinking. He developed close contact with Indian government officials on economic assistance matters. He also built a highly productive relationship with the Ford Foundation, especially Ford Mission Director Douglas Ensminger, as it came to play the key role in training Indian staff for the U.S.-assisted community development program. Phil Coombs continued to act as his liaison and advocate on economic assistance matters with sympathetic and influential figures in Congress, the State Department, and the Washington aid bureaucracy.

Bowles's hands-on approach to the aid program reflected not only his strong commitment to economic assistance but his conception of the role of an American ambassador. A chief of mission, he held, should take active charge of all phases of his post's operations. He derided ambassadors who preferred to focus exclusively on their traditional diplomatic roles of political reporting and negotiating and who neglected (either as beneath them or beyond them) major new programs such as economic aid, educational exchange, and information that had become important parts of the expanded postwar U.S. overseas effort. His approach was a forerunner of the Country Team concept he persuaded the Kennedy administration to adopt when he was under secretary of state in 1961. This system, still in effect, gives an ambassador responsibility for the conduct of all local U.S. government activities other than those that fall under major military commands.

Fortuitous timing allowed Bowles to exercise leadership over the aid program in an unusually powerful way. His appointment as ambassador coincided with the beginning of long-term, annually appropriated economic assistance under the Point Four program.[2] Although this program for assisting in the "improvement and growth of underdeveloped areas" had been proposed by Truman in his 1949 inaugural address—more than two and a half years before Bowles reached India—it had subsequently languished, "victimized," as Thomas Paterson has persuasively put it, "by bureaucratic warfare between Pennsylvania Avenue and Foggy Bottom, State Department lethargy, events which detracted from the program's importance, and congressional inertia."[3] A modest $26.5 million was appropriated for the entire program for Fiscal Year 1951, beginning July 1, 1950. The United States subsequently signed a $4.5 million agreement with India in December 1950, which funded the cost of American technical and economic advisers. As already noted, Washington also provided two million tons of grain, valued at $190 million, as a loan to meet India's emergency food requirements the following spring. But it was only in FY 1952 that substantial assistance to India was set up on a regular, long-term basis.

The $54 million appropriation was considerably less than State Department officials, led by George McGhee, had sought for India and was minuscule compared to the military assistance and economic aid sent to countries in Western Europe and the Far East. But it did allow Bowles to be present at the creation of the program in New Delhi. Unlike most ambassadors, who inherit established programs and must struggle with the Washington aid bureaucracy and their own aid staffs if they wish to change them, he had the opportunity to shape the main contours of the assistance program to conform to his own ideas.

Bowles made rural community development the core of the American aid program. He had been favorably impressed by Dr. James Yen's success with integrated rural development in China and wrote to him just before leaving for New Delhi: "I would like nothing better than the opportunity to put your ideas to work in India on a growing scale."[4]

The Indians themselves had been thinking and working along similar lines. In 1948, the government of the north Indian state of Uttar Pradesh had begun a program in Etawah, not far from New Delhi, that involved simultaneous introduction of new methods of fertilizing, better seeds, public health measures, primary education, and literacy courses in the district's villages. The project had been proposed to the Indians by Albert Mayer, an eccentric American architect and town planner who had become interested in the problems and potential of the Indian countryside when he was stationed in India during the Second World War as an officer in the U.S. Army Corps of Engineers. It was carried out primarily by village workers trained for the purpose. They were supported by a staff of specialists in agriculture, public health, and education, who were assigned a group of villages and were available to help the village workers when problems arose.[5]

Nehru had encouraged Mayer, and the Indian government had come to consider Etawah a showpiece of Indian rural progress. Foreign visitors interested in rural development were invariably taken to see it. Bowles went there a few weeks after his arrival in New Delhi and was greatly taken by what he saw: "As I listened to the hard-working, dedicated instructors in the village worker school and watched workers in the fields and villages, it seemed that this was the key to the future of India and Asia. Here was an administrative framework through which modern scientific knowledge could be put to work for the benefit of the hundreds of millions of people who have so long lived in poverty."[6] He was similarly impressed by Faridabad, an urban township south of New Delhi developed by the Indian Cooperative Union for refugees from Pakistan. Like Etawah, it followed an integrated approach combining economic productivity with social services.

Earlier in 1951, Nehru had been nettled by congressional criticism of the wheat loan. In a May 1 radio address, he had told the Indian public that "such help must not have any political strings attached to it, any conditions which are unbecoming for a self-respecting nation to accept, any pressure to change our domestic or international policy."[7] The prime minister had eventually recognized that the provisions of the loan would not impair Indian freedom of action and had accepted them. But the episode had led Ambassador Loy Henderson to be wary of going ahead with the pending new long-term aid program until the Indians reviewed and explicitly agreed to its terms.[8] When Chargé d'Affaires Loyd Steere subsequently went over the terms of the program with Nehru, the prime minister had accepted his assurances that U.S. aid was not given to foreign countries with any idea of exerting pressure on them to change their internal or foreign policies and had agreed to the establishment of the program under the standard terms and conditions Steere had spelled out to him.[9]

Bowles was concerned, nonetheless, about how Nehru would react when he went to see him on Thanksgiving Day in 1951, following word from Washington of India's share of the FY 1952 technical assistance program. This was one-third of the total annual budget of the Technical Cooperation Administration, which had been set up the previous year within the State Department to manage the Point Four program. Bowles thought it important to reassure the prime minister that there would be no political or economic strings attached to the aid package.[10]

On that occasion, Bowles gave Nehru a memorandum he had drafted outlining a "personal and unofficial" proposal for a nationwide plan of village development. As he stated in the memo, "[The proposal] represents simply my own views on how the experience already gained at Faridabad, Etawah, and other projects may be expanded into a dynamic, cooperative effort to raise living, health and literacy standards in all parts of India, within the next five–seven years."[11] He found Nehru much taken by the concept: "For nearly two hours we talked about the exciting possibilities. When I left [Nehru] thanked me earnestly for the help that the American people had offered. I said that we wanted no thanks and indeed that if India succeeded in raising her living standards by democratic means and demonstrated to Asia and to the world that men can have bread and freedom too, the whole free world would be in India's debt."[12]

The Nehru-Bowles discussion paved the way for the signing of a major bilateral aid agreement on January 4, 1952. Under the agreement, which Bowles had a major hand in negotiating, the two governments worked out a program covering fifty-five selected areas with a total of 16,500 villages and 11 million people, some 3 percent of India's total population. In the manner of the Etawah project in north India and Yen's efforts in China, the program focused on improving agricultural productivity, basic public health, and education. It also provided for control of malaria, then (and again today) a major problem in India. The United States agreed to contribute about $25 million for the program. The Indian government undertook to provide the equivalent of $72 million in rupees, mostly to pay Indian staff. Program administration was entirely in Indian hands; American experts acted only as advisers. The Ford Foundation took major responsibility for training over six thousand specialists and village-level workers. The U.S. government also undertook to fund high priority special projects outside the areas selected for the community development program, notably fertilizer plants, major irrigation works, the improvement of marine fisheries, and additional malaria control programs. Bowles was much less interested in these than he was in community development.[13]

Even before the agreement was signed, Bowles tried to share with the Indians the enormous enthusiasm he felt about community development and to persuade Nehru and his government to adopt his ideas about how the program could be most effectively run. He urged a strategy that would maximize self-help on the part of the rural masses, spread the program over as wide an area as available resources would allow, and assure high-level Indian government attention and support. He successfully headed off an Indian move to put more funds into selected districts, because this would have reduced popular responsibility for development and further limited the areas covered by the program. He was unable, however, to persuade the Indians to assign responsibility for the program to a cabinet-level official or to win approval for an autonomous TVA-like body to manage it. Despite these setbacks, he was reasonably satisfied with the way the program was operated under the direction of the young, American-educated engineer S. K. Dey and considered it a great success.[14]

▾   ▾   ▾

Bowles was untiring in his effort to build support for the program in the United States and to ensure that it was adequately funded. In private correspondence with influential friends, multiple mailings to congressmen and the media, official cables to the State Department and the White House, and articles for such major publications as the *New York Times Magazine* and *Foreign Affairs,* he issued from his New Delhi office a stream of copy designed to persuade other Americans that India was important to the United States and to heighten their awareness of the scope of the aid program, its effectiveness, and its crucial role in the struggle to meet "the Communist challenge to Free Asia." He supplemented these extensive mailings with two visits to the United States to carry on his campaign in congressional hearings, TV and radio appearances, and meetings with senior officials and others who could advance his efforts. He also collaborated with a New York firm headed by Edward Bernays, the famous public relations adviser. The Indian embassy in Washington had engaged the firm to help design a campaign to sell India to Americans, very possibly at Bowles's suggestion. The campaign included the further dissemination of his writings to American audiences.[15]

Bowles tried to persuade influential Americans both inside and outside the government to visit India and see its economic development and political dynamics for themselves, confident that those who did so would become more sympathetic to the programs and policies he favored. The poor response his invitations received disappointed him. He complained to newspaper columnist Walter Lippmann in November 1952 that there had been a stream of military visitors, and the heads of the U.S. Information Agency and the Technical Cooperation Agency had come out, but "no assistant secretary [of state] has been to India for nearly two years and no political officer of any importance since May 1951."[16] He was similarly unsuccessful in persuading important private Americans to visit, Lippmann among them. During the seventeen months of Bowles's first assignment as ambassador, the only really prominent private American who traveled to India was Mrs. Eleanor Roosevelt, in the spring of 1952.

Not all of the visits that did take place were unalloyed successes. Bowles recounted that when the commander in chief of U.S. Pacific forces, Admiral Arthur W. Radford, came to New Delhi in November 1952, Mrs. Radford found herself seated next to Indira Gandhi's husband Feroze at a dinner party at Bowles's residence. Catching only the last name of her Indian dinner partner, she breathlessly exulted to him that never in her life had she thought she would meet the great Mahatma Gandhi. Mohandas K. Gandhi had in fact been assassinated more than four years earlier. When one of those to whom he later told the story found it highly amusing, Bowles, who had no sense of humor about such things, sharply demurred. He said it was the worst day of his life.[17]

▾　　▾　　▾

Bowles made much the same pitch to all those he sought to influence, officials and private citizens alike. His public advocacy was unorthodox. Few American ambassadors have campaigned as openly and strenuously as he did for policies the administrations they served had not yet accepted. If some eyebrows were raised in the State Department and elsewhere about this approach, he did not let that deter him.

It is difficult to measure the effectiveness of these efforts. Senator Benton, for one, warned him against a tendency to oversell, an ad man's failing his old Madison Avenue partner was uniquely placed to spot. In their frequent correspondence, Benton also noted that while Bowles had added steam to the India program on Capitol Hill and had heightened the interest of the American people in the country, he should also keep in mind that "India is so remote from the Senate, in this political year [1952], that [it] is never mentioned at all."[18]

The flavor of Bowles's hard-hitting campaign comes through pungently in his early messages. "What happens here [in India] in the next three to five years may determine the future of democratic governments in Asia for several generations," he told Connecticut Senator Brien McMahon in January 1952.[19] Reporting on his consultations in Washington, he wrote President Truman later that month that "nowhere did anyone challenge my basic premise, i.e. that the loss of India will mean the loss of Asia, and the loss of Asia will shake the very foundation of the democratic world, including the military line which we are striving so urgently to build in Europe. . . . If U.S. assistance is not forthcoming, the odds will be strongly against the survival of the Nehru

Government in the next elections [scheduled for 1956]. . . . Even [Nehru's] most ardent supporters are grimly saying, 'This is our last chance'."[20]

Bowles used even starker terms in a memorandum ("The Crucial Problem of India") he sent to prominent figures in Congress and the press. He spoke of the "deadly cycle of events" which a Communist victory in India would set in motion. It would lead "to the loss of non-Communist Asia [;] and to many hundreds of millions of people in Europe, Africa, and the Americas, the loss of Asia would appear to be the handwriting on the wall." In his assessment, "the basic test of democracy in India will be the ability of the present [Nehru] government to raise the living standards of the people under the Five Year Plan."[21] Although the Indian Communist party and its allies had failed to develop an effective challenge to Congress at the national level and had won only 5.4 percent of the vote for parliamentary seats in the elections held in early 1952, it had scored gains in some of the south Indian states.[22] Bowles said that these "provide an ominous preview of what the next general election will be like if the Nehru Government is unable to meet this crucial test." In an underscored sentence he warned, "Let there be no mistake about it: if Nehru goes, Communism takes over."

While sounding these notes of urgent alarm, Bowles also cautioned that U.S. assistance, though crucial, could not alone save India from Communism. He told Ford Foundation President Paul Hoffman: "The real bulwark against Communism in this area must be built by the Indians themselves with whatever assistance we can give them. The most important thing of all is for the Indians to gain confidence in their own abilities and their own ways. They must develop a sense of accomplishment, the conviction that they are on their way towards a better life, and that basically they are succeeding through their own efforts."[23] To McMahon he wrote, "We in the United States cannot *determine* India's future, but with patience, understanding, and a moderate amount of economic assistance we can buttress the potentially strong anti-Communist forces which exist here [in India], and vastly improve the chances for a democratic success."[24]

The manner in which the United States provided aid was also important. "If our assistance is offered on the condition that the 'Star Spangled Banner' be played every time an American truck goes up the street, our efforts will not be successful," he wrote Hoffman. "But if we set as our goal the building of a new India through the leadership and efforts of the Indian people themselves, there will be plenty of good will for America, and most important of all, there will be a solid determination that India must never accept totalitarian rule, and that her ways must remain democratic ways."[25]

As these excerpts suggest, Bowles built his campaign for support for India and a well-funded U.S. economic program there primarily in terms of meeting the widely perceived Communist challenge. Given the climate that prevailed in Washington and elsewhere in the country in late 1951 and 1952, this made good sense tactically. With Communist China fighting U.S.-led United Nations forces in Korea and seemingly posing a threat to other parts of Asia as well, American opinion was likely to be more responsive to this appeal than to other approaches. Despite the ringing language Truman had used in proposing Point Four, the concept of economic assistance to poor countries as a good in itself generated only limited support on Capitol Hill and elsewhere, except when it was designed to meet emergency situations. As the debate over the Indian wheat loan demonstrated, even then acceptance did not come easily.

Only rarely in his correspondence did Bowles stress the more positive aspects of aid to India. A letter he wrote in January 1952 to Abram Chayes is one of the few that links Bowles's liberal view of America and its world role with need for economic assistance. During Bowles's term as governor Chayes had served as his legal adviser, and the two men shared many values. But even in that eloquent letter Bowles continued to stress the fight against Communism: "The single force capable of dealing with the Communist forces in Asia," he said, "is the United States, *operating within its best liberal traditions* [underscored in the original]. This calls for an America willing to share its wealth with countries which are willing to do their own share; an America free of racial prejudices and willing to accept men of all creeds and colors as their equals; an America keenly aware of the problems of defense but equally aware that we can not buy security with bombs."[26]

Looking back now at the failure of the Communist Party of India (CPI) in the 1950s and after to mount any serious bid for national power despite the country's continuing economic problems and often disappointing progress, a skeptic may conclude that Bowles's highlighting of the threat the Communists allegedly posed was a cynical effort on his part to develop support among Americans, whom he knew to be as fearful of the Red menace as they were uninformed about Communist strength in India. This would be wrong. Although Communist-sponsored insurgencies had been crushed and the party's turn to the parliamentary path had brought few dividends, many Indians and foreign observers believed that Communism represented a continuing danger. They feared that if the Nehru government failed to confront the country's development needs effectively in a democratic setting, the CPI might well win power, either through elections or by taking advantage of chaotic conditions caused by economic breakdown. For all its handicaps, which included its well-remembered support for the imperial British government as a Soviet ally after the Nazi invasion of Russia in 1941, the Communist party had a message that could appeal to the newly enfranchised and desperately poor Indian masses. If the Chinese and Soviets made the economic progress many predicted, this appeal would be enhanced. The Indian Communists had an experienced, if often divided, leadership, a cadre of dedicated party workers, and the advantage of Soviet funding and support. They would also benefit, it was feared, by the dimming over time of the appeal of the Nehru-led Congress as the party that had won independence for India.

Although Bowles at times characteristically overdramatized the Communist threat, he almost certainly shared many of these widely held views. He provided a candid assessment of Communist prospects in a letter he wrote in December 1952 to Donald Kennedy of the State Department's South Asian office, a confidant he had come to trust. "If Communism comes to India," Bowles forecast, "it will result from the gradual breaking down of the central government authority, the establishment of a few relatively autonomous Communist-governed states, the undermining of progress designed to raise living standards, and the slow resulting growth of chaos." He said that the takeover would not be sudden or dramatic, and assessed the chances of India's eventually going Communist at fifty-fifty.[27]

▾   ▾   ▾

Throughout his assignment Bowles engaged in an almost constant battle with Washington to get more money for the aid program and a long-term U.S. commitment to the First Five Year Plan. The account of the prolonged battle over aid levels that emerges from the endless messages drafted by Bowles and others in New Delhi and Washington has many of the familiar features of important bureaucratic struggles. Overstated arguments, appeals to higher authority, buck passing, differing interpretations of congressional attitudes, action-forcing events, mistaken signals, networking, and sudden, unexpected changes in position and prospects all figured prominently in those earliest days of U.S. assistance to developing countries. They still do today.

Bowles came to Washington in January 1952 to fight for the program. His goal at that point was an FY 1953 budget of $250 million as part of a four-year, $1 billion commitment. Half of this was to be for such programs as the drilling of tube wells, the transfer of U.S. Liberty ships for India's coastal shipping, provision of DDT, earthmoving equipment, and fertilizer, and the start-up of fifty additional community development projects. Foreshadowing the huge agricultural commodity transfers of the late 1950s and early 1960s under Public Law 480, Bowles wanted the other half used to pay for Indian imports of American cotton, milo, and wheat. The counterpart rupee funds generated from the sale of these commodities would be used to meet the local costs of the expanded community development program.[28]

Meeting with congressmen, Bowles got a mixed reception. Senate Foreign Relations Committee Chairman Tom Connally expressed strong opposition to increased aid and was abusive to Bowles personally because of what the crusty old Texan considered his unduly pro-Indian viewpoint. Bowles found a more sympathetic audience in the executive branch, where both President Truman and Mutual Security Director Averell Harriman seemed generally sympathetic to his proposals. Though he later recalled that Acheson was less supportive, the secretary's staff did pass on for appropriate action at the regional bureau level a memo recording that he had assured Bowles that he would help him push his ideas on the Indian economic program.[29]

As ambassadors often do after such consultations, Bowles left Washington feeling confident that he would get what he wanted. He was shocked when, soon after he returned to New Delhi, he was informed that the assistance level for 1953 would be only slightly higher than in the previous year. In the intensely Cold War atmosphere generated by the prolonged fighting in Korea, the administration continued to give much higher priority to military allies than to nonaligned countries like India, despite his arguments and the importance NSC 98/1 gave to the struggle against Communism in South Asia.[30]

Bowles struck hard for more funds and warned in dire terms of the consequences of failing to provide them. Truman was a prime target for his appeal. In a ten-paragraph cable to the president, he challenged the State Department's assertion that Congress was unsympathetic to the program—throughout Bowles's tenure a major concern of the administration in dealing with India. Besides, he told Truman in a moment of political naivete, "if the Republican Party refuses to support this program for India then the basic political motivation and dishonesty of their criticism of past Chinese policy will be dramatically evident." As compared with outlays for the comparatively minuscule populations of Taiwan and Greece, the funding he sought for India was cheap at the price, he added.[31]

Over the next months projected funding levels for India rose and fell as the administration found some additional money, only to see the entire aid budget slashed by Congress. The administration was concerned that the Indians were slow in using the money already appropriated. In light of the priority it gave to areas where Cold War threats seemed more ominous, it was reluctant to provide greater funding absent a critical emergency.

Bowles's second visit to Washington as ambassador, in June 1952, obliged Truman, Acheson, and Harriman to give personal attention to the issue, but it did not produce the results he had asked for. His call for an India-specific supplementary appropriation got a cold shoulder from the White House: though the president did follow his advice and issue a statement that focused on the problem Congress had created for U.S. efforts in India, he effectively killed Bowles's proposal by referring it to the Bureau of the Budget for review. When the dust finally settled, the program for India in FY 1953 totaled only $44.2 million. This was about eight million dollars *less* than the 1952 figure.[32]

This severe setback did not deter Bowles from resuming the fight when the FY 1954 budget battle began a few months later. Displaying both unabated fervor and his customary remarkable resilience, he weighed in with a long letter to Acheson at the end of October which went even further than his earlier messages in its apocalyptic assessment of the stakes involved. According to Bowles, India's continued existence as a free and friendly nation had become second in importance only to the survival of a free Western Europe. "Indeed," he warned, "it is wholly possible that these two great strategic areas may stand or fall together."[33]

Specifically, Bowles asked for $250 million annually for a three-year period, with $150 million earmarked for commodity grants (none had been voted the previous year, when many in the administration had felt that such grants were outside the scope of Point Four) and $100 million for other programs. He also called for a guarantee, "or as close as Congress can come to giving a guarantee," that American resources will be made available to give the Indian government the opportunity to meet its Five Year Plan goals before the 1956 parliamentary elections. "If we wait until the situation really begins to fall apart," he predicted, "Congress will undoubtedly vote any sum we request. But by that time it will be too late for effective action."[34]

By then in his last weeks in office following the Republican election victory in November, Acheson replied in a valedictory message to Bowles in early January 1953 that the outgoing Truman administration had decided to budget the Indian aid program for FY 1954 at about $200 million.[35] His successor as secretary of state in the Eisenhower administration, John Foster Dulles, refused to confirm this figure, however. Dulles was no friend of nonaligned India and was even less inclined than Acheson and others in the Truman administration had been to battle on India's behalf on Capitol Hill. Dulles doubted, he told State Department officials, that the amount was "either justified by the facts or could be justified to Congress." On his instruction, it was initially lowered to $140 million, a level Eisenhower approved despite further appeals from Bowles. Congress eventually made $89.1 million available.[36]

▾ ▾ ▾

By the time Bowles had completed his assignment in March 1953, 115 Americans had come to India to staff the economic assistance program. Most of them were technicians working outside New Delhi. Agriculture, literacy, and public health projects funded by the United States had reached 10,000 villages in the six months after the program's inception on Mahatma Gandhi's birthday in October 1952. Bowles highlighted that achievement in a letter to his designated successor, George Allen: "[Point Four] has enormous political significance and in the last year we have convinced the Indian Government and most Indian officials with [sic] the integrity of our operation and the sincerity of our approach." He warned Allen that "any effort by the administration or Congress to tie political strings to Indian aid or to force us to go out to 'claim credit' which really belongs to the Indians, will be disastrous."[37]

Economic assistance remained a major focus of Bowles's attention throughout his career in foreign affairs. He had advocated substantial aid to developing countries years before he was assigned to New Delhi. Out of office after leaving India, he was outspoken in urging the importance of economic assistance and in presenting ideas about how the program should be most effectively shaped. As a congressman in 1959–60 he worked to bring about some of the changes he had called for as a private citizen. In the Kennedy administration he played an important role in structuring the reorganization of what then became the Agency for International Development (AID), setting new criteria for its programs, and explaining to governments and key figures in the developing world the priorities and principles the administration had adopted. On his return to India as ambassador in 1963, he again devoted considerable attention to the aid program, by then greatly expanded in both funding and scope from the projects he had initiated in the early 1950s.

Bowles was not a development economist and displayed some impatience when those with academic credentials in that field tried to talk theory with him. He liked to divide economists into two categories: those he favored, who dealt with "people," and those who focused on "numbers." His lack of academic sophistication did not deter him from developing a set of guidelines he believed could maximize the benefits of economic assistance. He preached these consistently throughout his years in foreign affairs.[38]

As he had assured Nehru, Bowles believed that aid should be given "with no political strings attached." He defined this concept rather narrowly. He was convinced that efforts by the United States to use aid as a weapon to bring about significant changes in the international political or security positions of recipients were futile. They would either be rebuffed or, if accepted, would have limited value, because the pliant recipient government was unlikely to be able to bring its people genuinely to accept the changes. Bowles was thinking especially of the development of military agreements between the United States and Asian governments. He viewed such agreements with distaste and contended, correctly, that had the United States called for one as a *quid pro quo* for economic aid to India, Nehru would have had widespread popular support in rejecting it.

Bowles's clear preference for aid to popularly based Third World governments over help to authoritarian ones, especially right-wing regimes, reflected his strong belief in democratic values. He was convinced that only governments enjoying strong public support would be able to create the climate of popular enthusiasm required for successful economic development. The United States should offer its aid first to national governments that take the necessary steps to create such a climate.

Bowles spelled out his thinking on this sensitive issue in *Ambassador's Report*:

> If a government has no over-all plan to mobilize its own resources to the utmost, if there is an inadequate and unjust tax system which bears primarily on those least able to pay, if there are no controls over luxury spending in the midst of poverty, if there are no land reforms, the Ameri-

can assistance will go to perpetuate bad leadership and to increase inequalities. Such a climate makes substantial development impossible and Communism probable.

If America openly required a sound national plan, an equitable fiscal system, and land reforms as a precondition to aid, there would certainly be risks of antagonizing some governments. But would the risks be as great as they are now? On one side we are subject to blackmail by governments who let black markets run uncontrolled and refuse to tax their own wealthy people, and then come to us hat in hand pleading, "Help us quick or we will go Communist." On the other side we are easy targets for the Communists because of our support of just such governments.[39]

Although Bowles surely recognized that the economic criteria he mentioned were politically loaded, he avoided discussing them as "political strings." "There is a distinction," he claimed, "between political strings that spell out a new imperialism, and practical conditions which are simply necessary to assure that our funds are spent where they will produce the results intended." The strained definition seems a disingenuous effort to avoid using a highly pejorative term. Strings tied to domestic if not international political behavior were a basic element in Bowles's approach.[40]

Bowles conceded that the United States might decide in some cases that aid without reforms was more likely to strengthen democratic forces than no aid. He hoped such instances would be rare and urged that when they occurred a way be found "to make it clear that we are there to help the people." When aid was required to bolster, for U.S. security purposes, a country that failed to meet his criteria, that support should be clearly labeled military assistance and not confused with economic aid.[41]

Some of Bowles's other precepts were also provocative and controversial, as he no doubt had intended them to be. He argued that small-scale technical assistance, such as establishing training programs and sending American specialists, was not sufficient for the economic development of Third World countries. They required foreign exchange to meet their goals. As noted, he had sought to meet this need in India through a program of commodity assistance, which would have allowed the foreign exchange saved on food imports to be used for development requirements. He saw only a limited role for foreign private capital in the early stages of economic development. Nations emerging from colonialism were suspicious of foreign business, he found, and in any event only governments are in a position to address most of the basic infrastructural needs these countries face. (This opinion of his did not deter him from making efforts to open India to American investment when opportunities arose.)

He also favored increasing regional planning and participation, as far as practicable through the United Nations. Remembering the work of the Ford Foundation in India, he urged that nongovernmental organizations be encouraged to undertake their own projects. He valued the human links between the United States and the Third World such projects provided. This was a forerunner of the strong support he later gave the Kennedy administration's Peace Corps, which he also applauded for the exposure it gave young Americans to the developing world.

Exposure, however, had both its advantages and its challenges. The sudden arrival of over a hundred TCA technicians, few of whom had worked abroad before, had not been problem-free. As he wrote to George Allen:

> One of the major [staff] problems is TCA, which up to a few months ago did its recruiting largely on an evaluation of the individual's record by the Department of Agriculture. A Point Four specialist in India, in addition to knowing his specialty in agriculture, health, etc., must have extraordinary personal qualifications, and this also applies to his wife.
>
> We have been fortunate, perhaps, in having had only three or four duds. . . . We have tried to eliminate the weak ones, but this is not easy because their lack is usually not technical qualifications but in the kind of personal and psychological balance required for the unusually difficult work of a Point Four man in an underdeveloped country.[42]

With this in mind, Bowles made the careful selection and training of Point Four staff another cardinal point in his approach to foreign assistance. With tongue only slightly in cheek, he explained in a January 1953 *New York Times Magazine* article what criteria he had told a recruiter to use. "I suggested that he first carefully test the specialist's professional competence, then his patience and understanding of human beings, then his racial and religious attitudes. If this test were passed successfully, I suggested that he take the specialist and his family on a two weeks' camping trip, preferably in the rain with a leaky tent. If they all came through with a smile on their faces, the State Department could send them to India with confidence."[43]

The final precept in Bowles's list for foreign economic assistance was the one which had been so important to him from the time he began to think seriously about the issue: "Not mere anti-Communism but building strong democracies should be our main emphasis."[44] Although he had stressed anti-Communism to develop support for assistance when he was ambassador, his belief in the responsibility of the United States to promote abroad and at home the liberal, democratic values it stood for was at the heart of his approach to foreign policy. These values, he held, were readily exportable. Whatever their own political and cultural traditions, the peoples of Third World countries wanted to adopt them and would do so given the opportunity. He dismissed impatiently those who argued otherwise.

Bowles's belief in the global promise of democracy was paralleled, though in no way equalled, by a concern that professed anti-Communist regimes were taking the United States for an expensive ride. He often illustrated his points with anecdotes which he, at least, thought funny, as they might have been at their first telling a long time before. An often repeated favorite was the tale of the reported effort by the Monacans to get American funds. Unsuccessful because they had no local Communists they could use to scare Uncle Sam into producing a handout, the Monacans by Bowles's account asked the French to lend them a few surplus Reds. The French declined; they needed every Communist they had, for the same purpose.

Bowles put the issue more eloquently elsewhere in *Ambassador's Report:* "The challenge is to do what we ought to have done without the Communist challenge. But can we do what needs to be done out of fear and negation? We did not build our own country in order to oppose some foreign ideology but because we had a positive faith in our own. Only in that way can Asians build their new countries, and only in that spirit can our presence be of any real assistance."[45]

The China Card and an Asian
Monroe Doctrine

THE emphasis Bowles placed on China and its evolving relationship with the Soviet Union largely reflected the exchanges he had with Nehru. The prime minister recognized the critical importance for India of its relations with the People's Republic. His policy of support and friendship for Peking included a strong element of enlightened self-interest: India's need for stability along its long northern frontier. But there was also much idealism in Nehru's approach. As his biographer S. Gopal has pointed out, "[Nehru] hoped fondly that friendship with the new China would not only maintain peace in Asia but start a new phase in world affairs, with Asia giving the lead in a more humane as well as a more sophisticated diplomacy."[1]

This attitude was closely related to Nehru's faith in the resurgence of Asia, which he had made a pillar of Indian foreign policy. But he also remained wary of Peking's intentions, not least in the Himalayas, where Chinese assertion of control over Tibet in 1950 had aroused Indian concern. Aware that strong central governments in China had often sought to extend their power into adjacent regions, he bolstered India's position in the border areas by negotiating new security treaties with the small Himalayan states that lay between India and its possibly ambitious northern neighbor.

▾ ▾ ▾

Nehru and Bowles had their first serious discussion on China in early November 1951, when the prime minister drew the newly arrived ambassador aside at a dinner party to volunteer his ideas on prospects there. Bowles reported that Nehru considered China potentially aggressive and expansionist, though in the prime minister's view it lacked resources to take on more than it was already doing. The Soviets would likely try to use China by urging it into further adventures in other parts of Asia, but China had been hurt in Korea (where by then its troops had been engaged for a year) and would hesitate to embark on other moves likely to involve further fighting.

> The best hope was an attempt to divide Russia and China—or if this was not possible at least to modify China's viewpoint through outside contacts and thus convince China it did not need to depend entirely on Russia. . . . The best interests of India, the United States and the entire free world . . . lay in the policy of keeping the China door open. . . . The world had nothing to lose and much to gain in any effort to split China and Russia, or if that was impossible, at least to modify China's willingness to swallow the Soviet line completely.[2]

Nehru returned several times to this Sino-Soviet theme. "Over a period of time," he told Bowles in February 1952, "China might show the Soviets, perhaps by her actions, that she was not going to be a pliant junior partner."[3] In July 1952, the prime minister said he doubted that the Sino-Soviet association could last for more than a few years. Friendship with China was basic to Soviet strategy and Moscow would pay any price to maintain it. But as China gained confidence, differences were certain to develop: "There may be more chance of China running Russia twenty years from today than of Russia running China."[4]

Nehru had made similar assessments to others since the Communists had come to power in China, and Washington policymakers were well aware of his views. Bowles was obviously much taken by them nonetheless: they heightened his interest in China and influenced him then and later to look at the contentious issue of U.S.-Chinese relations in ways that often differed sharply from current perceptions and policy preferences. As noted, he had made the possibility of a Moscow-Peking split a major theme in the message he sent Acheson soon after coming to New Delhi. In private correspondence in his early months in India he dwelled on the implications of the potential division. Anticipating the "China card strategy" of the early 1970s, he wrote to William Benton that "if China should begin to wobble in her relations with Russia, the U.S.S.R. would be forced to make sweeping concessions to the West and there would be every hope for a broad settlement. This situation would give us the greatest bloodless victory in history, and we should make every effort to bring it about."[5] He was convinced that Moscow wanted to keep Washington and Peking embroiled and might have pushed North Korea to move south to this end. "If only the Chinese [Communist] Government will demonstrate its independence [of the Soviet Union] by making a peace in Korea possible," he wrote to Norman Cousins, "then we will start with a clean sheet of paper, and at least there will be a good chance that the present unhappy situation may be cleared up."[6]

The Truman administration did not respond to Bowles's call for efforts to help bring about a Sino-Soviet rift. He was urging on Washington a policy that had been carefully considered before. Senior officials were well aware of potential problems between Moscow and Peking: China specialists in the State Department had long brooded on this theme. In early 1949, as the Communists stood on the brink of victory in the Chinese civil war, Secretary Acheson had concluded that the goal of U.S. policy should be to prevent Soviet domination of China for strategic ends. One tactic he considered was to try to entice the Chinese Communists away from Moscow by developing trade relations. Another, contradictory, approach he contemplated was to cut off economic assistance and food supplies so as to coerce them into an orientation toward the West. Acheson continued to look for ways to promote an eventual Sino-Soviet split after the People's Republic was proclaimed on October 1, 1949.[7]

How fully aware Bowles was of the secretary's views and the high-level debate over China policy in the Truman administration is not clear. Although the possibility of promoting a Sino-Soviet division was widely discussed among Democrats in 1949 and 1950, he was caught up in Connecticut state problems in those years and was not focusing on foreign policy. In any event, hardening Chinese Communist and U.S. attitudes toward one another and, in late June 1950, the outbreak of the Korean War, swept away the possibility of pursuing a policy designed to encourage the rise of Chinese Titoism along the lines Bowles later recommended. By the time he reported Nehru's ideas and adopted them as his own, the dominant view in Washington was that the war, which the Chinese had entered in November 1950, provided incontrovertible evidence of the solidarity of Sino-Soviet ties and of a Communist design for world conquest.[8]

Although Bowles frequently leaned toward Nehru's views on China, and wanted the administration to encourage the prime minister's interest in "moderating" Chinese Communist policies (a recommendation the Far Eastern bureau of the State Department quickly shot down),[9] he was straightforward and patient in spelling out to the Indians the policy of the United States toward China and trying to get across to them in ways they would appreciate the challenge that the authoritarian People's Republic posed for them. Like other observers in India who assessed attitudes there toward China in the years the Communists were consolidating their power, he found the Indians confused and ambivalent. Nehru and others admired the Communists for uniting the country and building a strong nation with spirit and a sense of dedication. Although they feared that a powerful new China could become a serious threat to India and its other Asian neighbors, they also got what Bowles called a "subconscious and vicarious thrill" at the spectacle of a new, strong Asian power which had thrown off the domination of white Westerners and was able to deal with the West on equal terms. Bowles believed that India was in no position to stand up to this new China. India's economic development needs ruled out a major arms buildup, and it would have to find a basis for compromise with China in the Himalayan areas. He did not at that time foresee— nor did other competent observers—that Sino-Indian differences would come to focus on specific border claims, and that these would prove inexorable and provocative a decade later.[10]

Bowles continued to stress the importance of Sino-Indian economic rivalry that had figured so prominently in his message to Acheson, and seemed somewhat taken aback when Nehru took a more relaxed view of that competition. In calling for increased U.S. assistance, Bowles did not claim that India needed to outstrip China's economic performance. He believed—many with experience in Asia would disagree—that "Asians have been brought up in the democratic, liberal tradition. It is only if they feel that the democratic way has failed utterly to provide the decencies of life that they will abandon it." But he wanted the United States to take into account democratic India's inability to force its people to make the sacrifices the People's Republic could demand of its population and try to fill the gap between the two countries' capacity to mobilize resources.[11]

China also figured prominently in Bowles's thinking as a historical object lesson for U.S. policymakers. Repeatedly citing a statement attributed to Paul Hoffman that "India stood in 1952 where China had in 1945," he contended that the United States must learn from its mistakes in China and show in India the kind of imagination it had failed to demonstrate in its dealings with the Chinese during the crucial period of the 1940s. If the United States were to fail in India as it had in China, the results could be even more disastrous to its global interests.

He made his point most vividly in one of his last messages to Truman in December 1952, when the struggle over U.S. aid levels to India was again coming to one of its periodic boils. "I earnestly hope," he urged the lame duck president in an eyes-only cable, "you will . . . make sure our solid India program recommendation is turned over to the new [Eisenhower] administration. Then if we end up with another China on our hands at least we will have the satisfaction of knowing we met our clear responsibility." It was an appropriate valedictory note from an ambassador who might have become an Old China Hand to a president accused of "losing China."[12]

▾   ▾   ▾

Bowles pursued his interest in China and the broader Asian scene in correspondence with John Foster Dulles, initially when Dulles was a special assistant in the Truman/Acheson State Department and later when he had become secretary of state in 1953. He probably thought that Dulles, as the leading Republican foreign policy spokesman and authority on the Far East, was someone whom he could usefully trade ideas with and seek to influence. The relationship between the two men was at the time cordial though not warm, as it would remain through the first year of the Eisenhower administration. Their correspondence was largely one-sided, with Bowles doing most of the writing. He used the exchange to unveil some of the ideas which became standard fare in his approach to Asian issues.

One of these was his concept of Japan and India as joint pillars of a "vital democratic front" against Communism in Asia. In his first letter to Dulles, who in 1951 had negotiated the peace treaty with Japan, Bowles was not specific about the shape the front should take or the role of the United States as its backer. He confined himself to a call for stepped-up U.S. efforts to foster economic development and reform and to bring about increased Indian and Japanese confidence in the effectiveness of democratic practices. Without such confidence, and the economic well-being needed to bring it about, "pressure for military agreement alone . . . is bound to result in either flat refusal [to become part of such a front] or the signing of empty treaties which lack mass support."[13]

Bowles urged that "our policies in Asia should be built specifically for Asia and not simply adapted from our previous experience in Europe," where the historical background and political, economic, and social conditions were very different. He called for an expanded U.S. security role in Asia. "Strategically we should vigorously oppose aggression not only in Korea but in Indochina, Burma, and Nepal. . . .

The Chinese Communist government should be clearly, officially, and moderately informed that the United States (and hopefully the United Nations) will take vigorous action against future aggression, and that the fighting will not necessarily be limited to the area in which the aggression took place." Although Bowles conceded that "the hope for a more moderate attitude on the part of the Chinese Communists is not great," he urged that "we should carefully avoid any act or statement that would tend to strengthen Russia's grip on China and to support the Communist accusation that we are planning an all-out aggressive war on the Chinese mainland." There was a remote possibility that "if left alone, [the Soviet Union's and China's] varying interests and different stages of development will result in their gradually drifting apart." But even if this did not occur, "a moderate attitude on our part will give greater emphasis to the aggressive character of any overt acts on the part of Communist China, and convince the people of Asia that we have done our best to establish peace and understanding in Asia."

Dulles replied that he generally agreed with Bowles's approach to dealing with possible Chinese aggression. The United States needed to deter the Chinese from further attacks. But he was critical of Bowles's view that a "moderate" U.S. attitude toward Communist China would help bring about a rift between Peking and Moscow. The best way to promote a weakening of Sino-Soviet ties was to keep up the pressure on China and make life difficult for the Chinese as long as they remained in partnership with the Soviets.[14] Bowles politely disagreed. "Our best approach in dealing with Communist China," he insisted, "is to continue to make it emphatically clear that we are ready to fight aggression wherever it takes place and on our own terms; but at the same time we wish to avoid needless provocation, to hold the door open for peaceful negotiation, and to give the natural forces which are working constantly for a more independent China a chance to develop, if that is at all possible."[15] Gordon Chang has observed that the Bowles-Dulles exchange on this issue outlined the two strategies to promote Sino-Soviet differences that were debated throughout the years of the Eisenhower administration.[16]

Bowles continued to argue the case in his early 1953 letters to Dulles, by then Eisenhower's secretary of state. He urged Dulles to recognize that bringing about a Sino-Soviet rift was "a most basic objective of our foreign policy." In devising its Asia policy, the United States needed to determine the minimum conditions for living with the Communist Chinese. His own formulation was tough: "a fair settlement in Korea, plus an agreement calling for the withdrawal of Chinese support from the Viet-Minh, independence for Viet Nam, Cambodia, and Laos, an end to further Chinese Communist aggression in Asia, backed by a U.N. declaration that any future aggression will be immediately and forcefully dealt with at its source. . . . Under no circumstances could we agree to turn Formosa [Taiwan] over to Communist China." But he warned that if the United States was unwilling to live in peace with Communist China and was determined instead to oust the Communist regime, it would eventually have to undertake an all-out military effort involving large numbers of U.S. troops on the Chinese mainland. He judged that the American people would not support such a policy.[17]

In effectively ruling out the overthrow of the People's Republic while at the same time insisting that the Communists not be permitted to seize Taiwan, Bowles foreshadowed the "two Chinas" policy he later promoted. However, at this early stage he did not explicitly discuss the Chinese Nationalists with Dulles, except to report Nehru's assessment: "He still maintains a high regard for Chiang Kai-shek . . . [who] was the first head of a major government to go all out in support of India's independence, [but] feels that Chiang . . . has long since ceased to be an important force in the Asian situation, and believes that we tend to weaken ourselves by attempting to prop up a man who, in his opinion, has been so discredited."[18] Bowles's own views of the generalissimo were probably not very different from Nehru's, but it is likely he saw little purpose in directly urging them on Dulles.[19]

Bowles's conviction that India could play a leading role in helping meet the challenge of Communist China eventually led him to propose the concept of an Indian-led Monroe Doctrine for South and Southeast Asia. He spelled out this idea publicly in the fall 1954 issue of *Foreign Affairs,* but it also appears in the letters he wrote to Dulles from New Delhi in early 1953.

With his flair for historical analogy, Bowles likened India's position in the early 1950s to that of the United States 130 years earlier. Both were militarily weak countries that could play major roles in assuring the security of their regions only with the backing of a strong and supportive outside power. In the nineteenth century, the British, with their unrivaled fleet, had assured the effectiveness of the original Monroe Doctrine by barring the continental European countries from adventures in the New World. Bowles proposed to Dulles that the United States quietly stand behind India in the role he envisaged for New Delhi in deterring Communist moves in the twentieth.

This latter-day Monroe Doctrine should take the form of "a clear-cut statement that [New Delhi] would consider any infringement on the freedom of Burma, Thailand, Afghanistan, Pakistan and Iran a direct attack on India," Bowles proposed. The three Indochinese states could be included once the French had left and they had become independent. India should start by offering full support to Burma, Thailand, and Vietnam, the countries he considered most threatened. "Later as a solution to the Kashmir problem develops, India could work with Pakistan in the development of a similar guarantee for the strategically important area to the northwest." He had already tried out his approach with Nehru on an unofficial and personal basis, he told Dulles, and had found that, while cautious, the prime minister had not ruled it out. "He now understands with very real clarity the danger which India faces from the Communist nations to the northwest and the northeast, and for this reason my proposal has particular appeal."[20]

Bowles continued to promote the Asian Monroe Doctrine for many years after he left India. Whatever Nehru may at first have told him, he received no encouragement from the prime minister, nor from those in the United States who were otherwise attracted to his foreign policy views.

The concept in fact made little sense in the geopolitical setting of the 1950s. Nehru had no interest in playing the role Bowles saw for India as a leader in an anti-Communist Asian coalition. When Chinese policy forced him to recognize in the last years of the decade that his gamble on good relations with China had failed, he did not want to make matters worse by involving India in overt anti-Chinese moves not directly relevant to the defense of its own disputed and threatened borders with China and those of the small Himalayan states within its security perimeter. Nor were India's armed forces sufficiently strong to take on such a broader role. Any kind of entente with other Asian nations would also have violated strongly held Indian principles against involvement in multilateral security arrangements outside the United Nations and would have complicated India's important relationship with the Soviet Union. The mistrust of India's neighbors with regard to its regional ambitions was another obstacle, as was the unlikelihood that the United States would be either willing or able to play the quiet and self-effacing backup part Bowles had suggested. The American political process would have assured that the role was well publicized.

Nehru had quickly recognized that prospect. Bowles recalled a playful exchange on the issue with the prime minister. "This is a very interesting story," he reported Nehru had said when they had discussed the birth of the original Monroe Doctrine, "but how did the British react to your announcement that you were going ahead on this program unilaterally. Did various Members of the House of Parliament stand up to say that the Americans couldn't fight their way out of a paper bag and they're really relying on the British Navy to save them from European imperialism?" "Oh no," Bowles said he replied, "the British were very discreet, very sophisticated and very mature, and they didn't say a single word when they saw us carrying out their policy." "Well," said Nehru, "do you think you could trust your Members of Congress to show equal discretion and not point out to the world that you were in effect saving us from world Communism?" "Touché," Bowles responded, "Your question is quite apt. I doubt that we could control our people but I still think it's a good program."[21]

Dulles, for his part, never responded to the Monroe Doctrine proposal, nor did he offer any meaningful reply to other policy recommendations Bowles made in his early 1953 messages. The policies the secretary pursued in East and South Asia during his first years in office suggest that any hope Bowles might have had of influencing him had been misplaced.

▾   ▾   ▾

The Korean War continued throughout Bowles's assignment in New Delhi and was often a problem in U.S.-Indian relations. Angered in the latter part of 1950 and early 1951 by Indian diplomatic moves it regarded as favorable to the Communist powers, Washington remained mistrustful of India's motives and methods, particularly as these played out at the United Nations. During the 1952 General Assembly session V. K. Krishna Menon led the Indian government's initiatives on the Korean issue. His arrogant personality and frequently anti-U.S. views antagonized many Americans and became a stumbling block to better understanding between the two countries, at the U.N. and elsewhere, then and later.

Bowles did not share the view, strongly held by Acheson, that India was unlikely to play a helpful role in Korean War diplomacy. Indeed, he sought to interest the Indians in becoming significantly involved again, as they had been until early 1951. Gopal has stated that Nehru had avoided further involvement in the problem of a Korean settlement until Bowles and Eleanor Roosevelt, who visited India in early 1952, "pushed him into intervention."[22] Whether Bowles had acted under instruction is unclear, but seems unlikely in light of the skepticism about India's role then prevailing in Washington.

Bowles later recalled his role in prompting diplomatic activity by

India, which led to its sponsoring a General Assembly resolution on the sensitive issue of the repatriation of prisoners of war, the major obstacle to a cease-fire agreement in 1952. He claimed to have encouraged Nehru on a personal, unofficial basis to warn the Chinese and the Soviets in late summer that political pressures building up in the American presidential election campaign could lead to a major U.S. assault in Korea later in the year. As he remembered the episode, he asked the prime minister to urge the Communist powers to negotiate, or at least to show some willingness to negotiate. "Since no word of approval or disagreement came from Washington in response to my report of [this] first conversation, I urged Nehru a few days later to propose a new basis for a peaceful settlement among the U.N., North Koreans and Chinese when the United Nations met in October. This he did."[23]

If Bowles's account is accurate, he had, in approaching Nehru, helped spark an Indian diplomatic effort which the State Department saw as unhelpful and deceptive. Acheson has recalled his own strong opposition to the Indian move, "which Krishna Menon was hatching," and personally headed a determined campaign to persuade the British, French, and Canadians not to support the initiative, at least not in the form Krishna Menon had given it. Efforts led by the United States to amend the Indian draft to make it acceptable were only successful after the Soviets had publicly and angrily announced their rejection of it.[24]

On instructions from the State Department, Bowles helped convince the Indians to accept amendments Washington considered necessary. Fearful that Nehru might decide to drop the resolution after the Soviets had stated their opposition to it, he mentioned to the prime minister a press story reporting that the violent tone of the Soviet statement turning down the Indian resolution might indicate a difference of opinion between Moscow and Peking. He claimed that this helped move Nehru, who was always on the lookout for ways to divide the Soviets and the Chinese.[25] When efforts to develop language mutually acceptable to Washington and New Delhi were successful, he characteristically spotted a propaganda opportunity. Equally in character, he cautioned that it be handled with care and tact. "While giving full credit to India, we should not gloat over the fact that India took a position counter to that of the Soviet-Chinese bloc, nor should we imply that this indicates closer Indian alignment with the West." The United States should take advantage of the conviction in India that the Soviets prevented the Chinese from accepting the resolution and stress, as part of the effort to promote a Sino-Soviet rift, that while the Soviets wanted fighting to continue, it was to China's advantage to have it end.[26]

Although the General Assembly passed the amended Indian resolution by a wide margin, it was rejected by the Communist Chinese and the North Koreans. Another seven months passed before a cease-fire agreement was reached in July 1953. The prisoner-repatriation provisions in that agreement were in most respects similar to those in the resolution.

In his last months in New Delhi, Bowles's views on Korea continued to be strongly influenced by his conviction that the United States should do everything possible to encourage a falling-out between Moscow and Peking.

> I believe [he wrote Dulles in late February 1953] that the first immediate step towards the settlement of the Korean conflict is an intensive, persuasive appeal to the Chinese people to make peace. This appeal should emphasize that the Soviet Union used the North Koreans to start the war for its own selfish objectives and that when the invasion failed, the Chinese were asked to provide the cannon fodder with which to save the situation.
>
> It should be stressed over and over again that the Soviet Union now seeks to continue this war in order to test out its own weapons, to drain away Chinese military manpower, to delay Chinese industrial development which would become an economic threat to the Soviet Union, to eliminate any hope that Communist China may some day speak for herself in the United Nations, and to prevent the development of a peaceful, united and stable Asia.[27]

Bowles adopted a tough line on future U.S. military moves. In a message he had sent Dulles earlier in the month, he said that if, following a direct appeal to Moscow, "there appears to be no alternative to further fighting in Korea I would precede our stepped-up effort with a clear warning to the Soviet Union that the use of air power or further outside force will bring immediate retaliation against Soviet as well as Chinese sources of supply. . . . Although the Indian Government would undoubtedly be uneasy at the danger of broader conflict they would respect the logic of our position, and . . . might even accept it on an unofficial basis."[28] Given Nehru's abiding concern about the danger of the Korean War leading to a global conflagration, this seems wishful thinking.

Bowles left India four months before the cease-fire was finally negotiated in late July 1953. He stopped briefly in South Korea, where President Syngman Rhee ("a tired, hard, crafty old man") urged on him the need to reunify the peninsula by force.[29] The recommendations Bowles had sent Dulles from New Delhi on ending the war and furthering the possibility of a rift between the Soviets and the Chinese Communists were ignored by the Eisenhower administration. On Korea, as on other Asian matters, its agenda was different from Bowles's.

These differences included the issue of a role for India in a Korean settlement. The new administration's view was as negative as Acheson's had been when Bowles was promoting a diplomatic initiative by Nehru in 1952. Probably because there were few if any viable alternatives, the administration had agreed to India's chairmanship of the Neutral Nations Repatriation Commission, which was set up in June 1953 to supervise the disposition of Korean War POWs. This arrangement also provided for the exclusive use of the Indian military as custodian of those prisoners, a difficult role which it carried out with admirable professionalism. But at the urging of President Rhee, the administration insisted that India be excluded from the international political conference on Korea which met in 1954 in Geneva. Although some close U.S. allies argued for Indian participation, Washington was unwilling to change its position and the veto stuck.

▾   ▾   ▾

Bowles's Asian interests also extended to Southeast Asia. He visited the region in June 1952, at the midpoint of his assignment to New Delhi, and stopped there again on his way back to the United States following its completion. The observations he made generally confirmed the ideas he had developed as ambassador to India and earlier and helped persuade him that they had validity throughout Asia. They focused on the apparent threat to the area of Communist China and the indigenous Communist movements it supported. Bowles came away further convinced of the importance of nationalism and economic reform, linked together, in meeting this threat. His travels may also have strengthened his interest in a regional security arrangement with a prominent Indian role as the best defense against possible southward moves by China.

Bowles's liberal anticolonial convictions colored his approach to the problem of Vietnam and the smaller Indochinese states. During this 1952–53 period in the long Vietnamese drama, the figurehead Emperor Bao Dai headed a Vietnam state nominally independent within the French Union. Actual power remained in the hands of the French, who faced a Communist Viet-Minh insurgency led by Ho Chi Minh. Bowles contrasted French policy with British willingness to quit India: "Even the most ardent anti-Communists insist that French rule is no more welcome than Chinese, and . . . resent the proposal that they must negotiate in Paris for the freedom which they feel is theirs by right." He rued the way the French clung to both real power and its appearances, "hardly the way to convince the Vietnamese that they were a free people," and regretted that the United States had not been firm and decisive enough in pressing the French to state that they intended to clear out of Indochina once the Communists had been quelled. But following his second visit in mid-1953 he noted that French policy in Indochina had begun to undergo some encouraging changes, and expressed the hope—proved spectacularly vain when Dienbienphu fell a year later—that "these are solid steps on the road to full freedom for these three new nations [Vietnam, Cambodia, and Laos], and full defeat for the Communist forces."[30]

Bowles was convinced that the prospects for an anti-Communist victory in Vietnam would be crucially assisted by an effective land reform program. He sympathized strongly with the prime minister of the French-backed Vietnam government, who told him that the slowness of land reforms was one of the main reasons for the failure of the anti-Communist forces to crush the Viet-Minh insurgency, and wrote approvingly of the later French decision to allow peasants in villages recovered from Communist control to retain the landholdings the Viet-Minh had parceled out to them. By then land reform had become an article of faith for Bowles in Vietnam. He continued to stress its importance there long after the defeated French had withdrawn from the country. In the 1960s he sent a series of letters and telegrams to President Lyndon Johnson urging that speedy and effective land reform could undercut the Communist position in the rural areas and rally the Vietnamese peasants in support of the Saigon government. He was no more satisfied with U.S. and Vietnam government efforts to promote redistribution of landholdings in the 1960s than he had been with the attitude of the French and their Vietnamese associates toward such a program fifteen years earlier.

Difficult as it is to believe from the vantage point of today, Burma was of particular interest to Bowles. He was optimistic about its prospects for political stability and economic development under democratic government and had high regard for U Nu, its leader in the 1950s and early 1960s. He also saw it as a possible Chinese invasion route into India, and repeatedly warned Nehru that the Chinese might try to outflank the Indian army by slipping around the eastern end of the Himalayas through Burmese territory. These hopes and fears were never realized, as Burma fell increasingly into authoritarian rule, economic despair, and geopolitical irrelevance.

In visiting the countries east of India and meeting many of their national leaders, Bowles was doing more than satisfying his intellectual curiosity and finding additional copy for books and magazine articles. He was also adding to his foreign affairs credentials. He would be able to say, with some plausibility, that he had experience not only in the subcontinent but elsewhere in Asia as well. Such claims were later reflected in the blurb on the dust jacket of *Ambassador's Report* that called it "a remarkably human and hard-headed account of a successful mission involving not only the problems of India, but all Asia."

Following his return from New Delhi Bowles sought to project himself as a foreign policy expert and to play that role in the Democratic party. It seems reasonable to conclude that in returning to the United States via the Far East in early 1953, if not in traveling to Southeast Asia the previous year, he had that future role in mind.

6

Dealing with South Asia

DURING Bowles's first ambassadorship, the United States' relationship with Pakistan had not yet become a major problem in its ties with India. The Nehru government was troubled by what it considered Washington's pro-Pakistan tilt in United Nations efforts to resolve the Kashmir dispute. But the anger and concern provoked in India by the Eisenhower administration's establishment of bilateral and multilateral security links with Pakistan were still a few years in the future.

▼　　　▼　　　▼

Interest in a security relationship with Pakistan stemmed primarily from Washington's concern for the defense of the Middle East. In the view of Western strategists, the rising tide of Arab and Persian nationalism exemplified by British confrontations with Egypt over the Suez military base and the Anglo-Egyptian Sudan and with Iran over the nationalization of the Anglo-Iranian Oil Company had made that important area even more vulnerable to Soviet encroachment. The idea that Pakistan could play a useful role in Mideast security had been bruited about by the U.S. military as early as 1949, when a Joint Chiefs of Staff study noted that West Pakistan could provide a suitable site for air force operations. The availability of the well-trained but, at that time, still poorly equipped Pakistan army was also attractive to some military planners. By 1951, the Truman administration was actively considering a major military link with Pakistan within a broader organization that would include the United States, Britain, and regional countries. The Pakistanis, anxious to strengthen their security against India, let it be known that they were interested in participating.[1]

The administration had earlier agreed to a small-scale program of arms sales to Pakistan on a reimbursable basis. Bowles appears to have had no problem with the limited sale of weapons to the Pakistanis. It would have been awkward for him to have objected in light of the support he gave in the summer of 1952 to an Indian request for the purchase of 200 Sherman tanks, valued at $19 million. (The Indians at that time, and throughout the 1950s, acquired most of their imported arms from the British.) In a telegram recommending approval of the proposed sale at knocked-down prices, Bowles noted India's "growing security problems arising from Communist expansion in Asia." He thought these problems would encourage India to look to Washington rather than Moscow for military equipment and would probably contribute to improved relations. The availability of American arms would "help strengthen the Government of India's capacity to fight aggression, a factor which may eventually be of great importance to us here in South Asia." At the same time, however, he recommended that the State Department turn down India's request for 200 jet aircraft priced at $200 million. India should not be spending that kind of money on "unproductive military purchases," he argued. Washington approved the tank sale as well as a package of 54 C-119 transport planes valued at $54 million. It deferred action on the jet plane package and the Indians did not pursue the matter.[2]

But Bowles strongly opposed the much more significant military relationship envisaged as part of Pakistan's participation in a U.S.-sponsored regional security arrangement. He played an important role in stiffening the Truman administration's eventual unwillingness to move forward with the idea and gave himself credit for helping to kill it in Washington.[3] To his dismay, however, the concept surfaced again soon after the November 1952 presidential elections, when American press accounts reported that the incoming Eisenhower administration was considering it. In one such report, the *New York Times* stated that policy planners were going to ask the new president to decide whether there should be a shift in emphasis in foreign aid planning from Europe to Asia which would include "bringing strategically situated Pakistan into the free world's defense system."[4] Although the State Department tried to reassure the Indian ambassador when he inquired, concern in India mounted amid speculation linking U.S. interest in a security relationship with Pakistan with the more pro-Pakistan position that the Indians believed the United States had adopted on the Kashmir issue at the United Nations.[5]

During these last weeks of the Truman administration, Britain, reversing its previously negative view of a regional security role for the Pakistanis, suggested their possible participation in a projected Middle

East Defense Organization (MEDO). The State Department proposed to tell London that it was pleased with the idea and was prepared to support British approaches to Pakistan "if circumstances are appropriate." Replying to a request for embassy views, Bowles raised serious objections to this initiative. He forecast a strongly adverse Indian reaction. It would stem from fear that the West was building up Pakistan, suspicion of a deal with Pakistan on Kashmir, concern that the United States was shoring up a dying colonial order in the name of collective security, and apprehension about an increasing emphasis on military policy in the United States. As a result, India-Pakistan relations would become "explosive." There would be increased Indian questioning on broader issues such as Korea, NATO, and disarmament, and the loss of much of the cooperation built up over the past few months. Bowles also feared the move would increase Soviet pressure on Iran and Afghanistan. To mitigate this negative Indian reaction, he suggested a broadening of MEDO to include Iran, Afghanistan, India, and Ceylon (Sri Lanka). But he did not expect that such a step would be acceptable to India and probably recommended it as a way of killing Pakistani participation. (At that time, Washington would have been prepared to include India in MEDO, but, like Bowles, State Department officials did not think the Indians would be interested in forsaking their vaunted nonalignment to join.)[6]

Bowles weighed in forcefully with the incoming Republican administration in a letter to General Walter Bedell Smith, the former director of central intelligence who had been named under secretary of state by Eisenhower. He stressed again the strongly negative impact Indian opposition to Pakistan's inclusion in MEDO would have on U.S.-Indian and India-Pakistan relations. The change in the subcontinental balance would be attacked by Indians of every shade of opinion, Americans would defend their position, and "we will soon find ourselves in the same situation as the summer of 1951, with the air full of epithets, bitterness, and suspicion" and all the gains of the last year lost. The only silver lining he allowed himself was his assessment that "there is not the slightest chance that the Government will show any increased sympathy for Communism regardless of what we do."[7]

Nehru's view, Bowles reported, was that far from increasing the stability of the Middle East, the arming of Pakistan would gravely threaten whatever stability existed. Indian Foreign Secretary N. R. Pillai had added that regardless of the purpose for which the United States provided substantial quantities of arms to Pakistan, there was a very real possibility that they would eventually be used against India.

India would have to build up its own forces as a result. Bowles said he had argued with Nehru. He had told the prime minister he had understood his fears, but had also urged him to recognize that the United States needed to deal with the fact that the Middle East was soft and vulnerable. He had then suggested to Nehru that regardless of India's attitude toward the Cold War, it consider taking the leadership in the development of a defense organization covering the area from Iran through Burma. This initiative foreshadowed the Asian Monroe Doctrine approach Bowles brought up with Nehru and John Foster Dulles soon afterwards.

Bowles concluded his assessment with a peroration which summed up his approach to Asian security:

> If we are looking for military answers in South and Southeast Asia, we will not find them until these countries feel that they have something to fight for. More than that, if we attempt to force military answers on Asia we will lose whatever chance we have for economic stability and our hopes for winning the friendship of these hundreds of million of people. It may sound trite but it is nonetheless true, that tractors will do more than tanks to strengthen freedom in this part of the world. If we can instill confidence in the democratic ways in the peoples of Asia, I will trade that against all the easy promises of unrespected leaders. A promise by a leader whose armies will not fight is worse than useless since it deceives us and makes us rely on a strength that does not exist.

Smith assured Bowles in reply that early developments on the question of Pakistan's participation in MEDO were not expected and there would be plenty of time for everyone to weigh in. The leaks to the press, which had led Bowles to read about the resurfacing of the issue before receiving official word from Washington, had not been planned or premeditated, he said. He concluded with a compliment: "Neither should this unfortunate occurrence diminish in any way the feeling of satisfaction which you must yourself have for a job well done."[8]

Surprisingly, Bowles did not reiterate his strong opposition to a U.S.-Pakistan security link in the three long letters he sent to Secretary Dulles in February and March 1953, though it is implicit in the general approach he took to Asian security in that correspondence. He mentioned Indian concerns about MEDO almost in passing (on page eighteen of his twenty-page letter of March 20), noting that "Indians are worried about MEDO not because they fail to understand the dangers of the Soviet aggression in the Middle East, but because they fear the possible consequences of a stronger Pakistan army in the hands of what

they believe to be an unfriendly and dangerously unstable government." Pakistan did not figure in the approach he recommended the
secretary use with Nehru during the visit to New Delhi that Dulles was
scheduled to make later that spring.[9]

The Middle East Defense Organization proposal did not get off the
ground because of opposition to it in the Arab world. But the May
1953 visit to the Middle East and South Asia, which led Dulles to drop
the project because of problems the Arabs had with it, also prompted
him to conclude that there was considerable concern about the Soviet
threat in the region's "northern tier," that is, Turkey, Iran, and Pakistan. The stopover he made in Karachi left him with a fine impression
of the fighting qualities of the Pakistan army. The Dulles visit thus set
the stage for a series of military agreements in that region, including
an arms assistance pact between the United States and Pakistan, signed
on May 19, 1954. Later that year Pakistan joined the U.S.-sponsored
Southeast Asia Treaty Organization (SEATO). In 1955 it tightened its
links with the Western security system by joining the Baghdad Pact,
later renamed the Central Treaty Organization (CENTO). Although
not formally a member of this alliance, which included Iran, Turkey,
Britain, and, initially, Iraq, the United States was closely associated
with it. Pakistan thus became, as the Pakistanis themselves put it,
"America's most-allied ally."[10]

Bowles had left India well before reports reached there in late 1953
of the Eisenhower administration's expected decision. Indian reaction
was extremely negative, and even before the agreement was signed the
reliable stories that it was in the cards dealt a sharp blow to U.S.-Indian
relations and to India's relations with Pakistan. Writing as a private
citizen to Dulles in December 1953, Bowles added to the points he had
made to Smith at the beginning of the year and summarized his arguments in a hard-hitting paragraph:

> I believe we will isolate Pakistan, draw the Soviet Union certainly into
> Afghanistan and probably into India, eliminate the possibility of Paki-
> stan-Indian or Pakistan-Afghan rapprochement, further jeopardize the
> outlook for the Indian Five Year Plan [by leading the Indians to di-
> vert resources to an arms buildup], increase the dangerous wave of anti-
> Americanism throughout India and other South Asian countries, open up
> explosive new opportunities for the Soviet Union, gravely weaken the
> hopes for a stable democratic government in India, and add nothing
> whatsoever to our military strength in this area.[11]

The decision to move ahead with the security agreement was generally accepted in the United States, and Bowles found himself in rather

lonely opposition. He continued to regret the agreement as a major blunder, and his negative view of it was strengthened when many of the forecasts he had made of its impact on U.S. interests in India and Afghanistan came to pass. (The alarmist ones about the possible collapse of Indian democracy and the failure of the Five Year Plan fortunately proved well off the mark.) It is one of the many ironies of American relations with South Asia that Bowles was again ambassador in New Delhi in 1965 when the second war between India and Pakistan led to a breakdown of the U.S. security relationship with the Pakistanis that he had so strongly opposed at its inception eleven years before.

▾   ▾   ▾

If a U.S. security relationship with Pakistan was a potential problem for Bowles, the dispute between India and Pakistan over Kashmir posed a more immediate and pressing issue for him. Although the United States preferred the British to take the lead in seeking a resolution of the problem, Kashmir had become a major subject for American diplomacy at the United Nations. American ambassadors in New Delhi and Karachi were inevitably involved in the formulation of policies for dealing with it.

When Bowles arrived in India in 1951, the Kashmir issue had already been on the world's agenda for almost four years. The problem stemmed from the decision of the hastily withdrawing British to allow the rulers of India's five-hundred-odd princely states to decide whether to join India or Pakistan or, at least theoretically, to become independent when the *raj* ended. The maharajah of the large, strategically situated state of Kashmir was one of only three rulers who had not acceded to one dominion or another by the time the British quit India on August 15, 1947. An authoritarian Hindu prince of a state with a Muslim majority, the maharajah hesitated as communal passions in nearby parts of India and Pakistan boiled over into his territories. When tribesmen from Pakistan invaded in October, he turned to the Indian government for help. New Delhi agreed to intervene militarily provided he accede, and he quickly did so. But in accepting the maharajah's accession, the Indian government promised, in the words of Lord Mountbatten, by then governor-general, that "as soon as law and order have been restored in Kashmir and its soil cleared of the invader, the question of the State's accession should be settled by reference to the people."[12]

Indian armed forces were quickly sent to Kashmir and turned the invaders back, but fighting continued despite bilateral efforts to resolve the conflict. The Indians then turned to the United Nations Security

Council, where they charged Pakistan with a breach of peace and called for the withdrawal of the invaders. By the time the United Nations arranged a cease-fire in place on January 1, 1949, the Pakistan army had become openly involved in the fighting. The cease-fire left most of the state including the prized Vale of Kashmir under Indian control. But the repeated initiatives the United Nations took to resolve the dispute over the state's future status on the basis of the promised referendum foundered on two questions: the extent of administrative control the pro-India Kashmir state government should be allowed to exercise during the plebiscite period, and the number of military personnel the two sides could have at that time.

The U.S. and British governments had been in the forefront of efforts to resolve the issue despite what by 1951 seemed to many American policymakers poor prospects for success. The Indians, Nehru in particular, looked on this Anglo-American role with increasing disfavor, particularly as it appeared to equate the two claimants. India was the status quo power in control of the key areas of the state, and at best was in no hurry to resolve the issue. The Nehru government's position was that Kashmir was part of India as a result of the maharajah's accession and that Pakistan had been guilty of aggression. Moreover, the Indians considered Kashmir's inclusion in India a demonstration of the secular nature of their newly independent nation. In their view, for the state to join Pakistan because of its Muslim majority would undercut this claim to secularism, bolster Pakistan's contention that Hindus and Muslims were "two nations," and possibly touch off renewed Hindu-Muslim communal violence. Nehru himself took a very hard line on Kashmir. Many attributed this to his family's own Kashmiri origins, an explanation the prime minister dismissed.

The United Nations was making another attempt to bring about a settlement at the time Bowles became ambassador. Frank Graham, a former U.S. senator and president of the University of North Carolina, had been named special representative and charged with effecting demilitarization of Kashmir and preparing the way for a plebiscite. Bowles soon became closely involved in Graham's initiatives. The Kashmir issue was peculiarly important to him. The way it played out could have a major bearing on his efforts to bring about a substantial improvement in U.S.-Indian relations during his tenure in New Delhi. A resolution of the dispute was also a significant element in the achievement of his vision of an indigenous Asian anti-Communist defense arrangement, his Asian Monroe Doctrine.

Bowles was more persuaded than were other Americans involved in the Kashmir issue that India would be willing to move toward a reasonable settlement. His assessment stemmed from his conviction, which he believed the Nehru government shared, that India could win an honest and uninfluenced election in Kashmir. He was also probably moved by his natural optimism and by his general confidence in the motives and good faith of the Indian authorities he dealt with, especially the secretary general of the Ministry of External Affairs, Sir G. S. Bajpai. Bowles and Bajpai had quickly developed a warm personal and professional relationship, and Bowles, while hardly naive in his dealings with Indians on Kashmir, tended to credit Bajpai with a sincerity not always accepted in Washington. The fact that Bowles was a newcomer to the Kashmir issue and had not experienced the adroit diplomatic maneuvering of the Indians in dealing with it probably also bolstered his confidence in their professed interest in a settlement on terms the Pakistanis and the United Nations could accept.

While urging Washington to look more kindly on Indian intentions, Bowles also sought to limit the negative impact that continued failure to resolve the problem would have on U.S.-Indian ties. In a January 1952 cable, he urged that the United States "relax as much as possible and carefully avoid emotional involvement." We should "make up our mind that we alone cannot solve every problem and restrict our role on this issue to that of a friend to both countries which refuses to take sides but is anxious to help if at all possible." We should also "pray for Graham's success, but if he fails, keep our patience, refrain from moral judgements and adopt a position in the Security Council which . . . will be best calculated to advance a settlement between India and Pakistan, without aligning the United States with one side or the other."[13]

This approach reflected Bowles's recognition that Washington was likely to blame a continuing deadlock on Indian intransigence, whatever he might say to explain and justify the Nehru government's position. He probably reasoned that the less U.S. involvement—substantive and emotional—in the issue, the less intense the negative fallout would be. Carping at the Indians and passing resolutions they would interpret as critical would be counterproductive, he argued. So would U.N. efforts to impose formulas unacceptable to either of the two parties. It no doubt occurred to him that such evenhanded treatment would favor the status quo power, India.

Bowles's approach to Kashmir brought him into greater conflict with Washington than did differences on any other controversial issue. On such matters as economic aid levels there were sharp disputes, but

Bowles always had allies, particularly in the Bureau of Near Eastern, South Asian, and African Affairs of the State Department. On Kashmir, he seems to have had none.

The sticking point between Bowles and the department was his insistent advocacy of the partition of Kashmir as a means of bringing about a settlement. This approach, first proposed in 1950 by Graham's predecessor as mediator, Sir Owen Dixon, called for a plebiscite limited to the Vale of Kashmir, the area both sides regarded as crucial to their national interest. Other parts of the state—an amalgam of diverse regions joined together by dynastic ambition and historical accident—would be allocated to India or Pakistan according to the religious composition of their populations. The proposal had a certain logic, but neither India nor Pakistan had been willing to accept it at that time. In January 1952 Bajpai had revived it with Bowles, who touted it with growing fervor.

Though Bowles qualified his support with the warning that there was no assurance that the scheme would work, he soon found himself in conflict with Washington. Skeptical State Department officers doubted the *bona fides* of the Nehru government in reviving the idea, recalled earlier Indian objections to its implementation, and suspected that the Indians were using it as a delaying tactic or an additional excuse for obstructing a settlement. They also feared that encouragement given to partition would prematurely undercut efforts to move forward with demilitarization and an all-Kashmir plebiscite under the resolutions passed earlier by the United Nations. Repeatedly noting Graham's own opposition on legal and practical grounds to the approach, they regarded Bowles as naive, overoptimistic, and even dangerous in promoting it. For his part, Bowles claimed (without offering evidence) that Graham had been optimistic about what might be accomplished by broadening his terms of reference to include the partition plan. He blamed U.S. officials in Washington and at the United Nations for discouraging the mediator from moving in that direction, and regarded them as inflexible, unrealistic, and unduly legalistic.[14]

Bowles continued to urge the partition/limited-plebiscite approach until the end of his time in New Delhi, which roughly coincided with the conclusion of Graham's unsuccessful efforts. He faltered only briefly, when new-found interest on the part of Kashmir Prime Minister Sheikh Abdullah in possible independence for the state caused the Indian government to doubt its ability to win a plebiscite. At that time Bowles spoke about the possibility of India's agreeing to partition without a plebiscite, presumably an arrangement which would maintain something like the status quo. Once Abdullah and the Indian government had come to terms, he resumed advocacy of his earlier position.[15]

Bowles did not allow evidence of Nehru's intransigence on Kashmir to discourage him for long. The prime minister had registered his inflexible attitude most forcefully in mid-1952. The occasion was Bowles's involvement in what would later be called shuttle diplomacy. En route from Washington to New Delhi, he had met in Karachi with Pakistan Prime Minister Nazimuddin at the suggestion of Avra Warren, the American ambassador there. Nazimuddin had unveiled to Bowles and Warren substantial concessions on the Pakistani military presence in Kashmir that his government was prepared to make, provided the Indians agreed to the appointment of a plebiscite administrator, a major element in Graham's approach. The Pakistanis asked Bowles to sound out Nehru informally on their offer, and the department instructed him to do so "in the capacity of a friendly messenger."[16]

Despite an emotional personal appeal from Bowles, Nehru had rejected the offer. Reporting to Washington, Bowles concluded that "Nehru is acting in a wholly unreasonable manner and will probably continue to do so. . . . [He] definitely hopes the whole situation can be made to go away." He tried to explain the prime minister's reaction as the result of political problems in Kashmir and their repercussions elsewhere in India. But despite what he termed his bitter disappointment with Nehru's attitude, he was soon again calling for the partition proposal.[17]

After he left India, Bowles continued to contend that an agreement might have been reached on the partition/limited-plebiscite basis. In his long December 1953 letter to Dulles protesting the arms to Pakistan proposal, he called the failure to adopt the plan a "lost opportunity." Interestingly, he went on to acknowledge that India was morally wrong about Kashmir and had handled the situation clumsily and arrogantly. But "right or wrong," he continued in a passage which reflected his own thinking about Kashmir as much as it did the Indian government's, "Nehru and other Indian officials believe that American policy, instead of helping has hindered the rapprochement of India and Pakistan. They do not believe that we really understand their position on Kashmir, and they feel we have ignored their own explosive internal political problems in trying to settle the question."[18]

In retrospect, Bowles was probably unwise to have promoted the partition idea. Despite Bajpai's renewed sponsorship of it, Nehru would probably have been even less willing to go along with the approach than he had when Dixon had proposed it in 1950. The prime minister was determined to maintain control over the Vale, and with the loyalty of India's Kashmiri friends led by Sheikh Abdullah waning, there is little reason to believe that he would have been prepared to take the risk of a vote under arrangements acceptable to Pakistan and the United Nations. (A few months after Bowles had left India, Abdullah was deposed and jailed. For years afterward New Delhi entrusted the state to pro-Indian politicians, who enjoyed little support from a Muslim population that had increasingly come to favor either independence or union with Pakistan.) By pushing hard for the concept against the opposition of all other U.S. policymakers who dealt with Kashmir at a responsible level, Bowles only succeeded in making himself seem even more pro-Indian, and politically naive as well.

▾   ▾   ▾

Like other American ambassadors to India from 1947 until the late 1950s, Bowles was also accredited to Nepal. Although he inevitably had to treat the Himalayan kingdom as a sideshow to his far more important responsibilities in India, he took his role there seriously. He visited Nepal six times—on the first occasion crossing into the Kathmandu Valley from India by pony—and tried to see as much of the rugged countryside as time and the primitive transport facilities of the early 1950s allowed. His visits to Kathmandu were busy and purposeful, and he was able to develop good relations with King Tribhuvan and other Nepalese leaders. As most diplomats sent to Nepal do, he came to have a great affection for the country and its people.

Bowles's assignment to Nepal came at a particularly significant time in the country's history. Earlier in 1951, the long authoritarian rule of the feudal Rana hereditary prime ministers had been overthrown by an Indian-supported uprising, ushering in a period of more or less popular government under a resuscitated monarchy. As it had in India, the assignment also coincided with the beginning of U.S. economic assistance.

The development of the aid program became Bowles's principal interest, and he appears to have spent much of his time in Kathmandu dealing with it. His approach to aid in Nepal was similar to the one he took in India. The focus was on agricultural production, malaria control, road building, and basic literacy, in part through a community development program. The difficulties the U.S. development effort faced were compounded by the woeful backwardness of the country, the lack of trained Nepalese administrators, and the tough living conditions the American staff faced. Bowles dealt with these problems in his characteristically determined way, and was reasonably pleased with the quality and effectiveness of the aid program and its personnel.

Bowles believed that economic progress in Nepal, as elsewhere, depended importantly on the willingness of the government there to carry out reform measures, particularly to relieve rural indebtedness and establish a more equitable pattern of land distribution. In his final visit to Nepal as ambassador, he urged King Tribhuvan to move toward reform of the land tenure system. A passage of the address he read aloud to the king on that occasion reflected his basic approach to the process of economic development in the Third World: "Unless broad ownership of the land is developed, the cultivator has but little personal stake in its development, the benefits from increased yields will flow largely into the hands of the few, and the majority of the people will come to consider them a fraud and a delusion."[19]

He took a lively interest in Nepalese political developments, and the long and interesting letters he wrote to Donald Kennedy in the State Department following his visits are full of accounts of the maneuvering of the country's fledgling politicians. More hopeful than subsequent developments warranted about the prospects for democratic stability, he wryly maintained that the very lack of competent people was itself a stabilizing factor. "Although the government was presumably turned upside down in August [1952, when the prime minister resigned], the same people are actually running the various ministries in one way or another for the simple reason that there are no alternatives," he told Kennedy.[20]

Independent India, like imperial British India before it, regarded Nepal as part of its security perimeter and sphere of influence. Bowles was concerned that the Indians might become troubled by reports that the United States was exerting too much influence there, presumably to India's disadvantage. He tried in his statements and activities to quash Indian apprehensions. Given the primacy he attached to improving U.S. ties with India and his encouragement of a major role for New Delhi in regional security arrangements, he had no interest in having the United States perceived as a rival to India in Nepal, let alone becoming one.

During his tenure, he established a small American reading room in Kathmandu, the forerunner of the present United States Information Service program in Nepal. He believed, however, that frequent visits by designated American personnel assigned to New Delhi—not least himself—provided a way to deal with Nepal that was feasible yet less costly than the establishment of a resident mission there. Nepal was thus one of the few countries where the United States for years maintained an economic aid office but no diplomatic presence.

This anomalous situation ended in the late 1950s, when Ambassador Henry Stebbins took charge of a newly established embassy. Thus on his second assignment to New Delhi Bowles's accreditation was limited to India. He would have his hands full there. But he may well have regretted that the country to the north, which he found so fascinating, was no longer his direct responsibility.

▾   ▾   ▾

Eisenhower's victory in the November 1952 elections foreshadowed the end of Bowles's Indian assignment. By that time Bowles had become so highly regarded in India that the *New York Times* could report, in its roundup of international reaction to the election outcome:

> The chief topic in Indian political circles concerned the prospects of Chester Bowles continuing as the United States Ambassador. Some Indians refer to the popular American envoy as the "American Mountbatten," comparing his personal improvement of Indian-American relations to the achievements of Britain's last viceroy in cementing affections between India and London at the moment that Britain abandoned her long reign over India. Many Indians hope the new President will leave Bowles here even though the Ambassador is known as a prominent Democrat at home.[21]

This hope persisted as weeks passed and no word came from the incoming Republicans about a possible successor. Political commentators catalogued Bowles's accomplishments. Reflecting a widely held view, one leading paper, the *Times of India,* called on Eisenhower to retain the man who "had done more to encourage closer Indo-U.S. relations than all the powerful propaganda and publicity machinery of the United States was able to achieve in the previous four years."[22]

Bowles shared his Indian admirers' hopes. He had received mixed advice about his prospects from Americans who had visited New Delhi after the election, but was optimistic when replying on November 18 to a discouraging letter from Benton. The senator, who had just been defeated in his bid for a full term, had told Bowles that he ought to figure he would be replaced. The only reasons Bowles would be kept on, Benton said, were that Eisenhower might feel the need to have some top Democrats in the State Department or that Governor John

Lodge might fear a 1954 Bowles comeback bid and persuade the new president to keep him far away from Connecticut. Bowles agreed that Eisenhower, with a slim majority in the Senate, would want to demonstrate his nonpartisanship in foreign affairs by choosing a few Democrats. He wrote to Benton in reply that it was "wholly conceivable I will be asked to stay but that I would feel it was impossible to do so because of the policy attitudes which may develop" under the Republicans. He sought the lame duck senator's help in mobilizing Republican support for his continuing in New Delhi. "The chances are the situation within the Republican Party and in Ike's immediate councils is in a state of flux. A straight question from the right source as to his intentions here [in India] might result in a reassuring answer which his political associates would find difficult to undo later." New York Governor Thomas Dewey and Paul Hoffman, both Eisenhower Republicans, could be helpful on his behalf, he thought.[23]

Over the next weeks Anna Rosenberg (Hoffman's wife and a political personage in her own right), Henry and Clare Booth Luce, and even Indian Ambassador to Washington Vijayalakshmi Pandit, Nehru's sister, reportedly weighed in for Bowles with Eisenhower. It was an exercise in futility, and, as one Bowles associate has stated, in self-delusion. Eisenhower avoided making any commitment to Bowles's supporters. He eventually selected former Governor Val Peterson of Nebraska for the New Delhi appointment; but when both senators from the state opposed Peterson, he turned to the career service and chose George Allen. Very disappointed with the decision, Bowles later wrote that it was Governor Lodge and Senator Robert Taft who had eliminated the possibility of his staying on.[24]

As all politically appointed ambassadors are obliged to do, Bowles had submitted his resignation to the White House following the election of the new president. He was informed of its acceptance and the appointment of Allen as his successor in a curt note which came to him while he was vacationing in Ceylon (Sri Lanka). Returning to New Delhi to prepare for a March departure, he sent a glowing account of his ambassadorship to Connecticut State Democratic Chairman John Bailey:

> We will really feel badly to leave India. Steb and I have a great many friends here and it has been a most satisfying experience. I don't think I have ever been in any position which has been so completely free of conflict. Everywhere here, with the exception of the Communist fringe,

there is agreement on the goals that must be reached and the only difficulties are in how to reach them. We have very wonderful relationships with the people in the government, from the Prime Minister down, and also with many other people throughout India.[25]

▾   ▾   ▾

Bowles and his family left New Delhi on March 23 for the long trip back across the Pacific to Connecticut. His departure took place in the context of widespread agreement in India and the United States that he had done an outstanding job in his seventeen months as ambassador, particularly in his skillful use of his position to remove accumulated Indian misunderstandings about America and give a better tone to the dialogue the United States conducted with the country's leaders and the politically aware Indian public.

Several elements came into play to make Bowles the right man for New Delhi in the early 1950s. He had a warm and sympathetic understanding of India and a peculiar ability to convey to its people an intelligent concern about their views. Indians at all levels found this appealing both for its genuineness and its novelty in a senior diplomat. They sensed that Bowles really cared about them and saw India as more than a set of problems in bilateral relations, to be forgotten when he moved on. His deft use of public relations techniques heightened this perception. Some of his efforts to court the Indians went too far and were considered patronizing or silly, especially by the more Westernized. (Vijayalakshmi Pandit, for one, complained in her memoirs of the Bowleses' practice of serving Indian food at their dinners; she had looked forward to American fare.)[26] But such techniques as greater and more candid exposure to the press, a strengthened USIS program, and well-publicized travel to remote corners of the country contributed significantly to his successful effort to win friends and understanding for the United States at a time when both were in short supply in India.

Nehru put it well in an unusually warm tribute he wrote when he learned that Bowles would be leaving: "You have interpreted your great country in a manner which has been greatly appreciated not only by the Government but by large numbers of the people of India and as one wishing well to India. For those of us who have come into more intimate contact with you, your departure from India will be a matter for deep regret. We shall all miss you here greatly. But I am sure that the work you have done here will endure."[27]

The attractiveness to Indians of the positions Bowles was known to promote with force and persistence at the highest levels of the United

States government also enhanced his standing. The fact that his positions at times differed significantly from the policies Washington pursued looked to the Indians more like a welcome indication of his good will and good sense than a sign of his ineffectiveness. (In his second ambassadorial term, this positive assessment would change.) It helped him too that for Indians in the early 1950s it was an unusual experience to have an American ambassador of Bowles's calibre championing positions they found sympathetic and supportive.

The comments Sir Girja Shankar Bajpai made a few months before Bowles left India are worth quoting in this context. The ambassador had been successful, Bajpai told Escott Reid, "because he based his actions on four beliefs: India's foreign policy was its own affair; United States help to India was not charity but was in the interests of the United States; when India differed from the United States it was not necessarily being perverse; the way to detach China from the Soviet Union was to woo it." As the senior permanent official in the Ministry of External Affairs, Bajpai was likely to have been aware that of the four beliefs he found the basis of Bowles's successful diplomacy, only the one concerning the purpose of aid to India was accepted in Acheson's State Department. But Bajpai nonetheless believed that what Bowles had done was both praiseworthy and important, and this view was widely shared.[28]

Bowles's effectiveness as ambassador was of course not the only reason the Indians came to view their ties with the United States in a more favorable light during his tenure. The establishment of the economic assistance program at that time was very important and over the longer run had a far greater impact. It demonstrated both to the Indian leadership and the broader public that the United States could provide tangible benefits to the country, and that contrary to popular allegations and fears, Washington was prepared to help Indian economic development on a long-term basis without insisting that India abandon its independent foreign policy. Indian disillusion with the Soviet Union for its peremptory rejection of the resolution on the repatriation of Korean war prisoners proposed by Krishna Menon at the United Nations General Assembly—a Soviet move which Acheson at Bowles's urging promptly sought to exploit—and concern about the implications of Communist party gains in South Indian elections in early 1952 may also have led the Indian government to look more kindly on its ties with the United States. Relations probably also benefited, in the Bowles months, from the absence of any highly emotive political confrontations such as arose between the two countries about the Korean War in the fall and winter of 1950–51 or, to look ahead, by their clash over the implications for India of the U.S. decision to provide military assistance to Pakistan.

As Bowles had warned, that decision meant that the brighter view of the United States and of the usefulness of a more constructive relationship with it which Indians came to hold during his tenure would not last long after he left India. By the fall of 1953 the roller coaster which has so often characterized U.S.-Indian relations was moving downhill at a fast clip, to Bowles's dismay if not surprise. Indians would in consequence remember him even more fondly as an unusual American representative and view the limited time he spent in New Delhi as a brief respite from some of the misunderstandings and animosities which often seemed the normal environment of the bilateral relationship.

The impact Bowles had in the United States is more difficult to assess. His major accomplishment at home was to raise awareness of India as a nation of considerable importance to the United States which could be helpful in promoting American interests if its government and people were approached the right way. (The right way, that is, as Bowles defined and practiced it.) He was the first major American figure to project in this country the concept of a "new India," a changing land of great potential under enlightened and democratic political leadership, not the mix of arrogant pro-Communist elites, religious fanatics, and hopelessly impoverished masses which people from Truman on down had thought it was. His voluminous official and private correspondence, his many magazine articles, the public appearances he made during his visits home, and the good relations he cultivated with American reporters in New Delhi helped him make progress in changing the image of India in America. They also made him one of the best known American diplomats of his day.

Bowles saw his effort to raise American consciousness of the new India and its potential as an important element in his persistent campaign to maintain and enhance economic assistance levels. Although neither Congress nor the Truman administration (nor, of course, Eisenhower's) was as responsive to his enthusiastic advocacy as he had hoped, aid levels for India would probably have been lower if he had not weighed in. His effort also helped prepare the ground for the much larger assistance programs enacted in the later 1950s. He was less successful in his broader and more ambitious goal of bringing about a basic change in U.S. policy which would eventually lead to an implicit U.S.-Indian partnership to safeguard non-Communist Asia. Faced abroad by what it considered a dire Communist threat underscored by the continuing war in Korea, and beleaguered at home by right-wing critics, the Truman administration was neither in a mood nor in a position to put any significant confidence in a nonaligned India that seemed to many to lean toward the Communist powers. The Eisenhower administration was even less inclined to follow Bowles's advice.

Yet while few in the Truman administration were converted to the vision Bowles had of India's promoting U.S. interests in Asia, his efforts led many Americans inside the government and out to appreciate more keenly the considerable stake the United States had in keeping India out of the Communist camp. Before Bowles came on the scene, that objective had already been ranked as an important goal. His achievement was to dramatize the aim and link it to specific actions (such as high levels of aid funding) which could help the Indians remain democratic and non-Communist.

The important role Bowles apparently played in persuading the Truman administration not to move forward with a security link with Pakistan was another significant contribution. If he was unsuccessful in the similar effort he made when the Republicans took power it was not for want of trying. As Bowles foresaw, the U.S.-Pakistan security relationship introduced more liabilities than advantages to the promotion of U.S. national interests in South Asia. It heightened Pakistan-India tensions, distorted Pakistan's political and economic development, complicated U.S. relations with India and Afghanistan, and prompted a major increase in Soviet influence in Afghanistan which, over time, helped shape the circumstances leading to the 1978 Communist coup and the Soviet invasion the following year. Ironically, it was only after the invasion that the security relationship with Pakistan, revived by the Reagan administration in response to it, became an asset for the United States in South Asia and beyond.

In his approach to foreign policy during his New Delhi assignment, Bowles tried to look down the road to consider the long-term consequences of current options. His assessment of the Pakistan security relationship was characteristic of this approach. It was linked with his long view of India, and his confidence that Indian and American national interests in Asia were fundamentally compatible. As ambassador, he gave that assessment a legitimacy and respectability it had not enjoyed in the United States before. He differed with many other American ambassadors, whether drawn from the Foreign Service or outside, in using his position to press foreign policy positions that went well beyond the management of U.S. bilateral ties with host governments. His frequent airing of views on Communist China was the most obvious example.

▾   ▾   ▾

Bowles had come to some of his conclusions about foreign policy before he went to New Delhi. During his New Delhi tenure he developed fresh ideas, reworked old ones, and came to feel a greater sense of urgency in promoting his positions. Over the subsequent five years he further refined his thoughts in the books, articles, lectures, and position papers he prepared as a private citizen seeking to influence foreign policy during the Eisenhower administration. After returning to the United States, he moved with characteristic vigor to bring his positions to the attention of leading Democratic party figures and others who could help him win acceptance for them. His consuming interest in America's role in the world became the focus of his life and the guiding influence in shaping his political ambitions.

1. Bowles graduated from Yale with the Class of 1924 and remained a faithful Eli for the rest of his life. No scholar, he recalled that his most successful accomplishment in New Haven was his captaining the university golf team (bottom row, first on the right).

2. With William Benton, Bowles founded the advertising agency of Benton & Bowles in 1929. The firm's creative genius, he became one of the major figures in the golden age of radio of the 1930s.

3. Bowles was an expert yachtsman and found boating a relaxing distraction from the cares of business and public life. In 1937 he sailed to Bermuda on his 72-foot schooner *Nordlys*.

4. Under Bowles's leadership, the wartime Office of Price Administration became an effective instrument in containing inflation and ensuring fairness in the distribution of scarce commodities. He spent a good deal of time seeking, and winning, congressional support.

5. In Europe in 1948 as International Chairman of the United Nations Appeal for Children, Bowles meets with Czech children.

6. Bowles and Harry Truman campaigned together in 1948, when Bowles won the Connecticut governorship in an upset almost as great as Truman's reelection victory that year over Thomas E. Dewey.

7. Bowles initiated a thoroughgoing reform program during his two-year term as governor of Connecticut, only to see much of it stonewalled by state Republicans.

8. A longtime champion of civil rights, Bowles led the country in signing legislation in 1949 bringing about the integration of the Connecticut state unit of the National Guard.

9. One of the leaders in the liberal effort to dump Truman and make Eisenhower the Democratic party presidential nominee in 1948, Bowles welcomed him to Connecticut in 1950. Despite his strong distaste for the GOP, he remained on cordial terms with Eisenhower after Ike's election as president on the Republican ticket in 1952.

10. Unlike many Americans, Bowles was able to develop a warm relationship with Indian Prime Minister Jawaharlal Nehru, a man he came to admire greatly.

11. As ambassador to India, Bowles was an inveterate traveler who journeyed to remote areas where few senior diplomats had ventured.

12. Bowles's desire for closer relations between India and the United States is nicely symbolized by his rolling up his sleeves to help pull in the nets during one of his many forays into rural areas.

13. On his first assignment to India, Bowles was accompanied by his daughters Sally and Cynthia, his son Sam, and his wife Steb. Informality was their stock in trade.

14. Bowles's relationship with Adlai Stevenson (right, next to 1952 vice-presidential running mate John Sparkman) dated back to their boarding school days.

15. As a member of the House Foreign Affairs Committee, Bowles tried to blur his Third World image by displaying an interest in European affairs. In 1959 he traveled to Europe and met senior leaders including President Tito (Josip Broz) of Yugoslavia.

16. Bowles's relations with John Kennedy were never easy.

17. After two frustrating years on the New Frontier, first as under secretary of state under Dean Rusk, then as the President's Special Adviser on African, Asian, and Latin American Affairs, Bowles accepted Kennedy's offer of a second assignment as ambassador to India. He was sworn in by Chief Justice Earl Warren in June 1963, as Rusk stood by.

18. And during his second ambassadorship he had his difficulties with Lyndon Johnson too.

19. Indira Gandhi led the Indian government during much of Bowles's second assignment to New Delhi. She resented his avuncular attitude and his readiness to offer unsolicited advice.

20. Bowles's mission to Prince Norodom Sihanouk's Cambodia in 1968 briefly brought him back to the center stage of American diplomacy.

21. Steb Bowles was a constant help to Bowles through the ups and downs of his varied career.

22. Howard Schaffer (second from left) was second secretary in the New Delhi Embassy political section when Bowles was ambassador in the 1960s.

7

Exporting the American Revolution to the Third World

IN THE spring of 1953 the Bowles family returned to their home in Essex, an old and charming New England town a few miles up the Connecticut River from Long Island Sound. The large but unpretentious white brick house is beautifully situated on a bluff overlooking the river. Reached by a narrow private road that winds through a deep wood and opens suddenly on a broad lawn, it enjoys a magnificent view of the Connecticut countryside and, across a busy boat-filled cove, of the center of the little town to which the Bowleses had become so attached after settling there in 1939.

The house in Essex became Bowles's headquarters for the next five years. Halfway between New York and Boston, it was a comfortable and convenient gathering place for his political and foreign friends and acquaintances. Krishna Menon and Vijayalakshmi Pandit came up from the United Nations. Adlai Stevenson, Eleanor Roosevelt, and other national Democratic party luminaries were guests along with Harvard and Yale professors of similar liberal persuasion. Connecticut politicians drove down from Hartford on a road the state later turned into a turnpike it dubbed the Chester Bowles Highway. Conversations went on to all hours: Sally Bowles remembers the children complaining that they could not get to sleep. Staffers worked at the house collaborating with Bowles on the books, articles, and speeches he produced so prolifically. Bowles's colleagues and admirers came to have a warm and sentimental affection for the place, as they did for Bowles himself. The feeling was reinforced by an annual gathering at the house on the Memorial Day weekend, an occasion when people from his diverse incarnations could get together to compare notes and honor the head of what came to be called the "Chet Set."[1]

▼   ▼   ▼

Early 1953 was not a propitious time for a returning Democrat, especially not a Connecticut liberal eager to propagate fresh ideas about America's role in a revolutionary world. The Republicans had won both the presidency and majorities in the two houses of Congress on a platform which promised to make extensive changes in foreign and domestic policy. The Connecticut scene looked similarly bleak. Governor John Davis Lodge still had two more years of the four-year term he had won in 1950 with his victory over Bowles. The Republicans also held both U.S. Senate seats. For Bowles, the only silver lining on this dark political cloud was the absence from high office of any Democrat whose incumbency could bar the way should he seek to return to Hartford in 1954 or make a bid for the Senate in 1956 or 1958.

In Washington, the crusty, moralizing Wall Street lawyer John Foster Dulles had finally fulfilled his ambition to become secretary of state. Like Dean Acheson, he was a strong and outspoken personality who enjoyed the confidence of his president. Dulles had abandoned the bipartisan approach from which he had benefited as a special assistant to Acheson in the Truman administration and was anxious to assure right-wing Republicans that he was one of the faithful. He and Bowles enjoyed a decent if not close relationship at the time; Bowles even believed that Dulles had been prepared to agree to his staying on in New Delhi. But many of the positions Dulles adopted as secretary were fundamentally at odds with Bowles's view of the world and America's role in it. Bowles deplored Dulles's preoccupation with the security dimensions of the Cold War, his disdain for countries like India which practiced independent and nonaligned foreign policies, the low priority he gave to Third World economic development, the confidence he placed in military alliances, his apparent willingness to use nuclear weapons to defend U.S. interests, his inflexible hostility to the People's Republic of China, and his expressed conviction that the Communist bloc was a monolithic and demonic force for evil.

In the six years he was secretary of state, Dulles modified some of these positions. It also became evident that what he said for public and party consumption differed somewhat from his actual policies. His views on nonalignment and his attitude toward economic assistance to Third World nations which practiced it became more compatible with Bowles's concepts. He also adopted a more positive approach to the Nehru government, an important consideration for Bowles. But these changes, real and apparent, do not seem to have altered the basically distrustful and even disdainful attitude Bowles adopted toward Dulles early in his Foggy Bottom years. He had little good to say about the secretary once he had drawn his conclusions about the main lines of Dulles's approach.

Bowles quickly returned to the public stage. While traveling in Indonesia, he had accepted an invitation to be the featured speaker at the seventy-fifth anniversary dinner of the *Yale Daily News* in New Haven. He welcomed this opportunity to reinject himself into Connecticut in a nonpolitical, educational setting after his long time abroad. It was the first of many sessions he had at universities, foreign policy organizations, and political groupings as he sought a high profile role following the exhilaration and success of his Indian experience.

His first order of business was the completion of a book about his New Delhi assignment and his foreign policy views. He had planned the work while still in India and began dictating the text as he made his way home through Southeast Asia and the Far East. A potpourri of personal observations, political and economic assessments, historical tidbits, and policy recommendations, *Ambassador's Report,* published early in 1954, is a lively, easy to read book designed to appeal both to the general audience and to more serious students of American foreign policy and India. It was among the first popular book-length accounts written by postwar American ambassadors about their overseas experiences and the lessons they drew from them. The fact that Bowles was a highly unusual diplomat both in style and writing skill added to the appeal of his story. He emerges from the book as a very unorthodox American representative abroad, a personable and engaging figure with a great knack for relating to Asians.

The book's fundamental message, which Bowles repeated over and over again for the rest of his career, was that the history of the twentieth century would be written in an Asia stirring with revolutionary change. If the United States was to participate constructively in the unfolding of that history to the limited extent any outside country could, it needed to understand what was going on out there, not only among the elites but, even more important, in the villages where the vast majority of Asians live.

Bowles tried to provide an account of this new world and to spell out the policies and practices the United States should adopt in accordance with its own liberal ideals to influence Asia in a democratic direction. He stressed the positive. While he recognized the age-old problems of India and the new and enormous challenges it faced, the general tone of *Ambassador's Report* was upbeat. Bowles's enthusiastic description of India's first general elections and the excitement with which he wrote about the community development program and the First Five Year Plan are typical of the many passages in the book which convey a sense of forward movement and hope. He was for the most part sympathetic to Indian foreign policy positions, justifying nonalignment and putting a good face on Indian policies toward China, the Korean War, Kashmir, and Pakistan. He stressed again the central importance of India's experiment with democratic development: should India fail, he warned, "it will have a profound effect upon the future of every American and indeed of the world. The people of Asia . . . will turn to solutions of despair. . . . The balance of world power will shift fatally toward Moscow without a shot being fired."[2]

Ambassador's Report concluded with a chapter called "Policy for Americans" which summarized the elements Bowles thought most important in a viable U.S. policy for Asia. He gave major attention to relations with the People's Republic of China, calling again for "a policy of tough-minded but patient firmness coupled with willingness to meet any genuine Chinese concessions to the peace of Asia halfway." The United States should make the strengthening of democratic government in Asia its major objective, he said. It should take a clear stand against Communism in Indochina, abandon its support for discredited regimes, accept nonalignment, and step up economic assistance to developing countries. Recognizing the impact American practices at home could have on U.S. ability to act abroad, Bowles also argued that the United States could no longer permit itself the luxury of temporizing and evasion in its civil rights policies.[3]

Ambassador's Report sold well and was extensively and favorably reviewed in general and academic publications alike. Bowles was lauded both for his personal accomplishments as ambassador and his understanding of the Asian scene. Michael Straight said in the *New Republic* that "if more American ambassadors wrote reports demonstrating breadth of understanding and vision such as Mr. Bowles demonstrates in his new book, and if more American citizens and officials read and heed such reports, then indeed the millennium for American foreign policy would have arrived."[4] Bowles must have been even more pleased with the comment in *Pacific Affairs,* which succinctly summarized what he had set out to do: "The importance of the book is that it is implicitly a plea for principle in the making of American policy in Asia—a principle deriving from American notions of self-government, recognizing that the future of Asia can be determined in the long run only by the Asians, and that among them India, the largest self-governing democracy in the world, occupies a position of cardinal importance."[5] The *U.S. Quarterly* struck one of the few negative notes in finding that "this lively chatty book is not history, except incidentally and rather unsuccessfully, nor is it a full analysis of India's problems. . . . [It] is, rather, assertive, pictorial, and impressionistic."[6]

In preparing *Ambassador's Report*, Bowles was assisted by Abram Chayes and Harris and Clare Wofford. Chayes and the Woffords typify the bright, often brilliant younger people who worked with Bowles during his years in public life. One of Bowles's extraordinary strengths was his ability to discover talented people, persuade them to join him, and infuse them with the idealism that marked his own approach to public life. When in time they moved on, in many cases to careers of great distinction in politics, government, academia, the foundations, and the law, they helped Bowles spot fresh talent. Some of those he hired came back to work with him on a regular or ad hoc basis in a different setting; almost all retained links with him and were available for advice and assistance. With few exceptions, they looked back on their days with Bowles—as did many Foreign Service officers who worked with him—as among the best and most creative of their careers.

Unlike the many Bowles associates who had Yale backgrounds, Chayes was a Harvard College and Harvard Law School graduate. As governor of Connecticut, Bowles had recruited him as legal adviser on the advice of friends on the Harvard faculty. When Bowles became chairman of the Democratic Platform Committee in 1960, he named Chayes to head the committee staff. The association continued in still another form in 1961, when Bowles took office as under secretary of state and Chayes became State Department legal adviser.

The Woffords had studied in India and had written a book about Gandhiism, *India Afire*. Harris Wofford was completing Yale Law School when he and Clare worked with Bowles on *Ambassador's Report*. He accompanied the Bowleses on their trip to Asia and Europe in 1957. He later joined John F. Kennedy's presidential campaign, playing a major role there on civil rights issues. Wofford and Chayes figured in the ultimately successful effort to persuade Bowles to endorse and work with Kennedy. Both went on in their later careers to prestigious positions, Harris Wofford as president of two colleges and United States Senator from Pennsylvania, Chayes as a senior faculty member of the Harvard and Georgetown law schools.

Chayes was practicing law at Covington and Burling in Washington when he worked with Bowles on *Ambassador's Report*, and Wofford also later became associated with that leading establishment firm. They found time while there to collaborate with Bowles on his second major foreign policy book, *The New Dimensions of Peace,* published in 1955. Thomas Hughes, a Rhodes Scholar and Yale Law School graduate whom Bowles had recruited in 1954, joined them in that effort. Hughes, who had been associated with Wofford in the student world federalist movement in their high school days, came to be a central figure in the Bowles entourage. He remained with Bowles at Essex until the fall of 1955, then went to work in Washington for fellow Minnesota liberal Hubert Humphrey, returning to Bowles's circle as administrative assistant when Bowles came to Washington in 1959 as a congressman. Bowles later brought Hughes into the State Department, where he was successively deputy director and director of the Bureau of Intelligence and Research. He later became president of the Carnegie Endowment for International Peace.

For the rest of the decade Bowles worked, reworked, and built upon the points he had made in *Ambassador's Report* to develop a broad approach to foreign policy probably as far-reaching as any put forward by a practicing politician of the 1950s. In his effort to promote his ideas and win recognition as a Democratic party foreign affairs spokesman, he wrote several more books on foreign policy, pursued a strenuous schedule on the lecture circuit, and hit the newsstands regularly with articles in such favored periodicals as *Harper's, Foreign Affairs,* and the *New York Times Magazine.* His correspondence in those years with political leaders and other prominent figures in public life and the media fills many boxes of the Bowles Papers at the Yale University Library. The two long overseas trips he made in the winters of 1954–55 (to Africa and South Asia) and 1956–57 (to South Asia and the Soviet Union) provided him with fresh material and insights for his voluminous output and strengthened his standing as a well-informed senior figure whose foreign policy views deserved serious consideration.

As in his New Delhi years, Bowles's message to his varying audiences about foreign policy differed only in nuance. His positions were much the same whether he expressed them in the pages of *Harper's* or in memoranda circulated privately to Democratic party colleagues of various foreign policy persuasions. He often drew heavily on such "confidential" memoranda and other personal correspondence in writing articles designed for a much wider readership. He supplemented his analyses and recommendations on the substance of policy with memoranda and letters providing tactical advice to Democratic party leaders on the way issues could most effectively be played for political purposes.

Bowles's efforts earned him a wide and important audience in a party that was looking for new foreign policy ideas at a time when a popular Republican president was able to say that under his leadership America was no longer engaged in foreign wars. His ability to put novel ideas in nonthreatening ways acceptable to politicians and their constituents helped him. He was able to draw on a knowledge of American history for analogy in clothing his arguments in attractive and reassuring ways. His publicist's skill and background gave him important advantages as a wordsmith. He also benefited from the politicians' awareness that he too had faced the electorate and was likely to do so again. The result of this sustained effort, supplemented by extensive personal contact, was to pump Bowles's ideas into the mainstream of the Democratic party, where they found increasing acceptance over the course of the decade. His growing role as a liberal foreign policy spokesman gave him greater stature within the party and saved him from being forgotten during his long spell out of office.

Bowles's articles and memos were carefully prepared, and though first drafts were often the work of collaborators, the final product always bore a distinctive Bowles hallmark. James Thomson has vividly described the drafting process:

> What I did would be wrongly termed as ghost writing for the simple reason that the process itself was so peculiar, and so peculiarly Bowlesian. Chet would call me into the office and say what he wanted to do, or had been invited to do. . . . He would then talk quite rapidly and telegraphically, and I would sit there with a long yellow pad and take frantic notes, and after a half hour or so he would send me off to produce. What I produced . . . with much harassment from above as to why the draft was not yet in, would eventually be typed in triple space, wide-margined form and passed in to his desk. . . . What would emerge from his desk after he had gone over it was an entirely different animal. . . . He would put his total personal imprint on what had come from the helper on the first draft. It would then go back to a typewriter almost impossible to decipher except by a specially trained one of his secretaries. It would emerge from the typewriter, again triple-spaced, with wide margins, to be gone over by me, again to return to the typewriter and so forth. . . . In the very end [it] absolutely properly bore the by-line Chester Bowles, instead of any other by-line of his several helpers.[7]

Bowles drew on expert advice in preparing some of his material. Fellow liberal Democrat Arthur Schlesinger brought a Harvard historian's eye to such drafts as Bowles's survey of the American political, social, and economic revolution in *New Dimensions of Peace* and the 1954 *Foreign Affairs* article in which he called for an Asian Monroe

Doctrine. Less likely collaborators for a New Deal Democrat were senior members of the Central Intelligence Agency. Bowles met and corresponded with Allen Dulles, the director of central intelligence, whom he found far more congenial than he did Dulles's brother, the secretary of state. He had old Connecticut and wartime Washington ties with Richard Bissell, an economist who was chief deputy for Allen Dulles in charge of covert operations in the late 1950s, and a link with Robert Amory, a former Harvard Law School professor who was deputy director for intelligence at the agency. Bowles used to consult with Amory and his associates, and he would often use Amory as an entry point in the CIA for review of his memoranda. He was also on good terms with Sherman Kent, head of the agency's Board of National Estimates. His ties with Kent were linked to his relationship with Kent's brother Roger, Democratic national committeeman from California, where Bowles probably enjoyed greater popular standing than in any other state, including Connecticut.[8]

Bowles seems to have been well liked and respected at the agency, where he was regarded as a prominent Democratic spokesman whose intellectual attention was worth reciprocating. The agency at times even took the initiative in inviting him to come down for discussions. The mutually beneficial relationship gave Bowles considerable respect for CIA's analytical capabilities, however much he deplored some of its later covert operations such as the Bay of Pigs adventure.

He had no similar link with John Foster Dulles's State Department aside from an occasional exchange of letters with Robert Bowie, who chaired its Policy Planning Council. This lack of communication may have reduced further the already low regard he had for Foreign Service officers, with some notable exceptions. Nor did Bowles develop any significant relationship with the Pentagon, whose role in the formulation of foreign policy he viewed with considerable suspicion. His lack of confidence in State and Defense, and the few positive ties between him and the senior members of those agencies, had important consequences later when he entered the Kennedy administration.[9]

▾   ▾   ▾

The overarching concept in Bowles's approach to foreign policy was his belief that the principles on which the United States had been established and had prospered should guide it in understanding and dealing with the powerful, revolutionary forces sweeping what he termed in the early and mid-1950s the Afro-Asian "middle world." He believed the United States had quite rightly given Europe first priority in the 1940s. It could be proud of its success in helping bring about the economic recovery of its European allies and in warding off the threat the Soviet Union had posed to them. But it had failed to meet the daunting challenge posed by the developing countries and had consequently seen its prestige and power there decline. In coming to terms with the developing nations, the United States needed to associate itself with the aspirations of their leaders and masses and to recognize that these aspirations paralleled those that America had fulfilled in its own "continuing revolution." By doing so, it would recapture the traditional vision of America's role in the world.

Within this framework, Bowles called for an approach grounded both in military strength and in ideas and programs that would have a powerful political and ideological appeal to the developing countries. He took a very tough line on the importance of meeting the threat of Communist aggression. He demanded that the United States be well armed, with a balance of strategic air power and highly trained and well-equipped conventional forces, and he criticized as dangerous, morally unacceptable, and unworkable Dulles's 1954 announcement that Washington would in future confront any possible aggression by "a great capacity to retaliate instantly by means and at places of our own choosing."[10]

In Bowles's view, the Soviet challenge, if not the Chinese, was much more likely to come from the appeal Communist ideology had in the developing world than from a move by Communist armed forces across international frontiers. For that reason, the United States had to develop a more "positive" foreign policy if it was to avoid a potentially disastrous setback in its effort to contain Communism. As he put it in a 1955 memorandum, "if we continue to view almost every international problem primarily in terms of arms agreements, air bases, flight distances, and nuclear striking power, we are headed for a steadily growing series of setbacks which within the next two to three years may place us in a most dangerous situation."[11] What the United States needed instead was "a balance between ideas and defense; on the one hand, the bringing together under the banner of a militant new freedom of those people of the earth—and today they are by far the majority— who seek the goals we seek, self-determination, human dignity, and expanding opportunities, and, on the other hand the power of a massive competent defense to provide a screen behind which those goals can be vigorously pursued."[12]

Bowles's concern about Eisenhower administration foreign policy was heightened by increasing evidence in the mid-1950s of Soviet

flexibility. In *Ambassador's Report*, he had warned: "There are disturbing signs that Moscow's indifference to the possibilities of economic
assistance to the non-Communist underdeveloped areas may be changing and that a new period of 'ruble diplomacy' may lie ahead. . . . A
devastatingly effective Soviet version of Point Four could be financed
for less than one-third of the present $8 billion annual increase in
Russia's national income, which would amount to far more than we
are putting into our own Point Four effort."[13] The possibilities he
foresaw soon came to pass, not least in India, which the Soviets made
a particular target of their diplomacy and financial assistance.

The apparent development of a U.S.-Soviet nuclear balance had to
be taken into account as the United States calculated its approach to
the developing world, he also contended. Reviewing the outcome of
the 1955 Geneva Summit, he wrote that "if the [meeting] means anything, it means that at least as long as we maintain the present military
atomic balance a world war has been permanently outmoded by the
very frightfulness of modern weapons. If such is the case, a foreign
policy that gives almost automatic priority to the military factors and
minimizes the political, economic, and ideological forces which are now
writing history may prove to be an easy target for the new Soviet
tactics."[14]

Bowles pursued these and other themes in *The New Dimensions of
Peace*. The book was his most ambitious effort to spell out his conception of America's stake in the developing world and its relevance
to the Cold War and to provide general guidelines and specific recommendations about foreign policy. It appeared in 1955 just as Eisenhower suffered a heart attack, boosting (at least for a few months)
Democratic hopes of winning back the White House in 1956. This
fortuitous timing led *New York Times* columnist James Reston to note
that the book should be taken more seriously since "Bowles's thinking
is likely to have a considerable influence on his party's campaign next
year, and if the Democrats are elected, he is almost certain to play a
prominent role in the formulation of any Democratic Administration's
foreign policy."[15] But as Reston acknowledged, *New Dimensions* was
not a partisan book. Bowles was critical of American foreign policy in
the developing world as it was practiced *throughout* the postwar decade, predominantly a time of Democratic leadership in Washington.

New Dimensions is a more complex book than *Ambassador's Report*
and was more difficult to conceptualize and draft. It was designed to
appeal at several levels. As one of Bowles's collaborators has recalled,

"Chet was very conscious of audience, and one of the problems . . . was to produce a book popular enough for the political audience, intellectual enough for the academic audience, and generally insightful and responsible enough for Chet's growing reputation as a leading foreign affairs commentator and a potential secretary of state."[16] *New Dimensions* was less than fully successful in achieving those ends. To satisfy each of his different audiences Bowles tried to cram too much into a single volume. The mixture of historical surveys, philosophical considerations, policy proposals, recent travel experiences, and forecasts of the future gave the book a patchwork quality which at times obscured what he was trying to say.

Much of *New Dimensions* is given over to highly popularized accounts of the Russian, Chinese, and Gandhian revolutions and their appeal to the aspirations of emerging peoples newly aware, through improved communications systems, that they can make better lives for themselves. This approach, novel for a political figure, served to dramatize Bowles's long-standing contention that it was in the developing countries that the critical struggle of the twentieth century was taking place. It also underscored his faith that in that conflict the power of men and ideas was more decisive than the power of weapons, and it sought to provide historical justification for his thesis that the United States had to address the contest for the minds of the peoples in the emerging lands more seriously and constructively. The approach also reflected his fascination with history and projected him as a serious student of foreign affairs, prepared (unlike most politicians) to look at foreign policy issues from a historical perspective.

Bowles also used his survey of twentieth-century revolutions as a foil to cite the relevance of the American experience to the developing continents. For him, America represented the "complete democratic revolution," which had created a society that had come closer toward achieving political, economic, and social justice than any past civilization. He wished to see the United States help the emerging countries move toward similar achievements despite the limits to what it could do and the frustrations those limits would arouse. "I am deeply convinced," he wrote, "that the American Revolution, refreshed and strengthened and for the first time focussed on world affairs, can become a powerful political, social, and economic force affecting the lives of every man, woman, and child in the world."[17]

▾   ▾   ▾

Most of Bowles's commentary on foreign affairs in the 1950s focused on Asia. He visited Africa in 1955 and was one of the first well-known American foreign policy commentators to take an interest in African matters, but they remained a poor second on his agenda. European affairs were an even more distant third. While he recognized the security of Western Europe as the bedrock of U.S. foreign policy and was unhappy with the unimaginative way the Eisenhower administration dealt with the issue, he failed to develop serious expertise on Europe and largely left it to others to prepare specific policy proposals. The few pronouncements he made were generally in support of initiatives that he hoped might lead to a relaxation of Cold War tensions and strengthen relations between the United States and the Western European countries. They showed little originality and may have been designed partly to demonstrate that he was able to deal with policy problems outside the Third World. He surely had that objective in mind when he successfully applied in 1959 for membership on the subcommittee of the House Foreign Affairs Committee that dealt with Europe. These European sorties were not convincing; he continued to be regarded as an analyst whose interests focused on Asian and African countries and issues.

The limited attention he paid to European policies was paralleled by his unfamiliarity with Europe's leaders. Although he had met with Communist Party General Secretary Nikita Khrushchev at the Kremlin in 1957 and had had exchanges with a few other leading European figures, he was never really comfortable discussing European issues with senior Europeans. This contrasted with the easy rapport he was almost always able to develop with Asians and Africans.

Bowles showed similarly limited concern about the Middle East and, surprisingly, Latin America. He generally looked at the Middle East in the context of his interest in South Asia or as a Third World region whose problems were similar to those faced by other underdeveloped areas and merited similar responses. Although he had developed a friendship with Governor Luis Muñoz Marín of Puerto Rico and through Muñoz had come to know reform-minded presidents Betancourt of Venezuela and Figueres of Costa Rica, he made few specific references to Latin America. One possible explanation for his indifference to this region may have been the absence in Latin America of the Third World political issues he found so interesting in the Afro-Asian region—nonalignment versus alliances, the struggle against colonialism (rather than neocolonialism), and the development of new, viable nation states. Only at the end of the decade when he wrote about Latin

American land reform along familiar lines did he specifically focus on the area.[18]

▾   ▾   ▾

The visit Bowles made to Africa in 1955 came just a few years before the great burst of British, French, and Belgian decolonization changed the map of that continent earlier than almost all commentators had anticipated, himself included. But he saw clearly at that time that the handwriting was on the wall. The only point at issue in his thinking was how independence could most effectively and smoothly be brought about in light of the potentially explosive mix of African nationalism, racial tensions, and European stubbornness.

He spelled out his mid-decade ideas about Africa in lectures he gave at the University of California. These were subsequently published under the title *Africa's Challenge to America*. It was, like many of his works, a readable amalgam of personal observations and policy recommendations. His views largely reflected the approach to the politics and economics of the developing world shaped by his experience in Asia and his thinking about U.S. policies there. American national security objectives coincided with those of responsible African nationalists, he contended, and the United States should support these nationalists' aspirations and recognize that the pace of events on the African continent could no longer be controlled by "our European friends." Like the Asians, "what [the] new African leaders want most from us is the responsible reassertion of the democratic principles which have provided the primary energizing force behind America's growth and influence."[19] Not surprisingly, he found that U.S. policy had been much too timid in staking out positions because of the opposition of the colonial powers.

Although he was convinced that the age of colonialism was coming to an end, Bowles opposed indiscriminate support for African independence and favored instead a gradualist approach that would take into account the different levels of political and economic maturity in the various African colonies. He called for setting, at the earliest possible time, dates on which full independence would be granted, with increasing degrees of self-government to be developed as these came near. U.S. assistance for African economic development should be provided in ways beneficial to the indigenous populations, not to the colonialists. This could help bolster the political stability of the continent, which he recognized would come under strain. In an unusual wrinkle, he gave the United Nations special prominence as a potential key player in a program for the liquidation of colonialism. Appalled by the ignorance about Africa in the United States, he also urged greater attention to African studies in American universities and increased contact with Africa through cultural exchanges and diplomatic activity.

Bowles's interest in Africa grew as the pace of decolonization quickened at the end of the decade and in the early 1960s. His interest was no doubt heightened further when his son Sam and Sam's new wife went to northern Nigeria as teachers at that time. The rash of actual and impending political changes in what had been French, British, and Belgian colonial territories led the State Department to establish a separate Bureau for African Affairs. When Bowles became under secretary of state in 1961, he would give its activities special attention.

▾   ▾   ▾

But it was the fate of Asia that Bowles regarded as the key to the future. He held that the failure of the United States to recognize the contrasting historical experiences of Europe and Asia was a major flaw in its Asian policy. "When we used our military and economic power to fill the vacuum of Western Europe, we were moving chiefly among people who saw and responded to the same threat we did," he wrote in *New Dimensions*. "But when we acted to discourage Soviet intrusion into the Middle East and Southeast Asia, we were met with distrust. . . . The sensitive new governments of South Asia considered the threat of world communism remote, while their colonial memories remained vivid."[20]

The aim of U.S. policies in Asia should be the development of strong, independent nations whose political and economic foundations would be sufficiently solid to deal with the attraction Communism had for their intellectuals and masses, particularly in its promise of rapid economic development. Such nations would be prepared to fight against Communist aggression to maintain their own freedom, and their determination to do so was far more important than their attitude toward U.S. policies. Moreover, they could help relieve American defense burdens. "The key to the security of Free Asia," he believed, "lies in the development of dynamic centers of indigenous political stability and potential power which will lend their own growing strength to that of their neighbors—with the military and economic power of America and the Western alliance available, but discreetly in the background."[21]

This approach was reflected in Bowles's distaste for military pacts, evidenced earlier in his strong opposition to the U.S.-Pakistan security tie. Allies could not be bought, he repeatedly stated. He saw no possibility that an American-led and dominated anti-Communist front in Asia could be effective. The Eisenhower administration's policy of looking to the smaller Asian countries for partners and its seeming indifference to the popular standing of these newly allied regimes troubled him. He remained unreconciled to U.S. defense links with governments that did not enjoy broad support and was prepared to accept military assistance agreements with them only under very special circumstances dictated by pressing security requirements. "If I were asked to make one general criticism of our foreign policy under both [Truman and Eisenhower] administrations," he wrote to Paul Hoffman in December 1954, "it would be that we have lavished too much time, money and attention on nations which, although favorable to us, are inherently weak and vulnerable; and not enough on nations, which although often critical of our policies, have the potential power to shape history."[22]

Bowles continued to promote American acceptance of nonalignment as a reflection of deeply rooted anticolonial, nationalist attitudes. He warned against American overreaction to agreements between the nonaligned and Communist powers and hailed the landmark 1955 Bandung conference of nonaligned, pro-Western, and Communist Asian and African countries.[23] A 1957 formulation caught the basic thrust of his foreign policy: "The ultimate test is not what the 'Middle World' thinks of us, or of the Russians or Chinese, but what each Asian or African nation does within itself: Is it moving, however gradually, in the direction of increased political stability and individual freedom? Is it meeting its problems promptly enough and is it strong enough internally to resist violent revolution? Is it prepared to maintain an open friendly relationship with America and its Atlantic Community associates?"[24]

Anticolonialism was a constant theme in Bowles's message. He called repeatedly for a clear U.S. policy against vestigial Western colonialism and held that for the United States to sacrifice its moral position for a doubtful strengthening of its relations with old colonial European allies was a bad bargain. He shared what he called the common Asian view that the United States was violating its own principles when it compromised on the remaining colonialist issues. While he called for consultations with the allies when differences arose over colonial policy, and acknowledged that the United States needed to base its Asian policy on the assumption that the Atlantic pact was the cornerstone of its national security, he made clear what needed to be done. "Although our European allies are essential to our security," he wrote in 1955, "we cannot permit them to put a ceiling on our efforts to cope with these forces [of change in Asia]."[25]

▼   ▼   ▼

Bowles's Asian concerns centered on China and India. His old interest in China had been piqued by his New Delhi experience, and the question of the relationship between the United States and the People's Republic remained a major focus for his attention throughout the 1950s and beyond. His approach was more objective and farsighted than that of most of his political contemporaries. Unlike theirs, it reflected an awareness of the dynamics of modern Chinese history. James Thomson, to whom he often looked for advice on Chinese issues, has remarked that Bowles "always had a long-term understanding that the Chinese are really people; that China is really a place and not an ideological permanent enemy, not a permanent adversary; that Communism in China has its roots in a special indigenous situation."[26]

The positions Bowles adopted also reflected a courage of conviction not widely shared within the Democratic party, where many of those who believed Eisenhower's China policy unrealistic and even dangerous preferred to say so privately. His willingness to speak out on the issue is the more remarkable in light of the strong feeling on the subject in his home state. The powerful China lobby, which strongly supported Chiang Kai-shek and was implacably hostile to the People's Republic, enjoyed considerable support there, not least among the heavily Roman Catholic rank and file of the Connecticut Democratic party. Thomas J. Dodd, a member of the House of Representatives from Connecticut before he entered the U.S. Senate in 1959 after beating out Bowles for the Democratic nomination, was a leading member of the lobby.

By the time he returned from India, Bowles had come to several key conclusions about China, many of them similar to Nehru's. He believed that the People's Republic was well entrenched; under its leadership China had achieved political unity, ideological discipline, and economic and military strength, thereby adding to its prestige and influence throughout Asia. Unlike many of Chiang Kai-shek's American supporters, he found no convincing evidence that the generalissimo would be welcomed back to the mainland. Military measures to overthrow the Peking regime would require major American participation and would be extremely costly and probably unsuccessful. The unwillingness of the United States to recognize the Chinese Communist government and its claim to the Chinese seat in the United Nations merely strengthened Peking's ties to the Soviet Union. The Soviets valued and exploited

China's isolation, but over time China would come to pursue a line independent of Moscow. While the United States should do what it could to encourage such a split, it should also understand that China might well become more a threat to peace than the Soviet Union.

Over the decade Bowles was guided by these premises as he searched for ways the United States could live with the reality of Communist China short of recognizing the regime, an option he acknowledged had been made impossible by American political opinion and Chinese intransigence, especially the Peking regime's demand for Taiwan. While he agreed with the Eisenhower administration on the importance of containing the People's Republic (though he thought the policies it had adopted to accomplish this were wrong), he differed sharply with its objective of isolating Peking. He looked instead for ways of developing a relationship with the government and people of China that would go beyond the largely sterile and routinized talks that took place intermittently between U.S. and Chinese diplomats in Geneva and Warsaw after 1955. The United States should look for ways of assuring Peking that it was prepared to be "flexible and moderate"; he suggested to Allen Dulles in 1954 that the administration use Prime Minister Nehru's visit to China that year to get its message across.[27] It should also take a less bellicose public line against the People's Republic and explore the possibility of Western grain shipments to the food-short mainland, perhaps in exchange for the Chinese forswearing any aggressive designs against their neighbors.

Bowles recognized that Chinese hostility toward the United States limited prospects for a favorable response to such gestures, but he considered them worth making because rejection by Peking would shift the blame for stubbornness and inflexibility to the Communists. His attitude on the politically sensitive issue of a United Nations seat for Peking was tough—the United States should support the entry of the Chinese Communists only if they agreed to reasonable settlements on Korea, Indochina, and Taiwan and gave up their support for subversive forces. But it did not have the theological quality many other American leaders adopted on the matter.

The future of Taiwan figured prominently in Bowles's writing. Eager to have the United States disengage itself from the Chinese civil war (without abandoning Taiwan to the Communists), he wanted the administration to do more to oblige the Nationalists to withdraw their forces from the offshore islands of Quemoy and Matsu and looked with growing favor on the possibility of a separate Chinese state on Taiwan. He and Secretary Dulles locked horns on the Taiwan/offshore islands issue in 1959, when Dulles testified before the House Foreign Affairs Committee soon after Bowles had joined the committee as a freshman congressman. He told Dulles that it would have been unwise to have been forced out of Quemoy and Matsu the previous summer, when Peking was threatening to seize the islands—the second time in the decade that their fate had caused a major crisis. But, he said, "many of us [have] seriously questioned for a long time the wisdom of our being there in the first place." He asked Dulles: "What are you doing and what can you do, now that the situation is a little quieter, to liquidate what many of us feel is an unrealistic and dangerous situation out of which a major war can start that would gain us nothing, which might well bring in the Soviet Union, and which we would fight with no allies or friends outside of Chiang Kai-shek and Syngman Rhee?" He got no satisfaction from the secretary, who contended that there was no way he was aware of to liquidate the position at Quemoy and Matsu without at the same time liquidating the entire Free World position in the Far East.[28]

Bowles gathered together many of the elements of his thinking about China in a major article for the April 1960 issue of *Foreign Affairs*.[29] Contending that the time had come to end the myth that Chiang Kai-shek remained the ruler of 650 million mainland Chinese, he reiterated in unvarnished terms his earlier calls for the establishment of a separate state on Taiwan. Such an independent Sino-Taiwanese nation could eventually offer, as a contrast to the totalitarian People's Republic, a modernized non-Communist Chinese society that enjoyed an increasing measure of political liberty and offered expanded economic opportunities. While the security and prosperity of the island state would in the short run depend on U.S. military guarantees and economic assistance, in the longer term they would hinge on the attitude of other Asian nations, particularly India and Japan. He repeated his support for an Asian Monroe Doctrine in this context.

Bowles offered no specifics about how such a fundamental change in the government on Taiwan could be brought about, a major failing in his approach. He ruled out a plebiscite, which he had proposed earlier, since Chiang would reject it. He was similarly vague about the nature of the new Taiwan government (other than to say that it had eventually to be responsive to the Taiwanese majority on the island) and about what the United States should do in the event Chiang and the Kuomintang leadership refused to accept the proposed new arrangement.

Aside from advocating this "two Chinas policy" (which he preferred to call a "two nations policy"), Bowles also called for moves that could lessen U.S.-Chinese tensions and take advantage of differences between Peking and Moscow, by then becoming more pronounced. Continuing to rule out recognition, he noted, without elaboration, "that if ever it becomes practicable it will be in our national interest to restore our traditionally friendly ties with the Chinese people on the mainland." A first step should be the removal of obstacles to the movement of press correspondents between the two countries. (The administration had opposed this, then modified its position.) This could be followed by exchanges of businessmen, educators, and political leaders as well as consideration of trade ties. But he continued to mix such flexibility with toughness. The United States should make clear to Peking that it would oppose by all necessary means not only a move against Taiwan but any Chinese aggression in Southeast Asia as well.

Although by 1960 China policy could be discussed less emotionally than had been possible earlier in the decade, Bowles's formulation stirred up major controversy. He was denounced by the China lobby in the United States and by Chou En-lai in China. Ironically in light of his own initiatives eleven years later, Vice President Nixon reportedly told President-elect Kennedy soon after the 1960 election that because of the article he would forcefully oppose a Kennedy decision to name Bowles secretary of state. (Any support he received from Kennedy was at best *sotto voce*.) As often happened in his career, Bowles was perceived as too far out in front, and more cautious counsels carried the day.[30]

▾   ▾   ▾

The importance of India in Asia and the world continued to be a major article of faith for Bowles, and during the decade he was probably the most outspoken American advocate of stronger U.S.-Indian ties. He carried on a correspondence with Nehru, Bajpai, and other leaders, and followed Indian political and economic developments closely. His return visits to India in 1955 and 1957 were great welcome-home occasions when he could update himself in long sessions with his old friends and associates. He was widely recognized as one of the most important American authorities on India and South Asia and wrote and spoke extensively about them. Indians in the United States revered him as a father figure.[31]

Bowles continued to be a forceful supporter of high levels of American economic assistance for India. The worldwide assistance programs the administration carried through Congress in its first three budgets were largely directed toward the military, however. Except for a few development programs, economic aid unrelated to security considerations had been virtually eliminated by FY 1955. Though assistance to India was the largest in this small program of "pure" economic aid, it remained well below the annual $250–300 million mark Bowles had advocated from New Delhi.[32]

By 1955–56, however, the administration had begun to reconsider seriously its overall assistance strategy. The greater flexibility in post-Stalin Soviet policy toward the Third World, forecast by Bowles, was a major element in this reexamination. Moscow's new approach was highlighted by greatly expanded trade, low interest loans, and technical assistance. The administration saw it as an economic offensive that threatened to tie the developing countries closely to the Communist bloc.[33] The Soviet moves helped prompt Congress, too, to take a closer and more sympathetic look at economic assistance for nonaligned Third World countries.

India was a major focus for Soviet attention, and in the changing atmosphere toward economic assistance policy in Washington the launching of its ambitious Second Five Year Plan in 1956 provided a target of opportunity for advocates of higher aid levels to the Nehru government. Bowles was in the forefront in calling for U.S. support for the plan, particularly after a foreign exchange crisis in 1957 seriously jeopardized its prospects for success. The pleas for U.S. help for the second plan that he made in the media and in private correspondence with influential figures in both parties recall the impassioned messages he had sent from New Delhi advocating greater U.S. funding for the first plan. He accepted the second plan's emphasis on industrial development as a logical follow-up to the agricultural advances the first had helped bring about.[34]

As he had done earlier, Bowles depicted economic assistance to the Third World as a foreign policy tool, the same way the Eisenhower administration regarded it; but he also saw it as a manifestation of the liberal American spirit, a view much less widely shared. He argued that the main competition between Communism and democracy in Asia for many years to come would be in the development area and called for an economic program substantial enough to do for Asia what the Marshall Plan had done for Europe. He would later extend this Third World Marshall Plan to Africa and Latin America. Convinced that the American people were much more willing to pay for foreign aid than the Truman and Eisenhower administrations had estimated, he was scornful of efforts to curtail aid on budgetary grounds. "Let it not be said by future historians," he wrote in 1955, "that in the second decade after World War II freedom throughout the world died of a balanced budget."[35]

As the decade progressed, Bowles put more emphasis on the comparative economic performances of India and China. The competition, and its importance to the United States, had come to attract high-level attention. Even Dulles had cited it, in his 1954 congressional testimony supporting aid to India. In *New Dimensions,* Bowles went well beyond his earlier writings about the significance of the competition. He now called it "the battle of the century" and predicted that "more than any other single event short of war, [its] outcome may determine the path which the rest of the underdeveloped world ultimately chooses to take." He claimed that "underdeveloped countries throughout Asia, Africa, and South America, which are urgently seeking answers to similar problems, are watching this Chinese-Indian competition intently."[36]

In the political-military sphere, Bowles gradually moved to a position tantamount to calling for termination of the U.S.-Pakistan security arrangement. In a May 1956 memorandum he was still prepared to say that however mistaken the commitments made to Pakistan then appeared, they could not be disregarded. But he also called for a new regional military balance among India, Pakistan, and Afghanistan and noted that "if it would be helpful as a temporary expedient to make some modest equipment available to India on a long-term basis and without political strings in order to bring about a new balance, we should do so."[37] He went much farther in an early 1957 letter to Robert Bowie, the chairman of the State Department Policy Planning Council, in which he recommended that the United States propose a moratorium on all arms shipments to the Middle East, defined to include Pakistan. He candidly admitted that this was a stratagem designed to cut off military equipment to the Pakistanis. He later went public with the idea, suggesting a ten-year period for the moratorium.[38] (Ironically, by the beginning of 1957 Eisenhower was also expressing strong doubts about the Pakistan military assistance program.[39])

In correspondence and articles, especially those drafted in 1955 and 1956, Bowles often despaired of the future of U.S.-Indian relations and feared that Eisenhower administration policies had led to what he called an ominous change against the United States in the balance of power in Asia. Relations had in fact worsened during the first years of the administration. Foreign policy differences focused on U.S. military assistance to Pakistan; Eisenhower's assurances to Nehru that Washington would prevent Pakistan's using American-supplied arms against India did little to allay Indian concern. U.S. dissatisfaction with Nehru's enthusiastic championing of nonalignment and the closer ties India was establishing with the Soviet Union and Communist China also roiled the relationship. So did the Indians' dismay about what seemed to them U.S. support for colonialism, including Portugal's continuing control of scattered pockets of territory in India. As noted, economic assistance remained limited. Although the Eisenhower administration, like its predecessor, had acknowledged that aid to India and other South Asian countries could help prevent them from falling under Communist domination, its funding priorities initially lay elsewhere, as Truman's had.

The situation began to improve towards the end of Eisenhower's first term. The president had been gradually moving to a better appreciation of nonalignment, and Nehru's visit to the United States in December 1956, when the two men established remarkably good rapport, helped solidify his more positive view. (Dulles was somewhat slower in accepting the benefits of nonalignment to the United States, but by early 1957 he, too, was supporting it.) The prime minister's visit also heightened Eisenhower's willingness to help the Indian government with economic aid. The administration, already troubled by Soviet initiatives, soon moved forward with a much more generous program of assistance to India and other Third World nations.

The new approach was officially recognized in NSC 5701, approved by Eisenhower in January 1957. The document stated that the United States should "provide economic and technical assistance to India, placing emphasis on projects and programs having the maximum potential of support of the goals and aspirations of India's second five-year plan," described as "the best vehicle for action to promote U.S. interest in an independent India." It also declared that "the outcome of the competition between Communist China and India will have a profound effect throughout Asia and Africa."[40] Noting that the significance of the policy paper "rested in the fact that for the first time American officials at the highest level directly and emphatically drew the connection between economic development in Asia and American security," H. W. Brands has quite correctly quipped that "[it] might almost have been written by Chester Bowles."[41] Over the next four years economic assistance to India reached heights that dwarfed the levels of the early 1950s. As Dennis Merrill, another student of the period, put it, "India became for United States leaders a model nation where American-backed development was to be tested and proven efficacious."[42]

India welcomed the new importance the United States assigned to it, not least because of the serious impact of its foreign exchange crunch. Indian satisfaction with the U.S. position in the Suez crisis of 1956, its discomfort with the Soviet invasion of Hungary at that time, the sense that India had drifted too far from its nonaligned moorings in developing its close relationship with the Soviet Union, and, in the last years of the decade, concern about India's relations with Communist China also contributed to the Nehru government's interest in better ties with Washington. Although the problem of Pakistan had not gone away, by the time Bowles returned to office as Kennedy's under secretary of state in January 1961, U.S.-Indian relations were probably far better than he could have anticipated their becoming under a Republican administration.

8

Search for a Political Base

BOWLES'S interest in influencing the conduct of foreign policy played an important role in shaping his political plans following his return from India. This first became clear in 1954, when he had an opportunity to win back the Connecticut governorship he had lost four years earlier. The political signals early that year seemed propitious for Bowles. His performance in India—and the favorable publicity it had received, not least through his own efforts—had enhanced his prestige. He enjoyed what he thought was a good relationship and close friendship with Democratic State Chairman John Bailey, who would play a major role in determining who got the party's nomination. McCarthyism was on the wane, lessening a problem a Democrat of Bowles's liberal views faced in a state where the Wisconsin senator had exerted considerable influence. And in the normal off-year course of things the Democrats could be expected to make gains despite Eisenhower's continuing popularity.

Bowles's two years as governor had been exhilarating. Discussing his political ambitions in July 1952, when he was being sounded out about a bid for the U.S. Senate following the sudden death of senior Connecticut Senator Brien McMahon, he wrote Benton that "my principal interest is in policy making and the administration that grows out of it and that always leads to the governorship."[1] He had little regard for the way incumbent Governor John Davis Lodge had led Connecticut following the closely contested 1950 election. Winning a rematch would have given him great personal satisfaction, and it would also have offered him the opportunity to complete the ambitious reform program he had begun in 1949–50 and strengthen the liberal wing of the state Democratic party. It would also have made him a possible contender for the party's presidential nomination in 1956, as he would have been in 1952 had he won a second term.

But by 1954, and for the rest of the decade, he was tantalized by the prospect of becoming secretary of state in a Democratic administration. A natural objective for a senior political leader interested in foreign policy, that position was particularly attractive to Bowles, who had very firm ideas on what that policy should be. The secretaryship also offered him what he must have regarded as the satisfying prospect of again heading a large organization and running it in his own innovative way at a time U.S. power was its height. He had to determine the impact his returning to Hartford would have on these ambitions and on the increasingly prominent role he was building for himself as a Democratic party foreign affairs spokesman.

▾   ▾   ▾

After returning from New Delhi Bowles had become politically allied with Adlai Stevenson. In August 1953 he had written to Stevenson urging him to make another bid for the White House and to speak out against the foreign and domestic policy failures of the Eisenhower administration. He offered to help Stevenson in any way.

The Bowles-Stevenson tie went back to their days as boarding school students. The two men, both well-to-do establishment figures, had come together again as freshmen Democratic governors after winning election in 1948. They enjoyed a good if not really close personal relationship. Bowles regarded the Illinois leader as a fellow liberal who shared his views about the fundamental imperatives and goals of foreign policy. In this he was basically correct, although he probably thought Stevenson's ideas on international issues were closer to his own than was actually the case. "I always go along with Chet up to a point; then he becomes too soft and sentimental for me; and he always ends up with the implication that the solution lies in spending more money," Stevenson told Arthur Schlesinger in 1955.[2]

Bowles was ambassador in India during Stevenson's losing effort in 1952. He had told Benton earlier that year that had he been a delegate to the Democratic convention he would have voted for the Illinois governor. But citing his responsibilities in India, he had resisted the senator's suggestion that he come home to help in the campaign.[3] He and Stevenson resumed their close ties in 1953 following Bowles's return to the United States and the completion of Stevenson's postelection journey to Asia. (This included a visit to Kashmir, shortly after

Bowles left India, which had led to baseless but widely believed allegations that Stevenson had encouraged separatist political elements in the disputed state.) Aside from the one-on-one relationship they enjoyed through extensive correspondence and meetings over the rest of the decade, they were also associated in a high-powered study group led by former Air Force Secretary Thomas Finletter that was intended to be a brain trust for Stevenson.

The idea for such a group sprang from the sense shared by several of Stevenson's friends and advisers that in its unaccustomed opposition role the Democratic party needed a mechanism to generate new policy approaches. In the late summer of 1953, Bowles and Finletter, both highly critical of Eisenhower's foreign and security policies, had sought to meet with Stevenson to discuss these issues. Arthur Schlesinger and John Kenneth Galbraith were talking at that time at Harvard about the need for Stevenson to develop ideas between elections. (Galbraith later recalled that the group's primary purpose was to improve Stevenson's understanding of economic issues, which in his view had been sorely deficient in the 1952 campaign.) Galbraith wrote to Stevenson at the end of September urging the need for the Democrats to develop a program that could offer an alternative to Republicanism. The solution, he suggested, was "some organization in or adjacent to the Democratic Party" to formulate and discuss policies.[4]

Stevenson met with Finletter, former Ambassador to Moscow George Kennan, and Bowles at Bowles's house in Essex on the weekend of October 3–4, and launched what became known as the Finletter Group. The group met from time to time over the next three years, mostly at Finletter's New York apartment, and prepared papers on a variety of foreign policy and other issues. It carried on until the 1956 election, when its functions as a party think tank were taken over by the Democratic Advisory Council (DAC), a more institutionalized body affiliated with the Democratic National Committee. Bowles was also a member of the DAC, serving on its Foreign Policy Committee headed by Dean Acheson.

The Finletter Group gave Bowles his most sustained exposure to the Democratic element of the foreign policy establishment. He also played a role in the Council on Foreign Relations, which in the 1950s was the stronghold and symbol of that elitist, largely New York-based establishment. Bowles's relations with the foreign policy in-group were never easy. As both his associates and his critics have pointed out, many establishment figures looked down on him as an inferior intellect, a pleasant second-rater. Their condescension for his advertising background was pronounced. Some regarded him as fuzzy-minded and long-winded, an amateurish ideologue and simplistic idealist not tough enough to deal with Cold War realities and get things done.

Bowles's difficulties with the establishment were compounded by his ineffectiveness in dealing with his peers. Enormously successful in developing warm relations of mutual regard and useful give-and-take with younger people, he had trouble relating to people of his own age and social group, particularly at formal meetings that involved serious differences of view. To the consternation of his close colleagues, he tended in those circumstances to be withdrawn and to lack confidence in himself.

This inability to develop and maintain easy and confident relations with his peers seems paradoxical for a man who by that time had achieved success in positions in business and government where effectiveness in person-to-person contact was critical. Bowles recognized the problem but apparently did not try to resolve what appears to have been the manifestation of an inferiority complex rooted in past experiences. Some of his associates have speculated that as an essentially self-educated man with a Yale Sheffield degree, he felt intellectually inferior to the impressive lawyers, bankers, and academics he encountered in the 1950s and 1960s. In support of this theory, it can be argued that although Bowles came, as many of them did, from the Eastern establishment of the day, his work experience and the talents he cultivated in achieving his spectacular success in advertising were markedly different from the backgrounds and skills the others brought with them. In a sense, they and Bowles belonged to separate "establishments," and it is certainly conceivable that he might have been somewhat overawed when thrown into direct contact with them. Although he tried hard to cultivate them, his enthusiastic and optimistic approach differed sharply from theirs and had little of the sense of irony which was so often their stock in trade. He may well have found, as outsiders do in dealing with an established circle, that they spoke in a code which he could never successfully interpret. But this is at best well-informed speculation, and in the absence of any available systematic psychological analysis no conclusive finding seems possible.

There were major divisions on policy within both the Finletter Group and the DAC Committee on Foreign Affairs. Two important clusters among Democratic party foreign policy specialists and aspirants for secretary of state had emerged in the mid-1950s. Affinities were more or less sharply divided between the Eurocentric Dean Acheson–Paul Nitze wing, which emphasized the need for strong security measures and generally followed a tough, Cold War approach highly suspicious of Soviet intentions, and those like Galbraith, Schlesinger, and Stevenson himself who shared to a greater or lesser degree Bowles's position that a better balance had to be struck between America's security requirements and its concern for economic growth and humanitarian needs, especially in the developing world. Acheson and those who thought like him had little interest in that world and scorned the notion that its future was vital in the Cold War. While they did not exactly brand Bowles soft on Communism, they thought he was badly wrong in his assessment that a military confrontation with the Soviets was less of a threat to American interests than the appeal Communist ideology had for the poor nations of the world. Harris Wofford has phrased their attitude toward Bowles as a question: "Would you trust Chester Bowles to deal with Moscow?"[5]

▾   ▾   ▾

Bowles was torn over running for governor in 1954. Steb and a number of others close to him were convinced that it would be a mistake for him to go back into state politics. He wrote to Jean Joyce and Bernard Loshbough, who had remained in India, that he felt "the real ball game is being played on the international and national diamond and that there is a good chance that I would die of frustration in the Governor's chair in Hartford." "At the same time," he continued, "I know that the Governorship offers an opportunity to apply solid pressure on the development of the Democratic party on a national basis and at present I believe that this is particularly needed. If I ran for Governor and won, I would have a position in the Democratic party which perhaps would allow me to contribute in a major way beyond the confines of the state."[6] Thomas Hughes has put it more succinctly: "Speaking from Hartford on foreign policy was better than speaking from Essex."[7]

Discussing his options with Stevenson, Bowles tried to find a halfway house. He recalled telling Stevenson that "as Governor of Connecticut I could help him win at the nominating convention. If he won, I would, if he wished, resign the governorship to work in his new administration, presumably in foreign affairs." Stevenson did not agree. He believed it would be a mistake for Bowles to plan to resign in 1956 in the middle of a four-year term. He should make a choice: either run for the governorship and remain in Hartford for four years or stay out of the contest and work with Stevenson in the presidential campaign with the intention of taking a key position in Washington afterwards.[8]

In April Bowles decided to run for governor, but only if it was clear that he had the support of the party. He did not make an all-out effort to get the nomination, in part, he found, because he was emotionally not committed to taking on the governorship and giving up his interest in foreign affairs. When it became clear that Bailey would not fight in his behalf and that other important leaders were against him (some because of his outspoken opposition to Senator McCarthy), he decided not to make the race. He issued a statement in late May in which he asserted that his interest was focused on national and foreign affairs and that he had been willing to run only if it were overwhelmingly clear that his candidacy was essential for Democratic victory. He was now convinced that that was not the case. "It is entirely possible," he said, "that I may wish to run for national office, perhaps for the U.S. Senate in 1956." He turned down Bailey's suggestion that he run for congressman-at-large.[9]

Bowles recalled that he was subjected to heavy pressure to change his mind before the state Democratic convention by friends who were confident that he could win the nomination. It was only with great difficulty, he said, that he decided it was too late to reverse himself. He later concluded that his decision not to run had been one of the worst mistakes in his political career.[10]

It is not at all clear that Bowles could have won the nomination, especially in a fight against popular former Congressman Abraham Ribicoff of Hartford, even if he had declared his candidacy earlier and made a more strenuous effort. Ribicoff had run a good race for the Senate in 1952, though he lost to Prescott Bush; he enjoyed considerable support among the Democratic leadership and would probably have had the backing of John Bailey in a contest against Bowles. In mounting his campaign, Bowles would have been handicapped not only by the difficulties he had in abandoning for the time being his interest in high foreign policy office, but also by his distaste for the rough-and-tumble of successful political battles. As Hughes has observed:

[Bowles] had a kind of love-hatred of politics. His love of politics and insistence on high electoral office was combined with a chemical dislike for the hard, commonplace, people-to-people organizational activities. I think Chet either thought that others could do those things for him, or else perhaps that they were unnecessary in the last analysis. I think that disposition had a lot to do with the narrow victories over the years, and the narrow defeats. The strong, dominant but intellectualized political interest, contrasted, for instance, with . . . Humphrey, who organized things so well so easily, and had an unquenchable thirst for, and an active enjoyment of, popular politics. I think Chet lacked these attributes over the years. (I think he would agree that he did.)[11]

What does seem reasonably clear, however, is that Bowles would have been better off making the bid, even though the results of both the nominating process and the election were uncertain. (Ribicoff won the governorship by a little over 3,000 votes.) In making his decision he had put all his eggs in Stevenson's political basket. He had given up the only electoral option realistically open to him for another two years, and more likely four, and made the prospect for a major boost in his political standing and foreign policy influence largely dependent on Stevenson's getting the nomination, using him meaningfully in the campaign as a foreign policy adviser, winning the election, and making him secretary of state. In the spring of 1954 the prospect that all of these elements would fall into place was not at all good. In the event, the only one that materialized was Stevenson's winning the nomination.[12]

▾ ▾ ▾

In his correspondence with Stevenson, Bowles repeatedly stressed the importance of foreign policy as a political issue. On the eve of the 1954 congressional campaign he wrote that the Democrats had strong foreign policy arguments but that even if their position on foreign policy were weaker they would have a moral obligation as the opposition party to challenge the Republicans. "There is an excellent chance," he predicted, "that we may win the House this fall, and possibly even the Senate. Skillful, responsible handling of the foreign policy issue during the campaign may increase our chances and our margin. If we make foreign policy an issue in the campaign, and if we win additional seats in Congress our European allies and the underdeveloped countries would gain increased confidence in the United States and the Soviet Union would see that we are not likely to fall apart." Moreover, making foreign policy a campaign issue would more or less commit the Democrats to a position on foreign affairs which would carry over into policies the party followed in Congress during the two years leading to the 1956 election.[13]

Bowles participated in a late September 1954 meeting of the Finletter Group, which agreed with him that foreign policy should be an issue in the congressional campaign and developed suggestions for an effective strategy. He prepared drafts of campaign and postelection speeches for Stevenson. These pinned the blame for the negative policies of the

Eisenhower administration on the Republican Old Guard and called for "enlightened bipartisanship" in foreign policy. He urged Stevenson to continue the group. It should concentrate on specific fields and give special urgency to foreign policy. Anxious to play a role in what he was confident would be Stevenson's second presidential campaign, Bowles wrote him in October 1955 that if he did not run for the Senate from Connecticut he could be at Stevenson's service for three or four days a week beginning in mid-March. Stevenson hoped that Bowles would join him. Bowles also proposed to organize a second group to offer suggestions on foreign policy, to which Stevenson reacted favorably.[14]

Trying to counter the views of those who argued that foreign policy was unlikely to win the Democrats any votes in 1956, Bowles told Stevenson in October 1955 that "there is a deep underlying fear of war, and the candidate who seems most able to cope with it will have a good start toward victory." "Whether foreign policy will offer a major advantage for you or a relatively minor one will depend not only on our skill in shaping up the issues but perhaps to an even larger degree on the march of events."[15] He sought to bring his own skills into play, developing numerous strategy suggestions in letters, memos, and draft speeches he sent Stevenson. A typical example was his suggestion that instead of striking directly at Eisenhower, the Democrats should systematically go after members of the president's team. Most of them have no popular support, he said, and several are highly vulnerable.[16]

Among the many themes he proposed for Democratic campaigners was the charge that the Republicans had failed to take advantage of the favorable political situation following the death of Stalin in 1953 to negotiate a stable, peaceful Asia, but had instead been satisfied with the limited accomplishment of an armistice in place in Korea. "We will hear a great deal in the next few months about Mr. Eisenhower's success in bringing peace to Korea," he wrote Stevenson. "It seems to me important that we go on the attack early on this issue, because I think we are on strong ground and can further undermine the administration's position on foreign policy, and also because it will tend to lessen the effectiveness of the Republican portrayal of Eisenhower as a peace-maker. The administration settled for a truce which gave the Chinese and the Soviets a breathing spell and released their energies for the conquest of Vietnam a year later."[17]

Bowles's most formal expression of his views on foreign policy and the coming presidential campaign during the winter and spring of

1955–56 came in a confidential thirteen-page memo he circulated to Democratic leaders in December. Citing polls which showed that a sizable majority believed that foreign policy was the most important single issue before the American people and that two out of three Americans considered the Republicans better able to handle that issue than the Democrats, he argued that the prudent course was to proceed on the assumption that the party must clear the foreign policy record or face defeat. Rather than launch a head-on indictment of the administration's policies, however harmful these may have been, the party ought instead to develop a two-phase approach. In the first stage, the Democrats would detail the deteriorating international position of the country. (Bowles provided the details.) They would call on the administration to show the same leadership in dealing with the crisis the Democrats had shown in meeting a similarly critical situation in 1947. The country should be told that "if bold, feasible answers to the present challenge from the Soviet Union are proposed, we [Democrats] shall vigorously support them."[18]

This first stage would offer the public a sound evaluation while allowing the Democrats to appear before the electorate in a positive, constructive role. It would be more effective than wholesale condemnation in winning over independent and liberal Republican voters. Moreover, if the Democrats refrained at first from blatant partisanship, they would increase the natural divisions and pressures within Republican ranks. And when it had become abundantly clear that necessary action would not be forthcoming from the administration, as Bowles was sure would be the case, the Democrats would be speaking from an unassailable political position. At that point they would move into the second phase of their strategy by launching a forthright attack on administration policies with confidence that it would win public support and sympathy. The attack should focus on "the deeply-rooted divisions in the Republican Party which in fact prevent it from taking the kind of imaginative action which alone can assure the security of the United States in this dangerous and turbulent world."

Bowles stepped up his output after Stevenson had wrapped up the nomination. He had come to chair two committees—one, as he put it in a letter to James Thomson, "on [Stevenson's] general approach and what he calls 'the image' he is trying to put over to the party and to the public; the second, on foreign affairs."[19] He peppered the candidate with a constant barrage of messages on campaign themes and strategy. Most of these dealt with foreign policy issues and the way they could be most effectively woven into the campaign.

To Bowles's dismay, his efforts to persuade Stevenson to highlight foreign policy issues were largely unsuccessful. Stevenson concluded that it would be unwise to mount a major challenge to Eisenhower in an area he thought was the president's strong suit with voters. The only important foreign policy/national security issues he raised during most of the campaign were calls for an end to the draft and to the testing of hydrogen bombs. In a letter in October Bowles desperately tried once again to get Stevenson to "accept battle on the President's chosen ground and . . . make foreign policy and peace your principal issues from now until November 6." He argued that Stevenson's two initiatives stood outside any clearly stated foreign policy framework and "even many of your most ardent followers view them as little more than political gimmicks." (The ideas on the draft and hydrogen bomb had not originated with Bowles, though he had mentioned them in passing in a long memorandum in August and later sought to dress them up in ways he thought would be more appealing to voters.)[20]

His role in the election thus became a limited one. Only toward the end of the campaign, on October 19 in Cincinnati, did Stevenson hit foreign policy hard. Bowles drafted much of the speech, and it bears his clear imprint, especially in its catalog of the administration's failings and the attention it gave to Asia and India. He later said, immodestly, that the speech was in many ways the most effective in the campaign. "I think it convinced [Stevenson], but by then it was pretty late." Two weeks later Eisenhower won another smashing victory and Dulles carried on as secretary of state.[21]

Writing to Jean Joyce soon after the election, Bowles lamented that "the Democratic party failed to make the foreign policy issues clear or even to deal with them vigorously. Hence we failed even to contribute to the education of the electorate. . . . What has been lost is . . . America's capacity to influence in any important way the course of events at a critical stage in history."[22] Looking back in the early 1960s, he told an interviewer that the 1956 campaign had not been a very good one. "The American people were very concerned about the world, but a lot of people tried to persuade Stevenson that domestic questions would be decisive and not to pay any attention to foreign policy. And so he talked about domestic policy and didn't do it tremendously effectively or with any great drive behind it, and left the field which I think was the one everybody wanted to hear about."[23]

▾   ▾   ▾

Bowles had an opportunity to run in 1956 for the Connecticut U.S. Senate seat held by Prescott Bush—a move he had said he considered when he had dropped out of the contest for governor in 1954. Bailey and Ribicoff, now governor, appear to have been prepared to offer him the nomination. Bowles wrote Jean Joyce in April 1956 that most people around him said that if he wanted the nomination and really went after it he would get it. He later recorded that he could have had it "on a silver platter." His stated reason for turning it down despite his earlier expression of interest was that he preferred the possibility of working in the State Department in a Stevenson administration. If he ran in 1956 and won, he could not accept a Stevenson appointment if *he* won (however unlikely that possibility).[24]

Bowles explained his decision in a June 1956 letter to Yale Law School Dean Eugene Rostow, who had urged him to make the bid. He said Steb's illness had been a factor: she had undergone surgery for a brain tumor in December 1955 and had required lengthy recuperation and further hospitalization. But, he stressed:

> The principal reason lies in the fact that I feel the biggest contribution I can make in the next four years is in the administration of foreign policy. If the Democrats can win in Connecticut, they certainly can win nationally, and this will mean that I will have an opportunity to do the things that I want to do more than anything else in the formulation and administration of foreign policy. I've talked this over with Adlai at some length, and although, of course, I have never sought any commitment from him, I have no doubt that I would be able to fit into some major role where I could have a constructive part to play.[25]

Bowles's unwillingness to make the Senate bid also reflected political realities in Connecticut, as his letter to Rostow obliquely suggested. When the time came for him to make his decision in the spring of 1956, the Republicans were in a strong position. Bush was a popular senator and would clearly be helped by Eisenhower's reelection bid. The possibility that Bowles or any other Democratic candidate would win was poor. Under those circumstances, the Ribicoff-Bailey offer of the nomination to Bowles had a tainted quality. By 1956 his prominence and ambitions were becoming increasingly inconvenient to them, and they might well have seen his defeat in a futile Senate race against Bush as a way of crippling him to their own advantage.

The nomination eventually went to Representative Thomas Dodd. He was soundly beaten by Bush, as Bowles almost certainly would have been in that year's Republican landslide. Although Dodd, who had given up a congressional seat to run, lived to fight another day two years later, defeat in 1956 hurt him less severely than it would have damaged Bowles, not least because a beating by Bush would have made Bowles a two-time loser in state politics. He was wise not to have made the race.

▾   ▾   ▾

Well before he had dismissed the snare and delusion of a 1956 Senate race, Bowles's efforts to recover political standing, play a more influential role in foreign policy, and poise himself for greater responsibility when the political tide turned led him to seek appointment to a State Department position in the Eisenhower administration. This curious move was of a piece with his attempt to stay on in India following the Republican 1952 victory. It proved equally futile.

What Bowles had in mind was a role for himself as opposition party spokesman within the administration similar to the position of special assistant Dulles had held in the early 1950s. He thought that a prominent "shadow" secretary of state who was given some assignments by the administration in office (as the Truman administration had entrusted Dulles with the preparation of the Japanese Peace Treaty) would be helpful, especially in symbolizing and reinvigorating bipartisanship in foreign affairs, then in short supply. A strong advocate of bipartisanship, Bowles wrote forcefully and extensively in the mid-1950s calling for its revival.

He may have been encouraged to make the bid for an appointment by the cordial ties he enjoyed with President Eisenhower and several other senior Republicans. He was on good terms, for instance, with Paul Hoffman, C. Douglas Dillon, Christian Herter, Allen Dulles, Milton Eisenhower, Nelson, John, and David Rockefeller, and John Cowles, the newspaper and magazine publisher. He had enlisted the help of a number of friends in the GOP to help him continue as ambassador. In a December 1954 letter to one of them, Paul Hoffman, he contended that new, popularly supported Asia policies which could reverse the deteriorating U.S. position there required "the development of a bipartisan coalition consisting of the Executive Branch of the government, plus the bulk of the Democratic party and enough Republicans to provide a solid majority in the Senate and in the House. . . . At the risk of sounding like an applicant for the job," he said, "I suggest that the Administration would be extremely wise to set up two or three positions of importance for Democrats *who will dedicate themselves to the job of making bipartisanship work.* (underscoring in original) Without them the task will be immeasurably harder." The Bowles-Hoffman letter was shown to Cyrus Sulzberger of the *New York Times,* who published excerpts from it in his April 4, 1955 column.[26]

Although Thomas Hughes advised him early in 1955 that prospects for a major Democratic foreign affairs appointment in the Eisenhower administration looked unpromising, Bowles continued to express interest in the idea. He wrote Benton in February that "I would accept [a position] if I were asked, if the job was major, and if Adlai thought it would be helpful. That, I assume, would knock me out for the Senate in 1956, but not necessarily in 1958." He also took specific steps to strengthen his bid. An example was his drafting at the request of Nelson Rockefeller, by then a special foreign policy adviser to the president, of a speech Eisenhower could deliver on the occasion of the United Nation's tenth anniversary.[27]

Hubert Humphrey was one of several senators Bowles urged to take the lead in promoting the appointment. In August 1955 he told Humphrey that bringing responsible Democrats into administration foreign policy positions could neutralize a likely Republican effort in the wake of the successful Geneva Summit the previous month to project itself as the peace party and brand the Democrats as the party of war. Acknowledging that some Republicans would see the appointment of Democrats as a way to silence the party's opposition, he contended that this and other disadvantages would be outweighed by benefits the Democrats would gain.[28]

Nothing came of the bid. Dulles did not seem interested, and the Democratic congressional leadership which Bowles had hoped would press the idea was not inclined to urge it on the secretary. In any event, Bowles's interest soon diminished. After Eisenhower's heart attack in September he began to think less of bipartisanship and more of the State Department (in a Stevenson administration) and of the Senate, both much more feasible prospects if Eisenhower was not the Republican nominee in 1956. During 1956 he was tied to Stevenson both before and after the nomination, and though he certainly recognized with everyone else that Eisenhower's physical recovery made a Democratic victory less likely, he was in no position during the campaign period to press his interest in a Republican appointment. Among other things, Stevenson would have understandably taken a dim view of a Bowles assignment to an Eisenhower administration job, with all that that implied for endorsement of a joint program with the Republicans.[29]

Bowles's interest revived after the election. In a letter to Majority Leader Lyndon Johnson he even suggested that Democrats be named to the National Security Council and other key administrative and policymaking positions in foreign affairs. But the Republicans remained cold, and he finally gave up the idea in the spring of 1957 following discussions with Allen Dulles and the newly appointed liberal Republican under secretary of state, Christian Herter. According to Bowles, Dulles and Herter told him that while they personally favored bringing in Democrats, various factions in the GOP opposed the concept. He inferred that White House Chief of Staff Sherman Adams was the villain of the piece.[30]

Ironically, a few months before Bowles had begun his ultimately unsuccessful angling for high-level State Department appointment, the administration was considering the possibility of sending him back to India as a special envoy. The idea, urged by John Cowles in the summer of 1954, was dismissed by Dulles, who held that it would generate political controversy and undermine the standing of the regularly assigned ambassador, George V. Allen. When Eisenhower himself raised the prospect a couple of weeks later, the secretary of state succeeded in talking him out of it.[31]

▾ ▾ ▾

With the end of this will-of-the-wisp search for a base within the Dulles State Department, Bowles's interest in improving his political standing focused again on electoral politics. Since Ribicoff's reelection bid ruled out any possibility of Bowles's returning to the governorship, that meant a race for the Senate seat held by Republican William Purtell, the 1952 winner over Benton. A Catholic businessman, Purtell was not particularly popular. The Democrats, who seemed to be gaining strength across the nation in the recession-, inflation-, and scandal-plagued sixth year of the Eisenhower presidency, appeared to have a good chance to unseat him.

Bowles waited until early 1958 before taking the plunge. Well before that time, Dodd, who believed he deserved a second chance, had announced that he would make another bid. His conservative views and Irish Catholic background gave him a constituency markedly different from Bowles's, and there was no love lost between the two men. To Bowles's dismay, his longtime friend and associate William Benton, eager to return to the Senate after a six-year absence, quickly followed Dodd into the race. The decision of liberal New Haven Mayor Richard Lee not to run improved Bowles's prospects, however, and triggered his announcement that he would seek the nomination.

Bowles made numerous and personally painful efforts to persuade

Benton to withdraw. These were unsuccessful despite polls and surveys Bowles had commissioned (and shared with Benton) which showed Bowles far ahead of him both in convention delegates and popularity among Democratic voters. Remaining in the race, apparently in the mistaken hope that he would be chosen by the party organization as a compromise, "harmony" candidate, Benton split the liberal vote, made fund-raising more difficult for Bowles, and otherwise sowed confusion in a contest already complicated by religious, ethnic, ideological, and personal crosscurrents.

Despite Benton's insistence on staying in to the end, Bowles had high hopes that he could nonetheless beat out Dodd, the real competition. He assumed, incorrectly, that neither Governor Ribicoff nor John Bailey would support Dodd, for whom they had little regard. Their decision to do so at least covertly, which led to Bowles's narrow defeat at the state Democratic convention, probably reflected several political considerations.

One was the resentment which both Ribicoff and Bailey felt as a result of Bowles's decision as governor in 1949 to name Benton to a vacant U.S. Senate seat. Both men had wanted the appointment for themselves. Bailey appears to have been particularly keen to get it. He prized the prestige and respectability that Senate membership would afford him, and was prepared to take the seat with the understanding that he would not seek election in 1950 to the remaining two years of its term. Ribicoff, then a member of the U.S. House of Representatives from Hartford, had more far-reaching ambitions. But Bowles had not seriously considered either man. Their lingering resentment against him, and the impact it had on their political moves, was another reason—aside from Benton's own 1958 bid for the Senate seat—why Bowles later termed the Benton appointment the most foolhardy (as well as the most difficult) step he had ever taken in politics.

Probably a more important consideration for Ribicoff, however, was his interest, strongly shared by Bailey, in winning reelection by a massive majority. Ribicoff had performed ably as governor in Hartford, and by 1958 was ambitious to move on to a position in a national Democratic administration in 1961. He and Bailey were already in the Kennedy camp, and Bailey for his part wanted to become Democratic national chairman. A big, well-publicized win would help them achieve their aims, but it would be less impressive if the presence of the nationally prominent Bowles on the ticket shifted attention to the contest for the Senate. Dodd's candidacy did not have that handicap. In contrast to a Bowles (or Benton) nomination, it would also assure the governor of receiving the normal support from Connecticut's important Irish Catholic constituency, which would otherwise have been unrepresented at the state level of the party for the first time in decades.

Bowles's interest in becoming secretary of state also entered into the equation. Ribicoff was no doubt fully aware of this interest. He probably saw it as an obstacle to his own ambition to win high office in Washington. It must have been clear to Ribicoff and everyone else that two cabinet jobs for politicians from so small a state as Connecticut was an unlikely prospect. (Bowles, aware of the problem, thought in 1960 about the possibility of sidetracking Ribicoff to the Supreme Court.) A Senate seat would have made Bowles more competitive. Dodd, however, could be counted on to remain in the Senate.[32]

Finally, Bowles posed less of a potential problem for party unity than Dodd did. Connecticut allows any candidate who wins the support of more than 20 percent of convention delegates to request a popular primary contest in which the nomination is finally determined. Dodd had threatened to call for such a primary if he lost at the convention. Bowles, however, had given pledges to some delegates *not* to go the primary route. Ribicoff may have had these contrasting positions in mind when he decided to support Dodd. A bruising primary battle would have damaged the party and diminished the governor's prospects for winning big, as he surely recognized.

Although Steb and others urged Bowles to release those delegates who had agreed to support him on condition that he not enter the primary, and then go the primary route if necessary, he decided not to do so. Instead, to the surprise and dismay of many of his backers, he conceded the nomination to Dodd on the convention floor when Dodd, with Bailey's and Ribicoff's support, won the majority of delegates.

Looking back, Bowles acknowledged that he had made serious errors in political judgment in the contest for the nomination. He believed that if he had played his cards differently he could have beaten Dodd at the convention and then gone on to defeat him in a primary. Whether he would have done either is arguable. But from Bowles's own later viewpoint, his mistaken faith in Ribicoff's and Bailey's neutrality and his decision to rule out a primary fight ranked among the worst political mistakes he had ever made.[33]

▾   ▾   ▾

The contest for the Senate nomination was a particularly unhappy episode in Bowles's political life. In letters he wrote at the time, he called the defeat of his bid a disheartening experience which hit harder than any other setback he had suffered. Exhausted and disillusioned by the effort, he at first refused to consider the request put to him by Ribicoff and Bailey to run for Congress from the four-county Second Connecticut district in which Essex is situated. But he soon changed his mind, stuffed his pride in his pocket (as he wrote Jean Joyce), and accepted the arguments of many of his associates that he could play a useful role in the House, perhaps even emulating ex-President John Quincy Adams's performance there.[34] He told Thomas Hughes:

> The reason to run [for the House], of course, is to secure a solid platform in the next two critical years. Once in Washington I would want to spend my time and major efforts not only pushing the ideas that all of us have been pushing for these past years, but to do it in such a way that it will leave me in the strongest possible position in the event of the election of a Democratic president in 1960. This would require a certain kind of effort in the Congress and in my other activities which would perhaps call for some compromise here and there in order to achieve the larger end. However, I am so convinced that the public is hungry for the kind of ideas in which we have been dealing that I don't think too much of a compromise is involved.[35]

Bowles wrote Jean Joyce that Speaker Rayburn and House Majority Leader McCormack "strongly urged me to run on the grounds that in the House of Representatives there is almost no foreign policy leadership, that I could undoubtedly go immediately on the Foreign Affairs Committee and I would be assured of a leading role on foreign policy questions." Stressing that she keep the matter confidential since disclosure could lead to his defeat in the election, Bowles added that "it occurred to me that I might plan on only two years in Washington as a Congressman, using this opportunity largely as a basis of reestablishing my position in international affairs from an elective office from which I might move into a responsible role in a new Democratic Administration, if we can produce one in 1960."[36]

In *Promises to Keep*, Bowles pointed out another compelling reason to make the bid—the limited options available to him. "The alternative," he confessed, "was to return to the semiprivate life of writing and lecturing, of which I had had my fill." He also noted that election to Congress would put him in a better position to involve himself in the 1960 presidential campaign.[37]

The beneficiary this time of party support, Bowles easily got the nomination. He went on to win in the normally Republican district, defeating incumbent GOP Representative Horace Seely-Brown by almost 10,000 votes in the first victory of a Democrat there in ten years. At the same time, Connecticut voters reelected Ribicoff by an unprecedented margin of over 246,000. This paved the way for the realization of the governor's national ambitions, fulfilled two years later when he joined the Kennedy administration as secretary of health, education, and welfare. John Bailey accompanied him to Washington as Democratic national chairman at that time. Dodd's victory margin of about 144,000 was substantial but less impressive. Both Ribicoff and Dodd ran ahead of Bowles in his district.

Bowles's victory provided him the political base he had lacked after losing the governorship in 1950. Although election to a Senate seat would have given him stronger political standing, greater prestige, and a more impressive platform for the expression of his views on foreign and domestic policy, he had made the right decision in agreeing to run for the House. He was able to use his membership to good effect in the two years he remained there.

9

Freshman in Name Only

BOWLES had been swept to victory in 1958 in a national landslide which gave the Democrats huge majorities in both houses of Congress. The party picked up 15 seats in the Senate, for a total of 64 to the Republicans' 34. Among the more important Democratic members were 1960 presidential hopefuls Lyndon Johnson (who continued as majority leader), Hubert Humphrey, Stuart Symington, and John F. Kennedy, elected in Massachusetts to a second term by an unprecedented margin. The Democrats' majority in the House, 283 to 153, reflected a gain of 49 seats and was similarly lopsided. The party's performance in Connecticut was especially outstanding. All of the state's six congressional seats had been won by Republicans in 1956. The Democrats took every one of them in 1958.[1]

Perhaps the most prominent of the many newcomers in the House, Bowles enjoyed a wider national reputation than most members who had served there for several terms. He had developed good relationships over the years with Speaker Sam Rayburn, Majority Leader John McCormack, and other senior congressional Democrats. At a time when the House leadership still exercised enormous power over ordinary members, and freshmen in particular were expected to follow carefully instructions from on high, he was treated with unusual deference and respect. Rayburn and McCormack seem to have felt that Bowles was honoring the House with his presence. It became clear very early on that he was not just another first-termer who would get along only by going along with the leadership.

Bowles built an able staff, and under the direction of Tom Hughes his small, crowded office became a center of hectic activity. Pat Durand, who had worked with Bowles in Connecticut, came down to Washington as his principal secretary. She remained with him throughout his three years as congressman and under secretary of state in the Kennedy administration. Robert Downer, also from Connecticut, was recruited to look after congressional district matters. James Thomson, who had left Bowles's entourage in late 1958 to complete his Ph.D. at Harvard, returned in January 1960 to assist him on foreign policy issues, among many other responsibilities. He remained a key member of successive staffs until Bowles left for India in 1963. Another staffer recruited in 1958 who served Bowles through many incarnations was Brandon Grove, then awaiting appointment to the Foreign Service.

Hughes had joined Humphrey's staff after leaving Bowles in 1955, and in returning as administrative assistant he brought with him a first class knowledge of congressional operations and a wide acquaintance with key staffers on the Hill. While still in the Humphrey office he used his connections to ease the way for Bowles's appointment to the Foreign Affairs Committee. This was not the shoo-in Bowles had thought it would be, though in the end Hughes's friends and others helped McCormack and Rayburn recognize that Bowles's arrival was an opportunity for the House to enhance its reputation for serious consideration of international issues.

As Hughes tells the story, such high-level friends were necessary because two other newly elected Connecticut Democratic members also applied for the Foreign Affairs Committee, to Bowles's consternation. It is an amusing account of the way the House operated in those days:

Chet got hold of [Connecticut Democratic State Chairman John] Bailey, whose assignment was to speak to [Connecticut Congressman Frank] Kowalski. He called back later in the day saying that the sudden interest of the congressman-at-large in being appointed to the House Foreign Affairs Committee had evaporated as fast as it had arisen. Don [Connecticut Congressman Donald J.] Irwin, however, went to see Speaker Rayburn, explained that he spoke Spanish or something, and was very much interested in the House Foreign Affairs Committee. In due course Chet was summoned to the Speaker's office. Rayburn told Chet that an impudent young freshman congressman from up there in Connecticut had been in to see him expressing interest in the Foreign Affairs Committee. He couldn't remember his name. The Speaker just wanted Chet to know that he had told him that there was to be one man and one man only in the House of Representatives from Connecticut on Foreign Affairs, that New England statesman, Chester Bowles. So from opening day, Chet was supposed to be indebted to the Speaker for having demolished the other Connecticut applicant for the House Foreign Affairs Committee. And so he went in as the choice of the House leadership.[2]

Despite his warm welcome, Bowles was not happy in the House. His friends were in the Senate, and though the House afforded a less competitive forum for his talents than the star-studded upper chamber, he felt that he deserved to be there, too. For all his supporters' encouraging talk of a John Quincy Adams role for him in the House, he saw it as a kindergarten. He did not feel himself to be the free agent he would have been in the Senate, a more natural place for a man who remained essentially a loner in politics however diligently he tried to develop close party ties. The slow-moving machinery of the House frustrated him. So did his dealings with Thomas "Doc" Morgan, the stolid, small-town physician who chaired the Foreign Affairs Committee. Bowles found him too conservative and cautious. He also thought Morgan both less concerned and less well informed about foreign policy than he was himself.

Bowles was determined, nonetheless, to make the most of his House experience. He worked hard there, dealing with foreign and domestic issues in roughly equal proportions, and was able to make important contributions. He became a leading member of the newly established Democratic Study Group, an organization of party liberals which met to hear outside experts and to discuss such legislative issues as foreign aid, education, and housing, all of major importance to him. He also continued the heavy writing and speaking schedule he had undertaken during his years out of office and maintained his active role in the Democratic Advisory Council. The views he and like-minded colleagues promoted on the council's Foreign Affairs Committee were usually overshadowed, however, by those of its formidable chairman Dean Acheson and his deputy Paul Nitze. A number of Bowles's more important articles and speeches were put into the *Congressional Record* by colleagues. Senators Humphrey and Kennedy were among senior members who did so. This reflected their own ties with Bowles and, perhaps more important, the close working relationship between their staffs and the Hughes-led Bowles office. Bowles reciprocated the favors, further strengthening his image as a congressman freshman in name only.

The Bowleses led an active social life in Washington. Following Bowles's election, they rented a large house in the fashionable Georgetown section of the city before purchasing an even bigger place on N Street in the same neighborhood early in 1960. He and Steb put in a swimming pool, "one of the wisest things we ever did," and made the house a center for gatherings of interesting people who engaged in serious conversation. Bowles was always much more effective in such settings than he was in formal meetings. Guests included a broad cross-section of political figures, mostly of liberal persuasion, along with Third World types (for Chet), people in the arts (for Steb), and young people (for both). They made an unusually diverse mix in the Washington of the turn of the decade and enhanced the Bowleses' reputation for the unorthodox in their social activities.[3]

▾   ▾   ▾

Unusually for a member, especially for a first termer, Bowles made several carefully prepared speeches on the House floor that actually produced discussion and debate. Other important congressmen came on these occasions and took part in intellectual exchanges rare indeed for the House. At these times the leadership would occasionally say nice things, too. Majority Leader McCormack personally complimented Bowles from the floor following his February 26, 1959, maiden address, which McCormack called one of the best given in the House in his thirty years there. Even discounting heavily for congressional hyperbole and New England togetherness, it was a remarkable gesture from a veteran to a newcomer in that seniority-bound body.

Although that first speech focused on the need for domestic economic growth, long a major Bowles concern, he did not let the occasion go by without a bow to his foreign policy interests. Citing the challenges abroad which made new approaches at home even more important, he brought to the House floor for the first time his view of a postwar world changed beyond recognition by the revolution of rising expectations of the emerging nations, the militancy of Communist China, and the threat, as he put it, of Moscow "actively wooing the peoples of Asia, Africa, and Latin America with billions of rubles, thousands of technicians, and countless promises, backed by a skillful diplomacy."[4]

His first foreign policy address, delivered in the House in April, dealt with new directions for economic assistance.[5] Largely a reiteration of points he had made earlier on the need for recipients to reform their economic policies and administrative practices in order to qualify for aid, it also included a call for amendment of the preamble of the Mutual Security Act to reflect his view that assistance was a positive good, not solely a Cold War tool. His colleagues reacted favorably. The new language, eventually written into the law at his instigation, declared: "It is the sense of Congress that peace in the world increasingly depends on wider recognition, both in principle and practice, of the dignity and interdependence of man; and that the survival of free institutions in the United States can best be assured in a world-wide atmosphere of expanded freedom."[6] He was also successful in having the main body of the act changed to require that the administration carefully examine the efforts recipient governments were making to solve their own problems; only if these efforts were genuine would aid be forthcoming.

While he recognized the need for some flexibility to permit economic assistance for avowedly political or security purposes, he charged that military assistance had grown unduly large and often undermined regional power balances, diverted internal efforts from constructive development, inflated the power of the military, and propped up dictators: "We must determine precisely where we are heading with our military aid programs in Asia, Africa, and Latin America and establish more realistic standards for the granting of such assistance. . . . I do not propose that we recklessly repudiate old agreements. But . . . we should insist that they be shaped to new objectives and that agreements which fail to meet these standards should be ruled out."

Another Bowles-sponsored amendment required that military aid be used only to maintain a nation's independence and where it would not create regional instability or lead to an arms race. A reflection of his antipathy to the security agreements negotiated with Pakistan and other smaller Asian countries, it passed the House but failed in the Senate, according to Bowles because of pressure from the Defense Department.[7]

Bowles was active in promoting the cause of India in Congress. With Senator John F. Kennedy, Senator John Sherman Cooper of Kentucky (who had been Bowles's successor but one as ambassador), and Congressman Chester Merrow of New Hampshire, he introduced a concurrent "sense of Congress" resolution calling on the administration to invite other free and democratic governments to consult with the South Asian countries on their economic plans and assist them in carrying them out. In its original draft the resolution dealt only with India, whose "continued vitality and success [it said in language Bowles had made familiar] . . . is a matter of common free world interest, politically because of her 400 million people and vast land area; strategically because of her commanding geographic location; economically because of her organized national development effort; and morally because of her heartening commitment to the goals and institutions of democracy." According to Bowles, the resolution was prepared at the suggestion of Under Secretary of State C. Douglas Dillon who, like him, wanted the United States to help India cope with the foreign exchange crisis that had suddenly confronted her in 1957. At State

Department request the bill was later amended to include Pakistan, Afghanistan, Ceylon (Sri Lanka), Nepal, and Burma, apparently because of the department's concern that it would otherwise lead to charges of favoritism and complicate India's relations with its neighbors. It was adopted by voice vote in the Senate, but despite Bowles's efforts did not clear the House Foreign Affairs Committee because of the press of other business.[8]

Bowles was ranked last among the 21 Democratic members of the committee (there were 11 Republicans), and this limited his opportunity to question the many government and private witnesses who appeared at its hearings. Under the rules, senior members were called on first and they tended to dominate most meetings. But he did manage to get in his oar, and his higher-ranking colleagues sometimes yielded in his favor. He made good use of his experience and expertise in foreign affairs to put pointed questions to witnesses, whom he often used as foils to voice his own policy views. His sharp exchange on relations with Taiwan with Secretary of Defense Neil McElroy at a hearing in March 1959 is illustrative:

> Bowles: "For some years Chiang Kai-shek was presumed to be about to attack the mainland of China. Last October [1958] he announced that he was no longer planning to do so. Does our aid to Taiwan reflect this very different situation?"
> McElroy: "Our program, Mr. Bowles, never was a program which provided the equipment for him to do any attacking of the mainland."
> Bowles: "I am aware that it was a dream but this objective was publicly denied for the first time last October."
> McElroy: "And it was important dreams [sic] for the hopes of those people who were on the mainland."
> Bowles: "But I hope we will adjust our budget from such dreams to what is required for the total defense of the island itself. It could save us some money."[9]

At another committee hearing, in April 1959, Bowles took issue with William Rountree, the assistant secretary of state for the Near East and South Asia, over policy toward the Indian subcontinent. He succeeded in extracting from Rountree an admission that military assistance to Pakistan had created problems for the United States in its relations with other countries, though the assistant secretary stopped well short of finding that the U.S.-Pakistan agreement should be significantly modified or terminated. The exchange gave Bowles the opportunity to repeat in the House a warning of considerable future relevance he had often made elsewhere: "A British general said to me in 1957: 'I don't know how many thousand Britishers and Indians died to keep the Russians out of Afghanistan. But I do know that since the signing of the U.S.-Pakistan arms agreement Russia has made more progress in this area than it had in the previous hundred years.' I don't think this is an overstatement."[10]

As a member of the HFAC European subcommittee Bowles made a seven-country trip that included meetings with Tunisian President Habib Bourguiba, Yugoslav President Josip Broz Tito, and Jean Monnet, the father of the European Common Market. Thomas Hughes, who accompanied him, has recalled that Bowles was more interested in the discussions with Bourguiba and Tito than he was in the exchanges with the Western Europeans he met, a reflection of his unchanging focus on the Third World. (Tito was one of the leaders of the Non-Aligned Movement, the only European head of state who played such a role.) Following the trip, Bowles succeeded with some difficulty in persuading the subcommittee's tough chairperson, Edna F. Kelly of Brooklyn, to permit him to add a personal supplementary statement to its lengthy report, a very rare privilege for a freshman congressman.[11]

In the statement he complained that the United States was failing to exercise effective leadership in Europe. "I am deeply concerned," he wrote, "over the ironic image which America is so often presenting to the world. . . . I mean our national timidity in the face of all our past achievement, our national hesitation in the face of all our latent capacity, our national self doubts in the face of all the unfolding possibilities ahead of us." The country was fretful about balance of payment problems, susceptible to arguments for restrictive policies in trade and aid, and pessimistic about its economic competition with the Soviet Union. He issued a clarion call for the 1960s, a decade in which he hoped to play a major role in devising policies which would transcend such unwarranted attitudes: "I am convinced that historians of the future will look back in amazement at these ironies in American policy in mid-century. I also hope and believe that the same historians will be able to say that around 1960 we Americans began to grasp the full dimensions of the evolving challenge facing us, and began to meet it with all the sensitivity, inventiveness, and perseverance of which we are capable."[12]

As noted earlier, Bowles had sought membership on the European subcommittee to help dispel or at least modify his Third World image. His new interest in arms control may also have reflected this aim. He dealt with the issue in a carefully prepared speech, delivered in Los

Angeles on March 11, 1960, at a time when nuclear testing had been temporarily suspended and the United States, Britain, and the Soviet Union were seeking to find an acceptable formula for inspection and control. Eisenhower had made a test ban treaty, to be followed by some actual disarmament, a major goal of his presidency. He had announced a month earlier that he was willing to accept a pact that would end all testing, including underground tests "which can be monitored." He was still awaiting a Soviet response.[13]

In his address Bowles linked defense and disarmament. The United States had suffered debacles in both, he claimed—in defense because the administration had pursued a nuclear first-strike strategy, weakened nuclear retaliatory capacity, cut back conventional forces, and neglected air defense, anti-missile weapon development, and civil defense; in disarmament because of confusion created by the failure of the administration to provide a consistent lead to the various agencies competing in arms control policy. He called for simultaneous efforts to improve U.S. defense capabilities and develop fresh arms control formulas. But he had nothing particularly new to suggest other than to stress the importance of developing an effective research program designed to close the gap in U.S. ability to detect underground explosions. (In a memorandum distributed at about the same time, which in other respects paralleled his Los Angeles speech, he also proposed a one-year moratorium on the underground testing of small nuclear bombs as a quid pro quo for a treaty with a meaningful inspection system banning other forms of testing.) Concerned about the spread of nuclear weapons technology, he suggested that involvement within NATO of nonnuclear members in control, supervision, observation, and planning activities might stop them from seeking to emulate France, which had recently become the fourth nuclear weapons state. He called favorable attention to a study commissioned by the Senate Foreign Relations Committee, which suggested that in the long run the United States might find the Soviet Union cooperative in seeking to curb the spread of nuclear weapons. "This may appear extraordinary," he said in a far-sighted comment, "but it is in no sense impossible."[14]

Bowles followed through on his interest in arms control by cosponsoring with Senator Kennedy a proposal for an Arms Control Research Institute. This was not without potential political cost to him: Connecticut had an important military lobby, including many of his own constituents employed at the Electric Boat Company nuclear submarine shipyard at Groton. The Kennedy-Bowles bill, which never got out of committee, would have given the institute responsibility for a substantial new research effort on such problems as the detection of underground testing, which he had cited in his speech, and would have made it a clearing house for arms control proposals and the coordination of joint research activity with the Soviets. The unborn institute was in many respects the forerunner of the Arms Control and Disarmament Agency, established during the Kennedy administration.

▾　　　▾　　　▾

Like all other aspects of Washington life, Bowles's political (and social) activities became increasingly caught up in the preparations for the 1960 elections. As did many other Democrats heartened by the striking gains the party had racked up in the 1958 congressional and state races, Bowles saw 1960 as an opportunity to regain power and resume the liberal progress suspended during the Eisenhower administration. Probably more than any other Democrat, he thought 1960 could mark a turning point in American foreign policy. His thinking about the election was very much colored by this prospect for change and the role he was confident he could play in bringing it about.

He focused on what he believed was the critically decisive importance of the election in *The Coming Political Breakthrough*, published in late 1959.[15] An effort to influence the course of the upcoming campaign, the book was built around Bowles's cyclical theory of politics and was modeled on the Godkin Lectures he had delivered in 1956 at Harvard. There are tides in the affairs of man; revolutions spin their way out, or enter new phases. The nation had experienced great political change in 1800, 1860, and, most recently, in 1932. The Roosevelt Revolution, which had been sparked by the election that year, was over, and (he wrote thirty years prematurely) the Cold War period had ended. The new president, whoever he was going to be, would have an opportunity to develop new policies for a changing country and a changing world and to lead the kind of political breakthrough Jefferson, Lincoln, and FDR had spearheaded in their time. The question of what kind of leader might inspire the breakthrough and what he would do with his victory were major themes of the book.

Apart from the effort to place the 1960 election in the context of cyclical change, much of *The Coming Political Breakthrough* is a rehash of ideas on foreign and domestic policy which Bowles had set forth in more coherent and cogent form in previous writings. (The same could be said of *Ideas, People, and Peace*, a collection of essays Bowles published in 1958.[16]) The book was obviously and, judging from its content and style, hastily written to have as great an impact as possible on voters' thinking about 1960. It is basically an electoral guide book for liberals, and its choppy format makes it seem more like a campaign tract to be quoted from than a seriously considered political study. Not surprisingly, it was less well received by critics than other books Bowles wrote in the 1950s.

10

House Liberal in the Kennedy Camp

As a Connecticut politician, nationally prominent party liberal, and aspiring secretary of state, Bowles faced special difficulties in deciding whom to support for the Democratic 1960 presidential nomination. By 1959, Senator John F. Kennedy had become an avowed White House contender and the dominant political force among New England Democrats. With Bailey and Ribicoff solidly in JFK's corner, Bowles had to come to an accommodation with the Kennedy candidacy or undermine his standing in his own state. But he was also pulled to Adlai Stevenson and Hubert Humphrey, the liberal favorites. Stevenson had not declared his candidacy; Humphrey's hat was clearly in the ring. Bowles himself had been considered a potential contestant over the years, but seemed to have only a very remote chance of nomination by a deadlocked convention.

▼   ▼   ▼

Bowles has written that he felt a commitment to Stevenson and had told him so. Yet by the late 1950s he had soured on the two-time contender, in part because of the experience of the 1956 campaign. In a diary note he wrote on December 31, 1960, about the political events of the year just ending, he recalled:

> Although I always admired Adlai Stevenson he had demonstrated an inability to be decisive. In this respect his role in the campaign of 1956 was a dismal disappointment. Adlai knew as well as I did that foreign affairs was the primary issue yet he allowed himself to be talked into ignoring this most essential subject almost entirely. . . . The primary reason for our abdication of the foreign policy field . . . must be assumed by Adlai. . . . If he had been a stronger person he would not have allowed this to happen and this, it seemed to me, argued strongly against his

effectiveness as president. Moreover, Adlai while intellectually liberal is emotionally rather conservative. This is particularly true in questions regarding racial relationships, full employment, and until recent years even on colonial questions. Finally, as a practical matter Adlai had run for the presidency twice and had been badly beaten each time. This made it appear unlikely that he could win even though answers could be found to these other questions.[1]

Thomas Hughes, with whom Bowles consulted closely about his political course at that time, observed that

> after 1956 Chet had come to the conclusion that Adlai should not be president, even if he had a chance to win in 1960. . . . Even apart from the two defeats, many people, I think including Chet, had over the years reached the conclusion that Adlai was not cut out to be president, that there was more love of language than substantive commitment, that the aspiration was more social and cultural than [based on] deeper matters of policy, that the bona fides of his interest in the poor, the black, the Third World, were in doubt, and that the countryside of Illinois and the salons of Manhattan had far greater appeal—not to speak of London.[2]

Bowles and Humphrey had been associated in support of liberal domestic and international policies since the late 1940s and had many common friends and admirers in the Democrats' liberal wing. They were in close personal and political contact in the 1950s and established both a mutually beneficial collaboration and a warm friendship. In 1956, Bowles had shown his confidence in Humphrey's capacity for national leadership by encouraging him to run with Stevenson for vice president. He had also intervened with Stevenson on Humphrey's behalf. Writing to Humphrey after the Democratic convention had nominated Senator Estes Kefauver, he confided: "If he [Kefauver] had not been in the race, I think you would have been nominated, and what a ticket that would have been."[3]

There is no evidence that Bowles had any of the same later misgivings about Humphrey as he had about Stevenson. In an autobiographical note of 1962, Bowles said he felt politically closer to the Minnesota senator than to any other individual. His concern was about Humphrey's ability to win the nomination.[4] In his diary, he recorded that "the kind of qualities and convictions which it seems to me most necessary for a President were most nearly represented in Humphrey. Yet I was conscious that he lacked the personality, patience, and general approach that could assure him broad support."[5] He wrote later that "much as I admired and liked Humphrey, I did not believe that he could win the nomination in a contest with either Kennedy or Stevenson."[6]

Bowles's decision was hastened, if not forced, in October 1959 when Kennedy's chief aide, Theodore Sorensen, called at his Georgetown home for what Bowles remembered as a discussion of the political situation and likely campaign issues. A few days later Sorensen returned to tell him that Kennedy wanted him to become his foreign policy adviser. In notes he made later, Bowles wrote that "Ted was perfectly clear and blunt about his proposition; if I would really come out and work for Jack [Kennedy] and act as his foreign policy advisor I would be assured of Secretary of State."[7] (Thomas Hughes, who was present, remembers the offer differently. According to Hughes, Sorensen avoided language explicitly referring to Bowles becoming Kennedy's secretary of state.)[8]

Bowles and Sorensen discussed the sensitive issue of the role Bowles would play in the primaries. Bowles recorded that "I told Ted that regardless of whether I had what was required to be Secretary it should not in any event depend on my willingness to attack some of my oldest political friends [Humphrey and Stevenson] in a political contest."[9] The following week he informed Kennedy that he was pleased and interested in the proposal relayed by Sorensen but that because of his long and close association with Stevenson he could not agree until he knew Stevenson's 1960 plans.[10]

Bowles met with Stevenson in New York the day after his exchange with Kennedy. He has recalled that he told Stevenson about the offer and had stressed that his first commitment was to him. According to Bowles, when he went on to ask Stevenson about his own plans, Stevenson had replied that he expected to leave in midwinter for a long visit to Latin America and had no intention of seeking the nomination. He was unresponsive to Bowles's questions about what he might do later regarding a Kennedy candidacy and said that, while he appreciated his desire to support him, he should not feel obligated to him in any way.[11]

Later in October Bowles met again with Kennedy and accepted the foreign policy adviser offer. He recalled telling Kennedy that he was doing so without any consideration of the secretary of state job. "I said that it would be a mistake to make a deal of this kind and it might turn out later that he [Kennedy] might need Stevenson's support in order to get the nomination and an assurance to Stevenson on the Secretaryship might be a basic requirement. I also said that while I would like nothing better than to serve in that job my present decision was not based on that it any way." According to Bowles, he drove home the point by noting that if becoming secretary of state had been his basic motivation in deciding which candidate to support, he would have been better off coming out for Stevenson, who could not make himself secretary, or Senator Stuart Symington of Missouri, who was most unlikely to appoint Adlai. Despite the absence of any commitment, however, it must have been clear to Bowles that he could reasonably expect to become a leading contender, perhaps *the* leading contender for the job he had so long prized if Kennedy got the nomination and won the election. As Sorensen and Kennedy had both made clear to him, he was getting in on the ground floor. It was an attractive prospect to Bowles at a time when he was especially eager to play a key foreign policy role in the political breakthrough he had forecast for 1960.[12]

Kennedy and Bowles agreed that Bowles would announce his support for the senator immediately, with his role as foreign policy adviser to be announced early in 1960. Bowles remembered that as they walked together to the elevator from Kennedy's suite at the Carlyle, "Kennedy remarked that he was delighted that we would be working together. He added that I should not be unaware of my own potential as a candidate. If, he said, it became clear that he himself could not get the nomination, 'I want you to know that my support will go to those who were the first to support me.' I recognized this as a bit of political seduction, not as a serious statement of intent."[13]

Kennedy's motives in making the offer and Bowles's in accepting it seem reasonably clear. The senator saw Bowles's endorsement primarily as a breakthrough to party liberals. At that point in his bid for the presidency, Kennedy enjoyed limited support among them. Many liberals suspected his ideological credentials and questioned his commitment to principled liberal positions on issues important to them such as civil rights. They recalled his less than firm opposition to McCarthyism. They distrusted some of his political associates—including his outspoken and conservative millionaire father Joe—his youth, and the aggressive and expensive effort he was making to win the nomination. For some, Kennedy was an unwelcome intruder in a process they believed should lead to a third nomination for Adlai Stevenson. Stevenson's role as the intellectual and articulate standard bearer of liberalism in a decade of conservative dominance continued to make him attractive to liberals despite his two defeats. He enjoyed deep, often emotional support in the party, as Kennedy was well aware.

Although Bowles was not a political power broker in any conventional sense of the term, he did command great respect in the party's liberal wing. He was well regarded by politically important leaders of the labor movement such as Walter Reuther of the United Auto Workers. Throughout the 1950s, his extensive missionary work in promoting foreign policy views particularly attractive to liberals, his frequent contacts with the liberal faithful in extensive travels around the country, and, more recently, his well-publicized performance in Congress had added further to the reputation he had had at the beginning of the decade as a genuine and much honored liberal of the New Deal school. At a time when the *grande dame* of New Deal liberalism, Eleanor Roosevelt, was known to look very negatively on Kennedy's candidacy, and Hubert Humphrey was preparing to enter primary campaigns in which he hoped to win liberal support in battling the Massachusetts senator, Bowles's backing was a valuable asset to Kennedy.

Bowles was well aware of this. In *Promises to Keep,* he quoted approvingly a comment in the Waterbury (Connecticut) *Republican:* "Bowles could become the one to certify to his fellow liberals that Kennedy was close enough to being their kind of candidate, and thus, perhaps, lead a national break-up of the party liberals toward Kennedy which would clinch the nomination for him."[14]

Bowles's own motives were somewhat more complicated. From the political angle, the Kennedy offer was highly attractive. Basically, Bowles had nowhere else to go in his quest for a candidate with whom he could profitably and credibly align himself. Although he spoke of a commitment to Stevenson and could have waited for him to make up his mind about the 1960 race, the prospect of another bid by the indecisive former governor did not appeal to him. Thomas Hughes in fact maintains that by the time Bowles had his conversation with Stevenson about Kennedy, he would have taken the Kennedy route regardless of which way the discussion had gone. Hughes recollects that, astonishing as it may seem, Bowles even hoped for Stevenson's support for himself as a dark horse candidate. This shadowy and unlikely Stevenson-Bowles rivalry for the presidency prefigured their more substantial competition later for secretary of state.[15]

Bowles had also dismissed Humphrey's candidacy. According to Hughes, he was very honest with Humphrey about this. He had told Humphrey that, with Stevenson out of the picture, Humphrey was his first choice for president, but that he, Bowles, concluded that Humphrey could not win. Hughes says that Bowles told Kennedy the same thing.[16]

Other possible candidates had little political attraction for Bowles, either because their policy views and party alignments were unacceptable to him or because they had no real chance of winning. None, of course, had Kennedy's strong standing on Bowles's Connecticut turf. As for Bowles's own candidacy, to which Kennedy had seductively alluded, it was at best a very, very long shot. He recalled later that it was not a pertinent factor in his thinking at that time.

Although the foreign policy views of Kennedy and Bowles were far from congruent, they overlapped sufficiently for Bowles to feel intellectually comfortable in joining the Kennedy campaign. Like Bowles, Kennedy believed that the next president of the United States needed to exercise firm leadership in redirecting foreign policy. He shared Bowles's interest in the Third World, particularly in India; his call for U.S. assistance to the Indian Second Five Year Plan and his reference as a justification for such support to Sino-Indian competition ("for the economic and political leadership of the East, for the respect of all Asia, for the opportunity to demonstrate whose way of life is the better") could have been crafted by Bowles himself. The senator's insistence that America had a moral responsibility to relieve misery and poverty in the Third World and should not use economic aid solely for political purposes also paralleled Bowles's thinking. Kennedy's outspoken 1957 address opposing French policy in Algeria put him with Bowles in the forefront of American foes of colonialism. That the speech drew an angry rebuke from Dean Acheson would only have made it even more appealing to Bowles.[17]

But Kennedy was far more concerned than Bowles was with the Cold War struggle in Europe. As Bowles recognized, the senator's approach to this key confrontation with the Communist world included a focus on the uses of military power; this was a central element in the political status quo within which Kennedy was working. Moreover, Kennedy lacked Bowles's sense of conviction on foreign (and domestic) policy issues and the political courage of these convictions that had become his hallmark. These differences surfaced more markedly after the Kennedy administration took office.

Bowles tried to put the best face on the arrangement. Although he and Kennedy had worked together in Congress, cosponsoring both foreign policy and domestic measures, they had known one another only since 1954 and were not really close. As events in 1961 dramatically underscored, marked differences in personality and style characterized the crisp, ironic senator and his discursive and philosophical adviser. Kennedy was impatient with Bowles's practice of thinking aloud in voluble, imprecise, and sometimes outrageous abstractions.

He had a distaste for discussions of morality and principles, Bowles's stock in trade. He grew bored and annoyed when subjected to ideas and information he already knew, as Bowles was wont to provide. Bowles was unable or unwilling to adjust his style to Kennedy's, and remained throughout the relationship the master of the slow windup and the big picture, to his own disadvantage.

In his autobiography, John Kenneth Galbraith touched on Bowles's enthusiasm for ideas and the impact of this on Kennedy. "Often [Bowles] could not control this enthusiasm," Galbraith remembered; "one was informed at unnecessary length on what he had learned. One day, when he was Undersecretary of State, I went into the Oval Office just after he came out. Kennedy said, 'Chet tells me there are six revolutions going on in the world. One is the revolution of rising expectations. I lost track of the other five'."[18]

As he had in mid-decade with Stevenson, Bowles seemed, characteristically, to have persuaded himself that Kennedy and he were more like-minded than in fact they actually were on foreign policy issues, or at least that Kennedy's views were still sufficiently inchoate for Bowles to have a substantial influence on them. Kennedy on his side found much that Bowles was saying on foreign and domestic policy useful in shaping the appeal he could make both in the primary and presidential campaigns, and may also have been thinking ahead to some limited extent to the role Bowles could play in helping him run an administration. Although he never permitted the relationship to become closer than arm's length, he saw it as more than the cynical exercise in political manipulation Bowles would sometimes suspect it had been when he looked back at his career in later years.

The Kennedy-Bowles relationship was asymmetrical in terms of the relative stakes the two men had in it. Bowles had much the greater one. After he had opted for Kennedy, he was dependent on him politically; there was limited leverage he could bring to bear short of the highly dangerous if not totally unrealistic option of a dramatic break. He also had to depend on Kennedy to carry out the policies which had ostensibly brought the two into alliance. In his years with Kennedy, he at times seemed almost desperate to believe that the senator/president viewed the world through Bowles-colored glasses (to use a phrase popular later at the New Delhi embassy) and to find evidence to support that assessment. Kennedy had no similar stake in Bowles's opinions or political favors once he had joined the campaign.

The formal announcement that Bowles would become Kennedy's foreign policy adviser included the release of an exchange of letters between the two. These stressed the similarity of their foreign policy views and the great admiration they professed for one another. In his letter of January 29, 1960, Kennedy declared that "the search for a just and durable peace is the basic issue of the 1960 campaign." He had "long been impressed with your [Bowles's] own insights and your ability to articulate the fundamental foreign policy issues facing the American people."[19] Replying on February 12, Bowles wrote that he strongly agreed with Kennedy that the campaign should not concentrate on the many foreign policy errors of the Republican years but should focus on the need "for a fresh, affirmative, American leadership that will give direction, shape and tone to policies in the future." He lauded Kennedy's role in a way which made the candidate's views seem indistinguishable from his own:

> As a member of the Senate Foreign Relations Committee, you have been in the forefront here in the Congress in recognizing and proposing new policies to meet the challenges which already confront us. No other spokesman in foreign affairs today has done more to recognize the need to build a new framework for Free World assistance to India and other Southern Asian nations—to anticipate developments in Algeria, Africa, and Latin America—to suggest new policies to cope with the coming missile gap and the current economic gap between the rich and poor nations of the world—to suggest means of widening cracks in the Iron Curtain through loans, food and other assistance—and to propose ways of revitalizing old associations with our friends in Western Europe.[20]

"I am particularly anxious," he concluded, "that my own efforts may not only be of assistance to you in obtaining the nomination but also that they may help assure that your nomination will come in a way that will leave us as a united party, equipped to win and deserving to win, in November." This peculiar wording reflected Bowles's reluctance to engage in primary campaigns against Humphrey and Stevenson and an effort on his part to reconfirm the agreement he believed he had with Kennedy that he could opt out of such contests. In a "personal and confidential" letter he had written Kennedy the previous day, he said again that he could not campaign against those two old friends, and that his doing so would substantially diminish his effectiveness in Kennedy's behalf. It was essential to Kennedy's election that the senator secure the nomination through liberal support, he said, and the quiet talks he had had with liberal leaders were the best way he could promote the Kennedy candidacy with the party's liberal wing.[21]

Differences between Bowles and the Kennedy camp in interpreting the understanding on Bowles's campaign role became evident as the important and hard-fought Wisconsin primary battle between Kennedy and Humphrey came to a climax. There was an unwillingness on the part of the Kennedy campaign staff to accept Bowles's stand at face value, however firm the understanding he had made with the candidate and Sorensen seemed to him. Harris Wofford, caught in the middle, has written that while Kennedy and Sorensen had said they understood Bowles's position, "their understanding included the suspicion that Bowles did not want to burn his bridges in case Kennedy lost in Wisconsin."[22] Wofford found key people around Kennedy putting heavy pressure on Bowles to go into Wisconsin; Kennedy's brother-in-law Sargent Shriver, in charge of the campaign in the southern part of the state, asked Wofford personally to urge Bowles to take part. Painfully aware of the importance the Kennedy camp attached to total loyalty to the candidate's cause, Wofford tried to explain Bowles's position to Shriver. But, as he wrote to Bowles, the refusal to campaign was a difficult thing to understand. "As far as Humphrey is concerned, you are campaigning against him—accepting the foreign policy spot in the Kennedy campaign means exactly that. Your name is everywhere being used against Humphrey and for Kennedy. That is what it is wanted for. Surely you knew that when you made your decision."[23]

It looked to Wofford, he told Bowles, like "the very political self-inflicted handicap that you insist on on too many occasions . . . a certain disdain for the hard fights that are the heart of politics." He urged him to campaign all out for Kennedy and to take the line that while the other candidates were admirable, Kennedy was the only one who could win in November. If he did not come to Wisconsin, his prospects for power and influence in a Kennedy administration would be greatly diminished. Bowles would not be budged.

Wofford's forecasts were eventually borne out. Kennedy's so-called Irish mafia never considered Bowles a full team player after Wisconsin, and the suspicion that he lacked total commitment to Kennedy would haunt and damage him later. This questioning of Bowles's commitment was not confined to the nominee's staff, however. Discussing the pre-convention period, Abram Chayes recalled that Bowles "never came out wholeheartedly for Kennedy. . . . [Bowles] never really knew how fully he accepted Kennedy as a real exemplar of the liberal tradition in American politics or how fully he was accepted by Kennedy."[24]

▾   ▾   ▾

The suspicion that Bowles was less than fully committed was heightened by his unwillingness to turn off definitively the incipient Bowles-for-president movement that sprang up in different parts of the country in the spring of 1960. Bowles was pleased by this spontaneous movement, and did not firmly disavow it until the Los Angeles Convention in July. The interest in a Bowles candidacy had been stimulated by the increasingly frenzied search for a nominee by those who found the front runners either unacceptable or unable to win. In January, the *New Republic,* which saw eye to eye with Bowles on most issues, listed him as a "non-candidate candidate" and spoke of him warmly as an attractive possibility should the convention deadlock, as many then thought might happen. A campaign which was expected to revolve around foreign affairs and domestic economic issues would give the Bowles candidacy added appeal.[25]

The movement earned Bowles considerable publicity beyond the sympathetic pages of the *New Republic,* and he later wondered whether he ought to have encouraged the boomlet to give himself more muscle in his relationship with Kennedy. (The contrary outcome is far more likely: Bowles would have further damaged his standing in the Kennedy camp, which was already suspicious that he was playing his own political game. The movement would not have got far in any event.) Bowles insisted to well-wishers that he was solidly for the senator, but left an out by acknowledging the possibility of his candidacy "if lightning should strike." His closest associates differ about his attitude. James Thomson, responsible for scores of "lightning-strike" letters, thought that Bowles did not until very late lose his belief in the possibility of his becoming the compromise candidate of a deadlocked convention.[26] Hughes was less certain about how seriously he took the movement.[27] Bowles's own recollections suggest that he was torn about the possibility of becoming president and less than fully committed to the Kennedy candidacy. Describing his attitude as the Los Angeles Convention convened, he wrote in his 1960 year-end note:

> I thought that if the convention deadlocked there might be a chance. Johnson would try, then Stevenson, but neither would make it. With the support of Truman and some of the bosses I might have been in business. However, I am frank enough to know that my own thoughts and impressions were undoubtedly confused and to some degree in conflict. . . . I am comforted in the feeling that I handled the situation honestly and in a straightforward way, that is, if the proper decision was made in the first place.[28]

▾   ▾   ▾

No doubt to his relief, Bowles did not have to face any further demands for his participation in the battle for the nomination following the damaging Wisconsin episode. In late February, Democratic National Chairman Paul Butler offered him the chairmanship of the party's Platform Committee. Bowles seems to have recognized at once that the assignment could get him off the sharp and unwelcome hook the nomination struggle had become. He recalled telling Robert Kennedy that the Platform Committee chairman's involvement in preconvention campaigning could create difficulties for the platform itself. Robert Kennedy urged him to take the job and said that his brother, vacationing in the West Indies, would agree. He told Bowles that he understood the chairmanship would be a major restraint on Bowles activities on JFK's behalf, but that more would be gained by his accepting Butler's offer.[29]

By most accounts, Bowles's performance as Platform Committee chairman was highly impressive. It raised both his standing in the party and his public profile. He and many others regarded his platform accomplishments as one of his most important and successful political contributions. He was particularly concerned with the civil rights plank and the foreign policy section. Civil rights was again a potentially divisive issue, as it had been for years at Democratic conventions. Bowles was a leading advocate of strong civil rights measures. He had championed rights for blacks as early as his days in OPA, when under his leadership the organization won a reputation for taking more blacks in responsible positions than was the norm in the early 1940s. The first governor to integrate state National Guard units, he was early in recognizing the impact that treatment of blacks at home had on the achievement of U.S. foreign policy objectives in Third World countries. Moreover, racial discrimination was personally offensive to him. Working with Wofford at Los Angeles, he prepared a maximalist plank which reflected his own views but was actually designed to serve as a negotiating instrument. To his surprise, it was endorsed by the Kennedy camp. Although the Southern members of the Platform Committee placed a minority report before the convention objecting to it, the Bowles plank was adopted by the delegates without change and with little excitement.

In preparing the foreign policy planks of the 1960 platform, Bowles saw to it that the views he championed dominated. The basic platform he read out on the convention floor pledged opposition to armed Communist aggression, but also spoke of the inadequacy of a fragile power balance sustained by mutual nuclear terror and the need to "regain the initiative on the entire international front with effective new policies to create the conditions of peace." It said that "American foreign policy in all its aspects must be attuned to our world of change" and called for the recruiting of officials "whose experience, humanity, and dedication fit them for the task of effectively representing America abroad." A list of pledges to foreign peoples and governments was headed by one to the non-Communist nations of Asia, Africa, and Latin America to "create with you working partnerships based on mutual respect and understanding." Another stated in distinctively Bowlesian language that "in the Jeffersonian tradition, we recognize and welcome the irresistible momentum of the world revolution of rising expectations for a better life" and promised that American policy would be identified with the values and objectives of that revolution. There were also provisions pledging a revamping of foreign assistance programs, closer cooperation with Latin America, support for India and Pakistan (cited as "major tests of the capacity of free men in a difficult environment to master the age-old problems of illiteracy, poverty, and disease"), and notice to NATO allies of a proposed broader partnership that would go beyond common fears to recognize shared political, economic, and cultural interests.[30]

The Communist powers were told that their ideology was doomed to failure, but that a Democratic administration would be prepared to negotiate "whenever and wherever there is a realistic possibility of progress without sacrifice of principle." The platform also called for greater contact with the Communist world through exchange of persons, cultural contacts, trade in nonstrategic areas, and other nongovernmental activity. It reaffirmed opposition to "the present admission of Communist China to the United Nations" and pledged resistance to Communist encroachment on Taiwan. But it also stated that "although normal diplomatic relations between our governments are impossible under present conditions, we shall welcome any evidence that the Chinese Communist government is genuinely prepared to create a new relationship based on respect for international obligations."

If much of the substance of the basic platform reflected Bowles's own views and drafting initiatives, the way the platform was processed and presented was also largely his work. He developed many innovative ideas which reflected his skill and experience as a publicist. A decade before they had become commonplace, he organized preliminary local, state, and regional hearings designed to give interested citizens an opportunity to present their views to the party. The hearings attracted media interest, provided input to Bowles and the Platform Committee, and gave grass-roots Democrats a sense of participation.

The presentation of the platform at the convention was similarly novel. Bowles did this himself, reading out the basic platform, mainly comprising statements on major issues. He spiced his narration with film clips illustrating various points on foreign and domestic policy. A longer version of the platform, some 20,000 words, included most of the means the Democrats planned to use to implement their policy declaration. It was not read out; in Bowles's experience from his years in advertising the attention span of a 1960 TV audience was limited, and maximum dramatic impact could be achieved by shorter, jazzier presentations. As he observed, this format also meant that the TV audience received "an affirmative, not a negative statement." Most of the sharp attacks on the alleged failures of the Eisenhower administration were confined to the longer version. Bowles was even able to state that the short form did not include the word "Republican," in his view a history-making achievement.[31]

▾   ▾   ▾

Kennedy's victory at the Los Angeles Convention on July 13 raised the question of Bowles's immediate future. He had been renominated a few weeks earlier and could reasonably expect reelection to Congress. As in 1954, but under very different and much more complicated circumstances, he had to decide whether to make the bid or give up the prospect of further elective office in order to make himself more available for a senior Washington foreign policy position, preferably secretary of state.

Bowles visited Kennedy at Hyannis Port on August 1, and in *Promises to Keep* recalled that he discussed the problem with the senator at that time. He mentioned to Kennedy that he was confident he could easily win the congressional election and was reluctant to give up his seat without a clearer idea of what lay ahead. Kennedy had replied that he was counting on Bowles to devote a major share of his time to the national campaign and that he was confident that two or three weeks of hard campaigning in Connecticut would be enough to assure reelection. According to this Bowles account, Kennedy also raised for the first time the possibility of his becoming secretary of state. Discussions at the time with friends of the senator's led Bowles to believe that there was an even chance he would eventually be chosen.[32]

The Hyannis Port conversation was the opening feint in a shadowy game. Kennedy had an important immediate political stake in avoiding a discussion of Bowles's future. Bowles and Adlai Stevenson were widely regarded as front runners to head the State Department, and Kennedy's announcement soon after his nomination that he had designated them his foreign policy contacts with the Eisenhower administration had been seen as further evidence that one or the other would get the position. (Some observers also considered it an effort by Kennedy to reassure party liberals troubled by his selection of Lyndon Johnson as his running mate.) If Bowles's renouncing his congressional nomination was attributed to a Kennedy request, that would indicate that he and not Stevenson would become secretary, possibly leading Stevenson and his supporters to opt out of the campaign, an important consideration in what was expected to be a closely fought election.

Bowles's options were influenced by the situation in Connecticut. As in 1954 and 1958, the national political ambitions of Abraham Ribicoff and John Bailey came into play. Bowles believed that if he ran and both he and Kennedy won, the two state leaders would privately press Kennedy to leave him in Congress on the grounds that two senior appointees (themselves) from Connecticut were all the traffic could bear from that small state. Publicly, they would take the plausible position that Bowles should remain in Congress to continue to build a liberal political structure in traditionally Republican eastern Connecticut. Ribicoff, in fact, insisted that were Bowles to run for reelection, he would have to guarantee publicly that he would not resign to enter the Kennedy administration. The governor tightened the screws further by stating that he would not call a special election if Bowles *did* resign. According to Hughes, who was deeply involved in the negotiations to resolve the problem, Bowles even began to feel that Ribicoff was trying to keep him in the House so that *he* could become secretary of state.[33]

Bowles did not want to be trapped in Congress in the event Kennedy won, and was prepared to gamble that he would win. As he had written in *The Coming Political Breakthrough,* he believed that the administration elected in 1960 could, and should, make fundamental changes in the way the United States responded to foreign and domestic challenges. He wanted to play a major role in charting those new directions. To do that he had to become part of the administration. He could expect to contribute relatively little by a further term in the House, where the influential role he had been able to play despite his junior status would be markedly reduced once the Democrats regained the White House and a strong president made the executive branch the dominant voice in establishing policy for the party and the country.

With Bowles determined to quit the House, ostensibly to devote himself full time to the national campaign, the issue for Kennedy became one of presentation: how to announce Bowles's decision without its being seen to imply any commitment on the senator's part that he would make him secretary of state. Bowles, on the other hand, had a stake in having that implication conveyed as clearly as possible. According to Hughes, he wanted to release a letter strongly suggesting that he was withdrawing at Kennedy's request. Kennedy resisted this and, using Robert Kennedy to deal directly with the problem, countered by asking Bowles to state that there were no commitments or hidden obligations. Lengthy negotiations followed. Hughes recalls Robert Kennedy saying in the course of them that "we all know what we are trying to accomplish. We're trying to avoid the situation where the presidential nominee has to explain in public that he will never appoint Chester Bowles Secretary of State." Robert Kennedy claimed later that Bowles expected to lose the election and tried to make a deal, offering to resign if the Kennedys agreed to make him secretary.[34]

The language finally agreed upon put the responsibility on Bowles, who declared that he was withdrawing to devote his full efforts to the Democratic national campaign and had "no understandings or commitment with anyone, anywhere" as to possible future service in a Kennedy cabinet should the senator win the election. Senator Kennedy's brief statement combined appreciation for Bowles's help in the upcoming campaign with regret that he was leaving Capitol Hill. The *New York Times* story reporting this aptly noted that some Kennedy advisers were concerned that Bowles's abrupt withdrawal might indicate to Adlai Stevenson that Bowles had been assured the secretary of state job. "This, it was said emphatically, was not the case," the paper stated, without identifying sources for the denial. The *Times* also reported that Kennedy, backed by Ribicoff, had urged Bowles to remain in the congressional race.[35]

In the spin they gave to the story, Bowles's aides passed word that he had had great difficulty in making his decision and that he was not unaware that some Connecticut Democrats might feel he was deserting the state campaign to "bask in the national political spotlight," as the *Times* account put it. To dispel negative reaction to his move, Bowles emphasized that reports he had seen indicated that a substitute Democratic candidate was also likely to win. In the event, the Republicans took the seat, narrowly defeating Bowles's former campaign manager, William St. Onge, despite Kennedy's strong Connecticut showing. St. Onge won in 1962, however, and the district has generally been Democratic since then.

▾   ▾   ▾

With the announcement of his withdrawal, Bowles was free to throw himself full time into the campaign. He played a very active role in speaking and writing on behalf of the candidate. But he did not have a central part in delineating foreign policy issues and spelling out prospective handling of them. Although he sent Kennedy a series of memoranda, background notes, draft speeches, and statements on foreign policy issues, discussed immediate problems with him on the phone, and reviewed texts of speeches prepared in Kennedy headquarters, it became apparent to Bowles that he was just window-dressing.

Bowles said different things at different times about the impact his virtual exclusion had on the campaign. In 1965 he told an interviewer that he wasn't sure that Kennedy had really needed his assistance. "[Kennedy] made some very good speeches during that period," he recalled. "I disagreed very little with their content. If I had, of course, I would have spoken up very sharply. Occasionally, I might have differed on a matter of emphasis, but generally I felt that the ideas expressed were correct."[36] But closer to the event, in December 1960, he was less generous:

> Frankly, I was deeply concerned that our foreign policy presentation [during the campaign] was not much better than it was. There was really no ringing broad speeches of the kind of positive nature that I thought were [sic] so important. Instead we pecked away at such questions as Quemoy and Matsu, Castro, Cuba, Berlin, etc. . . . I am convinced that he [Kennedy] could have won by a substantially bigger margin if we had really sailed into some of the fundamental questions which the American people and the world are now called upon to face. This would not only have given us a much bigger mandate but it would also have given us a far clearer mandate.[37]

Bowles's limited role as foreign policy adviser may also have stemmed at least in part from his apparent unwillingness to muscle into the campaign. Abram Chayes has recalled his effort to get Bowles to join Kennedy on the campaign trail.[38] His view, a correct one, was that it was in the candidate's entourage where the key pronouncements were shaped and the key decisions made. Chayes says that Bowles tried to move in, but not very hard. Bowles's reaction to the suggestion was not surprising. He was not inclined to be aggressive in such situations, and his reluctance to force himself on the candidate was doubtless heightened by his own uncertainty about where he stood with Kennedy. This was a continuing problem for him; it became even more important as he sought to play a role in the Kennedy administration.

Bowles played a more significant part as Kennedy's liaison with senior foreign policy officials in the Eisenhower administration, particularly Secretary of State Christian Herter, who had succeeded Dulles in 1959. Bowles was initially skeptical about the value of regular liaison. In a letter to Kennedy, he recalled that when he had been ambassador to India he had concluded that access to highly classified papers added no more than two or three percent to the knowledge available to any careful reader of the *New York Times*. In his view, regular briefings would add almost nothing new; instead, they would "inhibit our criticism of administration policies, past, present, and future." He suggested to Kennedy that briefings be confined to information about important developments that might erupt during the campaign.[39]

Despite these negative views Bowles began to meet with Herter in mid-August, and their sessions continued on a regular basis through the campaign period. The two men got on well together. They were friends from their days as governors of neighboring New England states, and Bowles credited Herter and Under Secretary of State C. Douglas Dillon with improving the Eisenhower administration's conduct of foreign policy in its final two years. The White House was also skeptical about the briefings, but Herter was able to get around objections from that quarter by briefing Bowles not as Kennedy's foreign policy adviser but as a member of the House Foreign Affairs Committee who *ipso facto* had top secret clearance. The Bowles-Herter arrangement was smoothed by their meeting mostly at Herter's house in Georgetown, a comfortable private setting.

Bowles prepared a series of memoranda reporting the conversations.[40] He noted that, in their first discussion,

> at the outset [Herter] expressed the hope that no word of these meetings would get out. On this basis, he would be very glad to talk in complete frankness on any phase of our foreign affairs. I said I would be glad to abide by this arrangement and that I was as anxious as he that my own role in the meetings would not become known. (My unexpressed reason being the extreme sensitivity of Adlai's friends and hence my desire not to appear to have a special role from which Adlai was excluded.) As usual in such "briefings" there is very little information which I had not already known. The meeting, however, was helpful in that it gave me a clearer understanding of Administration thinking, which at least as far as Herter is concerned is more flexible than I had anticipated.

At this and subsequent sessions Herter and Bowles covered a broad range of major issues, including Berlin, Quemoy and Matsu, Latin

America, United Nations developments, the Congo crisis, African policy, and Sino-Soviet relations (seen by Herter as at their lowest ebb since the establishment of the People's Republic in 1949). There were several exchanges about Cuba. Bowles found Herter moderately hopeful that economic difficulties might create the basis for a countermovement against Castro. At no time, however, did the secretary disclose preparations for an invasion of the island. Kennedy only learned of these after the election, and Bowles much later.

Bowles found that the briefings enabled Kennedy and other Democratic leaders, including himself, to conduct their side of the campaign in a way that would not jeopardize national interests. The sessions also appear from his memoranda to have been useful in providing a channel for the two sides to discuss their concerns about the way the candidates and their supporters dealt with sensitive policy issues. For example, Bowles told Kennedy that following the highlighting of Quemoy and Matsu in the first Kennedy-Nixon debate, Herter had expressed acute alarm over the domestic political conflict that had developed over the islands. Bowles said he had defended Kennedy's reaction to Nixon's attack on his position. When Herter then expressed the hope that the question could be dropped, Bowles had replied that he personally felt Kennedy would be willing to do that provided there were no further attacks on the senator's position by Nixon or other Republican leaders.

According to Bowles, Herter repeatedly urged that the foreign policy debate be sober and restrained. Bowles said he told the secretary that this was entirely in Nixon's hands.

> I said that neither Senator Kennedy nor any of the rest of us had any desire to get into a demagogic debate on foreign affairs but that we felt bad mistakes had been made and that we had not only a right but also a responsibility to refer to them and to offer constructive proposals for improvement. I said that if the Republicans responded to these proper criticisms with charges that we were disloyal to our country, there would be no way that the fireworks which he and I both feared could be avoided.[41]

Despite such opportunities to pass word to the enemy camp and other benefits, Bowles's enthusiasm for the liaison operation remained limited. As he told Kennedy in mid-October, "although I have dictated reports on each [meeting] I have sent only one to you because I did not feel the others produced anything that was particularly relevant to the positions you are likely to take."[42]

11

Number Two at
Foggy Bottom

WHEN Bowles returned to Washington from Connecticut a few days after Kennedy's narrow victory, the president-elect asked him to act as his representative in meetings with foreign diplomats eager to make contact with the incoming administration. Despite his limited campaign role and his continuing inability to develop a close relationship with Kennedy, he still hoped he would be named secretary of state. Abram Chayes has recalled that when he himself went to Washington later in November to discuss a possible position in the new administration, he and Bowles had considered how he could best make a Bowles-for-secretary pitch to Kennedy. When he subsequently tried to do so, Kennedy said he was not ready to make up his mind yet. Kennedy did not actually come to a decision until well into December.[1]

Bowles's hopes were no doubt raised at a breakfast meeting toward the end of November when, as he recalled the exchange, Kennedy asked him hypothetically how he would organize the State Department if he were secretary. Bowles had replied that he would begin by asking Dean Rusk to become senior under secretary.[2]

A Rhodes Scholar who in the 1930s had been dean of the faculty of Mills College in California, Rusk had served as an army officer on the staff of General Joseph W. Stilwell in the China-Burma-India theater in the war. During the Truman administration he came to the State Department, where he headed the Office of United Nations Affairs before becoming deputy under secretary for political affairs and assistant secretary for Far Eastern affairs. He left government when the Republicans took office and became president of the Rockefeller Foundation. Rusk held that prestigious, high-visibility position in 1960 when his name came into play as a potential recruit for the Kennedy administration.

As a Rockefeller Foundation trustee, Bowles knew Rusk well. The two men had traveled together in India in 1957, and Bowles had been impressed by what he regarded as Rusk's sympathetic interest in the country. He had already touted Rusk for the deputy job in a memorandum to Sargent Shriver, whom Kennedy had put in general charge of the new administration's search for talent: "[He] would make an outstanding Chief of Operations in any government department, preferably in the Department of State. Although he is not primarily a policy innovator or experienced in dealing with the press and public, he is extremely intelligent, balanced and professional."[3] Bowles again recommended Rusk, along with Kennedy aide McGeorge Bundy and Paul Nitze, in a memo on senior appointments he sent the president-elect at his request soon after their breakfast meeting. Any one of the three, Bowles said, would make an outstanding alter ego for the secretary and at the same time provide Kennedy with a responsible and experienced source of information and advice with whom he could deal directly on specific questions.[4] A few days later, he described Rusk to Kennedy as "a competent manager, with broad experience and good judgment."[5]

James Thomson maintains that Bowles recommended Rusk only because he had learned that Kennedy was considering him for the secretary job he wanted for himself—thus damning Rusk with faint praise. Rusk's name had in fact been mentioned to Kennedy as a potential secretary of state by several prominent people. Former Secretary of Defense Robert Lovett, in turning down the secretary position himself, advised Kennedy to appoint him, a recommendation Robert Kennedy later said was very important to his brother. When the president-elect asked Dean Acheson for his suggestions, telling him, according to Acheson's account and no doubt his relief, that he did not intend to appoint either Stevenson or Bowles, the former incumbent recommended Rusk along with Chase Manhattan Bank Chairman John McCloy and veteran (but noncareer) diplomat David Bruce. According to Rusk biographer Thomas Schoenbaum, McGeorge Bundy and Walt Rostow, another Kennedy aide, were also high on him. A second biographer, Warren Cohen, has called Rusk "an obvious establishment candidate for Secretary of State."[6]

Kennedy moved toward the Rusk appointment in the first week of December. At a meeting of the Rockefeller Foundation Board of Trustees at Williamsburg, Virginia, on December 4, Rusk received a call from Kennedy who asked that he come to his house in Georgetown for a talk. Rusk asked Bowles, who was there as a foundation trustee, what he thought Kennedy wanted. Bowles replied, accurately, that Kennedy would ask Rusk to become secretary of state. He briefed Rusk about Kennedy over dinner at his home a few days later. When Kennedy and Rusk met soon afterwards, the president-elect was sufficiently impressed to offer Rusk the job the next day.[7]

The Kennedy-Rusk session had an ironic twist from Bowles's viewpoint. In the course of it Kennedy had not raised the possibility of Rusk's own appointment, but had queried him about the kind of person who would make a good secretary of state and had asked for suggestions. Rusk mentioned Stevenson, Lovett, Bruce, and Senate Foreign Relations Committee Chairman J. William Fulbright. When Kennedy queried Rusk about Bowles as a candidate, he replied, according to Schoenbaum's version of the conversation, that Bowles was not ready for the top job but would make a splendid under secretary. Rusk, of course, was unaware that Bowles had said much the same thing about him. He later recalled in his autobiography that he had thought the selection of the liberal Bowles as second in command would have helped limit objections to Fulbright, whose prospective nomination for the top State job had already aroused opposition from liberal groups troubled by the Arkansas senator's views on civil rights and the Arab-Israel dispute.[8]

Explanations for Kennedy's decision have included Rusk's strong background and experience in international relations, the favorable notices Kennedy received about him from figures in the foreign policy establishment, and the good impression he had made on the president-elect by his call for presidential leadership in foreign policy in an article in the spring 1960 issue of *Foreign Affairs*. There was much (accurate) speculation at the time that Kennedy intended to play the central role in foreign policymaking ("he will be his own secretary of state") and would thus pick someone whose experience qualified him for a supporting part. Warren Cohen wrote later in his biography of Rusk that Kennedy wanted to avoid becoming dependent, as Truman had, on a single foreign policy adviser and "deliberately . . . chose . . . a man whose temperament and modesty precluded his ever becoming an Achesonian presence in the Kennedy Administration."[9] John Kenneth Galbraith, no admirer of Rusk, has wryly maintained that Kennedy selected him "because of a common tendency in public affairs. We know the faults of our friends; others, whose faults are unknown, are assumed to be of purer stripe. Because [Kennedy] didn't know Dean Rusk, he didn't suppose him to have any drawbacks."[10] Rusk has said that Kennedy never told him why he had been chosen and that he had never asked.[11]

If Dean Rusk was a seemingly noncontroversial figure esteemed by those whose opinions Kennedy sought, Bowles was almost the reverse. Unlike Rusk, his outlook and record in foreign and domestic policy had made him highly suspect in many quarters. He had accumulated adversaries in Congress and elsewhere in public life and was held in low regard by foreign affairs establishment figures whose support Kennedy sought at that point. As noted in Chapter 9, Vice President Nixon had put Kennedy on notice soon after the election that he would forcefully oppose Bowles's appointment as secretary. Moreover, Bowles's political standing offered him a modicum of independence that could be inconvenient to a president determined to put his own stamp on foreign policy. These negatives overshadowed whatever claims Bowles may have had on Kennedy on the basis of his limited role as foreign policy adviser during the campaign, the considerable measure of congruence in their views of the Third World, Bowles's strong backing among party liberals, and his early support for the Kennedy candidacy (marred as this was by his attitude toward the Wisconsin primary and his unwillingness to snuff out support for his own nomination). Differences between the two men in style and personality probably also contributed to Kennedy's decision to look elsewhere.

Kennedy was prepared to offer Bowles the number two position at State, however. In a 1991 interview, Rusk recalled that when he met with the president-elect in Palm Beach and agreed to become secretary of state, he suggested to Kennedy that Bowles be named under secretary. According to Rusk, Kennedy agreed somewhat reluctantly. Rusk remembered that Kennedy had been annoyed by Bowles's feeling that the president-elect had an obligation to him because of his political support. "Bowles got off on the wrong foot with Kennedy" as a result of this, Rusk said. If Rusk's recollection of Kennedy's attitude toward Bowles at the time is accurate—and comments Robert Kennedy has made in his oral history statements about Bowles's "pushiness" lend further credence to it—this adds a very important negative to the considerations which led to Bowles's being passed over for appointment as secretary.[12]

Bowles was made aware of the decision to offer him the under secretary position on the same day Kennedy and Rusk had reached it. He was told to expect a phone call around nine that evening, December 11. Returning to his house through the icy Georgetown streets to take the call, Bowles fell down and hurt his back. He had to take to his bed and was there when the call came, Kennedy speaking first, followed by Rusk. It was not an auspicious beginning.

Accepting the offer, Bowles said he preferred to be responsible for political rather than economic affairs.[13] Aside from this, the scope of his duties was not defined. He reflected later that he had been too quick in agreeing to take the number two position: "This was the first of a series of errors, because what I should have done is said, 'I'll be delighted to consider this and think about it, but I would like to know a little bit more about the job, what it will consist of and what you expect of me.' I should have found out how I was to work with the Secretary and how I was to work with the President."[14]

These afterthoughts reflected the bitterness which often welled up later in Bowles when he looked back at his abbreviated tenure at the State Department. In the weeks after the president's December 12 announcement of the Rusk and Bowles appointments (and that of Adlai Stevenson as ambassador to the United Nations) his mood was fairly upbeat. He was disappointed at not being named secretary, but he did not let that undermine his characteristic determination to make the best of circumstances and his new role. He immediately began to speak well of Dean Rusk and to talk hopefully of the partnership they could establish.

There was no available guide or description which Rusk and Bowles could have used to spell out Bowles's responsibilities as under secretary. Each person who has held that office has brought his own stamp to it and has exercised its responsibilities in different ways. These have primarily reflected the incumbent's preferences and capabilities and what the secretary wishes him to do. The relationship of the second in command with the secretary is crucial not only in defining his role but in determining how effectively he will be able to carry it out. To an important extent, this relationship is a matter of personal chemistry. But it also obviously includes compatibility of general policy orientation and management style, as well as the secretary's ability to communicate his wishes and that of his deputy to adjust his own preferences to his leader's approach.

Meeting with him immediately after they had been selected, Rusk told Bowles that he wanted him to become his alter ego. He likened the projected relationship to the one in the late 1940s between Secretary George Marshall and Under Secretary Robert Lovett, to whom Marshall had delegated total responsibility for the day-to-day operation of the department. If Rusk meant this seriously, it was a prescription for failure, for neither he nor Bowles was temperamentally qualified to play Marshall and Lovett-like roles nor interested in doing so.[15]

Bowles recalled in a 1965 oral history interview his own approach to the under secretary's responsibilities at the time of his appointment:

I was really anxious to tackle the job of general management of the State Department and the apparatus of foreign policy. This is what I believed the Under Secretary to be. The Secretary saw him as alter ego. I saw myself with a specific definite role as general manager of the Department, building the procedures and putting the right people in the right spots (including the right ambassadors) and creating in the Department an instrument of foreign policy which would be an effective tool for the President. Of course, as Under Secretary, I expected to have some role in the formulation of policies. But the actual building of the instrument, the administrative instrument, was the thing I had my heart set on, and I thought the first thing was to be very sure my relationship with the Secretary was one of mutual trust and confidence which I tried so very hard to build.[16]

A few weeks after the new administration took office, Bowles made a formal effort to have his responsibilities defined. In a memorandum to Rusk, he spelled out the areas in which he believed he could most usefully concentrate: keeping fully abreast of the department's operations so he could step in and help the secretary on short notice; formulation and review of broad policy positions; participation in interagency meetings; overall administration; and, on an experimental basis, off-the-record press backgrounding. Rusk said he agreed. "This gives you a very heavy schedule," he noted, "but if we can get the right man as your Deputy Under Secretary, you can share some of this burden with him."[17]

▾   ▾   ▾

As is the practice during transition periods, the incoming team led by Rusk and Bowles was installed in small offices on the ground floor of the State Department where they worked before moving to the grander suites they would occupy once the new administration took over. Bowles plunged into his new job, focusing largely on the assignment of key personnel. This priority reflected the philosophy of management which he brought to the department. Samuel Lewis, a Foreign Service officer who headed Bowles's staff during his Washington years in the Kennedy administration, has summarized the philosophy well:

Bowles from his earliest experience with government (OPA) had been dissatisfied with organizations as they were when he found them, impatient with the career staff's endemic caution, and convinced that organization charts mean little in and of themselves. Rather, to him the key to executive management is the recruiting of a group of top-level people wholly sympathetic to the broad policy goals and concepts of the top man. Given the right key men, Bowles believes the organization and its charts will follow. He then is ready to rely heavily on delegation of authority, but only after this basic congruity between the top man and his chief aides has been assured. He also has faith in the power of talented men to make a real imprint on the tides of history if they boldly strike out to do so.[18]

Bowles had suggested this approach soon after the Los Angeles Convention, when he stressed to Kennedy "the need for fresh, able dedicated people" as "the indispensable key to everything else" and called for a careful preelection survey to identify "able men with whom we can work effectively" for the hundred or so key positions in foreign policymaking.[19] Much less inclined than Bowles was to think about the shape of an administration when he still had an election to win, Kennedy did not act on this recommendation. Bowles quickly returned to the theme after his appointment as under secretary. The selection of top policymakers should be "an extension of the Kennedy purpose," he told Rusk. The standards he proposed reflected his own view of what that purpose was, or ought to be. Policymakers "should have a broad understanding of the historical forces shaping the world and the practical problems of foreign policy-making and administration. . . . They should have the capacity for fresh affirmative thinking." This called for the appointment of fresh, competent individuals at all top foreign policy posts, down through the rank of assistant secretary. "With a minimum of exceptions, we [should] bring in people from the outside who are unhampered by past loyalties and associations, and who are in a position to inspire a new spirit and willingness among those who are working under them." Academia could be a prime source of ambassadorial talent. But Bowles also spoke well of the Foreign Service, which could be counted on for a "high degree of loyalty, intelligence and competent service . . . if we provide the necessary leadership, sense of direction and sensitivity to individual attitudes and problems."[20]

The selection of ambassadors became more important under the Kennedy administration because their responsibilities were expanded. Resurrecting the concept of an ambassador's role his New Delhi experience had prompted, Bowles had urged: "The ambassador should be an administrator responsible not only for the proper handling of his traditional responsibilities but also in a general way for the entire U.S. Government operations in his area."[21] Kennedy later signed a letter Bowles drafted instructing ambassadors that they were in charge of their entire mission and were expected to supervise all operations excepting those under the control of a U.S. military field commander. Bowles succeeded in getting this presidential imprimatur despite strong opposition from other agencies and departments; they did not want to have their overseas operations placed under someone they considered a State Department official. Some Foreign Service officers also fought the idea. The new approach was accepted by subsequent administrations and remains in effect.[22]

Bowles spent much of the preinaugural period and the first few months of the administration working up assignments for ambassadorial and key Washington positions. It is not clear how he got this responsibility. His associates assume that Kennedy approved the move. Rusk appears to have gone along. In coming up with names, Bowles generally followed the approach he had spelled out to the secretary, though he said that Rusk had given him only a vague verbal response to it.

Recruiting was one of Bowles's great talents, and the major task of filling top State Department positions at home and abroad showed him at his innovative best. Working from closely held master charts assembled by the inner circle of his staff, he spent long hours on the phone seeking out suggestions from contacts he trusted and getting further views about the candidates he had in mind. He did a good deal of personal interviewing, sizing up people and twisting the arms of those he wanted. Fresh information and impressions sometimes led him to last-minute inspirations, which introduced a certain amount of disorder in what was meant to be a systematic process.[23]

Bowles had to sell his ideas to the White House, and was in frequent touch with Ralph Dungan on the Kennedy staff in that sensitive exercise. Dungan sometimes blew his top over Bowles's last-minute changes, but the names sent over were usually approved and won him kudos as a talent spotter. The president, of course, had a few choices of his own. But most of the other assignments from outside the Foreign Service were Bowles's selections. Rusk apparently went along with these ambassadorial recommendations. The secretary brought in only two senior officials with him, both for assignments in the department: former ambassador and assistant secretary George McGhee, a fellow Rhodes scholar and old friend, as head of the Policy Planning Council, and Lucius Battle, Secretary Acheson's personal assistant and confidant, as executive secretary of the department.

Universities were a prime source in Bowles's talent search. At James Thomson's initiative he persuaded Harvard professor and Japan expert Edwin Reischauer to go to Tokyo. Bowles got the assignment through over a variety of objections: Reischauer's Japanese wife, his limited administrative experience, his past criticism of U.S. policy, and his association with Japanese leftists. (Bowles believed that the real basis for the objections was the desire of the department's Far East hands to keep the prized appointment for themselves.) Reischauer recalled that in urging the job on him, Bowles suggested that he could usefully become a super-ambassador to the Far East, using the Tokyo embassy as a base to advise Washington on policy for the whole region. Aside from the salesmanship involved, the idea probably was an echo of Bowles's own aspirations to play something of a similar role in his New Delhi days. Reischauer wisely adopted a go-slow approach in following up this suggestion when he reached Japan.[24]

Other academic figures Bowles found included former Amherst College President Charles Cole for Chile and Oberlin College President William Stevenson for the Philippines. Harvard economist Lincoln Gordon, whom Bowles initially wanted to become assistant secretary for inter-American affairs, eventually went to Brazil. John Badeau, for a decade president of the American University at Cairo, was named ambassador to Egypt.

Some noteworthy selections came from outside academic ranks. Bowles thought that special consideration ought to be given to retired Foreign Service officers who had left the service in good standing and still had something to contribute. He had come to know George Kennan well following Kennan's expulsion by the Soviets from the Moscow embassy in 1952, and had been influenced by his thinking about European issues. Dulles had forced Kennan into retirement in 1953; Bowles brought him back to become ambassador to Yugoslavia. Bowles also recruited as ambassador to Guinea William Attwood, a foreign affairs editor of *Look* magazine who had worked with him and Stevenson in the 1950s on foreign policy speeches and programs. Attwood had asked for the Guinea posting because he knew the West African country's maverick, anti-U.S. president, Sékou Touré, and thought he could work effectively with him. This was just what Bowles was looking for. He wanted noncareer appointees to take up assignments in the developing world, not only in the fleshpots of Western Europe, and had called for a determined effort to find people who could win the confidence of leaders in countries dominated by a single individual or a small clique. Guinea matched this description only too well.

The selection of Teodoro Moscoso as ambassador to Venezuela reflected another Bowles personnel policy objective: the breaking up—or at least leavening—of the ingrown group of Spanish language-

proficient officers who moved from one Latin American ambassadorship to another when they had reached the top rungs of the career
ladder. Bowles believed that many of these officers were out of touch
with new political forces challenging the Latin American power structure. At his request, Puerto Rico Governor Muñoz Marín made
Moscoso available from his own staff. The posting had the added
advantage, in Bowles's view, of placing a Puerto Rican in a key embassy
in South America. Other ambassadorial appointments which evidenced
his interest in bringing fresh blood into the Latin American circuit
included longtime Foreign Service Labor Attaché Ben Stephansky to
Bolivia, James Loeb, founder of Americans for Democratic Action, to
Peru, journalist John Bartlow Martin to the Dominican Republic, and
John Bell, former deputy head of the economic assistance agency, to
Guatemala.

Bowles also became deeply engaged in assigning career officers to
ambassadorships. This process involved a candid review of the current
crop of ambassadors and a search for talent further down the line.
Oddly, Eisenhower administration Assistant Secretary for Congressional Relations William Macomber, an upstate New York Republican
who had been John Foster Dulles's special assistant, played an important role in the sorting-out operation. So did J. Robert Schaetzel, a
senior Foreign Service officer whose comments about his colleagues
came, perhaps inevitably, to be known as the Schaetzel Shitlist. Since
Bowles and others new to the department who worked with him on
appointments had scant knowledge of the identities, let alone the
capabilities, of senior career people, both Macomber and Schaetzel
often had decisive influence.[25]

The selection process led to the forced retirement of many ambassadors who expected further assignments. Deputy Under Secretary for
Administration Roger Jones recalled that when he met with these senior
officers and explained the new approach Bowles wanted ambassadors
to follow, they generally agreed that the time had come to retire. The
attitude of most, he remembered, was that you can't teach an old dog
new tricks and that they were too old to pick up the new techniques.
Others "were inclined to argue that we couldn't bring about a revolution here, and that this should be an evolutionary thing, and they hoped
it wouldn't move too fast. Only one said he was owed another post."[26]
The forced retirement of ambassadors nonetheless prompted considerable bitterness against Bowles in the upper ranks of the Foreign Service.
This surfaced in the press, where unfriendly columnists later cited it as
evidence that he was destroying Service morale.

The hostility was heightened by his effort to assign to less sensitive overseas positions several career officers identified with the policies of the Eisenhower administration. He particularly wanted to transfer those he termed "old Dulles types" or "the Chiang Kai-shek group" out of the department. Thus J. Graham Parsons, whose role as assistant secretary for Far Eastern affairs in the final Eisenhower years Bowles viewed as particularly egregious, was sent off to Sweden. Instead of regarding these transfers as a way good people could be usefully kept on, which was what he intended, Bowles's critics saw them as unacceptable punishment of officers whose only crime had been their association with the Republican administration.

The wrath of the retiring and "exiled" senior men and their sympathizers was probably raised by Bowles's effort to assign younger and less experienced officers as ambassadors, particularly to the many posts then being opened in newly independent African countries. He was successful in blocking administration approval of the assignments of seven senior officers chosen by the Eisenhower White House on State Department recommendation to head missions in Africa. Looking back in 1965, he recalled that the selections were said to have been made deliberately in the belief that "these young, hot-headed African leaders would like to have a sober, white haired, old American Foreign Service officer that [*sic*] they could talk to all the time and get their advice." For Bowles, "it was just incredible."[27] His own strategy was to find the young to talk to the young. When scoffers protested that he was turning U.S. embassies in Africa into kindergartens, he would point out that Kennedy himself was only forty-three.

▾   ▾   ▾

Bowles faced greater obstacles in filling top-level State Department positions, especially the deputy under secretary for political affairs job and several at the assistant secretary level, than he did in winning approval for his ambassadorial recommendations. Anxious to avoid appointing individuals associated with Eisenhower-Dulles era views, he found that Rusk was often not prepared to go along with his suggestions for assigning "fresh thinking" talent to these Washington jobs. The secretary had a different approach to executive management. He did not share Bowles's view of the urgency and importance of staffing top department ranks with people of the "right" orientation. As Samuel Lewis put it, "Rusk was by background and bent a 'staff man' who believes in using the organization, in trusting the experts who make it up, and in getting the organization to function smoothly by cleaning up lines of authority and responsibility."[28] The secretary's long experience in the State Department had brought him into contact with those experts—arguably he had become one himself—and gave him confidence in the Foreign Service as an institution. (Bowles, in contrast, distrusted it.) Nor did he attach the same importance Bowles did to sweeping out Eisenhower policies and replacing them with new and different ones. Unlike Bowles, he was comfortable with many of these old policies, and in the Truman administration had helped formulate approaches in the Far East that were their forerunners.[29]

These differences became evident in the confrontation between the two men over the appointment of the deputy under secretary for political affairs. The position offered an incumbent powerful influence in developing and administering policy. Its primary responsibility was the coordination of the work of the regional bureaus and policy liaison with Defense, CIA, and the White House—functions crucial to the effective operation of the State Department. The job was ordinarily though not invariably held by a Foreign Service officer. (Rusk had himself held the position before volunteering to step down to become assistant secretary for Far Eastern affairs.) Bowles recognized its importance and wanted to fill it with someone who would bring to it the policy and management spin he favored, a "fresh thinker" who could shake the department out of its old and, to him, unsatisfactory ways. He looked principally outside the service for suitable candidates. He found that Rusk strongly preferred a career officer for the job, as he often did for other senior department positions.

Bowles's initial thought was to bring Richard Bissell over from CIA. This idea was bizarre even when measured against the innovative approach he used in developing assignments. At the same time, he and Bissell went back a long way together. Bowles was confident that Bissell had the imagination, competence, and real understanding of forces throughout the world that would make him extremely effective in the job. Thomas Hughes has said that it was never clear to him if Bowles ever really focused on what Bissell was doing at the agency, where he held the position of deputy director for plans under Allen Dulles. In January 1961, when Bowles sought to recruit him for State, Bissell was in fact in direct charge of planning the Bay of Pigs operation. Not surprisingly, Dulles told Bowles he could not let him go, but never quite explained why. Bowles was also warned from within the department of the inappropriateness of selecting a top CIA official for a key State assignment. The coup de grace was administered by Kennedy, who told Bowles that he intended to name Bissell director of central intelligence in July, replacing Allen Dulles.[30]

Bowles and Rusk squabbled over the assignment for months, creating a vacancy damaging to department operations. The job eventually was given to U. Alexis Johnson, an experienced senior diplomat long associated with Far Eastern policymaking in the department and overseas who was then completing an assignment as ambassador to Thailand. Johnson had been deputy assistant secretary in the Bureau of Far Eastern Affairs and had worked with Rusk there. He was cool, efficient, and thoroughly professional, but he was by no stretch of the imagination a representative of new thinking. Bowles was concerned by his close association with Walter Robertson, who as Dulles's initial assistant secretary for Far Eastern affairs had been a major architect of policies Bowles deplored. He later called the Johnson assignment "unfortunate and costly."[31] The description of Johnson he spelled out in a private memorandum he wrote later in 1961 tells why:

[Johnson] is a decent, dedicated Foreign Service officer. He is a good operator and has ability to get things done. However, he has no sense of purpose or policy orientation. His whole objective is to find ways out of difficult situations into ones which are immediately more tolerable, even though the maneuver has little to do either with our long-term interest or likely future developments. No one is harder working, nor is anyone better equipped with built-in insensitivity to block, divert, or stifle fresh approaches or new policies.[32]

In 1961, as it continued to do until recently, the State Department divided the world into five regions, each handled by a bureau headed by an assistant secretary. Assistant secretary positions are considered key policymaking jobs, though as with other senior department officials the power of these regional bureau chiefs depends importantly on the extent to which the secretary and the under secretaries look to them for advice and expertise.

Even before he had appointed Rusk and Bowles, Kennedy had selected the flamboyant liberal Democratic governor of Michigan, G. Mennen "Soapy" Williams, to head the recently created Bureau of African Affairs. Bowles has said that he had helped persuade Williams to accept the job; the disappointed governor had hoped to be named to a cabinet-level position. Bowles also played a role in the appointment of J. Wayne Fredericks of the Ford Foundation as Williams's principal deputy. Working closely with the bureau and very much in synch with the approach to Africa Williams and Fredericks favored, he considered it "a model in regard to the development and implementation of fresh plans, serving to highlight our mediocre success in staffing the other bureaus."[33]

Bowles's hand can also be seen in the appointment of Phillips Talbot, an academic authority on South Asia long familiar with its problems and principal players, as assistant secretary for Near East and South Asian affairs. Talbot was traveling in India when word of a possible appointment reached him.[34] A South Asian specialist may have been chosen in part to avoid nominating someone with possibly controversial views on the more sensitive Middle Eastern region for which the bureau was also responsible. The attractiveness of the appointment to Bowles was no doubt enhanced by an expectation that Talbot, who had lived and worked for many years in India, would subscribe to his own pro-Indian approach to South Asia. John Kenneth Galbraith, who has said he collaborated on the choice, also thought Talbot would be pliable.[35] When Talbot took a more evenhanded line between India and Pakistan, he lost Bowles's favor. Probably in consequence, Bowles came to have a much lower regard for the Near East–South Asia Bureau's performance under Talbot's management than he did for the Africa Bureau under Williams and Fredericks.

If Bowles soon soured on Talbot, he was unhappy from the start with the selections made in three other regional bureaus. He had been particularly anxious to ensure that leadership of the Bureau of Far Eastern Affairs was entrusted to someone who would help forge new approaches on China and Southeast Asia. As his attitude toward Alex Johnson and Graham Parsons indicated, he had a special animus against those he associated with Eisenhower administration Far Eastern policies. Despite these concerns, and the bureau's well-deserved reputation as a notorious stronghold of policy inflexibility, Rusk chose as assistant secretary Walter McConaughy, a pleasant veteran career diplomat whose service as director of the department's Office of Chinese Affairs and in a succession of Far Eastern posts had established him as a leading practitioner of the Dulles school of Asian diplomacy. Bowles considered McConaughy a "Taiwan-firster" emotionally involved in support for the Chiang Kai-shek regime. He soon pressed for his replacement by former New York Governor Averell Harriman, then roving ambassador, a recommendation Rusk (and the Kennedys) resisted. Ironically, when Bowles himself was forced out, Harriman was chosen for the position. McConaughy was appointed ambassador to Pakistan at that time. He was still there when Bowles returned to India in 1963, and their relationship was no better in the subcontinental setting than it had been in Washington.

The appointment of an assistant secretary for inter-American affairs was complicated by the presence of Adolf Berle as chairman of an Interdepartmental Task Force on Latin America. Berle had held the inter-American assistant secretary job in the Roosevelt administration, and it was difficult to find anyone willing to take the position until he was removed as a powerful bureaucratic competitor. The Bay of Pigs episode further complicated the recruiting process. Although Bowles was determined to find someone outside the Foreign Service Latin American circuit to take the job, he was obliged after a prodigious but unsuccessful recruiting campaign to agree to Robert Woodward, a career officer then ambassador to Chile. His efforts to bring in a new broom were similarly unsuccessful in the Bureau of European Affairs, where Foy Kohler, a Foreign Service officer who had been assistant secretary under Eisenhower, was asked to stay on despite Bowles's allegation that the bureau's policy positions had remained basically the same since Dean Acheson's heyday.

The recruiting effort to fill other department positions came out better from Bowles's viewpoint. He brought in Roger Hilsman, deputy head of the Congressional Research Service, to lead the Bureau of Intelligence and Research, his old Connecticut associate Philip Coombs to head the newly upgraded Bureau of Educational and Cultural Affairs, and a Republican, U.S. Civil Service Commission Chairman Roger Jones, to be deputy under secretary for administration. Harlan Cleveland, the head of the Maxwell School of Public Administration at Syracuse University, whom Bowles had wanted to run the economic assistance agency, was assigned instead at Adlai Stevenson's request as assistant secretary for international organization affairs. Abram Chayes's role in the Kennedy campaign helped win him the position of department legal adviser, an assignment Bowles warmly supported. Edward R. Murrow, Bowles's inspired choice to head the U.S. Information Agency, enthusiastically accepted that sensitive and important job, to the surprise of the many who doubted he would take the sizable pay cut involved in leaving the Columbia Broadcasting System for government work.

Like other assignments to senior department positions, these appointments involved considerable negotiation between the White House, Rusk, and Bowles. Looking back later in 1961, Bowles wrote: "I am astonished at the number [of senior personnel] I was able to get through the various hurdles thrown in the way." But he also believed that the appointments he had engineered or supported had had limited impact on the functioning of the department. Characteristically, he looked at the problem in terms of the generation of ideas, not of organizational efficiency. "Whatever fresh ideas [there are] around the place in regard to political affairs come from Harlan Cleveland, Abe Chayes, George McGhee, Adlai Stevenson, to some degree Roger Hilsman, and myself. The geographic bureaus (. . . excepting Africa) are largely dead."[36]

The problems Bowles had with Rusk went well beyond their disagreement on the selection of key personnel. It soon became clear that what Bowles had called "the partnership" was not prospering. As a senior official close to both of them has remarked, the two men were not made to work with one another.[37] Rusk was professional, pragmatic, low-key, very businesslike, very crisp, far less imaginative than Bowles. He was precise and focused on immediate problems. He had little time, in either sense of that phrase, for the long-range thinking and planning which Bowles thought so crucial to foreign policymaking, and limited patience for his deputy's lengthy discourses on historic developments in the Third World and other favorite themes. When they got together he wanted to deal quickly with specific issues, not get into long discussions of broad policy options and how these related to America's role in the world. Familiar from long experience with the rhythms and requirements of the bureaucratic process, the secretary was disturbed by what seemed to him Bowles's inability to deal promptly with papers that called for fast action.

These difficulties were heightened by more fundamental differences. Like many others in the new administration, Rusk paid much more attention to pressing national security issues than Bowles did. Perhaps because of his wartime service, he had a much higher regard for the military and its role in the resolution of foreign policy problems than Bowles thought was called for. Unlike Bowles, he tended to think of issues largely in terms of the threat of Communism. Although he had a warm and sympathetic interest in the Third World, he did not share all of Bowles's enthusiastic fascination for it.

Bowles tried his best to be loyal to Rusk. He deliberately avoided contacts at the White House and limited his relations with his political friends and with the press so as not to upstage him. He tried repeatedly to develop a dialogue, not only to discuss substance but to learn what it was the secretary wanted him to do. He got little satisfaction. As other senior officials in the department attested, Rusk was not good at letting his subordinates know what he expected of them. Because of Rusk's unwillingness or inability to communicate, Bowles never knew where he stood with him. Being listened to and responded to was very important to him, and he was troubled and hurt by Rusk's repeated brush-offs.

These difficulties were compounded by Bowles's unfamiliarity with serving as second in command. With the exception of his few weeks as Prentiss Brown's deputy at OPA in 1943, he had not been in a subordinate role since he had worked as an advertising copywriter in his twenties before setting up Benton & Bowles. He had run operations, and had run them the way he wanted to. He was a conceptualizer, not an implementer. It was hard enough for him to play a secondary role, especially to someone he believed less qualified than he was to be secretary of state (and who was well aware of the assessment). It became even more difficult when he found himself unable to learn what that role was to be or to get a lucid explanation from Rusk of the problems between them. He was prepared to do, or try to do, what Rusk required of him, but he never really knew what that was, for all the secretary's early reference to the obviously unworkable Marshall-Lovett model.

Increasingly, Rusk did not want to deal with Bowles. Bowles asked department Executive Secretary Lucius Battle what the trouble was. Battle suggested that the secretary did not react well to abstractions and recommended that when Bowles met with him he confine himself to consideration of specific issues. This excellent advice seemed to do no good. The two men talked less and less to one another and more through Battle, despite his pleas to them to work with each other directly and his suggestions about how they could best do so.[38]

Bowles's problems with Rusk inevitably affected his relationship with other senior department officials and his ability to function within the organization. Aware that he was not getting on well with the secretary, other officers paid less heed to him. Bowles compounded the problem by his bureaucratic style. He handled meetings poorly, regarding them more as opportunities for cheerleading and overwhelming any opposition than as occasions to draw people out and come to decisions based on the compromise of conflicting views. He was dismissive of those who took positions which did not fit into his concept of what policy should be. He did not recognize that the adversarial process can be a useful vehicle for working out decisions. Instead, he tended to personalize opposition and regarded as wrong-thinking those whose policy orientations and bureaucratic positions led them to adopt views with which he differed.

He also talked too much, too discursively, and to too little immediate purpose. He seemed to think of policymaking more in abstract terms than as a series of discrete decisions. "You could go to see Chet, say, to discuss a specific problem in Iranian relations," a senior officer remembered. "What you got instead was a long discourse on Iran and the role of the brown people and so forth. It was very interesting but not what was needed to make policy." Another recalled Bowles's "long, sentimental, emotional, and repetitive lectures" on the need to help the Third World. Colleagues found such long-winded and irrelevant performances a waste of their limited time and they went around him as they sought to get things done.[39]

Like many other senior officials who come to the department from outside, Bowles found State's machinery cumbersome, unresponsive, and strange. He had difficulty dealing with the flow of paper which comes across the under secretary's desk for decision. His staff worked hard—with considerable success, they claim—to get him to recognize that he had to focus on this. He tried to change the way decisions were reached and called for the scrapping of the time-honored but often very slow process of drafting papers at the working level before moving them upward to senior officials for final action. It should be replaced, he urged, by an arrangement in which the top people would get together, work out promising policy possibilities, and direct task forces to follow through. Rusk, comfortable with the old ways and uninterested in sitting down with Bowles to map out options, took no action on this proposal.

Some of Bowles's colleagues believe that his role in the department was further damaged by the way his office was staffed. Perhaps because of his low opinion of senior Foreign Service officers, most of whom he regarded as overly cautious, conservative, and unimaginative, and his preference for a talented personal entourage which did things the way he wanted them done, his staff comprised only people he had brought into the department with him, including Hughes (who soon left to become Roger Hilsman's deputy in the Intelligence Bureau) and Thomson, plus middle-grade and junior Foreign Service officers such as Sam Lewis and Brandon Grove.

As their subsequent records demonstrate, most of these people were unusually gifted. But they did not have the knowledge of the system and its major players that only experience within it can bring. "We arrived in that top spot of this enormous bureaucracy as totally innocent as you could imagine any babes in the woods to be," Thomson recalled. "Bowles was completely unprotected by his staff, partly our fault for being innocents, partly his fault for not bringing in the un-innocent."[40] Grove noted that Bowles "just was not—would not have been receptive . . . to the kind of staffing that subsequent under secretaries and his predecessors felt comfortable with; namely at least one senior Foreign Service officer who knows how the State Department functions, who is very sensitive to bureaucratic relations with other agencies."[41] Thomson contrasted the weak Bowles operation with the setup quickly established by Under Secretary for Economic Affairs George Ball, who brought in a strong team of competent and power-oriented people from inside and outside that made his office a bureaucratic and policymaking force to be reckoned with. The older and more experienced people Bowles recruited from outside the department did not come to work in his office, but were scattered around elsewhere in the building, and he could not use them to guard his interests in the way Ball used his staff.[42]

The inability of Rusk and Bowles to communicate in person prompted Bowles to send the secretary a long string of memoranda and letters, though their offices were only a few yards apart. (Rusk has recalled that he didn't think much of this practice but tolerated it. He also said that Bowles's memos were longer than they needed to be.) A compilation Bowles later prepared listed a total of ninety-eight memoranda he had sent to Rusk during the ten months they were together at State.[43]

Bowles wrote to Rusk in May in a further effort to define his own role after it had become clear that the February agreement with Rusk had not produced the desired results. Acknowledging that "the relation between the Secretary and Under Secretary of State is complex and imprecise under the best of circumstances," he listed areas where he should be given more independent authority. Not surprisingly, personnel came first, Bowles again making clear that assignments were central to his definition of management and administration:

> I do not feel that I now have the authority to make the personnel adjustments which I believe to be essential if the Department apparatus is fully to meet its responsibilities. . . . You and I can carry out fresh, affirmative policies only if the Assistant Secretaries and their deputies personally believe in these policies and are determined to see that they go into effect. In some bureaus this is not now the case. I have had a long administrative experience in business and government, and I am willing to assume as much administrative authority as you are prepared to give me.

Bowles said he could also be of greater help "in adapting our present policies . . . to longer-range requirements and realities." He could not do this effectively "unless I have the clear knowledge of your own views. This can only come from more frequent and deeper discussions than we have permitted ourselves so far." He warned again about the dangers of being boxed in by old assumptions and losing sight of the broad, historical context. "The President has a right to expect from us tough-minded answers, however unorthodox, controversial, or unpopular. If we fail to provide foreign policy leadership for whatever reason, the integrity, the realism, and the sense of moral direction which I believe to be vital to America's performance in world affairs will continue to be lacking."[44]

As events in the next weeks would demonstrate, this message, like Bowles's February memorandum about the responsibilities of the under secretary, was to no avail.

12

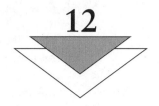

Running Afoul of
the Kennedys

JOHN F. KENNEDY had come to power determined to exercise strong presidential leadership in foreign policy and give it a new direction and vigor. A series of confrontations with Communist governments early in his administration prompted him to pay even greater personal attention both to overall policy direction and detailed strategy. This hands-on management of foreign affairs brought him into close contact with the State Department, from Rusk and other senior officials down to the office directors and country desk officers he phoned from the White House for detailed information. He looked to the department to play a key coordinating role in helping him deal with the problems his new administration soon faced.

Bowles's difficulties at the department played out against a backdrop of Kennedy's unhappiness with its performance. The president was increasingly disappointed with what he found at State. The department seemed almost the antithesis of his own way of operating. He thought it slow, indecisive, and unresponsive, its officers bland, conventional, and cautious. He derided its time-consuming bureaucratic processes, and despaired when after lengthy labor they brought forth an unimaginative, shopworn product. He made no secret of his dissatisfaction. His comment to Hugh Sidey of *Time* that the department was a bowl of jelly became one of the more quotable quotes of the first months of his administration.

It is ironic that though Bowles's own assessment of the department closely paralleled Kennedy's, some on the White House staff felt, and let it be known, that as under secretary he was part of the problem. He was not carrying out his responsibilities. At meetings where he was supposed to represent the department he often seemed to present his own views instead. (He was notorious in the department for failing to read briefing papers.) He was said to be miscast in his role and was charged with being a thinker rather than a doer, an allegation he always resented. The president himself voiced his dissatisfaction with Bowles's performance. In early May he told Arthur Schlesinger, by then a presidential adviser: "Chet is a fine fellow but he's just not doing his job. He was perfect as Ambassador to India. A job like that could use all his good qualities—his intelligence, his sympathy, his willingness to listen to difficult problems. But he is not precise or decisive enough to get things done. Because Chet isn't doing his job, Rusk is spreading himself too thin and is not able to do his job either."[1]

The tendency to blame Bowles for State's inadequacies stemmed in part from the apparent impression at the White House that the under secretary was responsible for the management of the department. This has not ordinarily been the case, at least not in the sense of the second in command taking charge of policy preparation and making sure that papers are properly staffed out and completed on time. That role has usually been entrusted to a senior official below under secretary rank. When Bowles spoke of wanting to tackle the "general management" job, he meant establishing new procedures and assuring that the right people were in key positions, not acting as paper-flow traffic cop, a responsibility which matched neither his interests nor his talents. If Rusk had really wanted Bowles to take on that duty, he never succeeded in making that clear to him.

Bowles's personal style and the way he chose to operate also damaged him. His moralizing, his constant call for high-level attention to broader, long-term issues, his readiness to talk about them at great length, and his lesser concern for the nitty-gritty of policy were out of place in a can-do administration that put a premium on fast, decisive action to deal with immediate problems and prided itself on being laconic and tough. He hurt himself further when he limited his contacts at the White House and with his politician and journalist friends in order not to upstage Rusk. He spoke with the president on the phone, and occasionally met with him at larger gatherings or social functions, but he did not try to arrange private meetings.

Nor did he have much social contact with the leading lights of the New Frontier. He was a serious, earnest, almost puritanical man, and the tastes of Camelot and the gaiety of its social whirl were not for him. He did not share the Kennedys' fondness for pageantry and was troubled when they used it to send what he considered wrong foreign policy signals. The gala reception at Mount Vernon for President Ayub Khan of Pakistan during Ayub's 1961 state visit was particularly appalling to him. The Sandhurst-educated Ayub represented for Bowles a particularly reprehensible type, the "brown *sahib*" unconcerned with the needs of the South Asian masses who could, over a stiff whiskey-soda, fool gullible Americans with bold talk about standing up to Communism.

The repeated confrontations which marked the first year of the Kennedy administration, and the way the president chose to deal with them, further reduced Bowles's potential for influence. The year 1961 was not a good one for policymakers given to thoughtful speculation about long-term trends and the impact present decisions could have on events five or ten years down the road. All too frequently, the name of the game was crisis management, never Bowles's strong suit. In playing it, the president was far more prepared than was Bowles to use, or seriously consider using, military force, whether this meant supporting counterinsurgency in Southeast Asia or plotting the landing of anti-Castro Cubans at the Bay of Pigs. Bowles believed in a strong military to deter Communist aggression, but he had long since concluded that there were narrow limits to its usefulness. The events of the year strengthened this important aspect of his approach to foreign policy and made him even less willing to change his stripes to suit the more military-minded preferences of the New Frontier.

This attitude set Bowles apart from those in the White House, led by M.I.T. Professor Walt Rostow (whom Schlesinger called, not inaccurately, "Chester Bowles with a machine gun"), who shared Bowles's view of the potential benefit to U.S. interests of nationalism and non-alignment in the Third World and the importance and urgency of economic development and "nation building" there, but also believed that this more "liberal" approach so long championed by Bowles was not sufficient. In some critical areas counterinsurgency measures were also needed to contain the perceived Communist challenge effectively. The militant line taken at the White House helped make Bowles seem odd man out, the ultimate fuzzy-minded, unreconstructed liberal in an administration that sought to develop a modern, flexible military capability and reserved special admiration for those tough and intelligent enough to use it to advance foreign policy objectives.

There were other important disconnects between Bowles and the New Frontier. Bowles's highly moral approach to foreign (and domestic) policy made him feel uncomfortable in the administration. He did not share the widespread admiration for its much vaunted pragmatism and thought of the president as a man of politics and power who had no principles or convictions which could not be shaken if circumstances called for a change.[2] "The question which concerns me most about the new Administration," he wrote privately in May 1961 after returning from a White House meeting, "is whether it lacks a sense of conviction about what is right and what is wrong."[3] Kennedy loyalists, for their part, questioned Bowles's willingness to be a team player. It was for Bowles a painful legacy of the resentment aroused by his reluctance to throw himself fully into Kennedy's preconvention campaign.

Beyond these problems was a generational difficulty. Bowles had come to political awareness during the Depression as a New Dealer. His view of foreign policy had sprung from the domestic political and social values he had acquired in those years. He had what by 1961 could be termed an old-fashioned idea of a world community, which derived from those values and from the vision of a better world inspired by the war. His visionary ideals were not shared by the rather cynical younger men around Kennedy. They saw their role largely in terms of dealing with the Communist threat on a day-to-day basis and gave little thought to Bowles's cherished brave new world.

Bowles might have reduced the cumulative impact of these handicaps had he been able to take charge of a particular part of the Kennedy administration's agenda compatible with his own interests and abilities. For all its preoccupation with immediate challenges and its susceptibility to military solutions, the administration made impressive progress in its first year in carrying out Kennedy's campaign pledge to devote greater U.S. attention and resources to long-range efforts to promote economic development and political stability in the non-Communist Third World. The Alliance for Progress, the Peace Corps, and the revamping of the management of economic assistance were landmark developments which were very much in tune with Bowles's thinking and had his enthusiastic support. Had he taken charge of the Alliance or the newly created Agency for International Development he would have become a more influential power in the administration (though not a central figure in it) than his nebulous and frustrating role as under secretary ever allowed. He might also have dispelled the widespread feeling that he was too concerned with long-range developments to deal with day-to-day problems. Although he seriously considered bidding for the AID job in mid-1961 and in 1962 was actually offered the Alliance (but without the overall responsibility for Latin American policy he insisted on), neither materialized.

▾   ▾   ▾

Bowles's differences with the New Frontier made him vulnerable to those who for ideological or personal reasons wanted him sidelined or removed from office. But none of his difficulties was as damaging to his White House standing as his role in the Bay of Pigs episode.

Like others at the State Department (aside from Rusk), Bowles had been kept in the dark about the projected CIA-directed operation to overthrow the Castro regime, learning of it only in late March when he was acting secretary during Rusk's absence overseas.[4] He was greatly troubled. As he later observed, "If I had been President when Allen Dulles first presented the plan, I would have told him, 'Allen, go back and take a cold shower, have a drink, and go to bed. You're crazy'."[5] Characteristically, he detailed his strong opposition in a memorandum to Rusk. The invasion, he contended, would violate the noninterventionist pledge in the Act of Bogota establishing the Organization of American States and "jeopardize the favorable position we have steadily developed in most of the non-Communist world by the responsible and restrained policies which are now associated with the President." He put odds on failure at two to one; they could only be reduced by commitment of direct U.S. military support, to him an unacceptable option. If Rusk agreed with him in opposing the operation, he urged, the secretary should voice his position personally to Kennedy. He thought that intercession would be decisive.[6]

Meeting privately with Rusk, Bowles added that if the president nonetheless decided to go forward with the plan, he would want to be informed so he could take his objections directly to him. Although Rusk agreed that the invasion would be a mistake, he remained silent (in the view of one of his biographers because he did not want to make common cause with Bowles when their relations were ebbing) and merely promised to pass on the memorandum to the president. Rusk has recalled that when he subsequently met with Kennedy in Florida he reported Bowles's opposition orally, withholding the memo because the president had already received several similar submissions from others including Schlesinger and Senator Fulbright. Returning to Washington, he disingenuously told Bowles that it was not necessary for him to see Kennedy since the plan had been greatly scaled down to a guerrilla operation.[7]

With the secretary again in charge, Bowles was no longer in the loop when the decisions to move forward with the operation were made. As rumors of an invasion grew, he became sufficiently alarmed to write out at home a letter to the president strongly opposing the project. Before the letter could be retyped the following morning, news that B-26s flown by Cuban pilots had attacked Havana airfield was already on the ticker. The invasion took place soon afterwards and ended ignominiously.

In any bureaucracy, it is often dangerous to have been right when your boss was wrong. Bowles had been right on the Bay of Pigs when the president, his brother, and many others had been wrong or had equivocated. But he was much more damaged by widely accepted reports that he had disclosed his position to the press. Rusk, for one, has stated flatly that when this story got back to the president, "it cooked Chester Bowles's goose with John Kennedy."[8]

Bowles, for his part, strongly denied to the president that he had leaked to the press, where word of his opposition (and Rusk's) appeared in the *New York Times* and *Time* magazine.[9] His secretary remembers that he privately blamed Arthur Schlesinger for the leak.[10] "The proper criticism against me," he told the editor of the *Hartford Courant*, "is not my willingness to make my views felt, but the fact that I kept my views so tightly within 'channels' that my voice proved ineffective."[11] From the press side, *New York Times* columnist James Reston has said that it was unfair to blame Bowles for leaking. "[The story about Bowles's opposition] was originally printed by this reporter and when I took it to Bowles for confirmation before publication, he refused to discuss it."[12]

Despite these disclaimers, it seems clear that Bowles had let his opposition become widely known, though he had not acted in a way which would justify *Time's* allegation that he had "deviously" leaked it. He admitted that he had told State Department colleagues, and though he later argued that such secrets could not possibly be kept in Washington, he surely could have been more tight-lipped about it and more aware of the sensitivity of the issue than he was. He compounded his problem by recalling his preinvasion opposition at an NSC postmortem. This had infuriated Robert Kennedy, to whom disloyalty was a cardinal sin. "I just said [to Bowles] that I thought it was a helluva thing to say now that this decision had been made, and so far as this administration was concerned, he should keep his mouth shut and remember that he was *for* the Bay of Pigs. . . . We didn't need somebody coming in and making sure that everybody understood that they weren't in favor of this [operation] in the first place. Everybody rather resented it."[13] As embellished by the press, Kennedy jabbed his finger into Bowles's body when making the point. Bowles has denied this.

Discussing the bureaucratic fallout of the Bay of Pigs episode a few days after the invasion, *Time* found that Secretary Rusk had improved his standing with the president because he voiced in advance doubts about the expedition and refrained afterwards from reminding his teammates that he had been right. By contrast, the much less circumspect Bowles was "way, way down" in the president's estimation.[14]

This perception that Bowles had fallen from grace apparently won widespread acceptance, weakening him further in an environment where knives are swiftly drawn against controversial figures who are seen to have lost White House favor.

▾　　　▾　　　▾

Bowles had more or less stumbled into the Bay of Pigs issue. His major policy concerns focused on U.S. relations with the Third World and China. He paid special attention to South Asia, where his recommendations reflected his well-known views that India was important to U.S. interests and that the security relationship with Pakistan had been a mistake. He did not take any single issue as his own, as other under secretaries have sometimes done, and as roving Ambassador Averell Harriman was doing in specializing on Laos. Although he continued to advocate a major reexamination of European policy, he left that task to others. European economic issues, for example, became largely the concern of George Ball, the under secretary for economic affairs who ranked just below him in the State hierarchy. When Berlin became the dominant European issue following Soviet Premier Nikita Khrushchev's challenge to Western rights there, Bowles took a moderate line and strongly opposed the confrontational approach spelled out in an NSC paper prepared by Dean Acheson. But his role in developing the administration's position—on this and other issues in the developed world—was marginal compared to that of other senior officials.

Laos, where the Kennedy administration faced its first major foreign policy crisis, was about as far from the developed world in every way as a policymaker could go. When the new administration took office, the remote but strategically located Southeast Asian kingdom of two million unwarlike people had been independent of French rule since 1954. The Eisenhower administration had become deeply involved in the country, as the Communist Pathet Lao and a variety of self-styled true neutralists, pro-Western neutralists, and anti-Communist rightists maneuvered for political position and occasionally engaged halfheartedly in armed hostilities. U.S. efforts to make Laos into what John Foster Dulles called "a bastion of freedom" collapsed with the military success in late 1960 of combined Communist and neutralist forces assisted by North Vietnamese cadres. The consequent danger that a Communist-dominated regime would take over the country brought the Laos issue to a critical stage just as Kennedy came to power. Fearful of the international strategic impact of a breach in the containment of China and the domestic political implications of "losing" Laos to the

Communists, the new administration was confronted with the unwelcome question of whether the United States should intervene in Laos, and if so, how.

Kennedy decided to explore the possibility of a political solution and sought an arrangement that would establish a truly neutral Laos. Bowles agreed with this, but differed with the president and with most of his State Department colleagues over the question of a U.S. military presence in the country. When Kennedy sought to make clear to the Soviets, the Chinese, and others by statements and messages through diplomatic channels reinforced by movements of American armed forces in the neighborhood that the United States was prepared to use troops if necessary, Bowles argued that the administration should not send them in unless it was seriously prepared to embark on a major land war with Communist China.

Bowles's position reflected his long-standing doubts about the wisdom and feasibility of direct Western military intervention in Indochina and his strong preference for the neutralization of the region with the cooperation and backing of India and other Asian countries. He believed that regional political stability and economic progress could best be promoted by sizable U.S. investment in the development of the Mekong River valley through a TVA-like authority, and had been dismayed by the Eisenhower administration effort to bring Laos into the Western camp.[15] Military intervention would place the United States in a colonialist position similar to that of the French in the early 1950s. Nor would China accept it. Drawing an analogy with Cuba, he wrote Kennedy less than a month before the Bay of Pigs: "If the situation were reversed and either the Soviets or the Chinese moved military forces into Cuba, there is little doubt that we would be under heavy political pressure for immediate and strenuous action to throw them out."[16]

Bowles thought it possible that the Soviets saw Cold War advantage in embroiling the United States with China in Laos, an argument that recalled ideas he had advanced a decade earlier about Soviet deviousness toward China in the Korean War. Stepping up his anti-interventionist efforts in April as the crisis lurched uncertainly toward a possible diplomatic solution, he maintained that a weak U.S. military position, lack of support from allies, and the anomaly of asking the American people to support military involvement in Laos but not in Cuba all argued against an armed U.S. presence. A better strategy would be to get maximum military and political support from other Asian countries and from the United Nations and to avoid doing anything that would tend to drive the Chinese and Soviets into closer cooperation.[17]

The arrangement of a cease-fire in early May and the convening of a conference at Geneva later that month eventually obviated the need to send American troops to Laos. Many contended then and later that it was only the U.S. threat to intervene militarily which persuaded the Communists to come to the negotiating table. Bowles never accepted this assessment, nor did he regret his opposition to sending in troops. In looking back, he found other persuasive reasons for the relatively satisfactory denouement of the crisis, especially the unwillingness of Moscow and Hanoi to have Laos "saved" by Chinese intervention.

Rather than convincing Bowles of the usefulness of saber rattling, the Laos crisis appears to have strengthened his conviction about the limits of military power in resolving issues. It heightened his concern that American policymakers were too ready to use armed force in ways which made little sense either logistically or from the viewpoint of broader U.S. interests. The episode also reduced further the scant respect he had for the role of the military in shaping foreign policy. During the crisis many senior officers had taken the position that the United States should intervene militarily, but only if it was prepared to commit large numbers of troops and be ready to use all-out force, including nuclear weapons, if actual fighting took place. This attitude was appalling to Bowles. Recalling his experience with the military mind in the first six months of 1961, he wrote: "I was concerned by the narrow military perspective that even some of our ablest military leaders brought to bear on what were primarily political questions. I was even more alarmed by their ability to influence what our government said and, in some cases, actually did."[18]

Bowles took much the same line on the broader issue of Southeast Asian security and stability as he did on Laos. The way to deal with the Communist threat to the region—which he saw largely in terms of Chinese ambitions—was to arrange for the guarantee of its neutrality and the territorial integrity of individual countries by a group of outside powers. While he held that in the longer run the Asian powers, especially India and Japan, should be in the forefront, his immediate idea, which he recalled putting to Rusk as early as February 1961, was to have the United States, the Soviet Union, France, and Britain, as well as these two favorite Asian countries, act as guarantors. The Soviets, he thought, might find the plan in their interest in keeping Communist China from absorbing the region into its sphere of influence. The idea was not accepted by the administration, and Bowles recalled that at the State Department it was suggested that in proposing it he was inadvertently playing the Communist game.[19] He put forward another proposal for neutralization in October 1961, when the military situation in Vietnam was seriously deteriorating, expanding his list of guarantors to include the People's Republic and the SEATO powers (aside from Thailand, which would be one of the countries guaranteed).[20] Although this was also rejected, Bowles continued to make the neutralization approach a major agenda item during 1962, when he was special representative to the president.

As he did in Laos, Bowles strongly opposed the introduction of U.S. combat forces in Vietnam. He spelled out his position most forcefully when General Maxwell Taylor and Walt Rostow returned from an October fact-finding visit there and urged on the president the stationing of as many as 10,000 American troops to stem the gains of the Vietcong and shore up the faltering Saigon government. Bowles argued that U.S. armed forces, like the French, would almost certainly be bogged down in a frustrating and costly struggle of white outsiders against "anti-colonial guerrillas." Fearful of Peking's intervention, he called again for the neutralization of the region, telling the president that "it is no more possible over the long haul for the U.S. to maintain a military power presence on the peninsula of Asia against the growing pressure of Communist China than it would have been for the Spanish to hold a military position in Florida in the face of the developing power of the U.S.A."[21] In *Promises to Keep,* Bowles recalled that he reintroduced his neutralization proposal in the fall of 1961 as an effort to transfer the debate from the military to the political agenda.[22] Kennedy eventually decided not to station American combat troops but to increase the number of advisers.

▾   ▾   ▾

Within the limits set by American public and political opinion and the stubborn positions taken by the People's Republic and the Nationalist government on Taiwan, Bowles looked for ways to modify the China policy the Kennedy administration had inherited from Eisenhower. He had been encouraged by Kennedy's enthusiastic, but private, endorsement in the spring of 1960 of his article in *Foreign Affairs* recommending a two Chinas policy. ("This was the first of several experiences in which I found Kennedy to be far more advanced in his private views than in his public statements," he ruefully conceded later.)[23] He was also buoyed when during one of the televised debates with Nixon Kennedy had echoed his views in questioning the need for a U.S.

commitment to the defense of Quemoy and Matsu and calling for their evacuation by Nationalist forces, though not at the point of a Communist gun. But Kennedy had quickly fuzzed his position following Nixon's sharp criticism, and aside from this brief and inconclusive encounter between the candidates over the marginal issue of the offshore islands, U.S. relations with China played a minor role in the election campaign.

The narrowness of his election victory reinforced Kennedy's disinclination to take politically risky initiatives on China, a position further strengthened when the departing Dwight Eisenhower told him that he would strongly oppose any attempt by the new administration to recognize the People's Republic or help it get China's United Nations seat. Bowles soon became convinced that the new president would only undertake major policy changes following a resounding reelection victory in 1964. He recalled that under those circumstances he was troubled but not surprised when Kennedy asked him to play down differences between his (Bowles's) ideas on China and the conventional position inherited from the Eisenhower administration at the confirmation hearing before the Senate Foreign Relations Committee in January 1961 for his appointment as under secretary.[24]

Bowles followed this advice, and the hearing, chaired by the sympathetic and supportive Senator Fulbright, proved a tame affair. Stressing the noncontroversial elements in his stand, such as his opposition to recognition of Peking and his call for the defense of Taiwan at all costs, Bowles mollified the senators further by citing Chinese Communist Premier Chou En-lai's negative reaction to the policy proposals he had made in the *Foreign Affairs* article. But while he shied away from suggesting any prompt, far-reaching changes in the U.S. relationship with the People's Republic, Bowles also asked the committee members to take a long-range view. "We have not only the problem of trying to contain China, we have the problem of how do you let the steam out of this boiler without an explosion. You can contain steam only up to a point; at some point it breaks the vessel in which you are trying to control it." The image became a favorite one with him.[25]

Aware of Kennedy's diffidence and Rusk's professed lack of interest in any significant change, Bowles focused as under secretary on approaches which would incrementally develop U.S. ties with the People's Republic and reduce its isolation.[26] He also wanted the United States to remove itself from the Chinese civil war by dissociating itself from responsibility for the defense of the offshore islands if it was not able to persuade the Nationalists to withdraw from them.[27] He sought ways to put on Peking the onus for U.S. policies which he understood the president himself regarded as irrational. "Instead of basing our refusal to recognize Communist China on her lack of 'peace loving' qualities," he suggested to Kennedy, "would it not be more persuasive to point out that we cannot accept the Chinese condition that we sell ten million Chinese Nationalists and Formosans [Taiwanese] down the river as the price of 'normal' relationships?"[28]

He did not advocate any loosening of the long-standing U.S. objective of containing Peking, however. As he put it in a July 1 memorandum to the president, the combination of the evangelical zeal of Marxism-Leninism, the recurrent force of Chinese imperialist expansionism, and the have-not demands typified earlier by prewar Japan and Germany made Communist China "a paramount threat to all the nations on its periphery." He argued again that the threat could be more effectively dealt with by enlisting India and Japan in the containment effort. He also recommended that Kennedy explore ways to involve the Russians in that effort. This advice was a follow-up to the suggestion he had made on the eve of the June 1961 Vienna Summit that the president raise the problem of Chinese expansionism with Khrushchev.[29] He saw no inconsistency between advocating the containment of what he considered a dangerously expansionist People's Republic and supporting closer contacts with it. He had followed this dual approach since he had first become interested in China policy ten years earlier.

Bowles found bureaucratic allies. He was delighted to learn that Edward Rice of the State Department's Policy Planning Council had prepared a highly classified list of possible initiatives on China policy. These included lifting the ban on U.S. citizens' travel to Communist China, the modification and eventual removal of the embargo on trade with it in nonstrategic goods, discussions with Peking on arms control and disarmament, the evacuation by the Nationalists of the offshore islands, consideration under certain circumstances of an offer of food grains to the Communists on a grant basis, some form of representation for Peking in the United Nations, and U.S. recognition of Outer Mongolia (the Mongolian People's Republic), a land-locked Soviet-dominated Communist state wedged between Siberia and China.[30] James Thomson, who shared Bowles's enthusiasm for Rice's daring and enterprise, has recalled that proponents of the initiatives believed the ideas might conceivably elicit a Chinese response. Even if they were rejected, they would nonetheless communicate a more moderate and flexible U.S. attitude toward Peking and lead eventually in the direction of

Sino-American accommodation. With Thomson as point man, the under secretary's office played a leading role in pushing some of these and other initiatives. The efforts were strongly opposed within the department by the Bureau of Far Eastern Affairs, where the Dullesian Walter McConaughy presided until November 1961 despite Bowles's efforts to have him removed. With Rusk inclined to let proposals molder in his in-box, and Kennedy unwilling to rally public opinion in favor of change, Bowles and those who shared his views were able to make only limited headway.[31]

Bowles's most important moves to develop a more flexible China policy were probably the campaign in the summer of 1961 to obtain U.S. recognition and United Nations membership for Outer Mongolia and the lengthier effort to make Western food available to Peking. The Mongolian initiative came to be particularly identified with Bowles. Its supporters argued that it would serve U.S. purposes in several ways. Coming at a time of increasingly evident hostility between Communist China and the Soviet Union, it would demonstrate that the United States was capable of making a distinction between Asian Communist countries that pursued reasonable policies (as Mongolia did in line with current Soviet positions) and the more aggressive rulers in Peking. It would also suggest that American policies in Asia were no longer dictated by Chiang Kai-shek, whose government strongly opposed the initiative. More directly, the move offered the United States a strategically located diplomatic listening post on China's northwestern frontier.

Although the proposal to establish relations with Outer Mongolia initially had Kennedy's support, strident opposition mounted by the China lobby, which feared that this could be a forerunner to U.S. recognition of Peking, prompted the administration to drop the idea. Proponents of the initiative were more successful on the issue of U.N. membership, but only because Mongolian entry had become linked to the admission of the West African state of Mauritania. Fearful that a Chinese Nationalist veto of Mongolia would prompt the Soviets to blackball Mauritania and that Mauritania's African friends, angered at Taiwan, would then retaliate by supporting Peking's U.N. membership bid, the administration persuaded the Chiang Kai-shek government to drop its opposition. But the price was a pledge by Kennedy that Washington would exercise its veto in the Security Council to block Communist China's admission if the General Assembly should vote to oust the Nationalists and seat Peking. The United States also agreed not to vote for Mongolia's admission; like the Nationalists, it abstained on the issue. This limited victory was further marred by concessions extracted by hard-liners on unrelated China issues. While it was a source of some satisfaction to Bowles, the battle probably was more damaging to him than it was worth. Old allegations that he was soft on Communism in general and the People's Republic in particular were trotted out by his adversaries on Capitol Hill and the press. Kennedy had little regard for those leading the charge against Bowles. But the aggressiveness of the attacks against the initiative and Bowles personally reflected the potency of the China lobby and increased the under secretary's post-Bay of Pigs vulnerability.[32]

Bowles had been interested in making Western food grain available to Communist China as early as the mid-1950s. He held that lifting the ban on grain exports, which could pave the way for further modifications in the trade embargo, could demonstrate to the Chinese and others that Washington was prepared to adopt a less hostile attitude toward Peking. He also linked it to the effort to contain the People's Republic. "Her dwindling margin of potential food expansion makes it likely that within the next ten years China may be sorely tempted to expand into the rich and relatively empty lands of Burma, Thailand, Malaya, and Sumatra," he wrote in March 1955.[33] Food supplies from the West might not only lessen Chinese propensity to move south; they could also provide an opportunity for the United States to exert leverage on Peking to modify its expansionist policies.

As under secretary, Bowles continued to stress the danger of a Chinese drive for *Lebensraum* and to urge the use of food as a means to thwart it, despite views expressed elsewhere in the department that a Peking move to seize Southeast Asian rice fields was unlikely.[34] Along with containment, he wrote the president, the principal objective in U.S. China policy in the years immediately ahead "must be to find effective methods . . . ultimately to relieve [her] food requirements and thereby to release her pent-up energy and hostility through channels other than conquest."[35] Less than three weeks after the new administration took office, he recommended that it consider offering the Chinese emergency food relief.[36] He also advocated the establishment, with American support, of an international commodity bank to provide a flow of food to the Chinese and linked this to efforts to persuade the Chinese to renounce territorial expansion.[37]

Despite the efforts of Bowles and his allies, the food initiative made little progress in 1961. The tide seemed to turn early in 1962, after Averell Harriman had replaced McConaughy as assistant secretary for Far Eastern affairs. Bowles, by then kicked upstairs to become the president's special representative and adviser on Asian, African, and

Latin American affairs (see Chapter 14), continued to play a leading role in the effort. In February 1962 he persuaded the president to authorize him to stop in Rangoon in the course of a planned Asian trip and use Burmese Premier U Nu as a friendly intermediary to pass proposals to the Chinese. According to Bowles, Kennedy had agreed with his recommendation that the United States sell a limited amount of wheat on an emergency basis without political strings and offer much larger quantities on a continuing, low-interest basis, provided China agreed to abandon its political-military pressures on its neighbors. Kennedy specified that the proposals be put as ideas that Bowles had discussed in general terms with him but which had not yet been formally approved.[38]

In one of those twists of fate which seemed to bedevil Bowles's diplomatic initiatives, the U Nu government was overthrown in a military coup the day he was scheduled to arrive in the Burmese capital. Over the next few months, neither his proposals nor those put forward by Harriman and others won administration approval. Opposition sharpened within the State Department, where the European Bureau argued that contrary to the view of Bowles and others, provision of food to China would increase, not lessen, its aggressiveness and would also prove beneficial to the Soviets. The Communists' negative reaction to an oblique but carefully worded press conference statement by Kennedy on the possibility of food supply was a further setback to proponents of the idea. By June 1962, when Rusk asserted that providing food to China would only play into Peking's hands, the initiative was dead. Other efforts Bowles supported suffered a similar fate.[39]

▾   ▾   ▾

Bowles was also an active player in administration policy toward Africa. As he had done before Kennedy took office, he continued to contend that the African continent merited high U.S. priority. Along with Assistant Secretary G. Mennen Williams, he was in the forefront of the "Africanist" group, which called for the United States to identify itself with the aspirations of the African people and to promote the independence of African territories still under the rule of colonial powers or of leaders considered European tools. The Africanists were opposed by the so-called Europeanists, who were concerned about the impact administration positions on African issues could have on U.S. ties with its European allies and were more prepared to defer to them in devising Africa policy. In the Europeanist view, relations with Western Europe had an importance that overshadowed the benefit of closer

ties with the emerging African nations or the alleged moral and domestic political advantages of helping bring about an end to colonial
or minority rule. The enthusiastic support for Africa of Bowles and
those who thought like him was ridiculed by the Europeanists. Harris
Wofford reported to Kennedy that a senior Foreign Service officer had
told him that "the trouble with Bowles and Williams was that when
they saw a band of black baboons beating tom-toms they saw George
Washingtons."[40]

Also at issue was whether and to what extent the administration
should accept nonalignment and even pro-Soviet policies practiced by
African governments rather than seek to enlist the new African states
on the side of the West. Bowles took the position that U.S. interests
would be best served by the neutralization of much of the continent
and its removal from the Cold War. "Africa," he wrote, "is too diverse
a continent, made up of too many conflicting cultures, tribal groups,
levels of development and historical psychoses to be dominated by
either the U.S.S.R or the U.S.A. We should resist the temptation to
classify Africans as 'good' or 'bad' or to place African countries into
'pro-West' and 'anti-West' categories."[41] Kennedy generally came to
accept African Cold War nonalignment, and though he sought to bring
pro-Communist Ghana into a more neutral position, he did not go
back on his decision to finance the huge Volta Dam project there (which
Bowles strongly supported) when it became evident that his efforts had
not been successful.

During much of Bowles's time in the Kennedy administration, its
focus of attention in Africa was the Congo (Leopoldville), now the
Republic of Zaire. Almost totally unprepared for independence by its
colonial Belgian masters, the huge Central African state quickly re-
lapsed into chaotic turmoil following the end of Belgian rule in June
1960. Its unity was severely threatened by secessionist movements,
most formidably in copper-rich Katanga in the south, where European
interests backed by white mercenaries supported the regime of Moïse
Tshombe.

With Adlai Stevenson and Williams, Bowles called for a firm U.S.
stand against the secessionists and their foreign backers, for whom he
had utmost contempt. (He once remarked that the mercenaries' con-
tracts no doubt provided that they were not obliged to fight anywhere
more than a thousand feet from a bar.) He was convinced that Tshombe
was widely regarded elsewhere in Africa and beyond as a quisling.
Returning from a visit to the Congo and other African countries in
late 1962 as the prolonged Katangan crisis seemed to be nearing a

climax, he urged Kennedy to provide military assistance to United Nations troops stationed in Katanga to enable them to break the back of the secession movement.[42] It was an unusual position for a man who generally was skeptical about the uses of armed force in the Third World, but as the historian Thomas J. Noer has pointed out, that was a time when "hawks became doves and doves talked like hawks."[43] Although Kennedy resisted any clear U.S. military commitment to the U.N. forces, they rapidly overcame Katangan resistance, to Bowles's great satisfaction but hardly surprise.

A second battleground between Africanists and Europeanists was U.S. policy regarding the continuing Portuguese presence in Africa. Bowles was outspoken on this issue. He wanted the administration to use its influence and resources to persuade the authoritarian Lisbon government of Antonio Salazar to give up its African colonies. He recommended that the United States and its European allies in effect buy out the Portuguese by offering to finance the modernization of their backward economy at an estimated one billion dollars on condition that Salazar agree to grant independence to the colonies within five years, possibly as part of a loose Portuguese-speaking commonwealth to include Brazil.[44] He also sought to reduce U.S. dependence on the Portuguese for the Azores air base—long an important element in Washington's, and particularly the Pentagon's, consideration of the U.S. relationship with Lisbon—by having it placed under NATO command.[45] The Kennedy administration offered the Salazar government $70 million in aid if it agreed to negotiate the eventual independence of the colonies, a paltry sum which the Portuguese leader rejected. It declined to tamper with the Azores base arrangement.

▾   ▾   ▾

Bowles also focused considerable attention on efforts to improve the organization of the foreign affairs agencies. Following the Bay of Pigs he called for the transfer of the CIA's overt intelligence gathering and intelligence assessment functions to the State Department, its paramilitary activities to the Pentagon, and its clandestine intelligence and covert operations to two separate agencies, each responsible to State for policy guidance.[46] (Kennedy eventually decided against any radical changes but cut back the agency's budget and replaced Dulles and Bissell.) Bowles's efforts to establish a new Bureau of Asian Affairs in the State Department responsible for both the Far East and South Asia, which reflected his own approach to Asian security, were similarly unsuccessful[47]. His interest in upgrading the department's Policy Planning Council led to the generation of more ideas and paper, but did not have the impact on policy he had hoped for.

He played a more successful role in the reorganization of the economic assistance operation, which led in October 1961 to the establishment of the Agency for International Development. This proved to be the most durable of what had until then been frequent new approaches in the way Washington dealt bureaucratically with foreign aid. AID, which took over the functions of several existing organizations, remains intact and under the same name more than three decades later.

Bowles helped draft Kennedy's message to Congress on the reorganization, which included many of the points he had long advocated. The new program, the president said, "should not be based merely on reaction to Communist threats or short-term crises. We have a positive interest in helping less-developed nations provide decent living standards for their people."[48] Kennedy urged that special attention be given to those countries most willing and able to mobilize their own resources, and called for the separation of economic and military assistance. The Act for International Development passed by Congress in October 1961 and still the basic legislation governing foreign economic assistance reflected this Bowlesian approach.[49]

Bowles was less successful in subsequent efforts to persuade the administration to adopt more specific criteria for economic assistance and further revamp the AID organization. Embodied in lengthy memoranda he sent the president in 1962, they were largely ignored by the White House.[50]

13

The Thanksgiving
Massacre

THE Bay of Pigs episode left Bowles upset and troubled. Aside from the body blow it dealt to his standing at the White House and the State Department—where his relations with Rusk became even more distant—it made him painfully aware of the differences he had with many of the president's other foreign policy advisers. He was alarmed by the way civilian newcomers to foreign affairs, especially those drawn from the universities, became "easy targets for the military-CIA-paramilitary answers which can be added, subtracted, multiplied or divided. . . . [These academics] operate . . . without any appearance of moral reference points whatsoever. Their whole attitude is one of proud pragmatism, and because they feel that the military people are inclined to look down at them as do-gooders and not the real elements of power, they make an effort to please them by almost outdoing the military minds in their own field." He had Walt Rostow particularly in mind.[1]

He continued to run afoul of Robert Kennedy, who called him a "gutless wonder," according to Harris Wofford, when Bowles opposed U.S. military intervention in the Dominican Republic following the assassination of longtime dictator Rafael Trujillo. The president's brother challenged the decision not to intervene made by Bowles in his capacity as acting secretary while Rusk was overseas with the president. Bowles found the attorney general's manner aggressive, dogmatic, and vicious, and made a record of what happened next: "I called [the president] in Paris and said, 'Am I acting secretary or is your brother?' He said, 'You are.' I said, 'Well, will you call your brother and let him know that?' He did." Although the attorney general ultimately backed off, the incident could not have done Bowles any good.[2]

As spring turned to summer, Bowles became increasingly concerned that the administration's opportunity to achieve major policy breakthroughs was slipping away. Less prepared than many others to view foreign policy as a mix of continuity and change, he feared that preoccupation with immediate problems had led to neglect of longer-range issues. By June, he later recalled, "I was convinced that unless the makers of American foreign policy could be persuaded to support a radical but essential shift in foreign policy, we would sooner or later be confronted with a disaster."[3]

Bowles expressed his concerns in two early July memoranda[4] in which he reiterated what had become familiar policy positions and urged greater State Department initiative in recommending actions to the president. He argued that while the administration had made substantial progress, it needed to do a great deal more. Though the increasing blurring of national and ideological identities had reduced American ability to shape events, the United States could still cushion the revolutionary new forces at loose in the world by applying its power pragmatically within a carefully defined framework of long-term goals.

He offered many suggestions. The administration needed to avoid rigid, doctrinaire approaches, and to seize and hold the initiative rather than merely respond to Soviet moves. The U.S. Information Agency and the economic assistance program should be more closely integrated within the State Department to make foreign policy operations more effective. Greater emphasis on the preparation of anticipatory crisis management papers could avoid the haphazard and emotional response to problems typified in the Bay of Pigs episode.

> [But] the danger [he concluded in his July 5 memo to Rusk] does not stem from our lack of knowledge or of experience. . . . Rather it comes from the failure of our colleagues both inside and outside the State Department to grasp the depth and power of the forces which are shaping history, from a readiness on occasion to sacrifice moral concepts of universal acceptance for a shallow "realism," from our failure as a rich, white and comfortable people to fully appreciate the feelings of the two-thirds of the world's people who are colored, poor, bitter and determined, and our inclination to postpone or reject critically important policies on the assumption that the American people are not quite ready to support what must be done, and that ugly critical speeches will be made on Capitol Hill.

If Bowles had any hope or expectation that his two long memos would have a positive impact on the secretary and help move policy and departmental organization in the direction he recommended, they were shattered—as was Bowles himself—when Rusk suggested to him when they lunched alone on July 6 that he become a roving ambassador. The proposal came as a complete surprise to Bowles. He reacted in stunned disbelief, finally managing to tell Rusk that he thought he could do the most good where he was.

That ended the discussion but not the problem. Over the next ten days, Bowles was attacked in several newspapers and magazines, the first major press criticism of him since comment on his Bay of Pigs role. *Newsweek* reported that there was a good deal of sniping at Bowles within the State Department. *U.S. News & World Report* alleged that Rusk was outraged by Bowles's end runs to the White House. (The secretary denied the report, but no retraction was ever printed.) Criticism of his performance by several influential columnists followed. Among them were Charles Bartlett and Joseph Alsop, whose close ties to Kennedy led many to conclude that their stories had been inspired by the White House. As James Thomson reported to Bowles, the articles had common themes: the under secretary's job should be that of chief-of-staff; Bowles was miscast in the under secretary's role; he was responsible for various forms of disarray; and he should be transferred to another assignment, preferably as a roving ambassador to underdeveloped countries. They referred to Foreign Service discontent, State Department "drift," and White House dissatisfaction, and termed the transfer of Bowles the logical solution to those problems.[5]

While this press onslaught was going on, Bowles met again with Rusk. The secretary pressed him to take the roving ambassador position or an embassy in Latin America and acknowledged that the idea had been Kennedy's. When Bowles lunched with the president the next day, Kennedy said, according to Bowles's unconfirmed account, that "he had often thought he had made a mistake in not making me Secretary of State instead of Rusk and that if he had done so things might have been different. However, Rusk was Secretary of State and he [Kennedy] was most unhappy because the State Department had not come up with the vigorous new policy approaches to the world which he had wanted. He said this was not my fault, but that some change had to be made, that I was the most likely candidate, and how would I like to go to Chile." Bowles said he expressed his surprise, spoke of his own unhappiness with the department's performance, and turned down the embassy offer.[6]

Arthur Schlesinger has recalled that he too was in touch with Bowles at Kennedy's instruction to suggest to him that he become ambassador to Brazil. Earlier Schlesinger had recommended that Kennedy tell Bowles he wanted George Ball to take over the administration of the department, with Bowles to focus on foreign and domestic persuasion, policy planning, and personnel, a suggestion he thought Bowles would welcome. According to Schlesinger, the president had replied that the idea wouldn't work and would only prolong the confusion and agony. Schlesinger has written that when he broached the Brazil assignment, Bowles had turned it down, saying he would do everything he could to make his departure from the State Department as graceful as possible.[7]

On July 17 the *New York Times* predicted in a front page article that when Kennedy met Bowles later that day he would ask him to resign and accept an ambassadorship in Latin America. Urged by his supporters to fight back, Bowles and his close colleagues had by then launched a counterattack. Articles critical of him were matched by friendly columns filed by liberal commentators. Political friends also weighed in. Adlai Stevenson, traveling in Italy, urged the president to keep Bowles on. Bowles's dismissal, Stevenson cabled, "might be disturbing to friendly people abroad and at home who believe [Bowles] has been right and has tried to introduce new people and attitudes in the department after the long Dulles regime."[8] At the White House, Harris Wofford contended in an eloquent memo to the president that dropping Bowles would damage U.S. standing in the Third World and hurt the administration with liberals at home. Bowles's ability to articulate foreign policy positions was an important asset and he should be encouraged to use his talents primarily in the field of ideas, policy planning, and personnel selection.[9] On the Senate floor, Joseph Clark, a liberal Pennsylvania Democrat close to Bowles, gave a strong speech systematically defending the embattled under secretary against the array of press charges and castigating those who had spread them.[10]

According to Bowles, when he met with the president, Kennedy once more urged him to take an embassy. Bowles rejected the idea and said that he intended to stay where he was until the president removed him. Kennedy eventually agreed to make a statement saying that Bowles was staying on and that the situation remained unchanged. He suggested that they review the situation after Labor Day, when Bowles had completed planned travel to Africa, the Middle East, and Asia.[11]

Reporting the following day that Bowles would remain under secretary, the *New York Times* stated that "the President has put off a change in the high command of the State Department that important administration sources believe to be inevitable."[12] Similar reports appeared in the *Washington Post* and the *Washington Star.* Offhand remarks by Presidential Press Secretary Pierre Salinger and Kennedy's ambiguous responses at his next press conference reinforced the view that Bowles had only been given a reprieve. Later recollections by those with whom the president spoke at the time support this conclusion. Senior White House staffer John Sharon remembered that Kennedy had been angered by the way Bowles had enlisted support to save himself. According to Sharon, who had put in a good word for Bowles, "[Kennedy] thought I was part of a great conspiracy that was campaigning for Chester Bowles's retention, and that he didn't appreciate at all the fact that there was this great campaign to keep Chester Bowles in the Administration."[13] Kennedy had also talked about the liberal outcry with *Time* editor Hugh Sidey. "What it did in my estimation," Sidey said, "was just solidify his determination to move [Bowles], because he ended that conversation . . . and said very casually, 'Bowles will go,' or 'He'll go.'. . . .There was such finality in that that I never had a doubt."[14] Bowles has written that he was satisfied with the president's press conference statement, though he must have recognized that it represented only a limited commitment. On a trip approved by Kennedy, he headed overseas to convoke regional meetings of senior American diplomats in Nigeria, Cyprus, and India.

Such sessions were useful both to the high-ranking Washington-based officials who traveled out to them and to the ambassadors and other Americans in the field who gathered to exchange views with the visitors. For Bowles, they provided both a forum to inform and inspire embassy staffers about the administration's new approach to foreign policy (as he chose to define it) and a welcome relief from the poisoned atmosphere of Washington. He was pleased with the exchanges and the warm reception the participants gave him. The travel was also an opportunity to meet with local leaders, hold press conferences, and address foreign audiences, no doubt a balm to him when he most needed it. But there was also a down side. Looking for ways to damage him further, Bowles's critics complained that the meetings were ego-satisfying junkets not worth the considerable bite they took out of the department's budget.

Both before and after his overseas travel Bowles sought to repair his links with Kennedy. Recognizing that his earlier diffidence had been a tactical blunder, he tried to involve the president personally in the reorganization of the State Department and raised with him for the first time his differences with Rusk over how the department should be run. His focus as always was on personnel. He was prepared to undertake the reorganization himself, he told Kennedy, but if the president preferred to have someone else do this he and George Ball could rearrange their responsibilities: "Once the right individuals have been selected and installed in key bureaus where our principal difficulties lie I would be in a position to divert a sizeable amount of my time to special policy problems in the Middle East, Southeast Asia, Northeastern Brazil, and elsewhere. I would also have time for more travel and for the essential task of explaining your policies in key nations abroad."[15] These efforts to work more closely with Kennedy were not successful. Instead, Bowles's relations with the president and key White House staffers became more tenuous during his last months as under secretary.

He also sought once again to define with Rusk his areas of responsibility. The secretary suggested to him in mid-August that he concentrate more on longer-range policy questions, overseas travel (particularly in connection with policies and operations in the developing world), public speaking in the United States, and high-level personnel and administration. In early September, Bowles recalled, Rusk assigned him these responsibilities. More of the cable and memo traffic on immediate problems was moved to George Ball. But the secretary was unwilling to announce the new delegation of authority, demurring on grounds that the timing was not right while the press was still discussing the difficulties of July. Bowles had told Stevenson earlier that he was doubtful about Rusk's willingness to establish clear lines of responsibility and skeptical about how the proposed changes would work out in day-to-day operations. As Rusk failed to move definitively, Bowles became increasingly concerned.[16]

Bowles was away much of late October and early November in connection with other regional conferences in Asia and Latin America. This complicated his efforts to work out his differences with Rusk and further divorced him from policymaking. In these difficult times, he was heartened by a report issued by the Senate Committee on Government Operations chaired by Senator Henry Jackson of Washington, which charged that the State Department was not doing enough to assert its foreign policy leadership and merely reacted to foreign policy problems as they arose. The committee concluded that the department needed good executive managers who were broadly experienced in dealing with the full range of national security problems. "This need for 'take charge' men is particularly urgent down through the Assistant Secretary level and at our large missions abroad. Round pegs in square holes are a luxury we cannot afford."[17]

Much of this was music to Bowles's ears. He resumed his effort to remove perceived round pegs, especially Assistant Secretary for Europe Foy Kohler and his opposite number in the Far Eastern Bureau, Walter

McConaughy. Bowles wanted Kohler replaced by George McGhee. His candidate to succeed McConaughy remained Averell Harriman. Rusk would not move on either recommendation.

▾   ▾   ▾

A few days after this unsuccessful effort, Bowles went to Connecticut for the Thanksgiving weekend and the Harvard-Yale football game, an annual fixture for a loyal Eli. On Saturday morning, Rusk phoned from Washington to ask him to return the following day. Mystified by the urgency of the request, Bowles reluctantly agreed. When he met with Rusk on Sunday, November 26, the secretary handed him a press statement announcing a series of major changes in the State Department. Bowles himself was to leave his post as under secretary to become roving ambassador in place of Harriman. The changes were to be announced within a few hours.[18]

Shocked and angered, Bowles said that he needed time to talk with Steb and his friends. Rusk then called Ted Sorensen, whom Kennedy, fearful that Bowles might resign in an uproar, had asked to stand by to hold Bowles's hand "as one 'liberal' to another." Sorensen came to the department. His account of his meeting with Bowles is poignant: "In the all-but-empty new State Department Building I found Bowles sitting disconsolate and alone in his office. He was hurt and angry at Kennedy, at Rusk and at the world. He had no intention of taking any post. He had his pride and his convictions, he said. He had been loyal and received no loyalty in return. He would resign and speak his mind."[19]

Bowles recorded that in their talk, "Sorensen used every device which a person in his position could be expected to use, from flattery to threat. The threat was that if I dropped out [and did not accept the roving ambassador offer], the charge would be made that I had failed to carry out my responsibilities." Bowles persisted in refusing the offer, but said that if Sorensen cared to discuss broader possibilities with the president, he would be glad to talk to him after conferring with his wife and others. Sorensen then phoned Kennedy, who agreed and said they would have a proposal together within twenty-four hours.[20] This eventually led to an offer of a position as the president's "special representative and adviser for Asian, African, and Latin-American affairs," where Bowles would be part of the White House team and report directly to Kennedy.

On hearing on the radio about the changes, Steb Bowles chartered a plane and flew from Connecticut to Washington. After anguished discussions with her and old associates at Abram Chayes's house in Georgetown, and negotiations over terms with Sorensen, Bowles accepted the offer.

▾   ▾   ▾

In July, *New York Times* columnist Arthur Krock had forecast correctly that "the next time the President decides to transfer Chester A.[*sic*] Bowles to a job more suitable to his considerable talents than that of under secretary of state, Mr. Kennedy will see to it that his inner advisory circle does not furnish advance billing."[21] In contrast to the premature disclosures of the summer, the White House had closely held word of what came to be called the Thanksgiving Massacre until it could be announced as a *fait accompli*. As Attorney General Kennedy later put it, "And then the President snuck up on him one day and got him fired before he knew it."[22] Bowles and his supporters had no opportunity to mount another counterattack. The administration had also limited the possibility of negative fallout to Bowles's ouster by making it part of a larger package that could be represented as general stock-taking and house-cleaning. The fact that the package included several appointments attractive to liberals such as the choice of Averell Harriman as assistant secretary for Far Eastern affairs, long recommended by Bowles, and the promotion of George Ball, a close associate of Adlai Stevenson, as Bowles's replacement further protected the administration against any repetition of the July outcry.

However packaged, Bowles's ouster in November reflected the same considerations that had led to the earlier effort to remove him. The strong feeling shared by the president and others at the White House that the State Department was not functioning properly and that its leadership needed overhauling contributed a great deal to the decision to sack him. Since the dismissal of Rusk so early in the administration would have suggested a serious error on Kennedy's part in appointing him secretary, Bowles became a natural target, especially because Kennedy saw him as a man who did not have the management skills and interest needed to move the department in the right direction. By contrast, George Ball, the new under secretary, had the reputation in the White House as someone who got things done.

But the perception of Bowles as a failed manager who would be better off somewhere else where he could spend his time thinking creatively or exchanging views with Third World leaders was only part of the story. The differences of personality, interests, and opinions he had with the president and others in the administration very probably

also played a role in his dismissal. They limited his standing and
influence at the White House and made him more vulnerable to the
array of enemies he had in Washington, including some close to Kennedy. Hard-line cold warriors like Joseph Alsop used their access to
the president to deride Bowles contemptuously as a bleeding heart who
advocated silly notions about the Third World and was soft on Communism. Dean Acheson aired his similarly harsh views in acid, witty,
and widely circulated comments. Senior State Department career
officers regaled their journalist friends at the Metropolitan Club and
elsewhere with tales about the way Bowles was ruining the Foreign
Service. Among the officers were such well-known people as "Mr.
Foreign Service" Loy Henderson, who had preceded Bowles as ambassador to India and was in charge of State Department personnel in the
last Eisenhower years. Aside from the damage such criticism inflicted
on Bowles, it may also have suggested to the president that if he wanted
to send a signal of his determination to be tough in a threatening world,
dismissal of his controversial, highly visible, "soft-line" under secretary
of state might be a good way to do it.

However, for all the problems Bowles had, or was perceived to have,
he probably would not have been dismissed had it not been for the
role he played in the Bay of Pigs episode. The event crystallized the
sense that he was less than totally loyal to the Kennedys and too ready
to offer his own views to the media and others to benefit himself. It
poisoned his relationship with Robert Kennedy; Wofford, close to both
men, has said that Bowles's role in the affair led the attorney general,
infuriated by Bowles's lack of anti-Castro militancy, to call for his
ouster.[23] Because it had obviously wounded him, the episode probably
prompted Bowles's adversaries to heighten their effort to discredit him
with the president. It worsened his relationship with Rusk and others
in the department, lessening his effectiveness there. If the Bay of Pigs
had not occurred, Bowles might well have been able to carry on as a
figure of limited influence until he had himself concluded that no
further purpose was served by his staying on in the administration.

Rusk generally shares this view. Looking back in 1991 at what had
obviously been a difficult experience for him, he stated that the decision
to dismiss Bowles was taken at presidential initiative and characterized
himself as the instrument who got the word to him. Rusk had found
this painful. He held that the decision to name Bowles had been a
mistake. He had not been a good under secretary. Even so, Rusk
maintained, Bowles was more of a plus than a minus in the position:
there were more good points about him than bad. He minimized the

policy differences he had had with Bowles and spoke of him warmly
as a person. No one, he said, was more disappointed than he that
Bowles had been unsuccessful. (Bowles seems to have been aware of
Rusk's sentiments. In an oral history interview in 1970, he said that
"I think that [Rusk] was genuinely distressed about his relationship
with me, because we had been good friends. And I think he's been
unhappy about the way it worked out.")[24]

Bowles's principal problem, Rusk asserted, was that he was an idea
man who would not get the day's work done. You can't run the State
Department unless the number two man reads and okays messages, he
said. He termed Bowles a "backlog man"—papers had to be blasted
out of his desk. Asked if he had ever discussed the problem with
Bowles, Rusk replied that he had mentioned to him specific problems
which needed action but had not generalized. He added, however, that
the backlog problem could have been dealt with over time. In his view,
too, the Bay of Pigs had been the major turning point in Kennedy's
(and his own) relationship with Bowles. He believed that absent that
episode Bowles "would have stayed on for quite a period."

Bowles later spelled out the difference he had with Rusk in *Promises
to Keep*. He and Rusk turned out to be poles apart. The secretary's
foreign policy ideas had been shaped by the early years of the Cold
War, and "although . . . he tried to take a less rigid view, he never
succeeded in seeing any international conflict in terms other than those
of the Cold War." Moreover, "he seemed to accept the vast and often
rigid State Department bureaucracy as a fact of life beyond his and my
capacity to change. His energies and efforts were invariably directed
at the problems that were presently on his desk, with little evidence of
concern about how and why they arose in the first place." Bowles
added, however, that "no man in public life . . . worked harder to meet
his responsibilities as he saw them" than Rusk did, and "if he was
wrong on Vietnam and other issues, . . . his conclusions were reached
in good faith."[25]

Characteristically, he was much tougher on Rusk in his private
discussions and writings than he was in his published comments. He
often complained to colleagues about the secretary's willingness to
adopt military solutions to deal with political problems and his undue
preoccupation with the confrontation with the Communist powers. In
a note Bowles prepared in early January 1962, when the bitterness of
his dismissal was still fresh, he found that Rusk had no sense of
administration, only an obsession with procedures. The secretary's
effectiveness was weakened by a blind respect for "the Service." Al-

though he had "an intellectual awareness of the political forces shaping events, he was almost totally insensitive to human factors." There was "no real quality of sophistication in Rusk's day to day reaction to events," which was often dominated by quick irritation with the Titos and Krishna Menons of the world.

When the chips are down and frustrations run high, Bowles asserted, Rusk is likely to come down in favor of the "Old World," though his excellent mind covered up this fundamental bias in situations not subject to emotional stress. "Because he has no clear commitment to any set of principles, he invariably avoids a potentially unpopular position. This was due partly to his own insecurity and partly because he rarely believes very deeply in whatever program may be at stake." Rusk, Bowles concluded, "is basically cynical."[26]

▾   ▾   ▾

For Bowles, the ten months as under secretary had been a frustrating time. Over the preceding decade—as ambassador to India, Democratic foreign affairs spokesman, congressman, and party Platform Committee chairman—he had advocated foreign policy approaches which he believed would make the world a better place for ordinary people and hence more congenial to the real interests and historic spirit of America. He had persuaded himself that Kennedy shared his views, or at least that as president he could be brought to accept them. Although disappointed that he had not been made secretary of state, he had accepted the deputy's role and had tackled it with the urgency, dedication, and enthusiasm he characteristically brought to his activities.

To his chagrin and further disappointment, Bowles had found that the walls of the old foreign policy had not easily tumbled down and, indeed, that despite his efforts they continued to be manned by many of the same guardians who had kept watch before. The urgency he felt in changing policies to reflect what he had heralded as the political breakthrough of 1960 was not fully shared by the president, let alone by the secretary and the senior Foreign Service officers Rusk preferred for high department positions. Instead of the new dispensation he had preached, he found that many of the old Cold War ways continued, and that preoccupation with immediate problems often crippled efforts to understand long-term developments and bring these to bear in policy formulation.

Despite his mounting impatience, Bowles had been unprepared either to quit or to adjust to the realities of Rusk's leadership of the department. Instead, he continued to urge, from within, the foreign policy approach he believed in, and to seek to bring like-minded people into key positions where they could help him change things. Severely handicapped by his bureaucratic failings and the administration's widely shared sense that he was a visionary unable to deal with the here and now, he had limited success in bringing about the policy transformation he sought.

His dismissal was a personal tragedy for this ambitious and sensitive man. Over the previous thirty years he had served with distinction in a succession of widely differing positions and had left his mark on all of them. He had repeatedly demonstrated that he could deal effectively with fresh and unfamiliar challenges. In 1960 his standing was such that he could be reasonably touted as a dark horse candidate for president and could hope to become secretary of state. Yet as under secretary he had failed—for the first time in his life—to tackle a job successfully. By the end of 1961 he was being forced out of the State Department by the liberal Democratic administration on which he had pinned his hopes for needed foreign policy change. For someone who had believed that there was so much to do, and who had been confident that he could play a major role in doing it, ouster was a bitter and unfamiliar pill. And though he and Kennedy tried to sugar-coat that pill with a new, eventually meaningless appointment, it was difficult for Bowles to swallow. Bowles's accomplishments did not end when he left the State Department, but it would not be too harsh a judgment to call the rest of his public life an anticlimax.

14

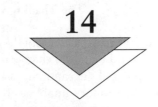

Inconsequential
Interlude

BOWLES'S responsibilities were spelled out in a memorandum of understanding obviously designed to make his new job look like a key foreign policy position. He was to report directly to Kennedy and Rusk on policy, long-range planning, and operations in the developing countries; promote the administration's foreign policies at home and abroad; and carry out specific missions for the president. The visual signs of office—ambassadorial rank, a White House car, and a salary boost—matched this impressive job description. The memorandum and an accompanying press release characterized Kennedy as delighted to have Bowles devote his full time and attention to his new and greater responsibilities in an area the president considered "second to none" in importance. A big White House swearing-in ceremony attended by Kennedy and all the foreign policy heavyweights in his administration was staged to underscore the seriousness of Bowles's new role.[1]

It is doubtful that many were taken in. Bowles certainly was not. He did not take the memorandum of understanding at face value even though he had helped draft it in lengthy negotiations with Sorensen. Kennedy tried to reassure him and told him, when Bowles raised the issue, that the difference in their personal styles posed no problem. Sorensen, exaggerating wildly, called the new job the Harry Hopkins slot in the Kennedy administration. Bowles remained skeptical and had strong reservations about his ability to work effectively with the president in what he recognized would be a "gadfly operation."[2]

Why did he take the job? Like his willingness to become deputy to Rusk, his acceptance of this appointment reflected Bowles's limited options. He had pretty well burned his bridges to Connecticut politics, and the only other feasible course if he wished to remain active was to resume his commentator's role of the 1950s, this time as a critic of his own party's conduct of foreign affairs. He was not prepared to do this. He had invested too much political and emotional capital in the Kennedy administration, and in his optimistic way continued to hope that he could help lead it to adopt the policies he favored. He probably recognized too that criticism of policy from outside the administration would make him seem a sorehead and be ineffective.

Despite his misgivings, Bowles tried to make the best of what he knew was an unpromising situation. The preoccupation of many of Kennedy's principal foreign policy advisers with Europe and Cuba led him to hope that he would find opportunities to shape policy on his Third World beat. Although neither the White House nor the State Department gave him specific assignments, he tried hard to carve out a role for himself as a policymaker, foreign policy spokesman, and, in effect, management consultant. His strategy, he said, was "to prepare a series of hard-hitting, direct memoranda dealing with specific situations in which our policies appear unrealistic, antiquated, or irrelevant; to develop precise recommendations of what to do in these situations and then to follow through regardless of the toes which almost inevitably will be stepped on."[3]

Bowles did all he could to carry out this strategy through extensive travel and seemingly relentless preparation of policy recommendations. It didn't work. As he had feared, his influence was limited during the year and more he was special representative. He was not a regular participant at meetings at which the major players thrashed out key decisions; and although his staff arranged for him to be cut in on important and sensitive cable traffic, he found himself even more excluded from the policymaking process than he had been as under secretary. The suite of offices he was given at the White House—a perquisite he had insisted on in his negotiations with Sorensen—did not give him the access he wanted to Kennedy, and he never became one of the President's Men despite earlier assurances.

Finding himself isolated in that unfriendly setting, he came to spend most of his time lodged rather ignominiously in a small room down a State Department corridor from the grandiose office where he had held forth as under secretary. While his travel abroad was useful in providing opportunities for contact and insight, especially since the farther he got from Washington the more important his title seemed to his interlocutors, it kept him even farther out of the loop. Rusk later called the job a makeshift appointment and the year which followed an inconsequential time for Bowles, almost a blank period in his life. "He was not in a position where he had any real authority so what he said didn't amount to much."[4]

▾   ▾   ▾

The policies Bowles recommended as special representative were for the most part updates of positions he had called for at the State Department and reflected the same premises, prejudices, and objectives as his earlier recommendations. His efforts to influence administration policy on China and Africa and his suggestions on the organization of the foreign affairs agencies were obvious continuations of the campaigns he had launched as Rusk's deputy. Among the other items on his agenda as special representative were a major initiative to change policy on Vietnam, and suggestions on relations with Pakistan and India that would recast significantly the U.S. approach to South Asia.

Bowles's recommendations for a change in Southeast Asia policy focused on a call for a "Peace Charter" for the region, which he suggested the president spell out in a major address. The proposed charter was to include guarantees by the great powers of the sovereignty, independence, and territorial integrity of the Southeast Asian nations following termination of guerrilla warfare, plus economic inducements, such as the development (with substantial American financial input) of the Lower Mekong River basin. He recommended that he be authorized to head a mission to meet with leaders in the region to win their support.[5]

His proposals were dismissed as impractical by Averell Harriman on the grounds that their implementation would require the United States to make international commitments without any assurance that the other side would do the same and with no workable enforcement procedures.[6] The Far East Bureau, which Harriman headed, also contended that the North Vietnamese government had not yet been given adequate incentive to call off its aggression in South Vietnam. In the bureau's view, it was this aggression that remained "the hard obstacle to the realization of our good intentions toward Southeast Asia."[7] In rebuttal Bowles pointed out that the chances for a clear-cut Saigon government victory in South Vietnam were no better than fifty-fifty. Under those circumstances the United States might be forced within the next year or so to choose between committing more and more American troops to what the president's political opponents would describe as "another Democratic war" or withdrawing in embarrassed frustration.[8] His pleas were to no avail.

All the while Bowles failed to deal with the fundamental flaw his critics had identified in his approach. The concept of the neutralization of Southeast Asia he laid out was a laudable goal, but it left unresolved the problem of the ongoing revolution and war in Vietnam. It was the war that polarized the region among the major powers and led to the increasing U.S. concern and involvement there. Bowles had no feasible proposal for ending it. The neutralization idea was thus not a plan but a lofty concept which lacked any mechanism for realistic implementation. His projected mission to Southeast Asia might have proved a salutary experience for him, but it would have failed.

Bowles's visit to South Asia in early 1962 led him to develop yet another strategy designed to undo the U.S. security relationship with Pakistan. He proposed that the administration force the Ayub government to agree formally that the purpose of the U.S.-Pakistan alliance was the containment of Communism—the U.S. objective in recruiting Pakistan into the Western alliance system—not the balancing of military power between India and Pakistan, which had been Pakistan's principal motive for signing on. To avoid misunderstanding, the two governments would formally spell out the aims, guarantees, and limitations of the alliance with regard to China, the Soviet Union, India, and Afghanistan. Bowles no doubt hoped that his proposal to strip away the ambiguity and uncertainty that had always surrounded the U.S.-Pakistan security relationship would lead to its breakdown.[9]

The Kennedy administration did not want this. Its conviction that the nonaligned countries could play a useful and important role in containing Communism was a major tenet in its Third World policy, and it was more interested than the Eisenhower administration had been in developing a strong relationship with nonaligned India. But it did not wish to dismantle the alliance structure that Dulles had developed. The Kennedy administration saw continuing value in the U.S.-Pakistan relationship and in early 1962 was making progress in restoring this to a reasonably even keel, after the dismay voiced in Pakistan by the efforts it had made during its first year in office to bolster U.S.-Indian ties. Kennedy was prepared to live with ambiguity, as Eisenhower had, and reckoned that a continuing security relationship with Pakistan need not inhibit progress in strengthening ties with the Nehru government. Bowles or others could produce no convincing evidence at that time to prompt the administration to conclude otherwise.

Bowles had been out of the country in the fall of 1962 when the eruption of severe fighting on the Sino-Indian border and the subsequent rout of the Indian army there profoundly affected the South Asian political equations as well as the prospects for a changed U.S. role in the region. He weighed in in a major way only in December, on the eve of President Kennedy's meeting with British Prime Minister Harold Macmillan at Nassau, where the two leaders were to consider policy toward India following the unexpected unilateral Chinese cease-fire and the withdrawal of Chinese troops from territory they had seized. The United States, Bowles recommended, should "pledge [its] efforts to the military defense of India against Chinese aggression provided the Indians accept the fact of Chinese expansionism in Asia as a common danger which requires both political and military discussions and ultimately cooperation."[10] Dubious on the basis of his past experience in India about the prospects of an India-Pakistan agreement on Kashmir, which Washington and London were then pressing, he suggested to the president that the administration should continue to urge a resolution of the dispute but avoid making aid to India dependent on a settlement.

Both the idea of a broader Indian role against the Chinese and the call for a more relaxed U.S. approach to Kashmir were hoary themes for Bowles, of course. He had continued to voice them as under secretary: one example already noted was his suggestion, at the time of Nehru's November 1961 visit to the United States, that Kennedy raise with the prime minister the possibility of an Indian role in an arrangement designed to guarantee the neutrality and independence of Southeast Asia against the threat of Chinese aggression. Like his proposals concerning Pakistan, Bowles's resurrection of his ideas on India at the end of 1962 are significant primarily as a preview of the major effort he would make to reformulate policy toward South Asia when he returned to New Delhi as ambassador in July 1963.

▾   ▾   ▾

Bowles eventually recognized the futility of his position as special representative. Privately (and accurately) he complained in October that his recommendations had made very little impression and concluded that "it was becoming obvious that my position at some point would prove to be impossible."[11] In December, after he had been on the job for a year, he decided to quit. His decision was hastened by Kennedy's unwillingness to defend Adlai Stevenson against allegations of softness during the Cuban missile crisis the previous month, which Bowles saw, probably wrongly, as evidence that the president was prepared to countenance, if not encourage, the departure of foreign policy liberals from the administration. (Bowles was in Africa during the crisis. It is most unlikely, in light of administration attitudes toward him, that he would have been asked to participate in the executive committee deliberations had he been in Washington at the time.)

In his letter of resignation, Bowles reflected on the ineffective role he had played despite his own earlier hopes and the president's assurances:

> I do not know how many of [my specific policy] recommendations ever reached your desk. However, there is little evidence that they received anything but the most cursory attention from your immediate advisors, who have been largely absorbed by the problems of Europe, the USSR and Cuba.
>
> While it is true that a number of these recommendations were eventually put into effect, this occurred only belatedly and haphazardly, less as a result of forewarnings than as adjustment to the pressure of crises which could have been eased or averted by more timely actions. As a rule, we have passed up numerous opportunities to take the initiative and shape the course of events—rather than be controlled by them. . . .
>
> There is still plenty for *someone* to do in Asia, Africa, and Latin America, and I would much rather work toward these objectives, which I believe you and I still share, as a member of your Administration than as an outsider. But, if there is no way I can more effectively bring my experience to bear in this context, there seems to be no alternative but to continue to work outside the Administration for the policies which I have been advocating for years.[12]

The president persuaded Bowles to hold off his resignation until the two of them had a further opportunity after Christmas to consider the situation. The imbroglio over Stevenson, which had earlier hastened his decision to resign, now led Bowles to delay it. He wrote later that although his instinct was to press the president, he decided not to do so because his resignation would have added to the difficulties Kennedy faced at that point over the unanswered accusations about Adlai.

While he was waiting for another session with the president, Bowles drafted a long letter to him in which he spoke of the curiously paradoxical situation the administration faced on foreign policy. He decided not to send it but instead to make the points orally since he thought it was not the kind of message Kennedy took easily.

The draft is worth noting for Bowles's assessment of the international situation as he prepared to move on. Beginning on a very upbeat note, he cited as promising developments the near-breakdown of Sino-Soviet relations, the virtual elimination of Soviet footholds in Guinea and the

Congo, "neutralist" India at war with Communist China, improved Egyptian policies, relaxation of Soviet pressure on Berlin, the Communists' need to build the wall there, the reduction of Moscow's military commitment to Cuba, the undermining of Communist influence throughout Latin America, and Khrushchev's "hoisting signals, however tentative, that indicate a desire for a bettering of U.S.-Soviet relations." But having lauded the president, he made it clear once again that more was needed: "Yet instead of seeing the growth of a national consensus rooted in these [advances], we are now encountering mounting pressures from individuals with great influence inside and outside of government to shift away from this successful approach."[13]

Bowles said he was profoundly disturbed by this hard-line challenge, particularly because the new year, 1963, might be Kennedy's last effective opportunity to forge a national foreign policy consensus before controversial issues became caught up in election rhetoric and maneuver. It was important that the president act promptly. By doing so, he could place himself in a strong position for the 1964 campaign and win a wider foreign policy mandate for his second term, the mandate that Kennedy told Bowles he did not have when Bowles urged fresh policy initiatives on China and elsewhere.

When Bowles met again with the president in January 1963, Kennedy did not again urge him to stay on as special representative. Instead, in yet another strange twist in Bowles's unusual career, he asked him if he would like to return to India as ambassador when John Kennedy Galbraith left New Delhi later in the year.

15

"Chester Bowls Again"

THE offer of a second assignment in New Delhi came as no surprise to Bowles. Although he had thought it more likely that the president would again ask him to head the Alliance for Progress, he knew that Kennedy considered him well suited personally and professionally for a Third World ambassadorship. Galbraith's leave of absence from Harvard was ending, and Bowles no doubt reckoned that the president would want to replace him with a strong appointee who would be well received by the Indians.

Bowles recalled in later years that the most persuasive argument for returning to India was the opportunity to develop a fresh and more realistic approach to U.S.-Indian relations following the 1962 Sino-Indian War and the deterioration of ties between China and the Soviet Union. These events had already produced major changes in the way Washington and New Delhi viewed one another, and Bowles was strongly drawn by the prospect of playing a key role in helping move them further in directions he had long advocated. Although his earlier experiences made him question how much he would be able to influence the administration, he concluded that as ambassador he would have more clout than he had had in Washington. "Cables from overseas often had a far greater impact on the White House and the State Department than even the most carefully prepared high-level interdepartmental memoranda." (This was wishful thinking. The persuasive power of a cable depends critically on the standing in Washington of the ambassador who drafts it. As Bowles found out to his disappointment later, his telegrams had no more impact on policy than had his earlier memos.) His interest in returning was quickened by the prospect of working again with Indian leaders he had known well in his first New Delhi incarnation. Remembrances of his personal happiness and highly regarded professional effectiveness also contributed to his decision, helping to balance the uneasiness he felt in deserting the liberal cause at home when it seemed to him to need all the assistance it could get.[1]

These recollections differed somewhat from the ones Bowles recorded at the time, when he was bitterly aware of his ineffectual role as special representative. He wrote in January 1963 that it would be good

> to get into an atmosphere where the situation is basically sympathetic and productive of some degree of confidence. . . . Two years [sic] in India would probably greatly improve my own position in the country as I would have access to the press, TV, Congress, etc., to reestablish my reputation which has been damaged by attacks levelled at me. In two years I will be able to return to the United States perhaps in a far better personal mood and in a position perhaps to move into some major role in the Administration and possibly be of some major influence in Kennedy's second term.[2]

Conspicuously missing from Bowles's written observations both in early 1963 and later, but surely not from his thinking when he contemplated Kennedy's offer, was a consideration by then only too familiar in his life in public affairs: the absence of viable alternatives. As in July 1958, December 1960, and November 1961, his choice was either to accept the position offered him or live as an outsider in Essex. His decision was made easier, as it had been at those earlier turning points, by his capacity to put the best gloss on events and to persuade himself that in his lesser role he would still be able to make an important contribution.

▾   ▾   ▾

Bowles waited until mid-February before responding to Kennedy's offer. He would accept, he told Kennedy, only if there was a reasonable prospect that his efforts in India would be effective. This depended, he said, on future American policy, the extent of his authority to recruit senior mission officials and direct the operations of all U.S. government agencies in India, the interpretation given to his appointment, and his ability to communicate with the president on matters not directly related to his assignment. Expressing once again his conviction that the United States had a historic opportunity to establish a close working relationship with India, he maintained that "unless there is a deeply rooted and clearly understood consensus on U.S. objectives and priorities in India and South Asia . . . shared by the New Delhi Mission and . . . Washington, I am clearly not the right man to represent the United States in India."[3]

The president seems to have had no difficulty with these conditions nor with Bowles's other terms. Bowles found his response forthright and reassuring but continued to have grave doubts about the support he could expect from Dean Rusk, whose expressions of exasperation with India's policies and skepticism about India's value to American interests had rankled him when the two had worked together at State. When Bowles raised his misgivings directly with Rusk, the secretary suggested that he outline the policies toward India and the rest of Asia he would advocate. The memorandum Bowles subsequently prepared covered familiar ground in stressing India's economic requirements, its primary role in South Asia, and its potential for working with other major Asian nations to develop a stable regional balance. According to Bowles, Kennedy agreed with his assessment and promised full support. He found Rusk less certain.[4]

Kennedy announced his intention to nominate Bowles in a warmly worded statement:

> No American has a deeper understanding of India and Asia. . . . India is engaged in a difficult, long-term struggle to preserve its independence and its democratic institutions. . . . I am therefore delighted that Mr. Bowles is willing to undertake this assignment. He has been a devoted, articulate, energetic public servant for over 20 years and he has served this Administration with particular effectiveness in our relations with less-developed continents.[5]

Bowles's confirmation sailed through easily, in contrast to the difficulties he had experienced in 1951, when Senator Taft had marshaled Republican opposition to his nomination. As Senator George Aiken of Vermont observed, this time with unconscious irony, "It takes a particular type of person to represent us in India and Bowles got along pretty well before."[6]

The nomination moved James Reston to make an incisive assessment of "the odd political record of Chester Bowles." Reston found that wherever Bowles went he left a trail of controversy, mainly because he was out of step with the political fashions of the day. "He is a talker among doers, a yearner among the cool-cats, a liberal among moderates, and an optimist among pessimists. His style and tempo are more in keeping with the New Deal than with the New Frontier. He not only thinks about things, which is bad enough here, but says what he thinks, which in this town is unforgivable. . . . Bowles," Reston concluded, "is simply a casualty of the Washington atmosphere, which is more a criticism of Washington than of Bowles."[7]

▾   ▾   ▾

The Bowleses returned to New Delhi on July 17 following an extended journey through Southeast Asia. They received a rapturous and emotional welcome from their old Indian friends. Some knowledgeable Indians questioned how effective Bowles would be in persuading Washington of the importance of supporting India, and contrasted his influence in the Kennedy White House unfavorably with the role the assertive Professor Galbraith had played there. But his first assignment still evoked warm memories, and he was seen as perhaps India's most sympathetic American friend. In Bombay, an Air India billboard caught the spirit with a cartoon of the returning ambassador on a cricket pitch tossing balls at a wicket defended by the airline's famous advertising trademark, the Little Maharajah. "Chester Bowls Again" was the caption.

India had changed greatly since the end of Bowles's first assignment there a decade earlier. The country's democratic institutions, though firmly in place, had been subtly altered as lower-caste, less educated groups were inducted into the political process and brought their own interests and attitudes toward government into play. Jawaharlal Nehru was still prime minister and the Congress party he headed remained the country's dominant political organization. But his political position and self-confidence had been seriously weakened by the Sino-Indian debacle and he was no longer the all-powerful figure he had been during Bowles's first tenure.

Despite his weariness, disillusion, and advancing years, Nehru was unwilling either to step down or to give any clear indication of his choice as successor. By the summer of 1963 Indian politics increasingly focused on the succession issue. "After Nehru Who?" was the subject of ceaseless maneuver and speculation as party bosses positioned themselves for the inevitable day and observers wondered if India's political system would be able to arrange a smooth transition.

Nehru's decline, the diffusion of political power, and the growing experience and assertiveness of Indian politicians and bureaucrats made for a more complex decision-making process than the one Bowles had dealt with when he first came to New Delhi. The U.S. mission had to use its powers of persuasion with a broader range of Indian officials, and it was no longer possible for Bowles to count on his relationship with Nehru to get his concepts across and, he hoped, accepted. Moreover, Indian leaders and administrators wanted to do things their own way and were increasingly sensitive about taking foreign advice.

Important changes had also taken place on India's economic front. Although the Second Five Year Plan (1956–1961) had been less successful than the first in meeting its targets, it had significantly added to India's industrial base, the plan's major objective. The government's decision to reserve the "commanding heights" of the economy to the public sector and to pursue a "socialistic pattern of society" had led to the establishment of many large state-owned industrial plants, often notorious for their inefficiency. The private sector continued to have a significant role in India's mixed economy, though it was subjected to extensive government direction and control. Agriculture, which had received fewer resources under the plan than those given to industry, had made some progress. But the gap between farm output and consumption had widened, increasing the dependence on imported grain; Indian planners (and Bowles) had expected it to end in the mid-1950s.

India had begun its Third Five Year Plan in 1961. This was another ambitious undertaking. The Nehru government sought to achieve as much during the third plan period as it had during the first two combined. The five years were seen as the first stage of a decade or more of intensive development leading to a self-reliant and self-generating economy. The key plan objectives were to increase income over 5 percent each year, achieve self-sufficiency in food grains, and expand basic industry so that the requirements of further industrialization could be met mainly from the country's own resources within ten years or so. The plan also sought to expand employment opportunities and reduce disparities in income and wealth. It depended heavily on foreign assistance for success. To achieve the projected goals, outside aid of over a billion dollars a year was required, almost 23 percent of total planned investment.[8]

Progress in the first two years of the plan had been disappointingly slow. Shortages of electric power, coal, transport, fertilizer, and foreign exchange had hampered the economy and led the government to lower some targets. Food grain production, which had reached 82 million metric tons in the 1960–61 crop year, had stagnated. In the subsequent three crop years—the first three of the third plan—it had averaged only a little more than 80 million metric tons. Grain imports had sharply mounted as India sought to feed a population growing by some 12 million people a year. Industrial expansion had also slowed, so that economic growth fell well below the targeted figure. The situation was worsened by rising prices. Expenditures resulting from the military buildup which had followed the Sino-Indian war had contributed to the strains the economy faced. The war had led the government to reorder its economic priorities, further reducing hope that the goals set in 1961 could be reached. A worsening balance of payments position, in part the result of military requirements, had increased India's need for foreign economic assistance. Despite substantial drawings against the International Monetary Fund, foreign exchange reserves were dangerously low.[9]

The Sino-Indian war had also obliged the Indians to make major changes in the way they interpreted nonalignment and had brought what seemed a stunning transformation in U.S.-Indian relations. Faced with the Chinese onslaught, Nehru had turned desperately to the United States and Britain for help. They responded promptly with arms and military air transport. Meeting in Nassau a few weeks after the fighting had ended, President Kennedy and Prime Minister Harold Macmillan solidified this support with a $120 million short-term military aid package funded in equal parts by the United States and the Commonwealth. A sizable U.S. military aid mission was set up. The presence on the streets of New Delhi of uniformed young Americans was a strange sight for old India hands and dramatized the greatly changed state of U.S.-Indian ties. In November 1963, a few months after Bowles returned, F-100s of the U.S. Tactical Air Force participated with some Royal Air Force and Australian aircraft in a highly successful air defense exercise with the Indian Air Force, until 1992 the only joint military exercise ever held in independent India.

Yet it was clear even before Bowles arrived that the goodwill which had been prompted by American support for India in the China conflict was fading. The Indians felt uneasy and crowded by their greater dependence on the United States. They wanted Washington to consolidate and significantly step up its military assistance program to help them expand and modernize their armed forces and defense production facilities, the Nehru government's top priorities after the Chinese debacle. But aside from a determination to confront the Chinese army more effectively in the Himalayas, they showed little interest in adopting policies which would be more supportive of U.S. objectives than those they had followed before China had attacked.

This was notably true in the way they dealt with Pakistan. Washington had long sought improved India-Pakistan relations, which it saw as critical to regional stability and the strengthening of South Asia against perceived Communist challenges. The desire of the Kennedy administration to promote strong ties with both India *and* Pakistan had heightened this interest. In the wake of the Sino-Indian border war, the United States and Britain had made another bid to resolve the Kashmir dispute, which was still the major issue poisoning relations between the two subcontinental rivals. Although the Indians had been willing to hold a series of bilateral talks with the Pakistanis, these had led nowhere. The initiative had instead sparked resentment against Washington and London among Indians who believed that the two Western powers were taking advantage of India when it was in a weakened and dependent position. Pakistan's evident pleasure over India's defeat at Chinese hands and its successful efforts to improve its relations with Peking had angered Indians and, along with Pakistani concern over India's postwar military buildup, had further strained India-Pakistan ties.

Nor had India curtailed its ties with the Soviet Union. After some hesitation, the Soviets had decided to favor India over China and had resumed the cultivation of the Indians which Khrushchev and Bulganin had flamboyantly inaugurated in the mid-1950s. The Indians valued this relationship not only for the military supplies, economic aid, and political support they received from Moscow, but also because of the assurance it provided against further Chinese moves. They saw strengthened Indo-Soviet ties as an important element in widening the increasingly evident split between Moscow and Peking. The Nehru government's obvious determination to maintain and strengthen its Soviet connection inevitably complicated India's relations with the United States.

Despite the assurances Bowles said the president had given him, the Kennedy administration was still undecided about the kind of relationship it wanted with India and the role it thought India might play in advancing American interests. It certainly gave U.S.-Indian political-security relations nothing approaching the priority and urgency Bowles called for and was not responsive to the appeals of Indian delegations that visited Washington seeking long-term U.S. military assistance at levels far higher than those agreed to at Nassau. As it had done before the sudden eruption of the Sino-Indian war, the administration focused its attention principally on the Soviet challenge in Europe and the Caribbean and the escalating dangers it saw in Southeast Asia.

At a meeting at the White House in late April 1963, both Rusk and Secretary of Defense Robert McNamara had resisted Bowles's call for enlisting the Indians to build a nonnuclear balance of power vis-à-vis the Chinese. Rusk contended that U.S. support for Indian security had to be made partly conditional on the course of India-Pakistan relations; McNamara believed that the Chinese army's threat to India was small. Both points had been frequently made by those skeptical about expanded, long-term military assistance to India. After hearing out the three men, the president had said he was inclined to agree with Bowles that the administration should go ahead promptly with an Indian program. But the size and scope of the program remained undecided. According to Bowles, the president had called him back into his office afterwards to confirm that he agreed with him and urge that he "go out to India and see what kind of a proposition you can get out there." Bowles said Kennedy told him to come back in November and "we'll see where we stand." By that time—which was only a few days before he was assassinated—Kennedy had met again with Macmillan, on June 30 at Birch Grove in Sussex. They had pledged a further year's funding of $100 million for military aid to India and had agreed to a joint radar training exercise. The question of a longer-term U.S. commitment was still on the table when Bowles arrived in India the following month.[10]

The administration was much clearer in its support for Indian economic development. Economic aid had increased sharply in Eisenhower's second term and grew further during the first Kennedy years. By 1963 new bilateral commitments to India reached $444 million. This funded a variety of projects and other programs as well as large-scale ($118 million) imports of surplus agricultural products under Public Law 480. These big outlays, and the prominent role the United States played in the World Bank-led Aid India Consortium, offered Washington the opportunity to influence economic policy in ways that went far beyond what Bowles had tried to do in the early 1950s.

▾   ▾   ▾

If India had changed, so had Bowles. He was sixty-two when he returned and had aged noticeably since his first arrival in New Delhi twelve years before. The official photograph of 1963 on display in the embassy's front office shows a grayer, more weather-beaten man than the 1951 version a few feet away beyond the pictures of the ambassadors who had served in the decade between his two terms: George Allen, John Sherman Cooper, Ellsworth Bunker, and John Kenneth Galbraith. He had gone through a lot in those years, and it had told on him.

The mission Bowles once again led was much larger than the one he had taken charge of with such enthusiasm in 1951. Since 1959 it had been housed in a stunning marble building designed by the American architect Edward Durrell Stone. Stone had brilliantly abstracted from traditional Moghul forms to create a masterpiece that had become one of New Delhi's prime aesthetic attractions. The expanded staff, crowded somewhat uncomfortably into this architectural gem, included State Department authorities on Soviet and Chinese Communism and specialists from other agencies on science, social welfare, and even fish and wildlife. The AID contingent was also much larger and more professionally high-powered than in Bowles's first ambassadorial term. The U.S. Information Service, also expanded, had taken over the more modest chancery building across town where Bowles had presided in those days. Aside from these core elements, the mission included a large military supply operation headed by a major general and a Peace Corps component, established in 1961 when the first contingent of twenty-five volunteers came to the Punjab to help in the development of the state's small industries and engage in agricultural extension work.

As always, Bowles was successful in enticing both up-and-coming younger people and well-established senior ones into working with him. Brandon Grove rejoined him as special assistant. Richard Celeste, a Rhodes Scholar from Yale then in his twenties, became his personal assistant and later took over Grove's responsibilities. Douglas Bennet, Jr., whose father had been a close confidant of Bowles's in OPA and Connecticut, was recruited initially for AID. Also in his twenties, he later joined Grove and Celeste in the front office as Bowles's principal speech writer. All these and a few others came to be known, good humoredly, as the local Chet Set. More experienced talent Bowles recruited included Council of Economic Advisers member John Lewis as AID mission director and Yale economist Charles Lindblom as economic adviser. Colonel Amos "Joe" Jordan came from the West Point faculty to serve as Bowles's special adviser on security matters. Williams College Dean Robert Brooks, who had worked with Bowles at OPA, joined him again, as counselor for cultural affairs.[11]

Bowles was accustomed to giving considerable responsibility to those in his inner circle, and at first there was some uneasiness between them and those he had not specifically recruited. This soon gave way to a generally shared sense of mutual regard. The Foreign Service officers at the embassy were themselves unusually talented, and many of them eventually became ambassadors and senior State Department and USIA officials.[12] They considered Bowles a remarkable man, an important and respected figure in India and the United States whose views would carry weight. Much friendlier and more approachable than the rather forbidding Galbraith, he was particularly encouraging to younger officers provided they shared his fundamental concepts about India and its importance to the United States. In his enthusiastic and open way, he was able to inspire in the mission staff a sense that something important was going on in the India of the 1960s and to make them feel that they were directly involved in major historic developments, not just observers. This sense of excitement—which the dramatic events of the time underscored—made New Delhi an unusual post. Those who worked there for Bowles look back on their experiences as among the most valuable and stimulating in their Foreign Service careers.

Many officers were concerned, however, by Bowles's bias in favor of India and what seemed to them his unduly sanguine view of developments there. The ambassador's familiar line—"you can look at a bottle as either half full or half empty"—sometimes appeared to be a pretext for slanting reports in ways that made India and the Indians look good. Bowles often said that Washington was full of anti-Indian officials looking for evidence to derail promising U.S. programs, and would warn embassy officers to be careful not to leap to conclusions that would provide these nay-sayers with ammunition. His own messages to the president and the secretary usually stressed the positive, or at least the potentially positive, in Indian political and economic developments.

Bowles's propensity to dramatize and repeat himself also tended to trouble (and sometimes amuse) his staff, as it did his Washington audience. In his reports, India was all too frequently reaching a crucial "watershed" which called for positive American action if the country were not to slide irrevocably down a "slippery slope." Unlike many embassy officers, including those who subscribed to his basic concepts, he was rarely able to view India with any degree of detachment, let alone humor. Despite these shortcomings, the staff never lost its affectionate regard for Bowles. To almost all of them, he was a great American and they were proud to serve under his leadership.

For his part, Bowles continued to take a jaundiced view of Foreign Service officers as a group, though he valued the work of many individuals among them. A July 1964 entry in his diary suggests that his opinion remained much as it had been during his first assignment:

The "service" is full of able people. Yet as a whole it is a dull, nervous, technically competent, but unfocused and unimaginative body. Although it shines in organizing funerals or a dinner, it retreats from the kind of sober, deep digging analysis that is so urgently needed. Our routine political reporting, in spite of my best efforts, deals with the froth of politics—who said what to whom, who fails to see eye to eye with whom—the basic forces which move events are largely ignored because they are intricate, dull, and controversial. The conspiratorial school of diplomacy and political reporting is well entrenched here as elsewhere, and as a result I spend a disproportionate part of my time trying to dig into the Indian political system to find out what moves it.[13]

In an effort to shake up the officers and broaden and deepen their way of thinking about the country, Bowles had them participate in large staff meetings at which mission members and outsiders gave presentations about significant developments in their fields. He would address the group himself from time to time. He asked more of the younger staff members to functions he and Steb hosted, putting them into contact with senior Indians they would not have otherwise met. Most important from his viewpoint, he undertook a major reordering of the way the embassy carried on its political and economic work.

Bowles had long held that in a developing country there was no real distinction between the political and the economic. Economics largely drove politics, and if the embassy did not know what was happening to the economic well-being of ordinary people all it would be reporting to Washington would be the politics of the drawing room. Concerned that in the standard embassy set-up officers covering the two fields were placed in separate offices and had little exposure to one another, he merged the political and economic sections into a political-economic division under a senior officer with the title of minister and made a distinction within the combined operation between affairs that were external to India and those that were internal. The novel arrangement had only limited impact on the quality of the embassy's output, however. Although it provided officers with fresh insights, this advantage was counterbalanced by the introduction of further layering, disruptive personality clashes, and confusion over responsibility. Bowles, pleased with the changes, was probably unaware of these problems or chose to ignore them. He thought the new arrangement important and successful enough to tout it to McGeorge Bundy and other senior administration officials.[14]

This decision to revamp the embassy's political and economic operations also reflected Bowles's determination, now that he was again in charge of an organization, to run it the way he saw fit. He had tried to introduce his own management ideas as under secretary but had been hemmed in by Rusk, who preferred a more conventional style. In

New Delhi Bowles had virtually full sway. He gave greater importance to the "country team" of agency and section heads, brought in special assistants, and recruited the people *he* wanted. As in the days before he was obliged to adjust to State Department orthodoxies, he gave those he trusted broad responsibilities and often disregarded the ordained pecking order. If all of this made life frustrating at times for the able and professional senior Foreign Service officer he had chosen as his deputy, Joseph "Jerry" Greene, Jr., it certainly enlivened the mission. That, of course, was what Bowles wanted.

Bowles tried to follow a life style much like the one he had adopted during his first assignment. He traveled extensively, discussing wheat yields with small farmers in remote villages, inspecting hydroelectric projects, chatting with state cabinet ministers and junior government development officials, and mingling with students, just as he had in the 1950s. In a dramatic demonstration of his continuing dislike for ostentation, he abandoned the imposing Roosevelt House ambassadorial residence on the embassy grounds and returned to the comparatively modest and far more comfortable bungalow where he had lived during his first assignment. He considered the abandoned "palace" a disaster that served symbolically to set Americans off from India and made them a ready target for charges that they were living callously in a poor country. He used it only for large gatherings and made it available to staffers for community functions. His own official entertainment was as informal as possible. Disdaining diplomatic pomp as much as before, he did everything he could to avoid attending the elaborate receptions and fancy dinners hosted by his fellow ambassadors and wealthy Indians of New Delhi's smart set. He encouraged other Americans to follow a similarly modest and low profile life style.

But Bowles's personal and professional life was profoundly affected by the onset of Parkinson's disease, apparently discovered in the year following his return to New Delhi. In 1965 he decided to undergo surgery. Without publicly disclosing the reason for his travel, he went to New York in June and was operated on at St. Barnabas Hospital by Dr. Irwin Cooper, a specialist in the treatment of the disease. The operation helped him temporarily. During his last few years in New Delhi, however, the symptoms of the ailment became more and more evident, and he felt obliged to cut back on his travel and public appearances. He worried a great deal about his physical condition. The many diary entries recording the state of his health, his hopes for recovery, and his fears of a future as a cripple are saddening testimony to the great emotional impact the disease understandably had on him.

Steb also resumed her old ways. Her natural empathy for Indians of all descriptions reminded some embassy staffers of the legendary Mrs. Moore in E. M. Forster's *A Passage to India*. Customarily dressed in a comfortable sari, she again put her energy and enthusiasm to good use in making contact with unconventional people and putting Chet in touch with them. If Bowles did not fully appreciate the thrumming of sitars and the beating of tablas at the musicales Steb organized as official entertainment, he recognized that the occasions were well received by the Indians and contributed handsomely to good public relations.

He continued to value the way Steb related to India and its people. One of her good Indian friends was the wife of Prime Minister Lal Bahadur Shastri, Nehru's successor, a rough-hewn north Indian woman who spoke no English and was the antithesis of the "brown *mem sahibs*" of the New Delhi diplomatic circuit. Steb, who knew some Hindi, accompanied Mrs. Shastri to Allahabad when she traveled there to scatter her husband's ashes on the Ganges following his death in 1966. Highly publicized in the Indian press, it was a diplomatic coup. As an embassy officer observed at the time, the Soviet ambassador's wife must have eaten her heart out.

16

Mission Unaccomplished

DURING his second assignment, Bowles's agenda continued to focus on the establishment of closer U.S.-Indian political and security ties and the promotion with American assistance of faster, more equitable Indian economic growth. Despite the many changes which had taken place in America, India, and the rest of the world in the decade between his two assignments, these objectives and the way Bowles pursued them bore many similarities to the approach he had followed when he was ambassador in the early 1950s. A decade later India's newfound hostility against China led him to seek a more active and visible U.S.-Indian security relationship than had seemed possible earlier, and Pakistan's greater friendship with Peking offered him fresh arguments against U.S. military ties with the Ayub Khan government. But the premises on which his recommendations about U.S. South Asian policies were based remained unchanged. And while he did eventually change the formulas he favored for Indian economic development, his close involvement in working them out and his determination to sell them to the Indian and American leadership were much the same as they had been during his first assignment.

▼　　▼　　▼

Before he could turn to the main items on his agenda, Bowles had to deal with two pressing and highly publicized problems, both rude reminders of the continuing limits on the further development of strong bilateral ties. Although their negative impact was cushioned by the goodwill generated in India by the American response to the Chinese attack the previous fall, they gave a discouraging tone to Bowles's second ambassadorship in its earliest days.

Bowles was on his way to India when an agreement was signed

between the Voice of America and the government-owned All-India Radio providing for U.S. funding of a medium-wave transmitter for AIR in Calcutta. In return, VOA was to get a daily share of the transmitter's broadcasting time over a five-year period. It would use this to beam its messages to Southeast Asia. The agreement had been enthusiastically promoted by Galbraith and accepted by Nehru.

Calling at the Ministry of External Affairs on his first full day on the job, Bowles was told that the prime minister and his cabinet had made a formal decision to renegotiate the agreement. The arrangement, it was explained, had come under unexpectedly strong domestic political attack as a breach of Indian nonalignment and had been badly received in Southeast Asia. The Indian government had (belatedly) found that the agreement would prejudice U.S.-Indian relations. It hoped that Washington would either lease it a transmitter or provide one outright with no VOA strings attached. Otherwise, the deal was off.[1]

Getting word of Nehru's reneging, a complete surprise to Bowles, was not the most auspicious way for him to resume his official relations with the Indian government. He shared the exasperation Washington felt about the decision and feared, quite rightly, it would have an adverse impact there on other matters on the U.S.-Indian agenda. His energetic efforts in public and private to persuade the Indians to change their position were ultimately unsuccessful, however. Nehru confessed to Parliament in early September that he had not recognized the implications of the agreement before it was signed and that "if it cannot be revised radically, we shall have to do without it." Since Washington—Bowles strongly concurring—refused to make such changes, the agreement was effectively dead.[2]

The second problem had been longer in the making. Well before Bowles's appointment, the Indian government's request for an initial $512 million loan to help finance a public sector steel mill at Bokaro in eastern India had led to a major controversy within the Kennedy administration over the project's technical feasibility and the ideological implications of such major funding for a state-owned operation. Bokaro opponents cited the recent report of a presidential commission headed by General Lucius Clay that assistance should not be provided to government enterprises that compete with existing private firms. Congressional consideration of the loan took place against a background of increasing doubt on Capitol Hill and elsewhere about the purpose and usefulness of foreign economic assistance. The skepticism of some congressmen about the technical feasibility and ideological advisability of Bokaro funding reinforced the opposition of those who were reluctant for political reasons to make a major loan to the Nehru government. President Kennedy, brushing aside the ideological considerations, said at a press conference in May 1963 that if Bokaro was an efficient project and met the requirements of the Indian economy it should be approved.[3]

Bowles had enlisted in the Bokaro campaign before he left for India and weighed in quickly by cable when he got there. Calling the project one of the "dramatic opportunities for action and policy initiatives which the Chinese attack had opened up for the United States not only in India but throughout Asia," he reported to Kennedy and Rusk that unwillingness to proceed would be regarded in India as evidence of a "doctrinaire attempt to force nations that we aid to conform to our pattern of economic organization" and, even more damaging, as the U.S. government's welshing on a commitment.[4]

Despite his efforts, and those of other Bokaro proponents led by Galbraith, congressional sentiment against the project continued to grow. In late August, the House administered the coup de grace by approving an amendment to the foreign aid authorization bill forbidding any expenditures on Bokaro during the current fiscal year. Reacting gracefully, Nehru wrote Kennedy offering to withdraw the Indian request for aid if it would be a continuing embarrassment to the administration. The president gratefully accepted Nehru's offer and assured him that the United States continued to favor extensive economic and military aid to India. In a friendly reply, Nehru said he was anxious, as Kennedy was, that the issue not come in the way of close U.S.-Indian friendship and cooperation in other fields.[5]

The outcome of the Bokaro struggle was a setback to Bowles's political and economic objectives, and he felt that keenly. The magnitude of the setback, and of his bitter regret about it, was greatly increased the following year when, despite its private assurances to him that it would not do so, the Indian government came to an agreement with Moscow providing for Soviet financing of the mill.

Nehru's negative reaction to an Anglo-American initiative to nominate a mediator to resolve the Kashmir dispute further complicated U.S.-Indian relations during Bowles's first few weeks in New Delhi. Bowles had resisted the idea, contending that such a proposal had no chance of acceptance and would reduce his effectiveness on other issues. "The pressure for affirmative action in regard to Kashmir at this moment is about as welcome [in India] as would be the effort of some foreign government to get us to recognize Castro and give up the

Guantanamo naval base," he told Galbraith. Washington was insistent, however, and Bowles's forecast of an Indian turndown proved correct. Nehru's sharp condemnation of Pakistan in Parliament soon after Bowles had reluctantly presented the proposal effectively closed off any prospect for progress on Kashmir. Kennedy's personal intervention to salvage the initiative and Nehru's rejection of the president's direct appeal made the episode even more damaging.[6]

▼　　　▼　　　▼

Bowles wrote Galbraith again in September to complain that "since you and [Galbraith's wife] Kitty left here in early July a major section of the roof has fallen in."[7] But he did not let the setbacks interfere with his effort to flesh out and sell the new approach to South Asia he had spoken of before leaving for New Delhi. His proposals, set out in cables he sent on September 9 and October 24, came as no surprise to his Washington audience.[8]

The overriding American objective in South Asia, Bowles contended, was to contain the India-Pakistan conflict within manageable limits and, optimally, to bring the two countries to work together to defend the subcontinent and contain Communist China throughout Asia. To achieve this goal, the United States needed to recognize that India was larger, stronger, more stable, and more democratic than Pakistan, give up the notion of balancing them as "power equals," and "not allow the irrational fears [about India] of [Pakistan's] leaders, however genuine, to dictate U.S. policies."

Bowles proposed that the United States limit its military assistance to the two countries to the hardware they could use against the Communist powers. This meant no tanks or high-performance aircraft for either country, a restriction he knew would be a major blow to Pakistan, which had built its military power around the U.S.-supplied Patton tank and F-104 fighter. The proposal represented a change, albeit temporary, from the position he had taken in August recommending that if the administration went ahead with additional F-104s to Pakistan, it should also let the Indians know it was willing to provide them with similar supersonic aircraft. He was prepared to support military aid to Pakistan at current levels only if the Ayub Khan government clearly acknowledged that the assistance was intended for use against the Communists. He supported continuing the high levels of U.S. economic support to Pakistan—on a per capita basis more than twice the amount India received, as he observed—but only if the Pakistanis respected American interests in Asia and avoided embarrassing the United States when they saw specific situations from a different perspective. This was a not particularly subtle way of saying that if Pakistan did not jettison its increasingly robust relationship with Communist China, it could no longer expect significant American largesse.

Bowles's recommendations for India centered on a proposed long-term U.S. program to modernize the Indian army to a strength of 16–18 divisions equipped solely for fighting the Chinese. Estimating that this would cost $100 million annually for five years, he warned that if the United States did not move to fill the military vacuum in India, the Soviets would. Military assistance should be conditioned on "India's willingness to work in harmony with the United States government in containing Chinese power not only in the Himalayas but in Asia generally." This did not mean a commitment of Indian troops to Southeast Asia at that time but rather "a close working relationship on political and intelligence matters looking toward military cooperation in future in opposition to a Chinese threat."

The United States could use military assistance to India and Pakistan as a lever to negotiate separate force level agreements with the two countries, Bowles held. He feared that if limits were not set, the Indians would proceed with a military buildup considerably greater than the level he recommended. This would lead the Pakistanis to undertake a parallel expansion, and a ruinous arms race would result. To make the arrangement more palatable to the two countries, he proposed that once Washington had successfully negotiated the force levels, it furnish the necessary equipment to both. In return, they were to agree that they would not acquire weapons for additional units from other sources. This arrangement would forestall the Indians from turning to the Soviets for arms.

The increased sense of security in India and Pakistan which Bowles hoped this approach could bring about could be further promoted by America's guaranteeing each country that it would come to its assistance if it were attacked by the other. Washington should also offer India the same guarantee of defense against Communist aggression it had given to Pakistan in the agreements reached in the 1950s, and station a naval task force in the Indian Ocean "to give emphasis and conviction to our assurances."

Bowles's formula for handling the intractable Kashmir issue was to deep freeze it. There was no chance of the dispute being settled in the present atmosphere, he said, so the United States should do what it could to persuade India and Pakistan to develop a moderate dialogue and wait for an opportune moment when the problem could be profitably tackled. A final settlement should take the form of an autonomous or semi-autonomous Vale of Kashmir, with the rest of the state partitioned between the two rivals. In the meantime, the United States should stay out of the line of fire and avoid raising the Kashmir issue with the Indians on a regular basis.

As Kennedy had reportedly suggested to him, Bowles returned to Washington in November. On the long flight back, he and Brandon Grove worked up a memorandum to the president outlining the security proposals. Grove recalled the experience as a typical Bowles drafting exercise, with Bowles radically amending and expanding the original product over his assistant's protests. The result was a five-page paper, probably more than Kennedy would have wanted but relatively concise by Bowles standards. In it, Bowles reduced the annual figure he sought for military assistance to India to $75 million. In discussions with him, the Indians had scaled down the requests for aid they had brought to Washington earlier, and he was able to claim that he had found a tentatively favorable reaction to his proposals in his discussions with defense, foreign policy, and economic affairs officials. Otherwise, the memo was essentially a reiteration of the main points in his earlier messages.[9]

Bowles met with the president at the White House on November 13. He recorded in his diary that Kennedy had read and fully absorbed the memo and was "wholly understanding and favorable to my proposals. . . . He understands [the memo's] implications and the interplay of the various components on the whole complex of Asian relationships. He asked me to see everyone with a voice and do what I could to persuade them. A National Security Council meeting would be held on the 25th or 26th [of November] . . . to nail down a decision. The implication was 'do your best to win agreement so that there will be as few dissensions as possible; in any event you can count on me'."[10]

Whether Kennedy's support was as firm as Bowles claimed is not clear. In a memorandum he sent the president on the eve of Bowles's call, NSC staffer Robert Komer had suggested that Kennedy "reassure him that we intend to go forward with India, while getting him to set his sights a little lower and more realistically."[11] Komer pointed out that the amount Bowles sought for the Military Assistance Program (MAP) for India was not much more than the $50 million a year the Pentagon had been thinking about, and asked Kennedy if he thought a five-year commitment should be made at that point. In dealing with Bowles, the president may well have been *too* reassuring, not an unusual event when a senior Washington official meets with a returning ambassador. Bowles, for his part, was notorious for hearing what he wanted to hear.

Komer, Assistant Secretary Phillips Talbot, and Deputy Assistant Secretary James Grant, all close to the issue, now agree that Kennedy would have approved a five-year package.[12] But no decision was ever reached by his administration on the size of the package or the conditions to be attached to it, let alone the package itself. The NSC meeting never took place: preliminary sessions were in progress at the White House when the president was assassinated. Bowles made a brief note in his diary: "Kennedy never really understood what I wanted to do—what I could have done for him." Then he watched the funeral cortege and returned to New Delhi empty-handed.[13]

▾   ▾   ▾

The new president, Lyndon Johnson, was understandably reluctant to move forward until he could review the situation. Bowles recognized that his proposal was at least temporarily stalled. He thought he had made little progress before the assassination in winning State Department support for it. Rusk had been "his usual, uncommunicative, polite self," the working level of the department even less sympathetic. "As I asked Phil Talbot's staff meeting," he recorded in his diary the day before Kennedy was shot, "how does the South Asia policy which we appear to have drifted into differ from the Dulles policy that I opposed vigorously throughout the Eisenhower years? . . . It seemed that I have been striving for a week to carry a double mattress up a narrow winding staircase."[14]

Despite Bowles's misgivings about State's receptiveness to his views, Rusk told Johnson a few weeks later that he, McNamara, and AID Administrator David Bell agreed that it would be well worthwhile to reach an understanding with the Indians along the lines of Bowles's proposal. But Rusk called for a more cautious approach that would allow Washington to gauge Indian responsiveness and Pakistani reaction before it made an explicit commitment. He agreed that in the meantime preparation should go forward within the U.S. government of a military assistance program in the $50–60 million annual range.[15]

Not surprisingly, Bowles found that this "modified Bowles proposal" fell well short of what he had in mind. He argued strongly that only by letting the Indians know at the outset what the United States government was prepared to do could they be persuaded to develop a realistic plan which linked their defense requirements and foreign exchange needs. He was dissatisfied with the lower figures Washington had worked up for projected support, and urged in particular a positive response to Indian interest in high-performance aircraft. This reversion to his earlier position reflected an awareness that acquisition of high-performance American planes (specifically the F-104) had become a prime Indian objective. He had also become even more troubled by the possibility that the Indians would seek to meet their high-performance aircraft requirements in Moscow, which had agreed before the Sino-Indian war to supply India with sophisticated MIG-21 fighters and had already sent a small number. Over the next months he came to see provision of American high-performance planes as crucial to the success of the grand design he had set out in his many messages to Washington.[16]

The new administration had confirmed Kennedy's request to General Maxwell Taylor that he undertake a firsthand assessment of the South Asian military assistance issue. Taylor submitted his report in late December following visits to India and Pakistan. Like Bowles, he favored a five-year military assistance program, provided the Indians limited their force-level goals and their diversion of foreign exchange from economic development, held down procurement from the Soviet bloc, exercised restraint in relations with Pakistan, and cooperated with the United States in the containment of Communist China. He recommended that the Indians themselves be charged with the responsibility for developing a satisfactory five-year plan, and that they be told for planning purposes to assume an annual U.S. contribution of $50–60 million. He did not specifically recommend provision of high-performance aircraft to India. But as Secretary Rusk pointed out in a favorable assessment of the report which he sent to the president, since Taylor had left it to the Indians to set priorities among the competing needs of their own services, the plan they devised might include a limited number of such planes from "free world" sources.[17]

Rusk had taken three weeks to comment on Taylor's report, and Johnson took another three before acting on the secretary's recommendations. Bowles nervously awaited the outcome of the debate. He was troubled by reports in late January that Johnson and McNamara were not supporting his initiative. "According to the Washington gossip which filters into New Delhi," he complained to Galbraith, "LBJ is indifferent, the State Department and the Pentagon are negative, and the support therefore is unlikely to be forthcoming."[18] He told Hubert Humphrey that if Johnson, McNamara, and Rusk did in fact view prospects for a strengthened U.S.-Indian security relationship differently from the way he did, it might be better for him to give up the ambassadorship.[19]

Deteriorating India-Pakistan relations complicated Bowles's efforts. The theft in December 1963 of a Muslim holy relic from a shrine in the Vale of Kashmir had triggered widespread disturbances. These led to the collapse of the Kashmir state government and major Hindu-Muslim clashes in East Pakistan and eastern India. In mid-January, Pakistan again asked the U.N. Security Council to take up the Kashmir issue, an initiative Bowles called an act of folly that would only worsen an explosive situation. He repeatedly recommended against U.S. support for the Pakistani position at the United Nations. Coming soon after the Bokaro decision and at a time when Washington was dragging its feet on military assistance, it would seriously undermine the U.S. position in India and limit his own effectiveness, he warned.[20]

On February 8 Johnson agreed, with caveats, to the recommendations Rusk had made on the basis of the Taylor report. The president had no objection to exploratory approaches toward five-year Military Assistance Programs, but he ruled out discussions with India and Pakistan about aid levels pending a better administration reading of congressional attitudes. Bowles was authorized to tell the Indians to develop an austere minimum five-year plan for defense against the Chinese Communist threat. Pending its completion, the United States was prepared to continue military assistance during FY 1965 at roughly the current $50 million level. Aid would be provided on a grant basis and would be subject to congressional appropriation. If the Indians inquired about high-performance aircraft, Bowles was to reply that it was up to them to include it on their priority list. The U.S. response would depend on a number of considerations, including Indian acquisition of Soviet aircraft and missiles and an assessment of the way Pakistan would react.[21]

Though he was not happy with the unrealistically low limits he believed it set, Bowles acknowledged that the decision pointed in the right direction. He continued to warn about possible Soviet arms supply and tried to dissuade key Indian cabinet ministers from looking to Moscow. He intended, he said, to tell the Indians that American supersonics and missiles might be available if they wish to give them priority, and asked for prompt assurance of one squadron of supersonics plus surface-to-air missiles as part of a general aid package. Washington instructed him to stick to his script. It opposed any large-scale preemptive efforts to head off Soviet aircraft and missile supply. Soviet experience in Egypt and Indonesia demonstrated that the road to political infiltration through the supply of fighter aircraft was a difficult one, Bowles was told. Moreover, an early offer to the Indians of the top performance aircraft in the Pakistani inventory—the F-104, which the Indians preferred—would substantially undermine relations with the Ayub government when U.S. interests on the subcontinent required acceptable ties with both India and Pakistan.[22]

Bowles took strong exception to this and was skeptical about Washington's suggestion that the British might provide the Indian Air Force with a suitable plane. He returned to Washington in late March to lobby for his position on aircraft and other aspects of the package he had proposed. He got Secretary McNamara to agree to a visit by Indian Defense Minister Y. B. Chavan in May for negotiations on the plan the Indians were preparing at U.S. suggestion, and came back with Chavan to take part in them.[23]

In *Promises to Keep,* Bowles recalled that after two weeks of negotiations the two sides had succeeded in producing a program satisfactory to India as well as to Rusk and McNamara. Johnson was also prepared to accept it, Bowles claimed, and the final meeting to nail everything down was scheduled for May 28. Word of Nehru's death early on May 27 disrupted these plans. Bowles, Rusk, and Chavan headed for India aboard a U.S. Air Force plane a few hours later.[24]

For the rest of his life, Bowles insisted that it was only the death of Nehru—as it had earlier been the death of Kennedy—that prevented the acceptance of a closer U.S.-Indian security relationship on the lines he had proposed. This is clearly an overstatement. Substantial agreement had been reached by May 27 on many important aspects of the package. These included $50 million in grants and a like amount in low-interest loans on a multiyear basis, subject to annual congressional approval, as well as specific limits (about $1.4 billion) on Indian foreign exchange expenditures for defense purposes. But Bowles was wrong in implicitly claiming that agreement on the all-important aircraft issue was virtually in the bag. A draft memorandum agreed to at the time had said only that "the subject would be examined further with a view to determining what U.S. assistance in this field would be available and appropriate."[25]

This language masked a serious disagreement between India and the United States about the type of aircraft India needed for its defense. As one of the American negotiators has recalled, the U.S. side urged the Indians to accept a used aircraft, the maximum speed of which was only the speed of sound. This appealed to the Americans because in their view it would be effective against the Chinese threat, less costly, and less of a problem for U.S.-Pakistan relations than the new high-performance planes the Indians sought. The Indians, however, did not accept this offer, thus leaving the crucial issue subject to later examination.[26]

In the days following Nehru's death, Bowles made every effort to persuade the key American players to move forward with the supersonic aircraft and to formalize the rest of the package. He tried to work on Rusk on the long flight to New Delhi, but the secretary, preoccupied with Southeast Asia, avoided the subject. Once on the ground, Bowles hosted a small dinner at which two senior embassy officers were to brief Rusk with the aim of selling him on the program. The stage-managed effort went awry when the secretary began telling tales of the Old South; these so disconcerted Bowles that he was unable to follow through with the scenario. Rusk flew on to Southeast Asia and the opportunity to engage his attention was lost.[27]

McNamara had remained in Washington. Bowles pointed out to him (and to Rusk, by then in Saigon) that the new Indian government would be dominated by moderates who would be under pressure from the Soviets and Indian leftists and would look to their friends in the West for moral assurance and material support. He proposed that once he and Chavan had initialed the agreement and the new government had been formed, he would inform the new prime minister and defense minister of U.S. willingness to proceed on the general basis of the agreement and express the hope that specifics regarding the high-performance aircraft could be worked out promptly.[28] Commenting on this message in a memorandum to McGeorge Bundy, Robert Komer said that he proposed to buck the issue up to the president. "It's worth the try," Komer noted, "though I'm not optimistic because Rusk and McNamara just haven't focused on Indian affairs."[29] But Komer also maintains that the Pentagon's opposition to providing F-104s was sufficiently strong that he did not think it necessary to put that question to Johnson.[30]

The understanding the two governments reached on June 6 sidestepped the aircraft issue; this, a joint communiqué stated, "would continue under examination by both sides."[31] Apparently undeterred, Bowles kept on pressing Washington and urged that he be given authority to outline to the Indians "one of the aircraft packages I have proposed."[32] He was put down by a June 10 telegram from Rusk, who told him that it had been decided not to go ahead with aircraft at that time. The secretary said he was convinced that "our interests dictate that we avoid any possible interference with the current truce in Indo-

Pakistan tensions. . . . However slim the hopes for accommodation may be, this could be an historic turning point on the subcontinent toward the type of cooperation on which all agree any lasting security must be based."[33] As subsequent events would make clear, it was nothing of the kind.

Bowles expressed limited satisfaction with what had been accomplished. He was particularly pleased with the agreement limiting foreign exchange outlays for India's defense budget. He thought this would keep the Indian army and air force at acceptable levels, one of the key objectives in his initiative. But his principal reactions were deep regret that the high-performance aircraft package was stymied, and heightened concern that the Indians, frustrated by American attitudes, would turn to the Soviets for the military hardware denied them by Washington. He was certain that when Defense Minister Chavan visited Moscow in August the Soviets would push hard to reach agreement on a package comprising surface-to-air missiles, large-scale production of MIG-21 fighter aircraft in India, and possibly even submarines for the Indian navy. "If the Soviet Union is prepared to put nearly one billion dollars worth of military aid into a confused situation such as Indonesia or into a relatively limited one such as the United Arab Republic [Egypt]," Bowles warned, "it would be foolhardy for the United States or Pakistan to assume that Khrushchev will refuse to invest equally sizeable amounts of semi-obsolescent military equipment in India in order to strengthen his political position in the one country in Asia which has the capacity to provide a significant counterweight to Communist China."[34]

He did what he could to head off the deal. He again tried—and again failed—to revive a U.S. aircraft package. He met with Chavan and other senior Indian officials to discourage them from accepting Soviet proposals. On the eve of the defense minister's departure he made a last-ditch effort with the new prime minister, Lal Bahadur Shastri. Shastri had been in office for only two months following a remarkably smooth transition in which he had emerged as the consensus candidate of the Congress party leadership. In his plea, Bowles argued that India was putting too much trust in the Soviet Union and called into question the apparent Indian strategy of using the deal to help assure Soviet support should China again attack. He pointedly suggested to Shastri that the arrangement would complicate U.S. efforts to carry through on its military assistance program to India.[35]

Bowles's efforts failed, and an arms agreement was signed in Moscow on September 11 making the MIG-21 the Indian air force's standard interceptor aircraft of the 1970s.[36] In an angry reply to a message from the American embassy in Pakistan apparently expressing surprise about the deal, Bowles recalled his many warnings. He pointed out that he had "consistently questioned whether it was in the interest of the Pakistan Government to block Western military aid to India over which we could exercise some control, only to see it provided by the Soviets with no strings on its use against Pakistan. However, because of Pakistan Government pressures we failed to win our case in Washington." He saw no reason to apologize to the Pakistanis for the Indian decision.

> Our task now [he concluded] is to minimize to the best of our ability the adverse effects of this agreement in both New Delhi and Karachi. This cannot be accomplished by an attempt to balance accounts by compensating the Pakistan Government by additional aid. Indeed the surest way to turn the situation which is clearly disadvantageous for the United States, Pakistan, and in the long run to the Indians as well, into an outright political disaster would be for the United States Government to become a party to a subcontinental arms race in which the United States Government backs Pakistan while the USSR backs India.[37]

At the same time, Bowles complained in his diary about the way the Indians had behaved.

> Perhaps the most unfortunate aspect [of the Indian-Soviet agreement] . . . is the lack of honesty which key Indian officials have shown in dealing with us. . . . [They] have been incredibly devious, not one, but many; not once but innumerable [sic] times. They said to avoid entanglements they would not get the Russians into Bokaro (the Russians could build the next, the fifth plant, instead); then VOA, then the cover-up on the SAM's; then the MIGs. Not once were we told the truth. We were allowed and indeed encouraged to assume . . . that the MIG deal was being held in abeyance awaiting our decision. Finally, when it was clear that the Indian desire to develop the Soviet split with China was going to take precedence over India's relations with us, they agreed with me to diffuse and fuzz up [the agreement]. Next thing we know, there is a Roman Holiday type commitment from Moscow.[38]

Bowles went on in the same diary entry to describe his dilemma with a candor he rarely displayed in discussing relations with India with his embassy colleagues or Washington:

> In regard to relations in general, we are caught in a bad situation. If I speak out bluntly at home, it would easily draw cheers from all the foreign aid slighters and isolationists. But it would be most damaging to do so. Any yet, if I remain silent, the Indians will continue to think they can

manipulate us to their heart's content. I am not disillusioned because I had no real illusions. But I dislike stupidity and here [the reference seems to be to both New Delhi and Washington] we have it in all shapes and sizes.

Despite the agreement with the Soviets, Bowles continued to urge that the United States provide high-performance aircraft and assistance for the production of planes in India. By early 1965 the Indians were expressing an interest in the F-5, a less sophisticated and less expensive jet than the F-104. While the administration deliberately dragged its heels, he argued strongly for moving forward. But his cable to the department on the eve of the scheduled visit of President Ayub to the United States in April indicated that he would accept a negative symmetry in the provision of American aircraft to India and Pakistan. He advised Washington that "if you believe that the over-all situation in the subcontinent and in Asia generally calls for a tough line by the President in dealing with Ayub Khan and if part of this tough line is to refuse or postpone new planes for the Pakistan Air Force, we are prepared to support similar action on F-5s for India until the political dust settles in the subcontinent."[39]

▾　　　▾　　　▾

The political dust did not settle; it only got thicker. India-Pakistan relations had worsened as the Indians adopted measures that further reduced the political and constitutional distinctions between Kashmir and other states of the Indian Union. The Pakistanis became increasingly concerned that the Indian military buildup undertaken after the Chinese debacle would turn the power balance against them and rule out a resolution of the Kashmir issue on any but Indian terms. Their flirtation with the Chinese, designed to bolster them against India, was viewed with growing dismay in Washington.

In mid-April 1965 the White House abruptly postponed the announced visits of President Ayub and Prime Minister Shastri to the United States. Johnson's disinclination to meet with Ayub precipitated the decision. He felt that Ayub's defense of Pakistan's relationship with China and his attitude on Vietnam would have an adverse effect on the aid bill and questioned whether the visit would improve U.S. relations with Pakistan. Because the president would not meet with Ayub, it was necessary to postpone the Shastri visit as well.[40]

Bowles was mortified when the "flash" cable came without any warning from Washington. He had worked hard to persuade Shastri to make the visit and to schedule it at a time most convenient to Johnson. The unwelcome message, delayed while Rusk sought unsuccessfully to turn Johnson around, did not acknowledge that Pakistan's behavior was to blame for the postponement; it merely cited "the delicate and pressing situation in Vietnam."[41] Bowles saw through this unlikely rationalization and tried desperately to persuade Johnson to change his mind. He urged that if the objective was to be tough with Pakistan, Ayub alone should be disinvited.[42] In turning Bowles down, Washington maintained that Johnson felt that neither he nor Shastri would be in a position to "talk turkey." The visit, it said, would focus unwelcome attention on bickering in South Asia and the apparent lack of economic progress in India despite large amounts of American aid. Bowles was not taken in by these *post facto* efforts to justify the postponement.[43]

Shastri took the brusque decision very badly, as did other Indians. Bowles thought the very negative reaction was heightened by U.S. failure to give the prime minister the opportunity to bow out gracefully on his own initiative.[44] A premature press leak had made it impossible for him to try to get Shastri to do so. He confided to his diary that although "probably no great disaster will befall us . . . damage has been done that will not be regained easily." The next few months would be good ones for the United States to lie low in India, he concluded.[45]

Bowles had had high hopes for the visit. In a long letter he sent Johnson just before he received word of the postponement, he said the coming discussions with Ayub and Shastri might affect the course of events in South Asia for years to come. With characteristic hyperbole, he advised the president that "in regard to India, after many years of effort we are approaching a watershed: either this vast and friendly nation with its already impressive economic and political structure will continue to grow in importance as a counterweight to Chinese power in Asia or we shall witness its gradual deterioration and estrangement from the United States."[46] The assessments and recommendations which followed contained little that Bowles had not said before about India and U.S.-Indian relations. The interesting twist this time was an appeal to the Texas populist in LBJ to win support for Shastri and Indian economic development.

The Indians were still reacting negatively to the postponement of the Shastri visit when an outbreak of fighting between Pakistani and Indian forces introduced another problem in U.S.-Indian relations. At issue was disputed territory in the remote Rann of Kutch in the western part of the subcontinent. The Pakistanis used some U.S.-supplied equipment (though apparently less than the Indians alleged), claiming later that their purpose had been self-defense and therefore permissible under the U.S.-Pakistan security agreement. Bowles angrily reminded Washington that he and his predecessors in New Delhi had repeatedly assured the Indians that the United States would act firmly to stop the Pakistanis from misusing U.S.-supplied weapons for aggressive purposes, as he was convinced they were doing in the Rann. He urged that Washington publicly chastise the Pakistanis and warn them that unless they agreed not to use MAP equipment in border disputes, such aid would be suspended. The administration found reasons to waffle on the issue.[47]

British-initiated efforts eventually brought about a cease-fire, and the two countries agreed to submit the Kutch dispute to international arbitration. By then the crisis and other developments in India and Pakistan had led Bowles to make yet another plea for a review of U.S. policy in South Asia, this time in a May 20 memorandum to Rusk. He offered nothing new aside from a proposal, prompted by the Rann of Kutch experience, to drop assurances to India and Pakistan that the United States would not allow military equipment supplied them under the assistance program to be improperly used. He suggested that Washington instead confine itself to a commitment to support each country through the United Nations, or unilaterally, if it were clearly the victim of aggression.[48]

Following up this message in an early July letter to Johnson, Bowles contended once again that India could be turned into a major political asset for the United States "if there is a clear understanding at the highest level of our government, first, of India's absolutely decisive importance to a favorable power balance vis-à-vis China in Asia and, second, of the very special nature of the Indian situation." Without specifying amounts, he called for military and economic support for India conditioned on its taking economic self-help measures and adopting a clear policy "not to make our task in world affairs any more difficult than it already is." He urged that an effort be made within the next sixty days to achieve the kind of basic understanding he had in mind.[49]

Johnson's reaction to Bowles's proposal was negative. He scrawled a note to McGeorge Bundy on the letter: "I just disagree. I think we probably need to transfer Bowles."

▼   ▼   ▼

When he wrote to Johnson, Bowles had been in Connecticut recuperating from surgery to cure his worsening Parkinson's disease. He went on to consultations in Washington and returned to India in early August. By that time, Pakistan had begun sending thousands of guerrillas across the cease-fire line in Kashmir in an effort to force the issue and gain control of the state.

Bowles became deeply involved in efforts to persuade the Indians not to overreact to the critical situation sparked by the armed infiltration. Publicly, he avoided actions which would suggest that the United States had concluded that a full-scale war might be imminent. To the dismay of his staff, he refused to allow the embassy to update its list of American resident "wardens" who would help coordinate evacuation plans should war break out. Measures to improve the security of the embassy against possible wartime anti-American demonstrations sparked by the U.S.-Pakistan relationship were quietly carried out without his knowledge. Meanwhile, as the tempo of the fighting mounted within Kashmir in late August, he called for a more vigorous U.N. approach to Pakistani infiltration. The United States should seek to avoid public intervention for as long as possible, he urged, but if the escalation continued he wanted the Pakistanis told privately that arms shipments would be suspended should the United States become convinced they were using American-supplied weapons.[50]

When the crisis reached a new and even more dangerous phase following the September 1 thrust of a Pakistani armored column into the southern part of Kashmir state, Bowles requested authority to tell Shastri that if the Indian government accepted the U.N. secretary general's call for a cease-fire and troop withdrawal and Pakistan refused, the United States would cut off all military assistance to the Pakistanis. He recommended that a parallel approach be made to the Pakistan government. He was told in reply that a decision had been made at the highest level not to engage in direct pressure on either country for the time being but to place primary reliance on the United Nations. (This remained U.S. policy throughout the 1965 conflict.) Moreover, Washington added, his idea wouldn't work.[51]

Thus when he saw Shastri on September 4, following an unsuccessful session with Minister of External Affairs Swaran Singh three days earlier, he had no specific carrots or sticks to offer, only moral suasion. He bolstered this with a history lesson, a favorite Bowles approach, and used the guns of August 1914 to illustrate the danger of taking the wrong course at a critical moment.[52] This last-minute plea failed. On September 6 the Indians responded to the Pakistani armored thrust with a large-scale invasion of West Pakistan.

The outbreak of war dealt a severe blow to U.S.-Indian relations, as

Bowles above all recognized. The United States cut off military aid and suspended further economic assistance to both India and Pakistan. This action damaged Pakistan more than it did India, which was less dependent on the United States, but it created considerable resentment among Indians. They were angry that in ending aid to both countries simultaneously and in adopting an "even-handed" approach in U.N. Security Council efforts to end the war, Washington had judged India and Pakistan equally guilty. They resented the inability of the United States to honor its pledge that Pakistan would not use American-supplied military equipment against India, and its failure to protest publicly when Pakistan did so.

Bowles seems to have worried at least as much about reaction in the United States as he did about the ugly mood in India. As the fighting escalated, he wrote in his diary: "I know pretty well what is going on, but LBJ doesn't and he will soon be asking, 'why should we subsidize a war?' What an utter, stupid, needless mess."[53] After the Indians had crossed into West Pakistan, he forecast to Galbraith that "even if the United Nations effort [to end the fighting] succeeds . . . there is bound to be a serious setback to all that you and I and all the others have tried to do on the subcontinent. . . . The situation," he feared, "is made all the more precarious by the fact that of the people who will be sitting around the cabinet table at the National Security meetings almost none will have been to India or possess any real understanding of the forces at work in this key area."[54]

But almost immediately after the full-scale war had begun, Bowles also began citing it as proof that his criticism of post–1954 South Asian policy had been correct, and as reason for Washington to adopt the different approach he favored. He continued to stress this theme, an obvious one for him, as efforts to end the conflict continued.[55] He recommended a joint U.S.-Soviet initiative to augment these cease-fire efforts and bring about a settlement of the Kashmir dispute. This was rejected by Washington. He blamed the turndown on "the Kremlinologists," who "are now running neck and neck with the Sinologists for being wrong."[56]

When the United Nations succeeded in arranging a cease-fire in late September, he was anxious to come home and weigh in as Washington picked up the pieces of its South Asian policy. "We have an opportunity to draw a much stronger and more confident India into closer political-military relations with us and at the same time to enable and encourage her to become an effective counterbalance to China in Asia," he cabled.[57] He wanted to be on hand to make the most of it. Komer's reaction was revealing: "Chet's recent reporting has been right on target—India won't give up Kashmir, so don't force it into Soviet arms. But Chet himself is the *worst* man to plead the case, especially with LBJ. So I see no point in his coming back now. We need him out there anyway."[58]

Ordered to remain at post, Bowles wrote a long letter to Johnson in October calling yet again for a "fresh and more realistic United States policy for the subcontinent." This was once more the same approach he had proposed to the president and Rusk earlier in the year, made more urgent by Soviet progress in India resulting from the war.[59] By late November, when he wrote to McGeorge Bundy in a similar vein, Bowles found the war almost a good thing. Indian attitudes toward the United States had greatly improved since the cease-fire, he said, and the greater Indian self-confidence engendered by success in the fighting had helped. He showed a new enthusiasm for administration policies; suspension of military aid to India and Pakistan had stopped hostilities in record time.

Ignoring the recommendation he had made at the end of September, when he called for a resumption of economic assistance, he reported that deferring new aid and food grain commitments "served to make India even more determined to do something about its food problem and [has] created a greater awareness of the obstacles to India's rapid industrial growth. . . . On balance, the ground we have gained by the President's policies of the last six months significantly outweighs the losses." He called on the administration to take advantage of the favorable turn in Indian attitudes to "gain a major political break-through in India and ultimately in Asia which can bring everlasting credit to the President and a new security and influence to our country."[60]

While he sought in his resilient way to put the best face on events, Bowles also worried with good reason about the state of affairs at home and his own influence there. He spoke in his letter to Bundy of his impression, a correct one, that there was deep-seated annoyance with India in Washington. The best adjective to describe his own position there was "lousy," he wrote in his diary. "The President, the Secretary, etc. have no understanding of Asia; they discuss my views as those of an 'Indian lover' (quote from LBJ) and then refuse to send someone out here whom they trust [as Bowles had suggested]. Indeed, if they did and he agreed with our judgment (as he almost certainly would) he, too, would be dismissed as an 'Indian lover'." He feared that LBJ might push him out in sudden irritation at his persistence, or that failure of U.S. policy might oblige him to resign.[61]

As usual, he was able to overcome such bouts of private despair. In his official messages, he continued to preach his familiar gospel. In March 1966, to cite one example, he was his old self in a long memorandum to the president advising about the approach Johnson should take with newly chosen Prime Minister Indira Gandhi when she made the trip to Washington that Shastri had not lived to make himself (he had died that January). Pulling out all the same stops, he again stressed the decisive importance an economically viable and politically stable India had for a stable Asia, and the key role the United States could play in bolstering the country. Like the aborted Shastri visit, Mrs. Gandhi's trip might also be crucial in determining the future of bilateral relations and the shape of events in Asia.[62]

▾   ▾   ▾

But by then Bowles was losing whatever Washington audience he had had. The 1965 war significantly changed the way the United States looked at South Asia. It crystallized the feeling among many in both the administration and Congress that the best approach to American political and security relationships with India and Pakistan was a plague on both their houses. The conflict seemed persuasive evidence that the two countries were too concerned with their antagonism toward one another to play a major, constructive role in helping the United States achieve its principal foreign policy objectives.

This view had been growing in the two years leading up to the war. Despite Bowles's efforts, there had been increased questioning among American policymakers of the usefulness to U.S. interests of bolstering India militarily against China. President Ayub's evident decision to reduce his country's dependence on the United States and develop closer ties with China, the nonaligned countries, and even the Soviet Union had led to parallel questioning about the rationale for maintaining the decade-old security relationship with Pakistan in any meaningful form. The war provided a conclusive response to this questioning. Outraged by the use by the two countries of U.S.-supplied military equipment against one another, and painfully aware of American ineffectiveness in dealing with the South Asian antagonists, policymakers in Washington came to believe that the United States should reduce its involvement in the affairs of the subcontinent.

For the rest of Bowles's assignment in India, Washington generally put South Asia on its political back burner. The growing urgency the Johnson administration gave to Vietnam speeded this reordering of U.S. priorities. The American view of New Delhi and its foreign policy role was increasingly seen through the prism of Mrs. Gandhi's perceived antagonism toward U.S. positions in Southeast Asia and her unwillingness to join in the effort to contain Communism there. Attention given to India came to be centered largely on economic development and famine relief. The idea of a broader political and security relationship in which the United States and India would cooperate in saving "free Asia" from the Chinese was definitively shelved.

Bowles was unflagging in urging the importance of India to the United States and calling for measures to strengthen U.S.-Indian political and security ties. But the ideas he proposed were less far-reaching than those he had campaigned for before the India-Pakistan War had ended whatever possibility there had ever been for acceptance of his vision of South Asia and America's relationship to it. The policy battles he fought were important in defining the shape of America's much reduced post-1965 political/security presence in the subcontinent, but they had limited significance in the broader scheme of things of an administration whose time, energy, and resources were increasingly focused on Vietnam.

The prolonged bureaucratic battle in 1966 and early 1967 over the resumption of military supplies to India and Pakistan was perhaps the best example of this downgrading of the administration's South Asian political concerns. Bowles felt so strongly about this issue that he seriously considered resigning if against his advice "lethal" U.S. military equipment was again made available to Pakistan. But in Washington the matter was regarded as far less important than problems the administration faced elsewhere and it attracted relatively little attention outside the circle of those who specialized in South Asian policy.[63]

▾   ▾   ▾

Looking back in *Promises to Keep,* Bowles called his failed effort to develop an enduring U.S.-Indian security relationship a lost opportunity.[64] He titled his diary for the period of his second ambassadorship "Mission Unaccomplished," no doubt with this failure in mind. He found various villains: mid-level State Department and Pentagon officers hopelessly wedded to old policies, senior officials ignorant of South Asian "realities," a secretary of state too bound up in Cold War rigidities to recognize the useful role India could play in helping the United States achieve its regional and global objectives, a malign fate which intervened with the deaths of Kennedy and Nehru.

Like so many other episodes in his public life, Bowles's record on the South Asian security issue reflected his chronic tendency to go beyond the politically feasible in reaching—it would be correct to say overreaching—for a "fresh approach" to an old problem. As had happened so often before, he failed to recognize that those who questioned his recommendations had genuine problems with them. He was unable to imagine that what was crystal clear to him was much more ambiguous to others, and that the opposition of many to his ideas stemmed from honest differences of view rather than from pigheadedness or an unwillingness to face the "realities" stemming from the "new forces stirring in the Third World."

Most of those who grappled with South Asian policy from 1963 to 1965 approached the issue from a different viewpoint than that of Bowles. They did not accept his contention that the United States could over time enlist India in the active containment of China elsewhere in Asia. Nor did they share his stark assessment of Pakistan. There was widespread recognition among them that the United States and Pakistan saw different purposes in their alliance and concern that it had been badly frayed as a result of improved U.S.-Indian and China-Pakistan ties. But a relationship regarded as valuable is not easily abandoned, however sour it has become, absent some dramatic turn of events. This is particularly true, as was the case in Washington in 1964, when important segments of the bureaucracy have developed commitments to it and remain hopeful that it will improve given proper handling. As long as the Pakistanis stopped short of truly outrageous behavior in their mesalliance with the Chinese and their relations with some of the more radical and less savory Third World countries, and some semblance of peace existed between them and the Indians, there was an understandable reluctance within the administration to cut ties or to insist on the redefinition of them that Bowles urged. His contention that a breakup of the relationship would be essentially cost-free to Washington was not accepted. What emerged from the debate his recommendations had helped spark was not a policy associating the United States with the anti-Chinese Indians and either abandoning Pakistan or forcing it to conform to new and more rigorous anti-Communist standards, but something much less black and white. The Johnson administration was willing to develop a long-term military supply link with India. But it was also prepared to live with its ambiguous relationship with Pakistan, as the Eisenhower and Kennedy administrations had done earlier.

In disparaging this result, Bowles was harsher on the Johnson administration, and himself, than was warranted. He had indeed got much less than he wanted, and the setback on provision of high-performance aircraft was particularly damaging to his policy goals. But the administration's willingness to agree to a multiyear arrangement was a considerable accomplishment for Bowles. In the 1960s such arrangements with nonaligned countries were unusual, and though India's war with Pakistan brought the military supply agreement to a premature end, neither the fact of the 1964 agreement itself nor the quite generous levels and terms it contained should be taken as lightly as he took them.

The record of the bureaucratic debate suggests that while Bowles played an important role in bringing about this limited outcome, he was often his own worst enemy. His repeated, eventually tiresome calls for radical changes in South Asia policy that would have made the U.S.-Indian security relationship the most important element in Washington's approach to the region heightened the widely held conviction that he was hopelessly pro-Indian. Although he was painfully aware of this reputation, and on at least one occasion apparently promised to mend his ways,[65] he never seriously tried to correct it. He might have served his own purposes better if he had sought greater balance in his recommendations and had acknowledged in more than an off-hand way that there were minuses as well as plusses in his approach. He might also have been better off if he had occasionally shared the dim view he took of some of the actions of the Indian government and not confined his misgivings to his diary.

Komer described Bowles's credibility problem well in a memorandum he sent to Bundy in June 1964: "You and I are among the few people in this town who read Bowles's epistles for sense. He's so drawn down his credit that neither the Department of Defense nor the Seventh [Executive] Floor of the State Department really focuses on his mail any more. Even the President seems to react adversely to Chet's over-bidding. This is Chet's fatal flaw."[66]

If anything, the problem became worse in Bowles's final years in New Delhi. As National Security Adviser Walt Rostow put it in a note to Johnson in 1966, "[Bowles] has a bad case of localitis which, in fact, serves neither India's interests nor ours."[67] Nor, Rostow might have added, did it serve the interests of Bowles himself.

17

A New Deal
for India

BOWLES had followed Indian economic development closely after leaving New Delhi in 1953 and was in the forefront of the successful effort to bring about high levels of U.S. economic assistance to India in the late 1950s and early 1960s. Though he supported the Indian government's ambitious designs for industrialization, his concern always focused on rural development. Long before many others, he had recognized that the building of a strong and prosperous rural economy was a prerequisite for sound industrial growth and orderly political progress alike.

On his second assignment as on his first, Bowles devoted a good deal of energy and attention to the economic aid program, especially those aspects of it that affected the Indian countryside. His strategy for persuading the Indians to adopt policies that he thought would lead to a more productive as well as a more just economy included frequent official and personal contact with the country's leaders and appeals in books, articles, and speeches to the politically literate public. These interventions helped bring about the Green Revolution in Indian agriculture. Bowles's role in that historic breakthrough was his most important and enduring accomplishment in his second assignment to New Delhi.

A remarkably able AID mission assisted Bowles in carrying out his ambitious plans. He leaned heavily from the start on Charles "Ed" Lindblom, a skilled and realistic Yale University economist who played a key role in persuading him to change his approach to rural development. Later, when veteran bureaucrat C. Tyler Wood had completed his assignment, he talked John Lewis into becoming head of the mission. A professor of economics at Indiana University and member of the President's Council of Economic Advisers, Lewis had lived in India and had done considerable work on Indian economic development.[1] Like Bowles a warm supporter of India, he shared many of his ambassador's views as well as his interventionist ardor. Bowles and Lewis joined forces to bring to the AID mission an outstanding team of senior professionals with a broad range of skills and experience. Confident in the mission's judgment, Bowles left day-to-day operations to Lewis and his staff and was less a hands-on manager than he had been in the 1950s. But the final decisions on major issues were always his.

Looking back, some of Bowles's associates contend that India's economic development and American assistance to it had a much higher priority for him than the political/security programs he pushed so hard during the early years of his second assignment. Bowles himself would almost certainly have said that the two efforts were closely connected. Only an India made strong through economic progress, and especially progress in the countryside, could play the major role he envisaged for it as an anti-Communist force. And only if India limited its military expenditures—and he had wanted the United States to exert its influence to that end—would it be able, with American and other foreign assistance, to continue its economic advance.

▾   ▾   ▾

Bowles's initial intention was to urge that Nehru revamp the community development program they had agreed to in 1951. Spread widely—and thinly—across India, the program had languished badly and had failed to fulfill the promise Bowles and others had seen in it in the early 1950s. As his associates sometimes said, Bowles stuck to old ideas the way a dog hangs on to a favorite bone. He was determined to revive the program, which by 1963 had come to encompass village self-government *(panchayati raj)*. Before leaving for India, he told Washington officials that he had in mind an intensive demonstration area approach in which a variety of rural development activities (for example, agricultural production, health, education, and road-building) would be given a well-funded, carefully integrated push in selected districts.[2]

Led by Wood and Lindblom, the senior AID staff resisted this approach. As Lindblom put it, the principal bottlenecks to rural development were Indian national and state pricing, procurement, and distribution policies; relatively little could be done through community development work at the district and village level. He and other AID officials believed that these policies needed to be changed to bring about substantial increases in India's faltering agricultural production. They favored approaches that would encourage food grain output through minimum price support programs for farmers, higher production and availability of fertilizer, more intensive irrigation, and the development and distribution of better hybrid seeds.[3]

At first Bowles was not moved by these arguments. He grumbled that if the AID staff did not help him prepare the memo he wanted to send Nehru on revamping community development, he would find someone else who could. As Lindblom reported at the time to his colleagues, Bowles wanted "a proposal for making better people and not just better producers. He [was] opposed to the idea that the best way to make better people is to first make them better producers."[4] Bowles sent Nehru a personal eleven-page memorandum in which he recommended an integrated program (education, health, public works, education, house construction, etc.) to be initiated in model areas in each Indian state.[5] He cut off all contacts with Lindblom for weeks.

Then suddenly he changed his position. Summoning Lindblom, who would not have been surprised if he had been sent packing to New Haven, he announced his conversion to a focus on agricultural production. "Ed, let's do it," Lindblom has remembered him saying. "Draw me up a program. I'll talk it over in Washington."[6] Bowles offered Lindblom no explanation, nor does any appear in his writings. Indeed, the account he gave in *Promises to Keep* of his first few months back in New Delhi omits any mention of community development and speaks only of the importance he attached to raising farm output.[7]

The AID staff and Bowles were not alone in concluding that major policy changes were required to boost Indian agricultural output. Their assessment was shared by influential figures within the Indian government and many of the multilateral government organizations and privately funded international foundations that were involved in the Indian agricultural sector. This dissatisfaction with ongoing food and agriculture policy was fully justified. The stagnation of grain production and the increasing need for food imports had long since become a well-recognized national problem and the subject of numerous studies. But although the Third Five Year Plan gave greater importance than the Second Plan had to agriculture, economic policy continued to emphasize the industrial sector, still seen as key to rapid development. Moreover, for political reasons, pricing policy was designed to make cheap food available to the potentially volatile urban masses at the expense of the farmers. This combination of government inattention and low prices conspired to keep agricultural production down, especially of food grains, which were less profitable for farmers than cash crops.

India's growing dependence on imports to meet its food needs was reflected in the U.S.-Indian PL-480 agreement signed in 1960. This provided for delivery of sixteen million tons of wheat and one million tons of rice over a four-year period and was the largest such agreement the United States had ever made. Critics correctly argued that the availability of such massive amounts of foreign grain on easy terms and with minimal and casually observed self-help requirements had inhibited India from adopting pricing, credit, and input policies that would stimulate domestic food production.

Once converted, Bowles attacked the problem with special zeal. He came to recognize that

> the most immediate needs . . . were to increase the use of fertilizer, to develop more modern techniques of irrigation, to adapt the extraordinary new hybrid seeds to India's climate and soil conditions, and to press for expanded rural credit at low interest rates. If the Indian Government could be persuaded to assure the cultivators year after year a price high enough to encourage them to take the risks involved in new methods and expanded production, we felt that there was reason to hope for a new dynamism in the largely agricultural villages.[8]

In their effort to promote this new agricultural strategy, Bowles and his staff were joined by other influential and forceful advocates. The World Bank, as chair of a consortium of countries that provided economic assistance, and a major donor itself, brought its influence to bear on the issue of price and incentive reforms under the leadership of its new president, American banker George Woods. The Rockefeller Foundation also played a useful part with its work on agricultural research and the use of high-yield varieties of wheat and rice. So did the Ford Foundation, which had developed package programs for boosting crop production in selected areas and was able to influence Indian thinking in furthering that approach. In Washington, AID Administrator David Bell strongly favored using U.S. resource transfers to encourage the Indians to adopt the new strategy.[9]

The most important figures in the American bureaucracy involved in the effort were President Johnson himself and his able and hard-charging secretary of agriculture, Orville Freeman. Johnson and Freeman had come to question the usefulness of the United States continuing to pour economic assistance into India while Indian food grain production remained stagnant. They believed the Indians had to do more to raise output. When Bowles met with Freeman in Washington in March 1964 he brought with him a memorandum prepared by Lindblom that laid out the AID mission's thinking on key agricultural issues, including fertilizer inputs and production, irrigation, extension and research, price supports, and land reform. He invited Freeman, an old friend and, like Bowles, a liberal Democrat and former state governor, to visit India. The secretary came out the following month.

Freeman subjected the Indians to critical questioning during his April 1964 visit. He had been interested in the agricultural economies of the developing countries for years, and the trip strengthened his concern about India's food problems. Under his determined direction, the Department of Agriculture was on its way to bureaucratic leadership of the planning and execution of overseas food aid programs (subject to the ultimate—and active—control of the president), and Freeman became Johnson's confidant and point man on Indian agricultural policy reform.

In the dialogue with the Indians, Johnson and Freeman were far more aggressive in their tactics than were Bowles and most of the other Americans involved. They were also much more skeptical about Indian performance. Both these aspects of the Johnson-Freeman approach were vividly evidenced in the president's adoption later of the "short-tether" policy on food shipments. The policy limited the duration and size of PL-480 agreements and mandated frequent, satisfactory review of Indian progress in adopting and carrying out self-help reform measures in food and agriculture policy as a condition for further deliveries.

On the Indian side, the lead in the development of the new agricultural strategy was taken by Food and Agriculture Minister C. Subramaniam. A dynamic South Indian politician who had served in Nehru's cabinet as minister of steel and heavy industries, Subramaniam was well known to Bowles and other senior Americans from the Bokaro negotiations. His selection by Shastri to take over the difficult portfolio seemed to indicate an interest on the new prime minister's part in adopting policy changes; Subramaniam, a skilled administrator, was known to be reform-minded and unlike his predecessors was seriously interested in doing something about agriculture. Over the next year and a half, he gradually put together a new reform policy, found political and bureaucratic allies, and developed a strong reform-oriented team. His key collaborators within the Indian government were Asoka Mehta, a recent arrival in the Congress party from the Socialists who had become deputy chairman of the Planning Commission, and the brilliant senior civil servant L. K. Jha, who held the important post of secretary to the prime minister. All three were on warm terms with Bowles.

Subramaniam faced strong opposition within the cabinet to the far-reaching policy changes he favored. A serious drought in 1965 fortuitously helped him in getting them adopted. The drought heightened the Shastri government's awareness of the need to adopt new approaches if the country was to avoid disaster. It also made India more vulnerable to American influence and pressure. As noted, the United States had suspended further economic assistance at the outbreak of the India-Pakistan War. The Indians recognized that if they were to get American concessional food grains flowing again in their time of need, they would have to demonstrate to Washington (and particularly to Johnson) that they were prepared to take adequate self-help measures.

What John Lewis has called the prolonged "transaction" on Indian agricultural reform was brought to a successful conclusion in November 1965. Meeting in Rome, where they were attending a session of the Food and Agriculture Organization, Freeman and Subramaniam reached agreement on a large and detailed package of policy reforms. The reforms were subsequently approved by the Shastri cabinet and Subramaniam then announced them in the Indian Parliament. To avoid suspicion that he had knuckled under to American pressure, he did not associate the package with the "Rome treaty," which remained secret for some years.

The agreement provided that investment in agriculture would be increased 40 percent in the coming year, and during the Fourth Five Year Plan (1966–1971) would be double the level in the third. It put particular stress on production and use of chemical fertilizers, encouraging foreign private investment in fertilizer plants and removing government-imposed restraints on distribution.[10] The new strategy also included a massive increase in the high-yielding seed program, more readily available credit for cultivators, and expanded and improved use of irrigation water. The Indians committed themselves to specific acreage and target tonnages for areas that would get first call on high-yield seeds, fertilizer, and other inputs. They also agreed to review pricing policies to ensure a favorable relationship between the price of food grains and the cost of farmers' inputs.[11]

When Mrs. Gandhi became prime minister a few weeks later in January 1966, she continued the strategy and kept Subramaniam on as minister. During her government, the provisions of the strategy were substantially implemented and contributed importantly to a sizable increase in Indian farm output over the next quarter century. By the 1989–90 crop year, this Green Revolution had boosted food grain production to over 170 million tons, more than twice the level of the early 1960s. Although this was less of a percentage gain than several other Asian countries achieved in the period, it is impressive when compared to India's performance in the years before the reforms were initiated.

The relative importance of the roles of the different players involved in bringing about the agricultural reforms remains a matter of debate. The Indians, Americans, and others associated with the reforms had many of the same goals in mind, but they often differed in matters of emphasis, detail, and tactics over the prolonged period that led to the enactment and implementing of the changes. Parceling out credit for the outcome is a difficult task.

It does seem clear, however, that Bowles was able to play a distinctive part. His close, well-informed personal involvement strengthened the position of the embassy and AID mission as key players in the "transaction" and encouraged the specialists on his staff in their efforts. His ability to bring his personal influence to bear was probably even more important than his formal ambassadorial interventions. Because he knew a good deal about rural development and was recognized as a longtime well-wisher of India with a special interest in the country's economic development, he could spell out to Indian officials some home truths about their policy failings and what they had to do to set them right. He did this in a persuasive, nonabrasive way, making a unique contribution to getting the reforms moving and ensuring their ultimate success. He was less effective in Washington, where the widespread perception that he was pro-Indian limited his influence with the president and others. Freeman, for one, has said that he never used Bowles's name in discussions for that reason.[12]

▾   ▾   ▾

The drought in the Indian 1965–66 crop year that provided impetus to the adoption of the new agricultural strategy proved to be the first of two consecutive failures of monsoon rains over large parts of northern and eastern India. Despite the urgent need for food imports created by this almost unprecedented disaster and the specific policy reform measures Subramaniam had agreed to with Freeman, Johnson maintained the practice he had initiated in the summer of 1965 of short-tethering PL-480 shipments.

The only significant break in this policy came in March 1966, when Johnson authorized a shipment of 3.5 million tons of wheat. This relaxation followed Mrs. Gandhi's visit to Washington. The president had been much taken by the prime minister at the time. His unexpected decision to remain at the Indian embassy for a formal dinner in her honor seemed to symbolize the success of the visit in promoting mutual understanding and good will.

This happy turn of events surprised and delighted Bowles. "The climax for me," he wrote in his diary, "was when LBJ closed his toast by saying, 'Missus Gaaandhi, Ah only hopes we can somehow be worthy of ya.' I rubbed my eyes in amazement."[13] A few months later, the practice of dribbling out food grain rather than authorizing its shipment in large tranches was resumed. It remained in effect until the famine was over.

The short-tether, or ship-to-mouth, policy and Johnson's role in it have been the subject of many studies and no detailed account is called for here. Economists and political scientists alike have been understandably fascinated by the spectacle of an American president becoming so deeply involved in the food assistance program that he insisted on personally approving every wheat delivery from U.S. ports to India and came to be regarded as an authority on grain ship sailing schedules.[14]

Bowles shared this fascination. But he was also appalled by the policy and argued that it was not only uncalled for but harmful to American interests. He wrote in a February 1966 diary entry:

LBJ's performance remains beyond comprehension or belief. . . . It is a cruel performance. The Indians must conform; they must be made to fawn; their pride must be cracked. Pressure to improve India's performance was sensible; but that had been assured in 1965 [by the Freeman-Subramaniam agreement]. Once the Indian commitment to modernize their own agriculture had been made was the moment for bold, effective, confidence-creating gestures. Instead came more pressure, more mystery with the poor State Department trying to explain each move or refusal to move as a logical result of India's failure to do all kinds of things that no sensible person ever expected them to do. It is in this way that distrust and hatred are born among people who want to be our friends.[15]

Bowles did what he could to change the president's position. He argued, unsuccessfully, that in demanding evidence of self-help measures, Johnson had failed to take into account the reforms the Indians had carried out despite the drought. He spelled out in stark terms the extent of the disaster and the urgent need for help. Aware that the president was receiving conflicting advice from the various departments and agencies involved in the food assistance program, he encouraged Johnson to send out independent observers and welcomed his decision to dispatch members of Congress to review the situation. (To Bowles's satisfaction, the delegation, which included Bob Dole, then a House member from Kansas, unanimously recommended that the flow of wheat should be continued.) In a noteworthy skirmish, he was able to sidetrack an ill-conceived presidential initiative to flood India with Department of Agriculture county agents, an example of Johnson's preference for dealing with the Indian food problem by tried-and-true American methods. Throughout these difficult months, he tried his best to soften the peremptory tone of Washington's messages to the Indians. He was convinced it could only harm the relationship at a particularly sensitive time.

As Johnson persisted in the short-tether policy, Bowles grew increasingly exasperated. Like many others, including LBJ's own White House staff, he speculated about the president's motives. "Dope sheets are flowing out of Washington which seek to explain the Great Man's intellectual and emotional prowess," he wrote in November 1966.

> But the most knowledgeable are baffled. Some say "because India is not trying to help itself," but the facts are clearly in the opposite direction. Others say "because we must ask Congress," but the new legislation which takes into account India's massive needs has just been signed. My guess is that the real answer is a combination of factors: (1) a deep distrust of Indians; (2) deep irritation about India's failure "after all we have given them" to support him on Vietnam, and (3) a sadistic pleasure in the display of power.[16]

Johnson himself had no regrets about the short-tether policy, and wrote later in his autobiography that he was convinced it had been successful. He claimed that without it India would not have adopted self-help measures, nor would other countries have contributed to the effort, as he had insisted they do because of the reduction in American grain surpluses. Congressional support could only have been assured by evidence both of India's progress in helping itself and of the participation of other donors in the food relief program. Pleased that he had been the key figure in an operation that in two years moved fourteen million tons of grain, the largest transfer of food from one country to another in history, he pictured himself as a strong and far-sighted leader ready to take tough measures to ensure that India's longer-term interests were met. If he did not specifically name Bowles when he scorned "Americans who considered themselves best friends" of India for pressing him to change his position, it was obvious that his ambassador to India fell in that category. "I decided," Johnson recalled, "I would have to live with the noisy but superficial criticism and do what I believed was right."[17]

Despite these claims, Bowles and other critics were correct in arguing that the drastic policy Johnson had pursued was neither necessary nor called for. The president's strategy doubtless made the Indians more aware of the importance of moving as rapidly as possible to self-sufficiency in food, not least to avoid putting themselves again in the demeaning position of beggars literally looking to a foreign country for the next meal. But like so much that Johnson did it was an exercise in excess, and was almost certainly influenced by considerations such as India's Southeast Asia policy, as Bowles, Freeman, and many others believed. Although the president liked to say that no one ever died as a result of his PL-480 policies, those policies had serious economic and political repercussions. A less drastic approach would have allowed the Indian government to plan distribution more rationally and thus avoided its having to cut back as severely as it did the amount of food grain it provided its citizens under its rationing program. It would also have avoided ill will toward the president and the United States government among Indian political leaders and officials.

▾   ▾   ▾

The efforts to persuade the Indians to adopt measures that would help raise farm output were part of a larger plan to use the assistance program to bring about major reforms in the Indian economy. At the request of its Washington headquarters, the AID mission in New Delhi enthusiastically developed in the spring of 1964 a Long-Range Assistance Strategy for India. Priority items in this strategy, which Bowles fully endorsed, included assistance to Indian industry and support for population control, as well as rural development. Programs in the industrial sector sought to increase incentives to private enterprise and improve the efficiency of government-owned plants, an objective Bowles believed could best be achieved by placing public projects under independent corporations where they would be free from bureaucratic interference.

The most noteworthy population program was assistance in the development of contraceptive manufacture. Like many concerned with Indian economic development at that time, Bowles had not been particularly interested in birth control measures during his first assignment. By the 1960s, however, when he had come to recognize that population limitation was needed to achieve development goals, he gave it the careful study and enthusiastic advocacy he had reserved earlier for rural programs.

Bowles and the AID mission followed up the Long-Range Assistance Strategy with a far-reaching proposal for bolstering the Indian economy. This was termed the Big Push. Prepared under John Lewis's direction, it reflected the approach advocated by Walt Rostow in his influential book, *The Stages of Economic Growth*. Big Push was based on the premise that if international donors provided enough additional foreign exchange to support a new growth-oriented economic policy for five to ten years, India could under favorable conditions achieve self-sustained growth by the late 1970s. As Bowles and others put it in their effort to win support from a doubting Washington, the road can be shortened by broadening it. The administration was considering the idea when the outbreak of the India-Pakistan War in the summer of 1965 led it to suspend—not double—new economic assistance.

After the war and the conclusion of the Freeman-Subramaniam agreement a few months later, the United States and India moved toward what Dean Rusk called "an economic bargain."[18] This meshed with the program promoted by the World Bank to invigorate the Indian economy in line with the conclusions of a high-level Bank mission that had visited India in 1965. Prepared at a time when donor countries were becoming increasingly dissatisfied with India's lackluster economic performance and concerned that their assistance was not being properly used, the mission's recommendations called for far-reaching reforms to liberalize the tightly controlled way the Indians managed their economy and move the country to a more pragmatic, market-oriented system. In return for these changes in Indian economic policies and administrative procedures, the members of the Aid India Consortium were to provide substantially higher levels of assistance, especially "program aid" (assistance not earmarked for specific projects) the Indians needed to restore their critically depleted foreign exchange reserves.[19]

In April 1966 Asoka Mehta, by then planning minister, came to Washington and negotiated an agreement with World Bank President Woods that included such Indian government commitments in economic management as a major liberalization of import controls and simplified procedures to speed up India's system of industrial licensing. Woods for his part pledged on the Consortium's behalf to attempt to raise the total aid level to $1.6 billion (including $900 million in program assistance) from its previous level of approximately $1.2 billion. Although there was no specific mention of the devaluation of the rupee in the agreement, both sides assumed that it would be a necessary part of the reform package.

Bowles staunchly endorsed both ends of the so-called bargain. The degree of his intervention with the Indians varied with his interest in individual issues. The reform of policy on food and agriculture, which the Indians had pledged to continue in line with the Freeman-Subramaniam agreement, remained at the top of his agenda. By contrast, his involvement in devaluation, carried out by the Indians on June 5 when they announced a 58 percent cut in the exchange rate of the rupee, was at most marginal. Like other senior American officials in Washington and New Delhi, he had strongly favored devaluation, but there is no available evidence that he played a significant role in trying to persuade Mrs. Gandhi and her advisers to agree to it.

Neither Bowles nor his senior colleagues foresaw the political controversy devaluation would create for the prime minister, then little more than four months in office. The measure was strongly denounced within the Congress party (most outspokenly by its president and kingmaker, K. Kamaraj), and by most elements of the political opposition, as knuckling under to foreign pressure. Despite the World Bank's lead role in promoting the reform package, many Indian critics of devaluation blamed the Johnson administration for conspiring to force it on the Indian government.

The political fallout in India was worsened by the failure of devaluation and other reform measures that accompanied it to bring about the higher levels of foreign assistance and the boost in exports that had been expected and used to justify them. Stunned by the negative reaction at home, Mrs. Gandhi lost faith in Subramaniam and Mehta, both strong devaluation advocates. Their fall from grace weakened the reformist faction in her government and Bowles's own influence there. Some observers, noting the joint communiqué Mrs. Gandhi and the Soviets issued in Moscow a few weeks after the devaluation announcement, trace her subsequent antagonism toward the United States and her willingness to challenge U.S. policy in Southeast Asia to the political difficulties devaluation and economic policy reform caused her. In this view, the uproar over these economic initiatives led her to conclude that she had to demonstrate her independence of the United States and the strength of her leftist political credentials. (See Chapter 18 for a discussion of the communiqué.)[20]

Bowles's efforts to get Washington to live up to *its* end of the economic bargain were reflected in his unremitting calls for high levels of U.S. economic assistance. He and other advocates did not get as much for India as they had hoped (and what the Indians believed had been promised them). Development assistance reached $415 million in FY 1966, the highest it had been except for 1962, but then declined. Figures for Bowles's last three years in India were $151 million (FY 1967), $292 million (FY 1968), and $176 million (FY 1969). Corresponding figures for total assistance, including food aid, were $1,130 million (reflecting wheat provided during the famine), $433 million, $629 million, and $439 million.[21]

A less important battle, but one to which Bowles devoted a great deal of attention, was his lengthy attempt to reduce the accumulation of rupees that had resulted from the sale of American food and fiber for local currency under the PL-480 program. Soon after he arrived in India, he developed the idea of a binational foundation that would use the rupees to finance projects in science, culture, and education. The proposal moved very slowly in Washington before Johnson suddenly agreed to it and formally offered the foundation to Mrs. Gandhi during her 1966 visit. She accepted the offer, but with little enthusiasm. Returning home, she found strong opposition to the concept from all parts of the Indian political and cultural spectrum and soon decided not to proceed with it. Bowles tried unsuccessfully for years to revive the idea. It was ultimately brought to fruition in the 1980s by Ambassador Harry Barnes.

▾   ▾   ▾

Bowles used his standing as a well-known friend of India to write unofficial letters and memoranda to senior Indian leaders and officials presenting his views on economic development. He hoped that packaging the ideas as his own rather than as official U.S. government positions would lead the Indians to consider them friendly advice from a recognized well-wisher rather than interference by a foreign government. It probably also occurred to him that if the messages were publicized, their having a personal cast would deflect allegations by anti-American political elements and others that the United States was bringing improper influence to bear. The technique allowed Bowles to transmit an array of thoughts that he could never have cleared in Washington. He often sent his messages directly to the prime minister with the reasonable expectation that they would then be disseminated to cabinet ministers, members of the Planning Commission, and others with important roles in economic development.

Although he sent memoranda to Nehru on agricultural policy and sought to move him on other issues, Bowles had recognized as soon as he returned to New Delhi that there could be no repeat performance of the relationship the two men had enjoyed in the 1950s. The prime minister, old and failing, had in fact only ten months to live at that time. Bowles found that he was dealing with a different man from the one he had known before. "In my first twenty-four hours," he noted, "it is apparent that I will be a witness to the collapse of an era, or rather I should say to its petering out. Nehru was 80 per cent of Indian government authority; now he must be 30 per cent as the struggle for supremacy is on with a vengeance."[22]

Bowles reckoned that he saw Nehru scarcely a dozen times in 1963 and 1964. He had met with him as many times in a month during his first assignment. He was often discouraged by their contacts. Nehru had become tired, old, and a bit confused, he commented in December 1963. "Why can't people leave rather than wilt and peter out?"[23] The prime minister's increasing frailty slowed the machinery of the Indian government and made it more difficult for Bowles to get any decisions, let alone the right ones. It was a major element in the VOA fiasco. Bowles was both frustrated and saddened. Looking back over the preceding months at the time he learned of Nehru's death, he remembered: "He was obviously so tired, so anxious to avoid difficult questions. . . . Only once or twice did I see flashes of the old humor and incisiveness."[24]

The problem had become worse after Nehru suffered a stroke in January 1964 while taking part in an annual Congress party session in eastern India. When Assistant Secretary Phillips Talbot and Bowles paid a courtesy call on him two months later, they were shocked by his mental and psychological deterioration. Nehru and Talbot knew one another well, but Bowles reported that the effort he and Talbot made to draw some response from the prime minister on several subjects that would normally have interested him was unavailing. "Based on this ten-minute visit," he concluded, "it is difficult for me to believe that he can last long as an effective political force in India."[25] Ten weeks later Nehru was dead.

▾   ▾   ▾

Bowles was very much taken by Lal Bahadur Shastri, who served as India's second prime minister from June 1964 to January 1966. During his second assignment the ambassador liked to divide Indian leaders into what he called "Adamses" and "Jacksons." In this division—which again revealed the amateur American historian in Bowles—the Adamses were people educated in Britain or the United States. Bowles found them anxious to prove that they were not pro-American or pro-West and willing "to go overboard the other way to prove they're not. They have one foot in Asia and one foot in Europe; charming, attractive and bright people, but they're not thoroughly Indian or deeply Indian."

By contrast, Bowles's Jacksons were India-educated, had rarely if ever been outside the country, and spoke locally accented "Indian English" if they spoke English at all. Although he continued to have many good friends and associates among the Indian Adamses, especially those whom he had known during his first assignment when the group held a stronger position, he came increasingly to admire and cultivate the Jacksonian newcomers and urged the embassy staff to do the same. He found them "more earthy and pragmatic, and closer to the masses of the people to whom they felt they belonged. . . . I have much more faith in that type person for the future," he told an interviewer soon after leaving India in 1969.[26]

Shastri's credentials made him a preeminent Jackson. He came from an ordinary lower-middle class, middle-caste Hindu family in the northern state of Uttar Pradesh. He had been educated entirely in India and, before journeying to Egypt soon after becoming prime minister, had never traveled abroad. A diminutive Congress party politician scarcely five feet tall, he came across as an unpretentious, down-to-earth, genuinely home-spun product of grass-roots India, almost the opposite of his worldly and sophisticated predecessor. Bowles hoped that a man of such modest origins would be responsive to his own strongly felt concerns about the lot of the common man, and would give them the same primacy he did in his approach to Indian economic development. He also thought that as a new incumbent Shastri might be more receptive to his advice than the jaded and tired Nehru. He tried hard to win his confidence and was successful in developing a warm relationship with him. This was reinforced by the ties Steb Bowles was able to cultivate with Shastri's wife.

Like many other observers, Bowles was impressed by Shastri's growth in office, his intelligence, and his political courage. He concluded later that had he not died after only nineteen months in power, he would have had an impressive career. He considered Shastri's performance during his abbreviated tenure extraordinary, and compared him to Harry Truman, another grass-roots political leader who had followed a great man and, to the surprise of many, had risen to the occasion.

Probably the most important of the messages Bowles sent Shastri was his October 1964 letter on economic development strategy. Written, or so Bowles claimed, at the prime minister's request, it is a compendium of recommendations for combining rapid economic growth and social justice, the indispensable twin elements in Bowles's vision of a New Deal for India that he hoped Shastri shared. The long list of proposals he set out for Shastri's consideration included the intensification of rural public works projects, vast new low-cost housing programs, expanded production of inexpensive building materials, and a host of other development schemes targeted at the poor. Taking issue with some development economists of the time, he also advocated greater availability of cheap and simple consumer goods, a prescription in his strategy for economic growth dating back to the early 1950s. This was needed to instill popular confidence in economic development and create incentives for higher production. Inevitably, he again gave prominence to land reform, which, he argued, could be most effectively carried out by enactment of a progressive land tax system. He was not deterred by the harsh fact that land reform was political dynamite in a country where well-to-do landowners played a key role in the ruling Congress party and that taxes on land in particular were anathema to that powerful group.[27]

Bowles stressed many of these same themes in his speeches and writing. One of his favorite techniques for getting out his message was to prepare a feature article for the *American Reporter,* the USIS monthly published in English and many vernacular languages. It would then be picked up by mainline dailies. Aware that the Indians were growing increasingly sensitive about the donor-recipient relationship, he usually dealt more in his public statements with the overall Indian development effort than he did with the role of the United States. He was especially careful not to crow about the expensive programs Washington funded.

The four lectures he gave at Delhi University in December 1963, later published as *The Makings of a Just Society,* are probably Bowles's most comprehensive public statement on economic development.[28] He wrote Rusk that in them "I plan to attack (in the tactful manner becoming an Ambassador) the clichés surrounding Indian development, to suggest a more pragmatic approach to attain economic growth."[29] Richard Celeste has recalled that Bowles saw the lectures as an opportunity to accentuate in particular the importance of rural development.[30]

With the cooperation of University Vice Chancellor C. D. Deshmukh, a former finance minister and old friend, Bowles had found an academic setting to get across his favorite point that in most developing countries only the expansion of agriculture offered any hope for a reasonable rate of capital accumulation. "Rupee for rupee, capital investment in the rural areas will affect more people and generate more growth than anywhere else," he argued. India should learn from Japan's successful experience in raising the income of the rural poor through redistribution of land and the development of small-scale, rural-based industry that had followed. He used the lectures to give his own definition of the essentials of nation building—adequate capital, enough goods and services to motivate people to make the personal effort required for development, adequate skills, curbing of population growth, and, finally, "a unifying sense of national purpose with effective communication between the people and their leaders."[31] He called for industrial growth, but insisted that it be combined with social justice. And in a final talk he returned to an old and favorite subject that he had been among the first to highlight, the competition between India and China. That rivalry would continue to draw world attention, and, "although no one can foresee the outcome, every person who believes not only in material progress but in the dignity of the individuals who create that progress has a personal stake in India's success."[32]

Bowles's critics have rightly charged that in working up his formulas for economic development, he paid insufficient attention to India's distinct economic, social, and political traditions and experience. As one student of Indian affairs has incisively put it, he treated India as a *tabula rasa* on which he could inscribe his New Deal ideas.[33] Although Dennis Merrill's observations in *Bread and the Ballot* concern Bowles's approach to economic policy during his first New Delhi assignment, they are equally accurate as an assessment of Bowles's views in the 1960s:

> Bowles assumed that America's style of welfare capitalism could be grafted easily onto the Indian setting. He clearly underestimated the historically rooted obstacles to the creation of a modern, consumer society: India's caste structure, underdeveloped industrial capacity, antiquated system of land tenure and ever-growing population—to list just a few. In addition, there was the question of whether the Nehru government possessed the political will to enact reforms and break down some of the

barriers. Bowles's go-getter style and natural optimism . . . simply led him to misjudge the seriousness of certain harsh realities.[34]

More fundamentally, Bowles's economic formulas reflected his view that people were much the same everywhere, whatever their cultural background and history. They shared the same basic economic and political goals and could be moved by the same incentives. Hence the same fundamental policies could be effectively adopted everywhere. Although Bowles knew a great deal about the politics and economics of India, it was a selective knowledge that ignored or minimized aspects of Indian life he found unpalatable. The gaps and mistakes in his information were at times the result of his tendency to hear what he wanted to hear. Blind-sided by his optimism, his universalist approach to people and institutions, and a tendency to regard opposition to his liberal views as obstructionist if not downright reactionary, he made important errors in judgment. Had he recognized how different India (and the Third World generally) was from his liberal vision of the United States, he might have revised his targets and spared himself many disappointments.

The record of a call on Bowles in 1966 by a Congress party parliamentary backbencher from a rural constituency near Madras provides an amusing illustration of how badly Bowles received information that conflicted with his conception of what was right for India. The M.P. considered himself a progressive farmer of pro-American political orientation and, like many others, wished to pay homage to the famous ambassador. Bowles was led to believe that an amicable meeting of the minds was in store. His long jaw fell as the M.P. detailed the advantages of organic fertilizer over the chemical varieties that Bowles promoted. It fell further when the visitor, apparently under the mistaken impression that the representative of the world's greatest capitalist power must be a supporter of "haves" such as himself, detailed how he had successfully evaded his state's land reform laws by the familiar stratagem of deeding land to his relatives. "Of course I believe in wider ownership of land," he confided to Bowles in the expectation that an American ambassador would fully approve. "I have transferred land to my wife, my sons, my daughters, my dogs, my cats. It was all very simple." Bowles was not amused, and the meeting quickly ended.[35]

▾   ▾   ▾

Indira Gandhi, who was prime minister during the last three years of Bowles's assignment, resented his practice of offering advice to government officials and the Indian public. To his surprise and dismay, his relationship with that prickly and cold-blooded daughter of Jawaharlal Nehru was far less satisfactory than it had been with either of her predecessors.

Bowles had known Mrs. Gandhi well since the early 1950s, when she lived in the shadow of her father as a member of the Nehru household. He had welcomed her decision to join the Shastri cabinet—her first experience in government office—and had been disappointed when she had been given the information and broadcasting portfolio rather than made minister of external affairs. When Shastri died, Bowles thought her a better choice as successor than her rival, former Finance Minister Morarji Desai, though he would have preferred the powerful Western Indian leader, Defense Minister Y. B. Chavan, who chose not to contest.

He was fairly sanguine that Mrs. Gandhi would be effective as prime minister. Unlike many others, including those in the Congress party "syndicate" of leaders who had maneuvered to bring about her election, he recognized that she was no "dumb doll," as some called her, who could be easily manipulated. "Once in office," he advised Washington, "Mrs. Gandhi may turn out to be much stronger than is generally expected." He added, however, that much would depend on whom she listened to. He was troubled by her inexperience with economic issues—she was an "economic neophyte"—but found some assurance in what he considered her close links with reform-minded ministers and civil servants such as Subramaniam. Describing her as a "persistent advocate of rebuilding relations with the United States," he discounted rumors of her anti-Americanism, but suggested that she might as prime minister be influenced by continuing Soviet flattery.[36]

According to the account of an embassy officer close to him, Bowles seriously damaged his relations with the new prime minister by blundering badly in his first communication to her after she had taken office. Failing to recognize that as head of the Indian government she would not countenance being treated as the young, relatively inexperienced daughter of Nehru he had so long considered her, he foolishly sent her a letter filled with avuncular guidance on economic policy. He compounded his mistake by addressing it to "Dear Indira." Apparently offended both by the gratuitous advice and the wording of the salutation, Mrs. Gandhi reportedly instructed one of her officials to call in a senior American embassy officer and inform him that the prime minister wanted never again to receive such a message from the ambassador.[37]

Like many other observers, Bowles recognized Mrs. Gandhi's weaknesses in her first year in office. He predicted to Rusk that following the 1967 general elections, in which he accurately anticipated major Congress party losses, her chances of returning to power were no better than fifty-fifty. He again hoped that Defense Minister Chavan would be the new choice.[38] Mrs. Gandhi hung on, however, weathered a succession of political challenges, and gradually bested the Congress party barons who had installed her. By the time Bowles completed his assignment, she was on the verge of engineering a party split that eventually led to her winning as strong a position of power as her father had enjoyed.

Contrary to Bowles's forecast, Mrs. Gandhi came to demonstrate the same mistrust of U.S. policies and motives her father had so often displayed. But unlike Nehru, she was not prepared to recognize Bowles as the exceptional American whose views deserved attention. Nonetheless, Bowles came to admire her skills, her courage, and her willingness to speak out. Not surprisingly in light of his own view of the purpose of public office, he regretted that she seemed to be too intent on achieving power for its own sake. He was also disappointed that he was unable to develop as good a relationship with her as he would have liked. Only when he was coming to the end of his assignment in 1969 and would no longer be around to offer her unwanted advice was Mrs. Gandhi prepared to restore the old, easier ties.

▾   ▾   ▾

If Bowles had his difficulties with Mrs. Gandhi as head of the Indian government, he also had his share of problems with his own leader. He admired much of Lyndon Johnson's Great Society domestic program, especially the president's bold and courageous stand on civil rights. But he had major problems with many of LBJ's views about foreign policy and was never able to develop a satisfactory connection with him.

Though Bowles and Johnson had both been young New Dealers who shared an admiration for Franklin Roosevelt, they had never been close personally or worked together in Democratic party politics. Bowles had remembered Johnson favorably as one of only two congressmen from oil-producing districts who had supported OPA, but the two men had nothing more than a casual acquaintance in the 1950s, when Johnson became Senate majority leader. In 1960, when several figures associated with the New Deal had supported Johnson's presidential bid, Bowles had strongly opposed it. He had also argued against the selection of Johnson as Kennedy's running mate. After Johnson became vice president, Bowles as under secretary of state helped him prepare for the overseas trips he undertook at Kennedy's request. He also arranged for the assignment of a State Department officer to the vice president's staff to work with him on foreign policy issues. But by the time Johnson succeeded Kennedy, Bowles had already gone to India as ambassador, and the two men never had a real opportunity to work closely together in Washington.

Richard Celeste has recalled that upon returning from Washington following John Kennedy's funeral, Bowles said he expected Johnson to be a good president. He believed that history would compel Johnson to promote far-reaching domestic programs, and, like many others, forecast that he would be able to win congressional support for them. But Bowles was less certain about foreign policy. He feared that Johnson might lean too far toward Pakistan, for the ambassador to India a most unwelcome prospect. He was reasonably optimistic about his ability to work with Johnson once the new president was on top of things. What Bowles knew he would lose with the change of leadership, Celeste remembered, was the special access to the senior staff of the Kennedy White House he had enjoyed despite his earlier difficulties with some of them.[39]

Bowles had a more basic uneasiness about Johnson, however. He did not like Johnson as a person and did not relate well to him. Their styles were even farther apart than Kennedy's and Bowles's had been. Bowles soon found the president vain, overconfident, and insensitive, and complained of his lack of historical judgment. He had told Celeste at the beginning of the administration that people respected Johnson because he knew how to exercise power. He shrewdly forecast that once things began to go wrong for the president "there will be few helping hands, and more ready to snicker or to cheer."[40] By the spring of 1966 he suspected that his prediction was coming true. After a meeting with LBJ that March, he wrote in his diary that "I saw in Johnson a man headed for deep trouble. A man feared but never loved or even liked, with the problem of an increasing obsession with his 'enemies' and steadily growing public disenchantment. . . . A break on Vietnam might save the situation; a disaster in Vietnam could speed the day."[41]

Bowles resented Johnson's approach to foreign aid, especially the president's view that recipients should be grateful to the United States and demonstrate this gratitude in their foreign policies. A diary entry of December 1964 presents a vivid picture of their differences. Recalling a White House meeting, Bowles wrote: "He more or less directed me to tell the Indians that we were tired of trying to help unappreciative people and seeing our libraries burned down, and if they didn't watch their p's and q's, we would walk out and leave them in the lurch. I explained that this would only serve to make us appear unstable and cause them to lean more heavily on the Russians and in any event, we had far more to lose from a chaotic world than did people who have grown up in chaos and privation."[42]

He was also troubled by what he thought was Johnson's lack of concern for India, which contrasted sharply with Kennedy's well-articulated interest in the country. He tried to win over the president to a position on the Kashmir issue more sympathetic to Indian concerns by comparing the disputed state's accession to India with the admission of Texas to the United States. No American, and certainly not LBJ, would want a plebiscite to determine whether Texas should be handed back to Mexico, he argued. He was painfully aware of Johnson's suspicion that he was too partial to India, and probably had heard of the president's reported complaint that the Indian government had two ambassadors to Washington—the diplomat assigned to its embassy there and Chester Bowles.

Bowles tried hard to persuade Johnson to take a more positive view of the Third World. Again playing the historian's role, he told the president in 1964, in the course of a conversation at the White House, that Third World demands in the 1960s were in many ways similar to the radical, non-Marxist reforms Johnson's populist father and grandfather had sought in West Texas in their day. He recalled stressing "the importance of building a bridge between the dynamic liberal tradition of the United States, on the one hand, and the yearning of hundreds of millions of people throughout the world for the ownership of their own land, for more irrigation water, for lower interest rates, for more schools and health clinics, on the other."[43] Johnson had expressed an interest in putting these ideas into a speech, and with Doug Bennet's assistance Bowles had provided a text. To his regret, the president never used it.

Over the years, Bowles sent many other policy suggestions and speech texts to Johnson and his White House staff. As early as March 1964, he had written in his diary that

my primary objective is to see if I can't give [Johnson] some simple conceptual ideas that will be persuasive within his experience. For instance, the Populist-New Deal-people oriented approach to domestic af-

fairs (which he seems to want to express) is the key to foreign affairs as
well. If I could influence him away from the McNamara-Rusk interpretation of foreign affairs which focuses on military power maneuvers
divorced from the political-social-economic forces which are shaping our
modern world, his populist inclinations . . . could become the key to a
people-oriented foreign policy that could look beyond the bemuddled
individuals who stretch across the front pages to the everyday folks who
feel the frustrations, generate the movements, and reach out for a better
future.[44]

Bowles doubted that he would succeed, but thought it worth a try.
"A man with genuine liberal convictions in regard to Boston slums or
Kentucky marginal farmers will almost certainly have good reliable
instincts in regard to the future of Portuguese imperialism in Africa;
India's third Five Year Plan; what to do about Calcutta; and what
course to follow in Latin America."

Following up on this idea, Bowles sent the president a proposal in
August 1965 for a worldwide campaign to identify him and his foreign
policy with, as Bowles put it, the "Populist-New Deal-Fair Deal tradition which under [Johnson's] leadership is demonstrating new vitality
in the United States." He spelled out a series of speeches he wanted
Johnson to give on such topics as the overall objective of American
economic assistance, greater food production, health programs, population control, and the Peace Corps. Striking a familiar chord, he
declared once again that "we are a people born in revolution, dedicated
to the continuing revolution . . . and living in a world of revolution."

> What I am suggesting [he wrote Johnson Special Assistant Bill Moyers]
> is that President Johnson should emerge as the prophet of this new era.
> This calls for a step-by-step effort to create the world image of a liberal,
> vigorous Lyndon B. Johnson who is carrying forward the continuing
> American revolution at home, who stands for similar objectives through-
> out the world, and who heads a people-oriented America which is pre-
> pared in our own tradition to help those who will help themselves.[45]

This Bowles vision of Johnson's role can be read as a projection of
the kind of president he himself would have wanted to be had "lightning struck" in 1960 or earlier. LBJ did not act on the recommendation.

▾   ▾   ▾

Important events in U.S.-Indian relations occasionally brought Bowles
and his embassy to the front pages of the world press over the years
of his second ambassadorship. The most dramatic of these was arrang-

ing for the escape from India of Svetlana Stalin, the daughter of the dead Soviet dictator. Bowles played an imaginative and courageous role in the episode. No discussion of his second assignment can be complete without at least a brief account of what happened.[46]

Bowles was sick in bed with flu the evening of March 6, 1967, when a neatly dressed woman carrying a small suitcase appeared at the main door of the embassy. Speaking good but accented English, she told the Marine guard there that she was a Soviet citizen and wished to talk to an embassy officer. Following standard procedure, the corporal called the officers designated to handle such "walk-ins." They found that according to her passport she was Svetlana Iosifovna Alliluyeva.

The woman told the officers that she was the daughter of Joseph Stalin by his second wife. She said she had come to India with the ashes of her common-law Indian husband, who was an uncle of an important Indian government minister close to Mrs. Gandhi. Long disillusioned with Communism, she had wanted to remain in India, but neither the Indian government nor the Soviets would agree. The Soviet ambassador had told her earlier in the day that she would have to be on the flight to Moscow that left New Delhi the following morning.

Recognizing that she would have no other chance of getting out of the Soviet Union, Svetlana had decided to appeal to the United States for help. That evening she packed a suitcase and took a taxi from the Soviet embassy to the American embassy down the street. She could not go back to the Soviet Union, she told the Americans who interviewed her, and was determined to live her life as a free person. If she could not get U.S. assistance, her only recourse would be to contact the press and appeal publicly for the help and support of the Indian and American people. She wrote out and signed a formal request for asylum in the United States.

Bowles and his officers were aware that the Soviet embassy was holding a large reception and that Svetlana's disappearance from the embassy compound had probably gone undetected. They calculated that they could count on no more than four hours before the Soviets discovered that she was missing. Once her defection was noticed and the Indian government informed, the Indians would almost certainly prevent the Americans from assisting her.

They quickly considered their options. Bowles immediately ruled out two of them—denying Svetlana assistance or spiriting her out of India covertly in the hope that the American role in her departure could be kept secret. The first would be completely contrary to American tradition and would lead to a public outcry in the United States and elsewhere once the embassy's refusal became known. The second was unacceptably risky since the possibility of her being a Soviet plant could not be ruled out. (The embassy had been unaware of Svetlana's existence, let alone her presence in India, and it was impossible to confirm her identity in the brief time at its disposal.) Moreover, the U.S. role would eventually come to light.

As Bowles saw it, the choice came down to keeping Svetlana in the embassy and informing the Indian government that she was seeking asylum in the United States, or helping her leave India as quickly as possible. He reasoned that if he chose the first course the Indians, under heavy Soviet pressure, would demand Svetlana's "release" to their custody. Since they could not be relied upon to permit her to remain in the country, he would have to refuse. The embassy would soon be besieged by the world press, and a first-class international donnybrook with an unpredictable outcome would become inevitable.

Bowles concluded that the best course was to help Svetlana to leave without officially deciding on giving her asylum in the United States. He had already prepared the way for this. At 9:40 P.M., only a little more than two hours after Svetlana had appeared before the surprised Marine guard, he told Washington in a "flash" cable that "unless advised to the contrary we will try to get Svetlana aboard Qantas flight 751 to Rome leaving Delhi at 1945 Zulu" (1:15 A.M. March 7 local time). She would be accompanied by a Russian-speaking U.S. embassy officer, Robert Rayle. Embassy officers told Svetlana that they could not guarantee her asylum in the United States, but were willing to assist her in leaving India for Rome immediately if she chose to do so. She was cautioned that this would mean burning her bridges behind her with no clear idea of what lay ahead. The officers assured her that if the United States could not grant her asylum, it would certainly continue to assist her until she did find a haven. Svetlana stated that she wanted to proceed to Rome.

The flight-to-Rome option, though risky, had a number of advantages in Bowles's view. It could be carried out openly and legally, since Svetlana's Soviet and Indian documentation was in order. This would protect the United States against charges of a CIA plot to kidnap her. (Revelations in the American press that the Asia Foundation and other apparently private American organizations operating in India were subsidized by CIA had recently rocked U.S.-Indian relations.) It would also provide a breathing spell in which Svetlana's future status could be considered without the direct glare of publicity or the involvement of the Indian government.

At about 11:30 P.M., less than two hours before Qantas flight time, Bowles approved issuing a U.S. visa to Svetlana (the airline would not have allowed her to board without some document for travel to the West) and confirmed the tentative arrangement for her departure for Rome absent any contrary word from Washington. At 12:15 A.M. she was driven to the airport by the head of the embassy consular section, accompanied by a Marine security guard in civilian clothes. The CIA station chief followed. They were met at the airport by Rayle, who had the tickets in hand. He and Svetlana passed through customs and immigration without incident. After what must have been an excruciating hour and a half in the departure lounge—the plane had been delayed by a leak in its hydraulic system—they departed at about 2:45 A.M. At that point the Soviets were apparently still unaware that she had left their compound. She arrived in Rome safely later in the day and eventually proceeded to the United States.

As Bowles had anticipated, both the Soviets and the Indian government were incensed by his action. The Soviets charged that the whole affair was a CIA kidnapping plot in which the Indian government must have cooperated. Caught in the middle, the Indian Ministry of External Affairs handed Bowles a note charging him with illegal procedure. In a letter to Indian Foreign Secretary C. S. Jha, Bowles replied that while he appreciated the concern of the Soviet Union that the note reflected, the Indian government had neither the legal nor the practical ground to sustain a protest to the United States. Jha should tell the Soviets of the American ambassador's assurance that the United States did not wish to embarrass Moscow; its course of action was determined not by a desire to create difficulties but to avoid them. "As you know," Bowles wrote, "no one feels more strongly than I do about the importance of closer relations between the United States, India, and the Soviet Union."[47] (This was an accurate statement. At that point, Bowles hoped that both the Indians and the Soviets could be brought to play a more constructive role in resolving the Vietnam crisis.) The Indians soon concluded that their interests would be best served by dropping the subject.

The Soviets apparently decided to demonstrate their displeasure by breaking off virtually all social contact with Americans in India. Previously made engagements were canceled without explanation and at social functions Soviet diplomats would ostentatiously turn and walk away as Americans approached. But roughly a week after Svetlana's departure Soviet Ambassador Benediktov and Bowles found themselves face-to-face at a formal "chiefs of mission" social gathering. With a stern look, the Soviet commented, "I suppose if anyone calls at your embassy in the middle of the night you give him a visa and a ticket to America." To which Bowles, with a smile, responded, "For you we will." This quick-witted rejoinder caused Benediktov to break out laughing in spite of himself. The next day Soviet-American social relationships in New Delhi were back to normal.[48]

Bowles had good reason to be pleased with the outcome of the Svetlana affair. He and his staff had recognized that they would have to move quickly and had shown good judgment in assessing the options and their political implications. Bowles had been aware from the start that he would have to make the decision. Familiar with the ways of the State Department, he knew that there was little if any chance that his cable would be answered before Svetlana left for Rome. Unlike many other ambassadors in similar situations, he did not hesitate to act as he saw best.

Svetlana settled in Princeton, married an American architect, had another child, and became a U.S. citizen. But unlike the princess in the fairy tale, she did not live happily ever after. Divorced and facing personal problems, she went to England in 1983 with her American-born daughter. The following year they moved to the Soviet Union. Svetlana was quoted at that time as saying that in her seventeen years in the West she had never been free and had lived tormented by guilt and longing for her children in Russia. The Soviet government sent her to the Georgian Republic, the Stalin family's old home. But there too she was unhappy. Her older children had rejected her and she could not adjust to Soviet life, which she found hard and uncomfortable. In 1986, after a year and a half in the Soviet Union, she returned to the United States. She now lives in England.[49]

18

Southeast Asia as Seen
from New Delhi

As PRESIDENT Kennedy's special representative and adviser on Asian, African, and Latin American affairs, Bowles had followed up his unsuccessful 1962 efforts to change Southeast Asia policy with a memorandum to Kennedy in March 1963 in which he highlighted the danger of the United States trying to prop up an unpopular Vietnamese regime. He called for a high-level review of the way U.S. military operations in Vietnam related to realistic political objectives there, and again urged that the administration lay the groundwork for a negotiated political settlement for the region as a whole.[1]

On his way to New Delhi that summer, he visited Saigon for the first time in ten years. He reported to the State Department that the Vietnamese political situation was explosive and that although the security situation was substantially better than it had been, no further improvement could be expected without political stabilization. He was convinced that South Vietnamese President Ngo Dinh Diem could not bring this about. Bowles and Diem had met for four hours, with Diem doing almost all of the talking.[2] In a private message to Kennedy, Bowles characterized the Vietnamese leader as "living in a world of his own and [seeming] completely out of touch with the situation."[3] He compared Diem to Chiang Kai-shek in the 1940s and recommended that the United States support his overthrow.[4]

After he reached India, Bowles continued to do what he could to influence U.S. Southeast Asian policy from his distant perch. His official messages and private records provide interesting insights into the thinking of a prominent liberal in the Johnson administration in the years when the Vietnam War was becoming a major point of contention between many liberals and the president. His evolving position needs to be assessed against the background of increasing American dissatisfaction with Indian policies regarding the Southeast Asian conflict. Although Bowles shared some of this dissatisfaction, he believed that in their dealings with the Indian government on bilateral issues the president and others in Washington gave a disproportionate importance to U.S.-Indian differences over Southeast Asia.[5]

In his first years back in New Delhi, Bowles continued to stress the importance of a new political approach in Southeast Asia. A first step, he wrote Hubert Humphrey in January 1964, might be a clear commitment to the economic and social development of the region "for the benefit of the people and not for a small number at the top."[6] After the August 1964 Tonkin Gulf incident he noted that the impact of "the forthcoming disaster in Vietnam" might be devastating for the conduct of foreign policy: "Instead of persuading American opinion of the futility of a narrow, negative militaristic approach, it may persuade them that everything we have been doing is futile."[7] He urged Johnson to get cease-fire negotiations started and suggested to the president in January 1965 that Indian sponsorship of a broadly attended conference might be the best way to move forward with talks.[8]

In March 1965, Bowles proposed a Johnson Plan for Southeast Asia that would call for a negotiated settlement without regard for the ideological complexion of the regimes involved, to be followed by generous economic support for the region from the United States and others.[9] He welcomed the speech the president gave at Johns Hopkins University two weeks later that included these elements, and recommended that Johnson follow it up with a brief bombing moratorium that would test Hanoi's intentions.[10] Later in 1965, he suggested that bombing be reduced to occasional symbolic raids "for the record," and American military operations in Vietnam limited to the protection of a strong defensive position.[11] Privately, he worried that by repeatedly urging Johnson to show restraint in military operations he was taking his political life in his hands.[12]

Bowles urged his Indian contacts to make what he called a decisive contribution in a common cause against aggression promoted and abetted by China. The rift between Peking and Moscow should allow India to play this role without jeopardizing its important ties with the Soviets, he told them.[13] He was privately scornful of the Indians when they proved reluctant to do so. "The Indians aren't helping the situation," he noted toward the end of 1964. "Although they are gentlemanly, orderly, friendly and correct, they are playing a narrow, selfish game which they feel is based on 'self-interest'. . . . It totally ignores the realities of the Soviet-Chinese relationship and it assumes that we can be counted on through thick and thin."[14] He does not seem to have sent such gloomy analyses of Indian thinking to Washington.

Although interest in maintaining good relations with the United States appears to have been one of the principles guiding Indian Southeast Asian policy in 1965 and 1966, not least because of India's need for U.S. economic assistance, the Johnson administration was unhappy with some elements of the Indian government's approach. It was troubled by New Delhi's repeated calls for a bombing halt, especially when these were made in joint communiqués with Communist countries, as happened during Prime Minister Shastri's trip to Moscow in May 1965. It was dissatisfied with the Indian tendency to separate the Chinese threat to India from the North Vietnamese effort to take over South Vietnam. The Indians dismayed Washington further by what it regarded as their niggling attitude as chairman of the three Southeast Asian International Control Commissions (ICCs) toward evidence of North Vietnamese intervention in South Vietnam, Laos, and Cambodia. Although there was also some understanding in the administration of the limits to what the Indians could do in Southeast Asia and a measure of appreciation for their quiet effort to move the Soviets to the peace table, these were usually outweighed by what it saw as the negative aspects of India's role in the region.

Washington used high-level visits to stress its dissatisfaction. The State Department suggested that when she came to the White House in March 1966, Johnson ask Prime Minister Gandhi where India would stand if, despite best U.S. efforts, the war in Vietnam led to direct American confrontation with Communist China.[15] Vice President Humphrey had asked Mrs. Gandhi to ponder the same question during his exchange with her in New Delhi earlier in the year. The department also proposed that the president tell the prime minister that "we need some clear sign that India recognizes our struggle in Vietnam serves Indian interests. We need a more forthright and effective Indian role in the ICCs. . . . And above all, India's leaders should refrain from taking public positions on developments in Vietnam that needlessly antagonize the U.S. Congress and public."[16]

Johnson apparently had only a very brief discussion of Vietnam with Mrs. Gandhi. If he reported it accurately, he adopted a very mild line quite different from the approach the department had recommended. Emerging from his one-on-one with the prime minister in the Oval Office, the president told waiting members of the American and Indian delegations in Mrs. Gandhi's presence that he had asked her to offer Washington recommendations from time to time on procedures to bring about peace in Vietnam and the rest of the world. He said he had made no request, had expressed his appreciation for Indian ICC participation, and hoped that someday we could find the answer to peace.[17]

In a speech afterwards at the National Press Club, Mrs. Gandhi said she had been "impressed by the sincerity of the president's desire for a peaceful settlement" in Vietnam. She also suggested that the Vietnam War was part of a struggle between democracy and the expansionism of Communist China. The *New York Times* reported that American officials were struck by the sympathy the prime minister expressed for the U.S. position. In their opinion, the *Times* said, she had gone about as far as she could go without explicitly endorsing American policies.[18]

A few months later, Mrs. Gandhi publicly launched a Vietnam peace initiative of her own. Reiterating her view that no military solution was possible, she asked Britain and the Soviet Union promptly to convoke another Geneva Conference similar to the session they had cochaired in 1954. She urged an immediate end to the bombing of North Vietnam followed by the cessation of hostilities and belligerent movements throughout Vietnam. Under her proposal, all foreign troops would eventually withdraw from Vietnam and the Geneva participants would guarantee the integrity, independence, and neutrality of the three Indochinese states.[19] American reaction to Mrs. Gandhi's initiative was equivocal. Washington welcomed the proposal to reconvene the Geneva Conference, but found serious deficiencies and ambiguities in her other points, not least the recommended ending of the bombing.[20]

This U.S. response was in sharp contrast to Washington's harsh reaction to the Indo-Soviet joint communiqué issued at the conclusion of Mrs. Gandhi's visit to Moscow later in July 1966. She and Soviet Prime Minister Kosygin stated that "imperialist and other reactionary forces" were responsible for a recent deterioration in world affairs. As Mrs. Gandhi had earlier, they demanded an immediate end to the bombing of North Vietnam and called for a settlement within the framework of a reconvened Geneva Conference. But this statement said nothing about a compensating deescalation by the other side following the bombing halt. Moreover, it described foreign bases as obstacles to peace.[21]

Both Johnson and Bowles took the communiqué very badly. It seems to have ended definitively the warm feelings LBJ had developed toward Mrs. Gandhi during her visit to Washington. Orville Freeman believes it led the president to tighten his short-tether food policy.[22] Bowles privately called the communiqué "obnoxious . . . deplorable, and indefensible"[23] and sent the prime minister a personal three-page letter of protest. He told her the statement seemed to blame the United States for the intensification of hostilities while totally ignoring the origins of the fighting and the responsibilities of the other side for a peaceful settlement. "Once again, my country has become the victim of a double political standard, of your government's saying one thing to us in private and another to the world in public. . . . While the communiqué endorses the policy of non-alignment (a policy which we fully accept and respect) it appears as on previous occasions to be 'non-aligned' on the side of the USSR."[24]

Indian government attitudes and pronouncements on Vietnam became an increasingly sore point in U.S.-Indian relations during Bowles's remaining years in New Delhi and a source of considerable frustration for him. He later recalled an exchange with an unidentified White House official to whom he had commented that in urging a bombing halt Mrs. Gandhi was only saying what the Pope and U.N. Secretary General U Thant had said over and over again. According to Bowles, the official had replied, "the Pope and U Thant don't need our wheat."[25] A diary entry in May 1967, when U.S. economic assistance had again been held up, further catches the flavor of his thinking about reaction in the White House to Indian policies in Southeast Asia and elsewhere:

> What Mrs. Gandhi said on Ho Chi Minh's birthday [she had sent the North Vietnamese leader greetings] or what the silly [Indian Minister of External Affairs] Chagla said in his nonsensical wooing of [Egyptian President Gamal Abdul] Nasser will not warrant a footnote in the history books. But what happens to India's economy and political system will fill volumes. It is a serious mistake to force (if we could do so) the Indian Government to shape their policies to fit LBJ's views or even to keep off his corns. Our objective should be not to pressure India to our way but rather to encourage them to look inward to their own economic and political ideologies, which will go far to determine what Asia is like twenty years from today.[26]

▾   ▾   ▾

In August 1966 Bowles decided to see the Southeast Asian situation for himself. Accompanied by Richard Celeste, he spent six days in Vietnam, Thailand, and Laos. It was an exhausting trip. Bowles traveled extensively across the Vietnamese countryside, looking at sensitive military areas, stopping at a "pacified" village, and calling at a special forces camp. He spent a night aboard the aircraft carrier *Independence* in the Gulf of Tonkin and was thoroughly briefed on the security and political aspects of the war by all the top people from General William Westmoreland and Ambassador Henry Cabot Lodge on down. Celeste has recalled that the problem of Communist military operations based in Cambodia figured prominently in the briefings.[27]

Bowles reported to the president that he had come away with a generally hopeful impression. He found that the war was being won, at least in a military sense, and lauded the performance of American military and civilian personnel. But he expressed concern about the danger of Chinese intervention with Soviet support and continued to urge a suspension of the bombing of targets in North Vietnam. He warned that the United States might achieve its military objectives yet find it impossible to create the indigenous administrative structure necessary to bring about stability. The war again demonstrated his old dictum that "military power has its own strict limitation in dealing with the burgeoning revolutions in Asia, Africa, and Latin America . . . upheavals [which] can be contained only if the masses have a genuine stake in the future." He was encouraged by the prospect of elections in South Vietnam and suggested the electoral process could be strengthened by a dramatic announcement a week or two before the balloting of a major land redistribution program.[28]

Characteristically, he tried to put Vietnam in an historical context. He was convinced that "the United States had embarked on an adventure in world politics which is leading us towards a watershed in American history." The adventure could lead to another world war. It could fail politically because of indigenous factors beyond U.S. control, and this setback could result in a new and catastrophic isolationism. But if the effort succeeded, he told Johnson, "as I hope and pray it does, you may have set the American people on a bold new course in world affairs which will have decisive implications for ourselves and for all mankind for generations to come."

In private notes he drafted about the visit, he was more specific, and less effusive, in describing what he meant by success:

> In the last 15 years, a substantial minority of us have been arguing that military power will not in itself succeed in crushing a revolutionary movement and that political turbulence can be eliminated only by the establishment of a sound society in which individuals are given a sense of participation, the right to own land, education, etc. . . . Vietnam *could* be the turning point in this situation. Hundreds of thousands of Americans . . . are having an opportunity to see with their own eyes the total hopelessness of a narrowly conceived effort to crush a revolution by

military means alone. Thus if we should succeed in South Vietnam the concept we have been pushing for so many years may suddenly emerge as a basic element of the common wisdom.[29]

The Southeast Asia visit made it easier for Bowles to speak out in India in support of U.S. policy. He did this in his own way. In sessions he sought with senior Indian leaders and journalists after his return, he was able to report firsthand how the Vietcong used terrorist tactics to impose their will on the countryside and to stress the danger posed by the Chinese. In a press release issued soon after his return, he expressed the hope that "the day will soon come when India and the non-Communist nations of Asia will themselves organize an effective effort to assure that the tragedy of Vietnam is not repeated elsewhere."[30]

▾   ▾   ▾

Over the next months, Bowles continued to offer recommendations to Washington. At the end of 1966, he proposed a suspension of the bombing conditional on (1) Soviet assurances to reduce their support to North Vietnam if it did not curtail its military activity following the bombing halt, and (2) a commitment by neutral nations that in such circumstances they would brand North Vietnam an aggressor. Washington found the proposal badly flawed and turned it down.[31]

Early in 1967, he stepped up his effort to persuade Johnson that a sweeping land reform program in South Vietnam could give the essential political thrust to U.S. efforts to win over the rural people to the fight against the Communists. He brushed aside objections that reforms would alienate landowners and cause administrative difficulties and that they could not be implemented in areas not controlled by Saigon. Similar arguments had been made against Lincoln's issuing the Emancipation Proclamation, he observed. He recommended that to win over the South Vietnamese government Washington enlist Chiang Kai-shek and the president of South Korea, both of whom he said had had extraordinary success with the kind of land reform he had in mind.[32]

Bowles's repeated calls for land reform got some high-level attention. The White House sent copies of his messages to Robert Komer, who by then was in charge of pacification at Embassy Saigon. Komer assured Bowles that his thoughts had been very helpful and that despite complexities that made Vietnamese land reform very different from the Taiwan-Japan-Korea model "we here [in Saigon] are pushing for every bit the traffic will bear."[33] Commenting to the president at the time on Bowles's initiative, Komer noted that "Chet has a good idea, but ignores all the problems of converting promise into performance." He added that despite handicaps more was happening on the land reform front than Bowles recognized. He promised Johnson that further efforts would be undertaken.[34] Johnson himself wrote to Bowles a few months later assuring him that great pressure was being exerted on the Vietnamese and progress was being made.[35] These efforts, in which U.S. Ambassador to Vietnam Ellsworth Bunker played a leading role, contributed significantly to the eventual passage, in 1970, of major land reform legislation.

Bowles apparently discontinued his diary in 1968. His entries had become more and more intermittent before then, and it is difficult to trace his thinking about Southeast Asia during his final years in India. He appears to have become increasingly unhappy with U.S. policy. He sent a gloomy letter to Humphrey in May 1967 in which he took sharp issue with many administration policies and assumptions about the war. He wanted the administration to make it "crystal clear to the Government of South Vietnam that our continued support will depend on its own determination to proceed vigorously with meaningful programs of land reform, eradication of rural debt, and national reconciliation." The administration should also indicate privately to the Soviets, the North Vietnamese, and others an upper limit in the number of troops that the United States would employ in Vietnam, "making it clear that this level would be reconsidered if an additional party [that is, China] were to intervene direct in the fighting." Consistent with the position he took in his messages throughout his New Delhi assignment, he asserted that he did not favor an American pullout from Vietnam.[36]

He also continued to send suggestions about policy changes direct to Johnson. Although the president never regarded Bowles as a significant player in Vietnam policy formulation, he apparently did consider one of his recommendations sufficiently important to mention in his autobiography. Sent from New Delhi in March 1968, this proposal called for a total bombing halt if other key governments and international bodies agreed in advance to take responsibility for bringing about meaningful negotiations and promised to cooperate with the United States and others in a postwar economic development program in Southeast Asia once a satisfactory settlement was reached. Not surprisingly, Bowles included India among the key governments. His proposal was linked in Washington with a recommendation sent in a few days earlier by Arthur Goldberg, the U.S. permanent representative at the United Nations. The administration eventually rejected the "Goldberg-Bowles" proposal.[37]

Bowles was careful not to reveal his opposition to ongoing policy to the Indian (or American) public. He pointed this out to Humphrey in a July 1968 letter in which he reiterated familiar positions in advising the vice president how he might best approach the Vietnamese issue in his campaign for the White House. "As U.S. Ambassador to India, I have meticulously refrained from making any public statement which could be interpreted as a criticism of President Johnson's policies just as you have," he said.[38]

Nor did he broadcast his views within the embassy. Although he had recruited specialists in Communist affairs for the political section, and his minister-counselor (later minister), Herbert Spivack, had spent many years in Southeast Asia, he did not tap these resources in preparing his formulations and kept these largely to himself. He took a relaxed attitude toward dissent on Vietnam policy. When the embassy was asked by USIA how it would react to a visit to India by an American professor known for his opposition to the official line, he warmly welcomed the proposal. And when American university students studying in India used the occasion of a visit by a congressional delegation to stage an antiwar demonstration outside the embassy, to the outrage of the congressmen and the delight of the Indian press, Bowles saw nothing wrong with their action.

▾   ▾   ▾

Bowles became directly involved in U.S. Southeast Asian diplomacy in January 1968. He was at his favorite South Indian beach resort near Trivandrum for the Christmas holidays when he got word that he had been selected to head a delegation to engage in negotiations with the government of Cambodia to resolve problems caused by North Vietnamese and Vietcong intrusion into Cambodian territory. Washington considered these Communist activities a direct threat to U.S. forces in Vietnam. Delighted to be dealing with a matter at the top of the administration's agenda and very important to him as well, he hurried back to New Delhi for further instructions.

Cambodian Head of State Prince Norodom Sihanouk had broken off relations with the United States in 1965. His indication that he was prepared to receive an American mission to discuss the problem of military intrusions by the Communists and their use of Cambodian territory as sanctuary was regarded as an important move on his part and a diplomatic windfall for Washington. Sihanouk had recently gone on record in favor of strengthened operations by the International Control Commission for Cambodia. He was well aware that American military commanders in Vietnam had been exerting increasing pressure for authority to engage in "hot pursuit" into Cambodia to root out Communist forces there, and many incursions had actually taken place. In several recent speeches he had asserted that he was "obliged to encourage the doves" to oppose these pressures.[39] Bowles believed that his mission to Cambodia was designed to head off just the kind of major U.S. intervention both Sihanouk and many in the Johnson administration feared.[40]

To avoid the need for intervention, the administration, like Sihanouk, called for the strengthening of the Indian-chaired ICC for Cambodia so that it would be able to deal more effectively with North Vietnamese and Vietcong violations of Cambodian soil. The three members of the commission were divided on how forceful a role it should play. The Western member, Canada, favored a more determined effort. Communist Poland strongly resisted this. India was reluctant to agree to any meaningful moves in the absence of unanimity, just as it was in analogous circumstances as chairman of the ICC for Vietnam.

By that time Bowles had been peripherally involved in Cambodian affairs for three years. In January 1965 he reported to the State Department that he had been approached by Cambodian Ambassador to India Nong Kimny. Recently arrived from Washington, where he had also been ambassador, Nong Kimny had told Bowles that he was eager to keep in touch with him on Cambodian matters. Bowles suggested to the department that he and Nong Kimny carry on a *sub rosa* dialogue in New Delhi. With Washington's blessing, he, or more often embassy Minister-Counselor Herbert Spivack, had then done so. According to Spivack, the pro-American Nong Kimny claimed credit for persuading Sihanouk to signal that he was prepared to receive the mission Bowles was chosen to head.[41]

If Presidential Press Secretary George Christian was aware of the Nong Kimny connection, he did not mention it when he briefed the media off-the-record on January 4, 1968. Christian told the newsmen that Bowles had been picked because he was an experienced diplomat, had been under secretary of state, had visited Cambodia before [in 1962], and was personally acquainted with Sihanouk.[42]

The fact that India was chairman of the ICC also figured, Christian said. The press reported later that Bowles had been in touch with the Indians in late 1967 about the strengthening of the commission. The

United States had made known that it was ready to provide the commission with helicopters and other equipment to facilitate its operations in the tough jungle country where the Communist incursions had taken place.[43]

Bowles arrived in the Cambodian capital of Phnom Penh by light plane on January 8, and discussions opened the following day.[44] He was not well and was obliged to rest every afternoon. His Parkinson's disease also caused trouble with his voice. According to Embassy New Delhi Press Attaché John Shirley, who had traveled with him, he was annoyed that the obviously crucial meetings with Sihanouk were not scheduled until he and his colleagues had conferred with Prime Minister Son Sann and Cambodian military commander General Nhiek Tioulong. Despite Bowles's reported pique, the mission was treated with utmost courtesy and kindness.

When Bowles and Sihanouk finally met at the royal palace, they got on well. According to Spivack, who participated in the session, the prince treated Bowles with the deference Cambodians give to an older man. This contrasted with the quip Sihanouk had made in a radio broadcast before Bowles's arrival, when he had suggested that Jacqueline Kennedy, who had recently spent a week in Cambodia, had been a more seductive emissary than Bowles was likely to be. Old Sihanouk-watchers recognized this as a typical Sihanouk pleasantry, not to be taken seriously.

Sihanouk had signaled the Cambodian position on "hot pursuit" to Stanley Karnow of the *Washington Post* in an interview published less than two weeks before Bowles's meetings in Phnom Penh. He had told Karnow that if "hot pursuit" carried American soldiers into uninhabited areas of Cambodia and did not harm Cambodian citizens or property, then the Cambodian government, seeing no evil, would not react.[45] In the meetings with Bowles, Sihanouk made a flat statement that the Cambodians would continue to send troops to engage any Vietnamese they found on their territory. But he noted that there were instances when he did not know that the Vietnamese had actually come into Cambodia. Bowles offered to provide intelligence about such instances, and Sihanouk said that when he had that information he would send in his own troops if possible. Otherwise, as he had told Karnow, he would close his eyes to the Americans attacking the North Vietnamese/Vietcong, provided they did so without harming Cambodians or destroying Cambodian villages. He dramatized his position by drawing his hand over his eyes. Bowles also reported that Sihanouk had gone on to say that while he could not admit it publicly, the United

States' adopting this course might even help him solve his problem. He later recalled that he doubted the prince had meant it.[46]

In the official report he cabled to Washington,[47] Bowles said he had accomplished three objectives. Sihanouk had reaffirmed in a formal, written message to the Indian chairman of the ICC his request for a strong, vigorous, adequately equipped commission with authority to operate mobile inspection teams and fixed inspection points backed by helicopter observation. The prince had specifically asked the United States to supply him on a regular basis with whatever information it had on suspected locations of North Vietnamese and Vietcong units on Cambodian soil. (As noted above, this request had followed an offer from Bowles.) Sihanouk promised to inform the ICC, to order his own troops to make a full inspection, and to move whatever intruders might be discovered off Cambodian territory. According to Bowles, Sihanouk also expressed the desire to reestablish normal relations with the United States and, when this had been done, to permit the U.S. military attaché to visit any part of his country as an additional safeguard. Only the first of these three points was mentioned in the communiqué issued at the conclusion of the talks.

Bowles reported that throughout the discussions, the prince and his ministers placed primary, indeed sole, emphasis on Cambodian national integrity. "I came away convinced, as on previous visits to Cambodia, that Sihanouk's decisions and attitudes, however bizarre, are shaped by intense and deeply rooted nationalism in which ideology has little or no part. The Prince stressed again and again that his is a small country caught in the middle of an unpredictable conflict and that Cambodia must strive to maintain a maximum degree of good will not only toward its neighbors, but particularly toward great powers."

Bowles was also persuaded that the Cambodian government's approach reflected a "significant change in emphasis" in its foreign policy to a position more suspicious of the Communists. He urged that the United States try to find some formulation on the recognition of Cambodia's frontiers—a critical issue for Sihanouk—that would provide a basis for the renewal of diplomatic relations. Sihanouk's sudden switches and unfair criticism would continue, but they should not deter the United States from the main business at hand: "to keep Cambodia neutral, to keep the Viet Cong and the North Vietnamese Army out of its territory, and, with an eye to the future, to improve our own relations with this small but important country."

In *Promises to Keep,* Bowles recorded that the talks had allayed

Cambodian fears of the consequences of "hot pursuit" by U.S. and South Vietnamese troops. "It never occurred to us," he recalled, "that two years later we would actually invade Cambodia."[48] By that time, however, the situation had fundamentally changed. Sihanouk had been overthrown, Vietnamese and local Communists had occupied large portions of the country and were threatening the capital, and the government of the newly proclaimed Khmer Republic led by the right-wing General Lon Nol was calling for help. More important, there was also a new administration in Washington.

It is difficult to tell whether Bowles's mission was a significant element in reducing the call by U.S. military leaders for intervention before that time. Its results were not such as would readily deter the hawks among them. Despite Bowles's generally upbeat report and the positive tone of the communiqué, subsequent developments undercut the gains that had been achieved in the Phnom Penh negotiations. In the end, the talks seem to have accomplished little aside from the arrangement under which the United States passed information on Vietnamese Communist infiltration to the Cambodian government. The Cambodians appear to have done little, if anything, with this information.

One early casualty was the hoped-for strengthening of the ICC. The Soviet Union, as cochairman of the Geneva Conference, and Poland, an ICC member, both firmly opposed acceptance of American aid to bolster the commission. Running true to nonaligned form, the Indians did not try to force the issue, and Sihanouk himself reportedly took the position that unless the Soviets agreed to the proffered U.S. assistance, he would not accept it.[49]

Nor did U.S.-Cambodian relations soon improve. Quite the contrary. The goodwill apparently generated in Cambodia by the Bowles mission was quickly dissipated when Assistant Secretary of State for Far Eastern Affairs William Bundy stated in Washington a few days after Bowles returned to India that the United States had not abandoned the right to engage Communist forces along the border and to penetrate into Cambodia. Bundy's assertion of this right, which he put in terms of self-defense, only spelled out what Bowles had deliberately left vague. (Bowles had told the Cambodians that the United States would do everything possible to avoid aggressive acts and incidents. The Cambodians had accepted these assurances.) But Sihanouk professed to take the statement very badly and publicly accused the United States of cynically disregarding the promises Bowles had made. He reportedly said that he regretted that so few countries had denounced "this scandalous arrogance and this scorn for a word of honor."[50] Back in New

Delhi, Bowles wrote in his diary that the success of his Cambodian venture had been undercut in Washington by Bundy and others. "We [Washington] are completely out of touch with reality," he complained.[51]

After this outburst, U.S.-Cambodian relations resumed their customary pattern of ups and downs. Sihanouk continued to pursue his policy of seeking to balance outside forces—those in neighboring states as well as the major powers—in order to strengthen his weak and exposed country's sovereignty and security. The resumption of diplomatic relations Bowles had hopefully promoted did not come about until June 1969, a year and a half after his mission and well after many other Western countries had resumed ties. By then, the United States had agreed to a vague formulation on Cambodia's borders that was acceptable to Sihanouk and presumably unexceptionable to America's allies in Bangkok and Saigon. Even then the two countries only exchanged chargés d'affaires, not ambassadors.

Despite this disappointing dénouement to his efforts, Bowles appears to have been gratified with the Phnom Penh assignment. He may well have felt that in contrast to his long and frustrating efforts to influence the Johnson administration's approach to Vietnam, he had been able for once to play a meaningful role, however limited his accomplishments. For a man who in his gloomier moments believed that he had been relegated to an exile's life in India and could have little impact on major foreign policy issues, this was not to be dismissed lightly.

19

"Only the Historians
Can Determine"

BOWLES completed his second Indian assignment in the spring of 1969, after the return of the Republicans to power under Richard Nixon. Although he had been impressed by Nixon—to his surprise—when the future president visited India as a private citizen in 1967, he did not repeat the unsuccessful effort he had made to prolong his first term as ambassador.[1] He was succeeded in New Delhi by Judge Kenneth Keating, an upstate New York Republican who had been a United States Senator before losing his seat in 1964 to Robert Kennedy.

Bowles's six-year assignment was unusually long but not unprecedented for a postwar ambassador. In his case it was probably too long. In his last years in New Delhi his role in foreign policymaking had diminished. Occasional episodes that briefly brought him back into prominence, such as the Cambodian negotiations, highlighted how far removed he had become from the main policy arena. The long period he had spent out of the country reduced the familiarity he enjoyed with the shifting cast of players on the Washington scene, and the narrow limits to the influence he had there did not go unnoticed among his Indian contacts. (As Washington came to know only too well, many of these Indians also wondered whether what he told them represented official U.S. government policy or only his own wishful thinking.)

At a time when the Johnson administration's interest in India had diminished, Bowles's insistence on the importance of U.S.-Indian relations seemed out of place. In this changed foreign policy atmosphere his reports were discounted, even more than they had been earlier, as reflections of his pro-Indian views or as familiar observations largely irrelevant to administration concerns. The lengthy memoranda he sent to Rusk and other senior officials went mainly unnoticed by those to whom they were addressed. The secretary might read a sentence or two before signing off on a warm and appreciative reply the India desk had prepared for his signature. The practice became part of a sad charade designed to keep an old man happy and out of the way.

The sadness of Bowles's final years was made more poignant by his increasing debility from Parkinson's disease. In 1967, when the symptoms of the illness were becoming more and more evident, he began taking the then experimental medicine L-Dopa that was sent to him by a hospital in New York. Like the surgery he had undergone in 1965, the drug helped alleviate some of the symptoms, but the beneficial effect again proved only temporary. He felt obliged to further limit his activities. The disease progressively affected his speech, handwriting, and gait. He gave up golf, no longer turned up on special occasions to play first base in embassy softball games, and wrote worriedly of his "snow shoe shuffle."[2] But his intellectual capacity seemed unaffected. That only compounded the tragedy of this enormously articulate man.

Some of his well-wishers thought then or concluded later that Bowles ought to have left India well before he did. But though he had himself felt at times that he should quit for policy reasons, he hated and dreaded the thought of retirement. "I would be bad at it," he wrote in his diary. "I would dry up like an old apple."[3] The options open to him were in any event even more limited than they had been earlier in the decade. And for all its professional shortcomings, the New Delhi assignment offered a pleasant life and had its rewards for him and perhaps even more for Steb, an important consideration in his thinking. Although he sounded out James Reston as early as 1966 about writing a syndicated newspaper column, he wound up staying on in India as long as he could.[4]

Before he left the embassy, Bowles sent a long message to the new secretary of state, William P. Rogers, outlining his views on India and U.S.-Indian relations. In many respects these echoed earlier messages he had sent to Johnson, Rusk, and others. He made the same pleas for high levels of economic assistance and greater understanding of Indian positions, and called again for visits by senior Washington officials, presumably to promote those objectives. He expressed the same optimistic views about the possibility of India's soon achieving economic self-sufficiency and the same warnings about its determination to hang on to Kashmir. No doubt recollecting Rusk's exasperated question to him years earlier—"What has India ever done for the United States?"—he explained to Rogers that it had survived as an independent democratic nation and a huge common market. He concluded, characteristically, that "the profound economic and political changes which are now taking place here will during the next few years determine this country's course for the indefinite future. Although the course of events here as elsewhere is unpredictable, my colleagues and I are persuaded that with boldness, ingenuity, flexibility, and, above all, understanding by the United States Government there is solid reason to hope for a major breakthrough."[5]

Bowles had drafted similarly dramatic conclusions to many cables he sent from New Delhi during his two assignments as ambassador. What stands out in his message to Secretary Rogers is the modesty of some of his positions. He had already scaled down his objectives after the India-Pakistan war. He no longer called for a revamped, comprehensive policy for South Asia but spoke instead of delinking India and Pakistan and treating each country in accordance with the respective American interests. He recommended that the United States not try to compete with the Soviet Union as a supplier of lethal weapons to India but instead help build up India's own weapons manufacturing capacity. And, he spoke more cautiously than he had in the mid-1960s and earlier about a possible Indian role in the effort to stem Communism in Southeast Asia.

▾   ▾   ▾

The completion of his second assignment in India marked the end of Bowles's long career in public service. On his return to Washington he was given the State Department's Distinguished Honor Award at a ceremony in the office of the secretary. The award cited his "exceptional contributions to international peace and understanding and to the strengthening of United States relations with India." Although awards are often given to retiring ambassadors who have served at major embassies and in high positions in Washington, the new Republican administration's presentation of the prestigious Distinguished Honor Award to a figure so closely associated with the Democratic party struck many as a very handsome gesture.

The presentation ceremony was a memorable occasion both for Bowles and those in the gathering who had worked with him over the years.[6] The affair seemed a throwback to earlier times. Secretary Rogers, recognizing that it was a Democratic show, quickly gave way to the senior leaders of the Kennedy-Johnson era who had come back to Foggy Bottom for the occasion. Among them was Averell Harriman, who told the throng that he was appearing as the representative of former governors to honor one of their number. But the principal figure was Dean Rusk, who made one of those gracious little speeches he could do so well. Bowles remembered him saying: "Chet Bowles has contributed many ideas which are now an integral part of American foreign policy. In regard to the many more ideas of his which were not accepted—only the historians can determine who was right and who was wrong."[7]

After his retirement, Bowles returned to Connecticut and the big white house in Essex. He continued to take a lively interest in foreign affairs and in India, and wrote about them from time to time. He visited India again in 1972, a final journey to his old haunts made difficult by his deteriorating physical condition, and stopped briefly in newly independent Bangladesh, whose struggle he had strongly championed the previous year in opposition to the pro-Pakistan policies of the Nixon administration. But he did not try to resume his old role as a major Democratic party spokesman, and his debilitating illness limited the influence he could bring to bear.

In January 1971 he completed *Promises to Keep,* the long narrative of his years in public life from 1941 to 1969 that has so often been cited in these pages. The book provides a good if somewhat uneven account of what Bowles was trying to accomplish and how he went about it. But it is not meant to be an autobiography, and it offers only a limited sense of his soaring ambitions for himself and his country and the often bitter disappointment he experienced when he failed to achieve them. In the book he was too kind and too gentlemanly in his treatment of his relationships with Lyndon Johnson, John Kennedy, Dean Rusk, and other major figures. He had made it a practice not to engage in public, personal criticism during his active career, and he stuck to that credo in *Promises to Keep.* "In reading over drafts of my book," he told an interviewer in 1970, "my friends accused me of being much too mild, of not being tough enough on the people with whom I had differences. But I feel there's been too much of that."[8] The assessments of people, policies, and events he expressed in his diary and in some of his private correspondence have been much watered down as a result, and the book is consequently both less valuable and less interesting.

In a six-page epilogue to his narrative, Bowles wrote poignantly of what he considered the dismal state of national and international affairs and the awesome array of problems the United States faced at home and abroad in 1971, when American life seemed dominated by the war in Vietnam. He noted with understanding the alienation many younger people felt toward the American political, economic, and social structure. But as he so often did in his life, he insisted that the crisis could be overcome, as Americans had overcome other crises in the past: "Two hundred years of American history have demonstrated the incredible ability of human beings in a free society somehow to make their way through seemingly impossible dilemmas and to improvise effective responses to new forces. It is, I believe, within our capacity to do so again."[9] It was a distinctively Bowlesian last hurrah.

▾   ▾   ▾

Bowles died in Essex on May 25, 1986, at the age of eighty-five of complications arising from his twenty-two-year struggle with Parkinson's disease. He had suffered a stroke the week before. Many of those close to him regarded his death as a release as much as an occasion for grief. In the decade before he died the symptoms of his malady had progressively worsened; visitors to Essex in the early 1980s would find him sitting hunched in a wheelchair, unable to speak or, so it seemed, to recognize the caller. His death briefly recalled his unusual, so often controversial career to the attention of a public which had largely forgotten him. The *New York Times* front-paged a lengthy obituary, and in Connecticut Governor William O'Neill, the latest to sit in his old Hartford seat, ordered that flags on state buildings be flown at half staff for thirty days. Large numbers of his friends and admirers paid tribute to him in a moving memorial service at the Yale chapel. He was buried in Essex in a plot overlooking the Connecticut River.

In his last years, before Parkinson's disease finally made him mute, Bowles sometimes wondered aloud if his life had been a failure. His questioning reflected the urgency and importance he attached to what he had been trying to accomplish. Beneath his bland features was a driven man, greatly worried about America and the world and his own seeming inability to do more about changing them. His associates tried to reassure him when he raised the question; some of them were angered by his asking it. They had good reason to react the way they did. For despite all of his shortcomings and failures, Bowles had made significant contributions both to the way Americans thought about foreign policy and to American foreign policy itself.

Perhaps his most important contribution was his role as the visionary of a more equitable, democratic world that the United States could help bring about by abandoning its support for the status quo and becoming instead a driving force for political, economic, and social change. He took the lead in his time in reasserting the primacy of traditional American liberal values as the basis for foreign policy, and was confident that such a principled approach could win broad support among the American people. His conviction that those values were shared by people overseas and his insistence that the United States had an obligation to itself and others to promote them was a mid-twentieth-century manifestation of a foreign policy viewpoint rooted in the early decades of the Republic. The most noteworthy spokesman earlier in the century of this liberal-idealistic tradition, Woodrow Wilson, had inspired Bowles in his formative years. His admiration for Wilson had later been an influence in leading him to forsake his Republican heritage and join the Democratic party.

Bowles brought a new orientation to this idealistic approach. Earlier, the focus of those who championed it had been for the most part on Europe. The breakdown of the colonial order after the Second World War led to the emergence in Asia and Africa of independent and would-be independent nations with no experience of rapid economic growth and only rarely of genuinely democratic political institutions. Bowles dedicated himself to this non-European Third World. His recommendations for dealing with the developing countries went beyond what most of his predecessors in the idealistic tradition had called for in their foreign policy formulations, and differed also from the views of many of his liberal contemporaries. He insisted on nothing short of strong American support for the radical transformation of the structures of Third World governments and societies. The United States not only needed to bring its influence and resources to bear to promote self-determination and democracy, as Wilson had urged. It also had to do what it could—and Bowles was convinced it could do a lot—to assure that political institutions truly reflected the popular will and that ordinary citizens benefited from economic development, in his view the key to a more just and stable political equilibrium.

This new and far-reaching interpretation Bowles gave to the precept that America should export its values because they are right and applicable everywhere was starkly different from the approach many of his contemporaries favored. Some of those who professed similar principles did so largely for tactical advantage. Bowles had only contempt for that attitude. In a noteworthy passage in *New Dimensions* he wrote: "The difference between asserting moral principles for limited purposes of psychological warfare and of living them because they are the warp and woof of our national life is necessarily the difference between manipulation and genuineness, between tactics and truth."[10] He was able to clothe his ideas in language that made them seem less revolutionary than they actually were to those he was trying to win over. But what he said and wrote reflected the abiding views of this unreconstructed New Deal liberal about the purposes of America.

His most cogent explanation of what these purposes were came in an entry he made in his diary in 1965 when he was ambassador to India:

> I have been thinking a good deal recently about my own attitudes toward America and I have come to see something very fundamental. I am devoted to the view of a sensitive, effective, productive, democratic America not as an end in itself but as an instrument in the creation of a truly world society. A good America, a strong America is a vehicle for the betterment of life in all corners of the world. It is our task to build such an America, not as a triumph in its own right, but as a means to the broader world-wide objective.[11]

For the many Americans who believed in Bowles's time, and believe today, that their country has a higher purpose in the world than the pursuit of national self-interest, his idealistic message was an inspiring one. The rejection of Communist ideology and the establishment of democratic institutions in the former Soviet Union, Eastern Europe, much of Asia and Latin America, and a growing number of African countries has given fresh salience to that message and new meaning to the role Bowles played in acting as the standard bearer of American idealism at the height of the Cold War.

▾   ▾   ▾

If Bowles's approach to foreign policy echoed a familiar idealistic strain, boldly reinterpreted by him for the postwar, postcolonial world, it was also designed for that Cold War. Bowles was a product of his times in believing that there was a serious Communist threat to the "free world," promoted by Moscow and abetted by Peking. With almost all of his American contemporaries in the postwar quarter century, he was convinced the United States needed to take the lead in containing Communist expansion. Although he held that the United States should be flexible in dealing with the Communist powers and avoid the highly charged rhetoric favored by many in his time and later, he saw Communism as an evil system. It seemed to him all the more dangerous because it might appear better able to meet the aspirations of Third World peoples for economic growth than the liberal, capitalistic, market-based strategy he favored, or other social and economic policies developed in a democratic framework. Like most of his contemporaries, he did not foresee that the failure of Communist economies would be a major element in the eventual triumph of democratic values in Cold War competition. Instead, he found that the apparent attractiveness of the Communist economic model to some

Third World countries made an effective containment strategy even more urgent. He saw his policy recommendations for the reworking of liberal foreign policy principles as the basis for that strategy. They need to be assessed in that context.

Two elements in Bowles's general approach to foreign policy were most central to his containment strategy. The first was his stress on the key role nationalism could play in stopping the spread of Communism, and eventually in weakening it by fostering national Communist regimes in countries where Communism had already been established. The second was the priority treatment he gave the Third World in his analysis of the nature and scope of the anti-Communist struggle.

In accepting nationalism and the independent, nonaligned foreign policies it had prompted in Nehru's India and elsewhere in Asia and Africa as ineluctable, legitimate, and potentially beneficent forces, Bowles proved to be both unduly optimistic and superficial. In the years since he articulated his views, nationalism has provided an important ideological basis and platform for opposition to Communism. It has also contributed significantly to tensions and divisions within the Communist world—rifts that he had urged the United States to encourage in its dealings with Peking and Hanoi. But Bowles did not fully recognize how destructive rival nationalisms could be and was disappointed when instead of working together in rational ways to improve the lot of their people, the governments of Third World countries turned on one another, to loud popular acclaim. "What a stupid war," he had said of the India-Pakistan conflict of 1965. He would have been appalled by the Iran-Iraq war of the 1980s and other armed struggles that scarred Asia and Africa in the years after he left public life.

The record of many of the leaders of the newly independent countries would have seemed equally disconcerting to him. He had pinned high hopes on those representatives of the "new forces" stirring in the Third World to which he so often referred. In his optimistic way, he did not foresee how selfish, brutal, and narrow-minded many of the leaders would be. In power, few of them were attracted to the liberal American ideals he thought had broad appeal in the Third World. The satisfaction he expressed in *Promises to Keep* with the newly established leadership in the Congo (Zaire) of President Mobutu, one of the most corrupt and heinous of the lot, is a sad but accurate commentary on the way Bowles often allowed his hopes to cloud unpleasant Third World realities.

In dealing with the new nations and their leaders, Bowles failed to grapple with two key questions that faced those who advocated American acceptance and encouragement of nationalism as a force that could be mobilized, or would mobilize itself, against Communism: What measures can the United States reasonably take to assure that the forces of nationalism will be led by the "right" leaders—that is, those who will meet popular aspirations and develop strong non-Communist regimes—without violating the principles of self-determination and non-interference that recognition of nationalism implies? And what certainty is there that a nationalist, non-Communist regime fully accepted and supported by the United States would be helpful to American interests?

Bowles was naively sanguine in dealing with both these questions, mostly shrugging them off. He was unduly confident that patriotic nationalist leaders would come to the fore, pursue properly progressive policies ultimately beneficial to American interests, and remain in place—provided that the United States did not support outdated feudal and other reactionary forces, as he thought the Kennedy administration had done in Peru despite the precepts of its Alliance for Progress. He was a dedicated interventionist on economic issues and was insistent that the beneficiaries of U.S. assistance put their economic houses in order in accordance with standards he repeatedly spelled out. But he does not appear to have favored a significant U.S. role, clandestine or otherwise, in identifying and helping bring to power progressive nationalist figures who, like Magsaysay in the Philippines, could carry out programs to develop the "strong, self-confident countries" he saw as key to the containing of Communism.

His confidence that all would be well as the right leaders materialized from nationalist movements and carried out reform measures at U.S. suggestion may have reflected his exposure to India. For Bowles, India under the leadership of Nehru and his successors was the very model of a nationalist country pursuing policies that offered its people the stake in remaining part of the "free world" he believed vital to containment strategy. He did not seem to recognize the special nature of the Indian experience and its limited applicability to other emerging countries that lacked its popular and responsible leaders, trained administrators, and viable political and economic institutions. Perhaps in consequence, his formulations provided only a very sketchy guide to how progressive nationalist forces could be encouraged and sustained in the anti-Communist struggle without the United States itself taking over the leadership of that effort.

Bowles was similarly complacent in addressing the issue of the foreign policies of the nationalist regimes that he urged Washington to bless. He often contended that what was important was that these countries had not slipped into the Communist orbit. They would cause problems, but the United States could live with those. It was better to be squabbling with an independent Third World country than with a Communist one.

Though consistent with the stated foreign policy priorities of the day, this attitude did not reflect the dismay and worse that Bowles and others in the Kennedy and Johnson administrations experienced when, despite U.S. acceptance of nonalignment, Third World governments pursued policies regarded in Washington as pro-Soviet and hostile to American interests. This was notably true regarding India, which for its own reasons sought strong ties with Moscow and, partly because of the importance it attached to them, rejected the supportive role in Southeast Asia Bowles had contended it could be brought to play. Third World nationalism and nonalignment proved much less beneficial to the United States than he had claimed, and the Kennedy administration in its first years had hoped. He would have been more persuasive had he simply argued that in the case of most Asian and African countries these unhelpful policies were inevitable, and the United States had no choice but to deal with them as best it could.

Bowles did not invent the notion that the Third World was an important area in the containment effort. The Truman and Eisenhower administrations had been concerned with real and potential Communist gains there through Moscow-supported "national liberation" struggles and had tried to devise strategies to prevent these. But Bowles gave the region as a whole a primacy that few were prepared to afford it in the 1950s. He helped persuade many Americans to recognize, if more dimly than he wished, that something significant to U.S. interests was going on in remote, newly emerging countries of which they had known and cared little or nothing. In highlighting the differences between the problems the United States faced in dealing with Europe and those it confronted in the developing countries, and calling for policies that stressed "positive" actions such as economic assistance rather than "negative" ones reflected in military alliances, he offered a new approach to the Third World as a whole that was influential within the Democratic party and elsewhere.

While Bowles's stress on the Third World provided a useful corrective in helping to win for the emerging nations more attention than they had been given earlier, his insistence that they would be the arena where the struggle against Communism and the fate of the globe would be determined proved to be vastly overstated. His assessment that the relative economic performances of authoritarian China and democratic India would play a key role in determining the effort to contain Communism in what he termed the "battle of the century" was also faulty. Neither country's development strategy has been seen elsewhere in the Third World as a model to emulate. Besides Japan, the most economically successful of the Asian countries have been those smaller powers of East Asia that have gone much farther than India has in adopting market-oriented policies. The prosperity they have achieved has been significant in warding off any Communist challenge to their governments and has made them much more important to the United States. Bowles had denigrated them and thought U.S. efforts to cultivate them mistaken. It was not there, he said, that the history of the twentieth century would be written.

This stress on the primacy of the Third World made Bowles vulnerable to charges from the foreign policy establishment of the day that his strategy to contain Communism was incomplete. He tried to refute such allegations by speaking out on the fundamental importance to the United States of the security of Western Europe and by taking measures to demonstrate that his concepts went beyond his Third World concerns. But he continued to be seen, correctly, as a Third World–oriented figure.

His unwillingness to become involved in the details of European security issues and his unfamiliarity with European leaders strengthened that impression, which was reinforced by the limited interest he took in security policy generally. This attitude probably reflected his conviction that well-equipped armed forces were an indispensable element of America's security but that the militarization of U.S. foreign policy had gone much too far. In a period when military issues were often at the heart of the concerns of other foreign policymakers and analysts, he never became more than peripherally involved with such important questions as the nature of an American military response to Communist aggression (though in 1958 he went so far as to call, quite foolishly, for such a reaction to the crossing of international frontiers by Communist armies *anywhere*), the size and equipment of U.S. armed forces, and the way U.S. military needs should be financed. What seemed to many his one-dimensional approach led to Bowles's being taken less seriously as a foreign policymaker and containment strategist and limited his influence.

▾   ▾   ▾

This assessment of Bowles's approach to containment should not obscure the other contributions of his foreign affairs years. Those he made to U.S. policy toward Third World economic development were especially important and influential. He recognized before most others the importance of rural development for economic progress, industrial growth, and political stability. In the decades that followed, many who earlier put their faith in rapid industrialization as the magic wand of development have come around to his way of thinking. Many of the guidelines he spelled out for the provision of economic aid remain valid today. And, three decades after it was passed, the legislation he championed is still the basic framework for U.S. foreign assistance.

Like his approach to economic development, Bowles's other major recommendations and forecasts often reflected his insistence that policymakers take a long view of the direction the world was moving and what that portended for American interests. His scorecard was uneven. He was surely correct in his analysis in the 1950s of future difficulties in Sino-Soviet relations and the opportunities these offered the United States, though his claim that only a very few others shared his foresight was considerably overstated. His call for a more realistic U.S. approach to Communist China was wise and courageous; the "two Chinas" policy he promoted has in effect come about. That Kennedy would have gone farther in accepting the advice of Bowles and others on China following a resounding reelection victory in 1964, as Bowles hoped and thought he would, is by no means certain. In any event, Bowles himself seems to have been much less interested in pushing for change in China policy following the outbreak of fighting along the Sino-Indian border in late 1962.

Later events were to prove his early, strongly expressed concern about the perils of U.S. armed intervention in Vietnam prophetically accurate, though the most important formulation he put forward to resolve the crisis, his 1962 regional peace charter proposal, was probably unworkable. His recognition that a military solution in Vietnam was not possible and his efforts to promote policies designed to enhance prospects for an acceptable political one need to be read in conjunction with his unwillingness, while holding office in the Johnson administration, to speak out publicly against its Vietnam policies or to advocate at that time the withdrawal of U.S. forces. His often expressed fear of a drive southward by a famine-stricken People's Republic, an important element in his thinking about China and Southeast Asia, was well off the mark.

Bowles's record in India and his ideas on U.S. policy in South Asia have been reviewed in the chapters on his two assignments as ambassador. He was much more successful in his first posting, when the circumstances of the early 1950s offered a special opportunity for him to use his talents to heighten mutual understanding and improve bilateral relations. Referring to that time, John Kenneth Galbraith, who was ambassador in New Delhi between Bowles's assignments there, has cogently observed that he "brought to India a determination first to understand the needs and problems of the young republic and then to show that the United States could be a firm, informed, and undeviating friend. . . . Those of us who followed him," Galbraith went on to say, "lived gratefully on the Bowles inheritance."[12]

Bowles faced a different situation when he returned to India a decade later. His second assignment coincided with a marked lessening of U.S. interest in South Asia as a region of importance to American global concerns. Although the second term was a disappointment to him, it included significant accomplishments, notably in the part he played in helping persuade the Indians to reform their economic policies and launch the Green Revolution. He set high standards for other men assigned to the often difficult New Delhi post, and almost a quarter century after he left he was still much admired in India as a warm friend and advocate.

At important points in his campaign to strengthen U.S.-Indian relations Bowles was plagued by a well-founded recognition that he was unduly biased in India's favor. He was correct in warning about the negative consequences to American interests in South Asia of the U.S.-Pakistan security relationship established over his strenuous objection in the 1950s, and lived to see India gain in the 1971 breakup of Pakistan the subcontinental preeminence he had long called on Washington to acknowledge as the basis for U.S. South Asian policy. But he had a more sanguine view of India's potential world role than its performance to date has warranted. Nor have subsequent developments justified his conviction that U.S. and Indian interests were fundamentally congruent. Bowles would probably have argued, incorrectly, that the fault rested primarily with the United States for failing to deal with India along the lines he had so often advocated. He rarely acknowledged that there were far-reaching differences in perception, experience, and objective between the two countries that led them to approach issues in dissimilar, sometimes inimical ways.

For all the allegations that he failed to manage State Department operations effectively, Bowles can be credited with important contributions to the administration of foreign policy. The most outspoken critics of his performance as under secretary acknowledge the success of his efforts to recruit high-calibre people for overseas and senior Washington positions. His style as an envoy, which broke away from traditional diplomatic practices, continues to influence American representatives in the developing world. His insistence that ambassadors assume responsibility for all aspects of their missions' operations has been made mandatory.

He was much less successful in his efforts to persuade Kennedy, Rusk, and others to look beyond immediate problems and deal with foreign policy issues in longer-range perspective. But in seeking this different approach, he was challenging the long-established Washington practice of dealing with problems on an ad hoc basis or, at best, calibrating the management of foreign policy to a short-term political cycle. Like others before and since who refused to accept the old saw about long-range planning being an oxymoron, he could not change the system. The conduct of U.S. foreign policy would have been more effective had he been more able to do so. He deserves credit for his persistence at a time when immediate confrontations with the Soviets led the Kennedy administration to focus on day-to-day problems, and when the narrowness of the president's election victory had made him cautious in initiating major changes in policies on China and other issues.

But there was something well beyond these achievements that may be Bowles's greatest legacy to governance. This was the inspiration he gave to generations of talented young people to play a role in public life. He offered them his vision of what needed to be accomplished and gave them remarkable opportunities for making their mark. As Richard Celeste said at the memorial service held for Bowles in the Yale chapel, he played the role of mentor well before that term came into popular use. Many of those he imbued with his unique sense of idealism and mission hold prominent positions today. They, and the country, owe a great debt to him for the way he helped mold them and for what he helped them aspire to and attain.

▾   ▾   ▾

The foreign policy of the United States would have looked quite different had Bowles become secretary of state, or, even more so, had "lightning struck" in 1960 or earlier. One could speculate endlessly about the scenarios that would have flowed from his stewardship of Foggy Bottom or the White House. Perhaps a more appropriate question is whether, having failed to become either secretary or president, he could have done more to bring his ideas to fruition. Or was he, as George Ball has put it in discussing Bowles's performance as under secretary, simply "too noble for life in the bureaucratic jungle" to have been able to accomplish more than he did?[13]

He might within limits have modified his way of operating. If he had taken as his own an immediate issue, as Averell Harriman had with Laos, he might have dispelled the widespread and damaging suspicion that he was too concerned with long-range developments to deal with day-to-day problems. He ought to have tried harder to blur his exclusively Third World image, and to limit the perception, at a time most Americans believed there was a dangerous Communist challenge to the "free world," that he was more interested in what was happening in obscure Asian villages than he was in areas more immediately and obviously important to U.S. security and well-being. He might have benefited as an advocate of the cause of closer U.S.-Indian ties if he had been more cold-eyed and candid in his assessment of Indian government positions and motives and avoided Johnson's alleged quip that he was New Delhi's second ambassador to the United States. Had he been tougher and more cynical in dealing with those who opposed him, less willing to place his confidence in colleagues whose moves too often surprised and disappointed him, less the decent and congenial person all who knew him found him to be, that too might have worked to his advantage.

But he could only have gone so far. He was never prepared in the interest of "pragmatism" to modify his principles or forsake the moral compass that guided them in his dealings with issues and people. Efforts by his associates to persuade him to change his style and water down his positions had only limited success. In his practices, as in his policy agenda and the philosophy that governed it, he always remained Chester Bowles, a New Dealer in the Cold War.

Bibliographic Note
Notes · Index

Bibliographic Note

In addition to the material detailed in the notes, this book draws from a range of interviews conducted, roughly, between 1989 and 1991. A list of the people interviewed appears below, followed by a list of people whose oral histories I consulted in the Bowles Papers at Yale.

Interviews

GEORGE W. BALL, Princeton, New Jersey: under secretary of state for economic affairs, 1961, and under secretary of state, 1961–66.

LUCIUS D. BATTLE, Washington, D.C.: executive secretary of the State Department in the Kennedy and Johnson administrations.

DOUGLAS J. BENNET, JR., Washington, D.C.: worked with Bowles in New Delhi during second ambassadorship.

ALFRED M. BINGHAM, Salem, Connecticut: worked with Bowles in OPA; family friend.

BIMLA NANDA BISSELL, New Delhi, India: worked with Bowles in New Delhi during second ambassadorship.

JOHN BISSELL, New Delhi, India: family friend.

DAVID H. BLEE, Washington, D.C.: worked with Bowles in New Delhi during second ambassadorship.

SALLY BOWLES, Essex, Connecticut: daughter of Bowles.

MCGEORGE BUNDY, New York City: assistant to the president for national security affairs under presidents Kennedy and Johnson.

CAROL LAISE BUNKER, Washington, D.C.: officer in the Bureau of Near Eastern and South Asian Affairs and ambassador to Nepal during Bowles's second ambassadorship.

HENRY A. BYROADE, Washington, D.C.: assistant secretary of state for Near Eastern, South Asian, and African affairs in the Truman and Eisenhower administrations.

RICHARD F. CELESTE, Columbus, Ohio: worked with Bowles in New Delhi during second ambassadorship.

ABRAM CHAYES, Cambridge, Massachusetts: worked with Bowles in Connecticut and at the State Department.

CLARK M. CLIFFORD, Washington, D.C.: special counsel to President Truman; secretary of defense in the Johnson administration.

PHILLIP H. COOMBS, Essex, Connecticut: worked with Bowles in Connecticut; assistant secretary of state for cultural and educational affairs in the Kennedy administration.

CARLETON S. COON, JR., Washington, D.C.: officer in the Bureau of Near Eastern and South Asian Affairs during Bowles's second ambassadorship.

JANE A. COON, Washington, D.C.: worked with Bowles in New Delhi during second ambassadorship.

EVERETT DRUMWRIGHT, San Diego, California: worked with Bowles in New Delhi during first ambassadorship.

ORVILLE FREEMAN, Washington, D.C.: secretary of agriculture in the Kennedy and Johnson administrations.

J. WILLIAM FULBRIGHT, Washington, D.C.: United States Senator from Arkansas, member and later chairman of the Senate Foreign Relations Committee.

JOHN KENNETH GALBRAITH, Cambridge, Massachusetts: deputy administrator, Office of Price Administration; Democratic party adviser; ambassador to India, 1961–63.

LINDSEY GRANT, Washington, D.C.: worked with Bowles in New Delhi during second ambassadorship.

JOSEPH N. GREENE, JR., Lyme, Connecticut: deputy to Bowles in New Delhi during second ambassadorship.

BRANDON H. GROVE, JR., Washington, D.C.: worked with Bowles in Congress, the State Department, and New Delhi during second ambassadorship.

SELIG HARRISON, Washington, D.C.: journalist in New Delhi and Washington during Bowles's ambassadorships.

JOHN R. HUBBARD, New Delhi, India: worked with Bowles in New Delhi during second ambassadorship.

THOMAS L. HUGHES, Washington, D.C.: worked with Bowles in Connecticut, Congress, and in the State Department.

PAT DURAND JACOBSON, New York City: worked with Bowles in Connecticut, Congress, and the State Department.

U. ALEXIS JOHNSON, Washington, D.C.: deputy under secretary of state for political affairs in the Kennedy and Johnson administrations.

JEAN JOYCE, Washington, D.C.: worked with Bowles in OPA, Connecticut, and in New Delhi during first ambassadorship.

ROBERT W. KOMER, Washington, D.C.: National Security Council staff member during Bowles's second ambassadorship.

JOHN P. LEWIS, Princeton, New Jersey: worked with Bowles in New Delhi during second ambassadorship.

SAMUEL W. LEWIS, Washington, D.C.: worked with Bowles at the State Department.

CHARLES E. LINDBLOM, New Haven, Connecticut: worked with Bowles in New Delhi during second ambassadorship.

EDWARD J. LOGUE, Boston, Massachusetts: worked with Bowles in Connecticut and in New Delhi during first ambassadorship.

INDER MALHOTRA, New Delhi, India: journalist in New Delhi during Bowles's second ambassadorship.

GEORGE C. MCGHEE, Washington, D.C.: senior State Department official and ambassador in the Truman, Kennedy, and Johnson administrations.

JAGAT SINGH MEHTA, Austin, Texas: senior official of the Indian Ministry of External Affairs during Bowles's second ambassadorship.

JOHN Y. MILLAR, Washington, D.C.: worked with Bowles in New Delhi during second ambassadorship.

DILIP MUKHERJEE, New Delhi, India: journalist in New Delhi during Bowles's second ambassadorship.

BRIJ KUMAR NEHRU, New Delhi, India: Indian ambassador to the United States during Bowles's second ambassadorship.

PAUL H. NITZE, Washington, D.C.: Democratic party adviser; senior Defense Department official in the Kennedy and Johnson administrations.

JAMES RESTON, Washington, D.C.: columnist for the *New York Times*.

WALT W. ROSTOW, Austin, Texas: senior official in the Kennedy administration; national security adviser in the Johnson administration.

DEAN RUSK, Athens, Georgia: secretary of state in the Kennedy and Johnson administrations.

ARTHUR M. SCHLESINGER, JR., New York City: Democratic party adviser; historian at Harvard; White House official in the Kennedy and Johnson administrations.

DAVID T. SCHNEIDER, Washington, D.C.: office in the Bureau of Near Eastern and South Asian Affairs during Bowles's second ambassadorship.

JOHN W. SHIRLEY, Washington, D.C.: worked with Bowles in New Delhi during second ambassadorship.

HERBERT D. SPIVACK, San Francisco, California: worked with Bowles in New Delhi during second ambassadorship.

PHILLIPS TALBOT, New York City: assistant secretary of state for Near Eastern and South Asian affairs in the Kennedy and Johnson administrations.

JAMES C. THOMSON, JR., Cambridge, Massachusetts: worked with Bowles in Connecticut, in Congress, and at the State Department.

M. GORDON TIGER, Washington, D.C.: worked with Bowles in New Delhi during second ambassadorship.

NICHOLAS A. VELIOTES, Washington, D.C.: worked with Bowles in the State Department and in New Delhi during second ambassadorship.

T. ELIOT WEIL, Washington, D.C.: officer in the Office of South Asian Affairs during Bowles's first ambassadorship.

LEONARD WEISS, Washington, D.C.: worked with Bowles in New Delhi during second ambassadorship.

MORRIS WEISZ, Washington, D.C.: worked with Bowles in New Delhi during second ambassadorship.

Oral Histories of Bowles at Yale University Library

ROBERT R. R. BROOKS: worked with Bowles in OPA and in New Delhi during second ambassadorship.

RICHARD F. CELESTE

ABRAM CHAYES

PHILLIP H. COOMBS

BRANDON H. GROVE, JR.

THOMAS L. HUGHES

PATRICIA DURAND JACOBSON

JAMES G. ROGERS, JR.: business, OPA, and Connecticut associate of Bowles.

JAMES C. THOMSON, JR.

WILLIAM WEATHERSBY: deputy to Bowles in New Delhi in second ambassadorship.

HARRIS WOFFORD: worked with Bowles in Connecticut; adviser to Senator John F. Kennedy; official in the Kennedy administration.

Notes

Introduction

1. Chester Bowles (hereafter CB) diary, March 21, 1965, Box 395, Bowles Papers, Yale University Library (hereafter Bowles Papers).
2. CB, *Promises to Keep: My Years in Public Life 1941–1969* (New York: Harper and Row, 1971), p. 367.

1. Manhattan, Washington, and Hartford

1. *Promises to Keep*, p. 3.
2. CB Oral History interview, Columbia University (1963), Box 396, Bowles Papers.
3. *Promises to Keep*, p. 5.
4. *History of the Class of 1924, Sheffield Scientific School, Yale University* (New Haven: Class Secretaries Bureau, 1924).
5. Selden Rodman's article "Chester Bowles" in the April 1946 *Harper's*, based in part on Rodman's interview of Bowles, has some particularly interesting insights on Bowles's career in advertising and other aspects of his early life.
6. James G. Rogers, Jr., Oral History interview, Box 398, Bowles Papers.
7. *Promises to Keep*, p. 10. According to Sydney Hyman, Benton's biographer, when Benton & Bowles was organized, Bowles made a verbal agreement with Benton to buy Benton's stock if the firm prospered so that Benton would be at liberty to enter other fields. The account states that Bowles never expected Benton to leave the firm (*The Lives of William Benton* [Chicago: University of Chicago Press, 1969], p. 129). Hyman's biography includes a number of interesting passages on the Benton-Bowles relationship. Not surprisingly in a book that Benton reportedly helped fund, the characterization tends to make Benton look good and Bowles less so.
8. Author's interview with David H. Blee, April 1990.
9. David S. McLellan and David C. Acheson, eds., *Among Friends: Personal Letters of Dean Acheson* (New York: Dodd, Mead, 1980), p. 143. The letter to Rostow is dated August 14, 1958.

10. CB Oral History interview, Columbia University.

11. In *Washington Goes to War* (New York: Ballantine Books, 1989), David Brinkley deftly describes the setting in which OPA operated. Bowles's achievements receive prominent notice (see pp. 133–36).

12. *New York Times,* July 15, 1943. Galbraith, no doubt high on Maxon's list of impractical, leftist professors and theorists, later wrote a short analytical study explaining why OPA's price controls had been effective; see John Kenneth Galbraith, *A Theory of Price Control* (Cambridge, Mass.: Harvard University Press, 1952/1980).

13. CB's testimony before the U.S. Senate Banking and Currency Committee, April 15, 1946.

14. Bowles summarized his position in his letter of resignation (CB letter to Truman, June 28, 1946, Box 47, Bowles Papers).

15. *Time,* March 12, 1945.

16. *Promises to Keep,* p. 163. CB diary, July 23, 1958, Box 392, Bowles Papers.

17. CB letter to Roosevelt, June 20, 1944, Box 10, Bowles Papers.

18. Roosevelt letter to CB, July 7, 1944, in ibid.

19. CB diary, July 23, 1958.

20. Bowles's radio campaign put to political use the singing commercial techniques he had developed at Benton & Bowles. His most effective song, "Truman and Bowles," written by Steb to the tune of "Buttons and Bows," was belted out by a singer in the tradition of Ethel Merman.

    Bowles recalled that in the 1948 campaign, the Republicans tried to smear him for his Unitarian religion and his divorce. Similar efforts were made in 1950 and (by fellow Democrats) in the contest for the party's nomination for a U.S. Senate seat in 1958. In 1948, voters were told that Unitarians did not believe in God. A photograph of the October 1948 wedding of Bowles's daughter from his first marriage, Barbara, was front-paged in the state's Republican newspapers to call attention to the divorce. Barbara was described as "the daughter of Chester Bowles, candidate for Governor, and Mrs. Winchester of New York." (The first Mrs. Bowles had also married again, to John G. Winchester, a New York banker and investment adviser.) Bowles remembered with some amusement that "the picture was a very lovely picture of my daughter, who is a very attractive girl, and I always thought the Republicans lost on this deal" (CB Oral History interview, Columbia University).

21. Discussing the cooling of his interest in ADA in *Promises to Keep,* Bowles recalled his regret that the organization was "unable to communicate more effectively with the voters. Gradually it emerged as a group of elite liberals, who seemed more interested in analyzing political problems on a lofty abstract level than in working at the grass roots to develop [needed] fresh political concepts. . . . Although I agreed with ADA's position on most issues . . . and indeed was asked to become its first chairman, I felt I could be more effective working within the Democratic Party in Connecticut" (p. 170). Closer to the event, Bowles wrote in March 1948 that he thought the ADA had concentrated too much of its time on opposing Communism and not enough in opposing the Republican party, which he considered the greater threat in the United States at that time (CB letter to Eleanor Mishnun, Box 31, Bowles Papers).

Bowles may also have backed away from the ADA because he sensed that association with it could be a political liability in Connecticut. In the 1950 gubernatorial campaign, to cite one well-remembered example, Republican candidate John Davis Lodge charged that Bowles, as an ADA member, was soft on Communism and favored U.S. recognition of Communist China. These allegations, vividly televised, probably hurt Bowles in a close race.

22. CB, *Tomorrow without Fear* (New York: Simon and Schuster, 1946).
23. CB Oral History interview, Columbia University.
24. Thomas Hughes Oral History interview, Box 398, Bowles Papers.
25. See Philip Coombs Oral History interview, in ibid.
26. Among these recruits were several who figure importantly in Bowles's later career, including Douglas Bennet, Sr., Abram Chayes, Philip Coombs, Jean Joyce, Edward Logue, and Bernard Loshbough. Bennet and Joyce had worked with Bowles in OPA. Bowles also appointed his former Madison Avenue and OPA associate, James Rogers, Jr., to serve as a member of the commission to reorganize the state government.

2. From America Firster to Liberal Interventionist

1. *New York Times,* November 9, 1950.
2. *Promises to Keep,* p. 244.
3. E. J. Kahn, Jr., *The China Hands* (New York: Viking Press, 1972), p. 279.
4. Wayne S. Cole, *America First* (Madison: University of Wisconsin Press, 1953); Michelle Flynn Stenehjem, *An American First* (New Rochelle, N.Y.: Arlington House, 1976); and Justin D. Doenecke, *In Danger Undaunted* (Stanford: Hoover Institution Press, 1990), are good sources for the America First Committee and Bowles's role in it.
5. Cole, *America First,* pp. 8–10.
6. *Common Sense* (magazine), December 1941.
7. Ibid.
8. Albert Horlings, "Who Are the Appeasers?" *New Republic,* 104 (1941), p. 110.
9. CB letter to R. Douglas Stuart, October 22, 1940, AFC Papers, quoted in Stenehjem, *An American First,* p. 53.
10. Rodman, "Chester Bowles."
11. CB letter to Taft, May 28, 1940, Robert A. Taft Papers, Library of Congress.
12. CB letter to Stuart, July 15, 1941, AFC Papers, reproduced in Doenecke, *In Danger Undaunted* (hereafter Doenecke), p. 280, as Document 85.
13. CB letter to Sidney Hertzberg, January 16, 1941, in ibid., p. 390, Document 115.
14. Ibid.
15. CB letter to William Benton, October 27, 1941, William Benton Papers, University of Chicago Library. Benton had by then become assistant to the president of the University of Chicago, and he and Bowles corresponded intermittently about foreign policy and other matters.
16. CB letter to R. Douglas Stuart, September 19, 1941, Doenecke, pp. 391–92, Document 116.

17. CB letter to R. Douglas Stuart, November 28, 1941, Doenecke, pp. 107–9, Document 12.
18. *Common Sense,* December 1941.
19. CB letter to Stuart, November 28, 1941, Doenecke, pp. 107–9, Document 12.
20. CB letter to Stuart, April 25, 1941, Doenecke, pp. 281–82, AFC Document 86.
21. CB letter to Stuart, October 16, 1941, Doenecke, p. 20.
22. CB letter to Hoover, November 28, 1941, Hoover Library. Bowles had sounded out William Benton earlier about the proposal and the possibility of using Hoover to launch it. See CB letter to Benton, November 19, 1941, William Benton Papers, University of Chicago Library.
23. Hoover letter to CB, November 29, 1941, Hoover Library.
24. CB letter to Robert E. Wood, December 22, 1941, quoted in Stenehjem, *An American First,* p. 118.
25. See Thomas Hughes's diary, October 14, 1960.
26. James C. Thomson, Jr., Oral History interview, Box 398, Bowles Papers.
27. CB letter to Truman, November 22, 1945, Box 47, Bowles Papers.
28. CB letter to Y. C. James Yen, March 17, 1948, Box 51, Bowles Papers.
29. CB letter to George Marshall, March 28, 1948, Box 41, Bowles Papers.
30. CB speech, "Our Chance to Turn the Tide," Freedom House, New York City, January 17, 1947, Box 59, Bowles Papers.
31. CB speech, "America's Food in a Hungry World," Supermarket Convention, Chicago, May 25, 1947, in ibid.
32. *New York Times Magazine,* April 18, 1948.
33. CB letter to Acheson, January 12, 1949, Box 3, Bowles Papers.
34. Bowles hesitated a long time before naming Benton, and did so only after other candidates, including Columbia University Professor Philip Jessup and Hunter College President George Shuster, had declined to be considered. The problems the appointment of Benton later caused Bowles are outlined in Chapter 8.
35. CB letter to Benton, April 13, 1951, Box 33, Bowles Papers.
36. In a letter he sent to Eisenhower on March 31, 1948 (Box 37, Bowles Papers), Bowles wrote that he had little confidence in Truman. Our only hope, he told the general, was to find someone who can be a substitute as Democratic presidential nominee. "As far as I am concerned, you come much the closest of anyone to filling the bill and I only hope you will not close your mind to the possibility." In a nationwide radio broadcast the following day, Bowles said Truman's chances of winning were slim to the disappearing point and that Eisenhower had proven his ability as an administrator and as someone who could get along with people. "If, in the next few months it becomes clear that Eisenhower's economic, social, and political views are progressive and in key with the difficult times we live in, then I believe that the people of this country will *demand* that he accept the Democratic presidential nomination" (CB speech to the Groton, Connecticut, Democratic organization, April 1, 1948, Box 59, Bowles Papers). Defending his opposition to Truman's nomination, Bowles wrote William Benton that "Truman hasn't a chance in the world of winning, and I believe a Republican sweep, with all its implications

in Congress and the Cabinet and the influences around the White House, could well be disastrous" (CB letter to Benton, May 12, 1948, Box 32, Bowles Papers). Bowles's interest in the party's dropping Truman was no doubt heightened by his own intention to make a bid for the governorship of Connecticut in the 1948 election. He must certainly have calculated that his chances of winning would be much better were the Democratic ticket headed by the popular general rather than the seemingly failing president. Robert J. Donovan has an interesting account of Bowles's role in the "dump Truman" effort and the president's reaction to it in *Conflict and Crisis: The Presidency of Harry S. Truman, 1945–1948* (New York: W. W. Norton, 1977), chap. 40.

37. Author's interview with Clifford, February 1990.
38. There is a rough draft of a letter to Truman in Box 47, Bowles Papers, in which Bowles reviewed the aborted Philippines and roving ambassador assignments. Dated January 17, 1951, the letter was apparently never sent to the president. There is no record of it in the Harry S. Truman Library.
39. *Promises to Keep,* p. 246.
40. CB letter to Truman, February 5, 1951, Harry S. Truman Library.
41. CB letter to Benton, February 13, 1951, Box 33, Bowles Papers.
42. Benton letter to CB, February 2, 1951, in ibid.
43. Memorandum of telephone conversation between CB and Acheson, January 16, 1951, Papers of Dean Acheson, Harry S. Truman Library.
44. CB letter to Harriman, May 4, 1951, Box 38, Bowles Papers.
45. CB letter to Benton, April 13, 1951.
46. *Promises to Keep,* p. 247.
47. CB Oral History interview, Columbia University.
48. Letter to author from Stephen P. Cohen, University of Illinois, April 17, 1992.
49. *Promises to Keep,* p. 247
50. Author's interviews with Jean Joyce, September 1989, and Edward Logue, February 1990.
51. CB letter to Eleanor Roosevelt, August 27, 1951, Box 45, Bowles Papers.
52. CB letter to Dean, September 6, 1951, Box 36, Bowles Papers.
53. CB letter to Kefauver, October 9, 1951, Box 39, Bowles Papers.
54. See, for example, the *Hartford Courant* and the *Hartford Times,* both of September 13, 1951. The newspapers were quoted by William Benton in a speech he made on the Senate floor on September 14, 1951, supporting Bowles's nomination (*Congressional Record,* vol. 97, 82nd Congress, 1st Session, p. 11366).
55. *Executive Sessions of the Senate Foreign Relations Committee (Historical Series)* (Washington: U.S. Government Printing Office, 1976), vol. 3, pp. 26–46.
56. *Congressional Record,* vol. 97, October 9, 1951, pp. 12841–52.
57. Clipping from unidentified newspaper, June 19, 1952, Box 117, Bowles Papers.
58. CB letter to Aiken, October 19, 1951, Box 31, Bowles Papers.
59. CB letter to Rockefeller, October 8, 1951, Box 44, Bowles Papers.
60. CB letter to Cousins, October 12, 1951, Box 36, Bowles Papers.
61. CB letter to Humphrey, September 20, 1951, Box 39, Bowles Papers.

3. A Connecticut Yankee in Mr. Nehru's Court

1. Government of India, Ministry of Information and Broadcasting, *India, First Five Year Plan,* 1953. See also Michael Brecher, *Nehru, A Political Biography* (London: Oxford University Press, 1959), p. 524 and following, and A. H. Hanson, *The Process of Planning* (Oxford: Oxford University Press, 1966), p. 98.
2. Jawaharlal Nehru, *India's Foreign Policy* (Ministry of Information and Broadcasting, Government of India, 1961), "Future Taking Shape," broadcast from New Delhi, September 7, 1946, p. 2.
3. Ibid.,"We Lead Ourselves," speech in the Constituent Assembly, March 8, 1948, p. 31.
4. Ibid., "Future Taking Shape," p. 2.
5. Brecher, *Nehru,* p. 566.
6. See Gary R. Hess, *America Encounters India, 1941–1947* (Baltimore: Johns Hopkins University Press, 1971), especially chaps. 1 and 8. Discussing U.S. wartime policies toward the quest for Indian independence, when Roosevelt proved unwilling to challenge Churchill's tough position on nationalist demands voiced by the Indian National Congress, Hess concluded, "In its first test [in facing the challenge of responding to Asian nationalist movements directed against its European allies] the United States substantially failed. Because of its equivocation the nation appeared uncertain of its own espoused ideals, and seemed to be a partner in imperialism" (p. 183). As will be seen, Bowles sought to improve that record by his insistent advocacy of a U.S. approach that stressed support for the independent foreign policies favored by India and other newly emerging Third World states and opposition to colonialism and neocolonialism.
7. For a particularly insightful study of the power of stereotypes, see Harold R. Isaacs, *Scratches on Our Minds* (Westport, Connecticut: Greenwood Press, 1958).
8. NSC 98/1, January 22, 1951, *Foreign Relations of the United States* (hereafter *FRUS), 1951,* vol. VI, p. 1650–52.
9. As popularly understood, the term "loss of China" carried the implication that the United States could somehow have prevented the Communists' coming to power. It was often used by critics of the Truman administration's Far Eastern policies. Despite this implied meaning, the term was used in NSC 98/1 and other government documents of the time. In a sense, Bowles picked it up for his own purposes when he called on Washington to prevent the "loss of India."
10. H. W. Brands, *India and the United States: The Cold Peace* (Boston: Twayne Publishers, 1990).
11. NSC 48/1, December 23, 1949, National Security Council records, National Archives.
12. *FRUS, 1951,* vol. VI, p. 1651.
13. CB memorandum to Acheson, December 6, 1951, in ibid., p. 2191–2202.
14. Bowles had written earlier to Assistant Secretary of State George McGhee about Sino-Indian economic competition, but the memorandum to Acheson

appears to be his first formal presentation of what was to become a familiar, and widely accepted, argument (CB letter to McGhee, November 18, 1951, Box 96, Bowles Papers).

15. In 1962 Bowles's staff asked the Library of Congress to check the accuracy of this quotation and was told that no evidence could be found that the Soviet leader had ever uttered it. By then, Bowles had used the phrase countless times in his writings and speeches. Apparently unabashed by the disclosure, he told a National Press Club luncheon audience: "Scholars assert that Lenin never made such a statement. I would reply that he should have—and would have with the assistance of better speech writers. For I know of no sentence that describes more cogently the thrust of Soviet strategy" (Box 62, Presidential Office Files [hereafter POF], JFK Library).

16. *New Republic*, November 26, 1951.

17. CB letter to Benton, December 11, 1951, Box 81, Bowles Papers.

18. *Ambassador's Report* (New York: Harper and Brothers, 1954), p. 300. The book is Bowles's account of his first assignment to India.

19. CB letter to Bailey, February 27, 1952, Box 81, Bowles Papers.

20. *New York Times*, November 6, 1951.

21. Author's interview with a former embassy New Delhi officer, November 1989.

22. CB letter to Allen, March 7, 1953, Box 93, Bowles Papers.

23. CB letter to Kennedy, December 15, 1952, Box 95, Bowles Papers.

24. David E. Lilienthal, *Venturesome Years, 1950–1955* (New York: Harper and Row, 1966), p. 101.

25. Escott Reid, *Envoy to Nehru* (Delhi: Oxford University Press, 1981), p. 266.

26. CB Oral History interview, Columbia University.

27. The quotations are drawn from *Ambassador's Report*, chap. 9, and *Promises to Keep*, chap. 38.

28. *Ambassador's Report*, p. 103.

29. Bowles devoted a full chapter in *Ambassador's Report* to the importance of land reform and the shortcomings of the Nehru government in carrying it out (pp. 173–94).

30. See, for example, New Delhi telegram 1458, October 6, 1952, *FRUS, 1952–1954*, vol. XI, p. 1667.

31. New Delhi despatch 149, July 17, 1952, National Archives.

32. Bowles Oral History interview, 1971, Jawaharlal Nehru Memorial Library, New Delhi.

33. Dean Acheson, *Present at the Creation* (New York: W. W. Norton, 1969), p. 336.

4. Spotlighting Economic Assistance

1. CB letter to McGhee, November 8, 1951, Box 96, Bowles Papers.

2. Jonathan Bingham, *Shirt-Sleeve Diplomacy: Point Four in Action* (New York: J. Day, 1954) provides a good rundown of the early days of the assistance program. The Bowles and Bingham families were on close terms in Connecticut. When Bowles went to India, Bingham was assistant director for Non-European affairs in the Office of International Security Affairs in the State

Department, and soon afterwards became deputy administrator in the Technical Cooperation Administration (Point Four).

3. Thomas G. Paterson, *Meeting the Communist Threat* (New York: Oxford University Press, 1988), p. 150. According to Bowles, Truman had told him that Senator Brien McMahon of Connecticut, Presidential Special Counsel Clark Clifford, and Bowles himself were the people who persuaded him to include Point Four in the inaugural address. (See CB letter to Under Secretary of State C. Douglas Dillon, December 18, 1958, Box 130, Bowles Papers, and *Promises to Keep*, p. 246.) There is no corroborating evidence for this. Clifford does not mention a role for Bowles in his *Counsel to the President* (New York: Random House, 1991), which includes an extensive discussion of the origins of the program (pp. 247–53), nor could he recall any such role when the author queried him in a 1990 interview. Paterson similarly does not cite any Bowles influence.

4. CB letter to Yen, September 18, 1951, Box 51, Bowles Papers.

5. For a detailed account of the Etawah project, see Albert Mayer and Associates, *Pilot Project, India: The Story of Rural Development in Etawah, Uttar Pradesh* (Berkeley: University of California Press, 1958). Dennis Merrill, *Bread and the Ballot* (Chapel Hill: University of North Carolina Press, 1990), pp. 80–88, includes some excellent fresh insights on Bowles and community development, as well as on Bowles's broader views of economic development.

6. *Ambassador's Report*, p. 198

7. *FRUS, 1951*, vol. VI, p. 2153 fn.

8. See New Delhi telegram 3165, May 10, 1951, ibid., pp. 2161–62.

9. See New Delhi telegram 3362, May 25, 1951, ibid., pp. 2164–66.

10. *Ambassador's Report*, p. 199.

11. "Tentative Proposal for Economic Aid and Development," November 22, 1951, Box 98, Bowles Papers. Bowles had foreshadowed his approach to Nehru in a letter of November 17, 1951 to George McGhee (Box 96, Bowles Papers).

12. *Ambassador's Report*, p. 200.

13. For the text of the agreement, see *United States Treaties and Other International Agreements (UST)*, vol. 3, pt. 2, p. 2921.

14. CB memorandum, "A Progress Report from India," April 7, 1952, Box 93, Bowles Papers. CB letter to Phillip Coombs, March 18, 1952, Box 84, Bowles Papers. To resettle refugees from Pakistan, S. K. Dey had developed the new town of Nilokheri, another community development project Bowles much admired.

15. See the correspondence between Bowles and Edward I. Bernays in Box 82, Bowles Papers. Bernays remained on the Indian embassy payroll only until May 1952, when he found the embassy impossible to work with and gave up the account. Bernays letter to Indian Ambassador B. R. Sen, May 26, 1952, in ibid.

16. CB letter to Walter Lippmann, November 21, 1952, Box 87, Bowles Papers.

17. Author's interview with David H. Blee, June 1990.

18. Benton letters to CB, February 25, 1952; March 23, 1952; April 15, 1952, Box 81, Bowles Papers.

19. CB memorandum to McMahon, January 3, 1952, Box 88, Bowles Papers.
20. CB letter to Truman, January 31, 1952, Box 96, Bowles Papers.
21. CB memorandum, "The Crucial Problem of India, A Personal Report by Chester Bowles," February 1952, Box 93, Bowles Papers.
22. In the 1952 Indian elections, the Communists and their allies won 5.52 percent of the parliamentary seats, having received 5.4 percent of the vote. Comparable figures for the Indian National Congress were 74.0 percent and 44.9 percent. The Communists and their allies did marginally better in the elections for the state legislative assemblies. The southern states in which the Communists and their allies scored relatively well were Hyderabad, where they won 42 of 175 seats in the state legislature (to Congress's 93), Travancore-Cochin, part of present day Kerala (32 of 108, to Congress's 44), and Madras (62 of 375, to Congress's 152).
23. CB letter to Hoffman, November 14, 1951, Box 86, Bowles Papers.
24. CB memorandum to McMahon, January 3, 1952.
25. CB letter to Hoffman, November 14, 1951.
26. CB letter to Chayes, January 15, 1952, Box 83, Bowles Papers.
27. CB letter to Kennedy, December 15, 1952, Box 95, Bowles Papers.
28. Phillip Coombs memorandum, "The Difference of Views between Ambassador Bowles and the State Department on the Amount of Aid for India in Fiscal 1953," February 25, 1952, Box 84, Bowles Papers. CB letter to Truman, January 31, 1952, Box 96, Bowles Papers.
29. *Executive Sessions of the Senate Foreign Relations Committee*, vol. 4, pp. 62 ff. *Promises to Keep*, p. 45. "Memorandum by the Deputy Director of the Executive Secretariat (Barnes) to the Staff Assistant to the Assistant Secretary of State for Near Eastern, South Asian, and African Affairs (Hemba)," January 18, 1952, *FRUS, 1952–1954*, vol. XI, p. 1633.
30. Of the $7.9 billion foreign aid budget the administration presented to Congress in March 1952, over $5 billion was allocated to military aid for Europe. Allocations for Asia and the Pacific were increased to slightly over $1 billion, but $610 million of that figure was for military assistance. Most of the remaining economic aid for Asia went to perceived security danger points in East Asia, nearly one-quarter to the Chiang Kai-shek government on Taiwan. (Merrill, *Bread and the Ballot*, p. 90, and Senate Committee on Foreign Relations, *Hearings: Mutual Security Act of 1952*, 82nd Congress, 2nd session, 1952, p. 8.)
31. New Delhi telegram 3003, February 21, 1952, *FRUS, 1952–1954*, vol. XI, pp. 1635–39.
32. "Memorandum by the Secretary of State and the Director for Mutual Security (Harriman) to the President, Subject: Bowles Program for Additional Aid for India," June 5, 1952, ibid., pp. 1646–48. Truman letter to CB, July 1, 1952, ibid., p. 1653.
33. CB letter to Acheson, October 28, 1952, ibid., p. 1670.
34. Ibid., p. 1675.
35. Acheson letter to CB, January 8, 1953, ibid., p. 1683.
36. "Memorandum by the Secretary of State to the Under Secretary of State (Smith)," March 4, 1953, ibid., p. 1692.

37. CB letter to Allen, March 7, 1953, Box 93, Bowles Papers.
38. Bowles outlined his precepts in chap. 20 of *Ambassador's Report,* "Role of Foreign Aid," pp. 322–47.
39. Ibid., p. 335.
40. Ibid., p. 334.
41. Ibid., p. 335.
42. CB letter to Allen, March 22, 1953, Box 93, Bowles Papers.
43. *New York Times Magazine,* January 4, 1953.
44. *Ambassador's Report,* p. 342.
45. Ibid., p. 343.

5. The China Card and an Asian Monroe Doctrine

1. S. Gopal, *Jawaharlal Nehru: 1947–1956* (Cambridge, Mass.: Harvard University Press, 1979), vol. II, p. 139.
2. New Delhi telegram 1661, November 7, 1951, *FRUS, 1951,* vol. VI, pp. 2186–91.
3. CB memorandum of conversation with Nehru, February 1952 (no date), Box 98, Bowles Papers.
4. New Delhi despatch 149, July 17, 1952, National Archives, Diplomatic Branch.
5. CB letter to Benton, December 11, 1951, Box 81, Bowles Papers.
6. CB letter to Cousins, November 29, 1951, Box 84, Bowles Papers.
7. Gordon H. Chang, *Old Friends and New Enemies* (Stanford: Stanford University Press, 1990), pp. 16–21. Valuable earlier studies of this period in U.S.-Chinese relations include Foster Rhea Dulles, *American Policy toward Communist China, 1949–1969* (New York: Thomas Y. Crowell, 1972); Dorothy Borg and Waldo Heinrichs, eds., *Uncertain Years* (New York: Columbia University Press, 1980); Warren I. Cohen, *America's Response to China* (New York: Alfred A. Knopf, 1980); and Nancy Bernkopf Tucker, *Patterns in the Dust* (New York: Columbia University Press, 1983).
8. Chang, *Old Friends,* p. 80.
9. New Delhi despatch 149. State Department, Bureau of Far Eastern Affairs memorandum, July 25, 1952, National Archives, Diplomatic Branch.
10. New Delhi despatch 149.
11. *Ambassador's Report,* p. 329.
12. New Delhi telegram 2341, December 8, 1952, National Archives, Diplomatic Branch.
13. CB letter to Dulles, March 10, 1952, Box 94, Bowles Papers.
14. Dulles letter to CB, March 25, 1952, in ibid.
15. CB letter to Dulles, April 23, 1952, in ibid.
16. Chang, *Old Friends,* p. 84.
17. CB letters to Dulles, February 5 and February 25, 1953, Box 94, Bowles Papers.
18. CB letter to Dulles, March 20, 1953, in ibid. In this last letter of his early 1953 series to Secretary Dulles, Bowles worked up a long analysis of Nehru's

views, having in mind Dulles's forthcoming visit to India, which took place in May after Bowles had left the embassy.

19. Bowles was almost certainly unaware of the disdainful attitude toward Chiang which Dulles was expressing privately at the time.

20. CB letter to Dulles, February 25, 1953.

21. CB Oral History interview, Columbia University.

22. Gopal, *Jawaharlal Nehru,* p. 139.

23. *Promises to Keep,* p. 492.

24. Acheson, *Present at the Creation,* p. 700ff.

25. New Delhi telegram 2213, November 26, 1952, *FRUS, 1952–1954,* vol. XV, p. 687. An account Bowles provided ten years later in an interview for an oral history gives a more dramatic version of this episode. Bowles said at that time that he told Nehru the angry Soviet rejection represented the first indication of daylight between Moscow and Peking, which up to that point had been noncommittal toward the Indian initiative. "This was the Soviets telling the Chinese that Stalin wanted no truce, and they had better get in line" (CB Oral History interview, Columbia University).

26. New Delhi telegram 2272, December 2, 1952, *FRUS, 1952–1954,* vol. XV, p. 701.

27. CB letter to Dulles, February 25, 1953.

28. CB letter to Dulles, February 5, 1953.

29. *Ambassador's Report,* p. 376.

30. Ibid., pp. 366–68. CB letter to Sir G. S. Bajpai, June 5, 1953, Box 97, Bowles Papers.

6. Dealing with South Asia

1. For an excellent, carefully researched, recent account of the genesis of the United States-Pakistan security tie, see Robert J. McMahon, "United States Strategy in South Asia: Making a Military Commitment to Pakistan, 1947–1954," *Journal of American History* 75 (December 1988), pp. 812–40.

2. New Delhi telegram 639, August 13, 1952, *FRUS, 1952–1954,* vol. XI, pp. 1660–61. The volume includes several other messages on the proposed sales (see pp. 1658–65).

3. Foreign policy participants and competent observers give Bowles major credit for stopping the development of a United States-Pakistan security relationship during the Truman administration, as does Bowles himself. Canadian High Commissioner Escott Reid, who overlapped briefly with Bowles in New Delhi, has recalled Bowles telling him during their first talks in December 1952 and January 1953 that "some time before there had been a proposal that Pakistan should join a projected Middle East defence organization but that Archibald Nye, then British High Commissioner to India, had killed it in London and [Bowles] thought that he had killed it in Washington." (Reid, *Envoy to Nehru,* p. 101.) Bowles recalled his strong opposition to the proposal in 1951 and 1952 in a memorandum dated May 28, 1956 (Box 166, Bowles Papers). In an interview in February 1990, Henry A. Byroade, who had been assistant secretary for Near Eastern, South Asian, and African affairs in the late Truman

and early Eisenhower administrations, told the author that Bowles had been a forceful and effective opponent of the relationship. (Byroade himself became one of its principal proponents.) William J. Barnds, in *India, Pakistan, and the Great Powers* (New York: Praeger Publishers, 1972), p. 92, and Selig Harrison, in the first (August 10, 1959) of a series of articles in the *New Republic,* "Case History of a Mistake," also credit Bowles with an important role. Curiously, there are no available messages sent from New Delhi by Bowles discussing the issue before November 1952, when the Indians (and Bowles himself) became alarmed at the prospect of the incoming Republicans reviving the idea and the British had come to favor it.

4. *New York Times,* November 10, 1952.

5. Department of State telegram 1477 to New Delhi, November 10, 1952, National Archives, Diplomatic Branch. New Delhi telegram 2063, November 17, 1952, *FRUS, 1952–1954,* vol. XI, p. 1302.

6. Department of State, circular telegram 544, November 13, 1952, Harry S. Truman Library, Papers of Dean Acheson. New Delhi telegram 2119, November 20, 1952, ibid. For further documentation of Bowles's efforts to hold off a move by the lame-duck Truman administration to develop a security tie with Pakistan and his reporting of negative Indian reaction to that prospect, see New Delhi telegram 2063, p. 1303, and "Memorandum of Conversations in New Delhi and Elsewhere Between October 20, 1951 and March 20, 1953," Box 104, Bowles Papers, p. 11. Robert McMahon concludes ("United States Strategy in South Asia," p. 830) that the Truman administration's decision not to proceed with the Pakistan linkup in its final months in office had less to do with Bowles's impassioned arguments than with the administration's lame-duck status.

7. CB letter to Smith, January 15, 1953, Box 96, Bowles Papers.

8. Smith letter to CB, February 6, 1953, in ibid.

9. CB letter to Dulles, March 20, 1953.

10. For Dulles's radio address on his Middle East-South Asia trip, see *Department of State Bulletin,* vol. XXVIII, no. 729, June 15, 1953, pp. 831–35. For his June 1, 1953, comments to the National Security Council, see *FRUS, 1952–1954,* vol. IX, pt. 1, pp. 87–88. In addition to the United States and Pakistan, the members of SEATO were Great Britain, France, Australia, New Zealand, Thailand, and the Philippines. The members of the Baghdad Pact were Great Britain, Pakistan, Iran, Turkey, and Iraq. Iraq withdrew in 1958 following the overthrow of its pro-Western monarchy, and the organization was then renamed the Central Treaty Organization (CENTO).

11. CB letter to Dulles, December 30, 1953, Box 130, Bowles Papers. Bowles received a perfunctory, rather patronizing reply from Dulles: "As you know from your own experience, one rarely has the luxury in diplomacy of being able to choose a course of action which is all on the 'credit' side of the ledger and entails no 'debits' at all." With respect to the subcontinent, Dulles said, "we shall do our utmost to see that the benefits of any action we take outweigh the difficulties" (Dulles letter to CB, January 14, 1954, ibid.).

12. A great deal has been written about the dispute over Kashmir. Among the

better studies are Sisir Gupta, *Kashmir, A Study in Indo-Pakistan Relations* (Bombay: Asia Publishing House, 1966); Josef Korbel, *Danger in Kashmir* (Princeton: Princeton University Press, 1954); and Alastair Lamb, *Crisis in Kashmir* (London: Routledge and Kegan Paul, 1966). Lamb has followed up his account with a valuable but controversial broader study of the Kashmir problem. The book brings the issue forward to the late 1989 outbreak of the insurgent movement in the state, which returned the question of Kashmir's political future to world headlines: *Kashmir: A Disputed Legacy, 1846–1990* (Hertingfordbury, Hertfordshire, England: Roxford Books, 1991).

13. New Delhi telegram 2718, January 30, 1952, *FRUS, 1952–1954,* vol. XI, p. 1184.
14. For a useful discussion of the Dixon proposal and reactions to it, see Gupta, *Kashmir,* pp. 217–23. Bowles laid out his position in a series of New Delhi telegrams, including 2426, January 10, 1952 (*FRUS, 1952–1954,* vol. XI, p. 1167); 2851, February 12, 1952 (ibid., pp. 1188–90); and 3976, April 28, 1952 (ibid., p. 1240). The difference between Bowles and the department is spelled out most clearly in an exchange of letters he had with Assistant Secretary of State for United Nations Affairs John Hickerson, ibid., pp. 1233–38 (CB letter to Hickerson, April 28, 1952) and pp. 1251–57 (Hickerson's reply of May 29, 1952).
15. See, for example, memorandum of conversation, June 13, 1952, ibid., pp. 1257–59. Bowles returned to Washington that month for consultations. The memo records a discussion he had with Hickerson and others at the time.
16. Karachi telegram 1577, June 26, 1952, ibid., pp. 1264–65. State Department telegram 31 to Karachi, July 4, 1952, ibid., p. 1269.
17. New Delhi telegram 100, July 5, 1952, ibid., pp. 1271–76. New Delhi telegram 155, July 11, 1952, ibid., pp. 1278–79. CB letter to Donald Kennedy, July 31, 1952. Box 95, Bowles Papers. Bowles told Kennedy that because of the disaffection of Nehru's longtime political ally, Kashmir Prime Minister Sheikh Abdullah, and the outcry of the Hindu political right, "the last thing [Nehru] wanted to be confronted with was a reasonable offer from Pakistan which was likely to bring the situation to a head at that particular time."
18. CB letter to Dulles, December 30, 1953.
19. *Ambassador's Report,* p. 294.
20. The Bowles letters to Donald Kennedy are in Box 95, Bowles Papers. The quotation is from the letter of November 5, 1952.
21. *New York Times,* November 6, 1952.
22. *Times of India,* January 1, 1953.
23. Benton letter to CB, November 8, 1952, Box 82, Bowles Papers. CB letter to Benton, November 18, 1952, ibid.
24. Author's interview with a former New Delhi embassy officer, 1990. *Promises to Keep,* p. 248. Although Benton thought Lodge might want Bowles to remain outside Connecticut in 1953 and 1954 so as to diminish his prospects for a political comeback, Bowles apparently concluded that the governor was more fearful of the prestige his reappointment as ambassador by a Republican president would give him among the state's voters.

25. CB letter to Bailey, February 12, 1953, Box 81, Bowles Papers.
26. Vijayalakshmi Pandit, *The Scope of Happiness* (London: Weidenfeld and Nicholson, 1979), p. 261.
27. Nehru letter to CB, February 6, 1953, Box 98, Bowles Papers.
28. Reid, *Envoy to Nehru,* p. 12.

7. Exporting the American Revolution to the Third World

1. Author's interview with Sally Bowles, July 1990.
2. *Ambassador's Report,* p. 391.
3. Ibid., pp. 380–99.
4. *New Republic,* January 18, 1954.
5. *Pacific Affairs,* September 1954.
6. *U.S. Quarterly,* June 1954.
7. Thomson Oral History interview.
8. Schlesinger made an interesting comment in a letter to Bowles dated July 16, 1954: "A major difficulty with the thesis was that it really applied more to China than to India and this, in a sense, strengthens the case for a Peking-sponsored Monroe Doctrine." He contended that "[China's] relationship to the USSR as far as Asia is concerned is not dissimilar to the United States' relationship to the United Kingdom at the time of the Monroe Doctrine; and the role of the United States in Asia today has all too many parallels to that of the Holy Alliance in Europe." (Arthur M. Schlesinger, Jr., Papers, JFK Library). Schlesinger's analysis did not deter Bowles from pressing the idea as he had originally conceived it.

    Bowles's confidence in Bissell and Amory was reflected in his effort to place them in the State Department. When he became under secretary in the Kennedy administration, he tried unsuccessfully to have Bissell as deputy under secretary for political affairs. (Chapter 11 details this effort.) Earlier, he recommended Amory to replace Robert Bowie as head of the department's Policy Planning Council. Writing to Hubert Humphrey to support that move, Bowles noted that "during the recent [1956 presidential] campaign, [Amory] was enormously helpful at several key points and I have no personal doubt as to where his heart lies. He is a person of integrity, ability, and experience, whose approach would closely coincide with yours and mine" (CB letter to Humphrey, July 20, 1957, Fulbright Papers, University of Arkansas).
9. In the July 20, 1957, letter to Humphrey just quoted, Bowles spoke of Bowie as "one of the few in the Department who has had the courage to speak up to the Secretary [Dulles] on some of the more critical and difficult problems."
10. Bowles spelled out his opposition to Dulles's so-called "massive retaliation" policy in an article in the *New York Times Magazine,* February 28, 1954, "A Plea for Another Great Debate." The State Department apparently considered Bowles's criticism sufficiently important to refute point by point. A memorandum to this end was prepared in the department for the use of Senator William Knowland of California, a leading Republican hard-liner. See Dulles Papers, General Correspondence and Memoranda Series, Box 2, Eisenhower Library.
11. CB memorandum, October 19, 1955, Box 166, Bowles Papers.

12. CB speech, "America Must Redefine Its Purpose," Cleveland Council of World Affairs, April 18, 1956, Box 171, Bowles Papers.
13. *Ambassador's Report,* pp. 330–31.
14. CB, "The Crisis That Faces Us Will Not Wait," *New York Times Magazine,* November 27, 1955.
15. *New York Times,* October 30, 1955.
16. Thomas Hughes, Oral History interview, Box 398, Bowles Papers.
17. CB, *New Dimensions of Peace* (New York: Harper and Brothers, 1955), p. 383.
18. "The Cry for Land in Latin America," *New York Times Magazine,* November 22, 1959.
19. CB, *Africa's Challenge to America* (Berkeley: University of California Press, 1956), p. 96.
20. *New Dimensions,* p. 17.
21. CB memorandum, "The Ominously Changing Balance of Power in Asia," March 22, 1955, Box 166, Bowles Papers.
22. CB letter to Hoffman, December 31, 1954, Box 138, Bowles Papers.
23. See CB letter to Nehru, May 2, 1955, Box 148, Bowles Papers.
24. "The Challenge of the Next Decade," *New York Times Magazine,* April 21, 1957.
25. CB memorandum, October 19, 1955.
26. Thomson Oral History interview.
27. CB letter to Dulles, September 21, 1954, Box 191, Bowles Papers.
28. House of Representatives, Committee on Foreign Affairs, *Briefing on Current World Situation, Hearings,* 86th Congress, 1st session, January 28–29, 1959, pp. 27–29.
29. "The 'China Problem' Reconsidered," *Foreign Affairs,* April 1960.
30. See John Sharon, Oral History interview, JFK Library, and author's interview with Thomas Hughes, March 1990.
31. Bowles's welcome was less warm at the American Embassy in New Delhi. When he visited India in 1955, the embassy staff in the absence of the ambassador deliberately limited their contacts with him and offered him few of the courtesies ordinarily made available to a former envoy. They were apparently wary of being regarded in Washington as helpful to a leading Democrat who was highly critical of administration foreign policy.
32. Burton I. Kaufman, *Trade and Aid, Eisenhower's Economic Policy 1953–1961* (Baltimore: Johns Hopkins University Press, 1982), p. 58.
33. Ibid., pp. 60–65.
34. See, for example, the letters (all in the Bowles Papers) he wrote to President Eisenhower (January 26, 1957, Box 131), New York Governor Thomas E. Dewey (October 10, 1957, Box 130), Vice President Nixon (October 8, 1957, Box 149), and Dean Acheson (September 26, 1957, Box 118).
35. CB, "The Crisis That Faces Us Will Not Wait."
36. *New Dimensions,* pp. 165–66.
37. CB memorandum, May 28, 1956, Box 166, Bowles Papers.
38. CB letter to Bowie, January 26, 1957, Box 123, Bowles Papers.
39. At a January 3, 1957 meeting of the National Security Council, Eisenhower

observed that "we had decided some time ago that we wanted Pakistan as a military ally. In point of fact we were doing practically nothing for Pakistan except in the form of military aid." In the president's view, "this was perhaps the worst kind of plan and decision we could have made. It was a terrible error, but we now seem hopelessly involved in it" (*FRUS, 1955–57,* vol. VIII, pp. 25–26).

40. NSC 5701, "U.S. Policy toward South Asia," January 10, 1957, ibid., pp. 29–43.

41. H. W. Brands, *The Specter of Neutralism* (New York: Columbia University Press, 1989), p. 106.

42. Merrill, *Bread and the Ballot,* p. 137. Professors Walt W. Rostow and Max Millikan at the M.I.T. Center for International Studies were especially effective in influencing opinion in favor of assistance to India as part of a greatly expanded foreign aid program and in treating India as a model aid recipient. See Walt Rostow, *Eisenhower, Kennedy, and Foreign Aid* (Austin: University of Texas Press, 1985).

8. Search for a Political Base

1. CB letter to Benton, July 30, 1952, Box 82, Bowles Papers.

2. John Bartlow Martin, *Adlai Stevenson and the World* (Garden City, N.Y.: Doubleday, 1977), p. 247.

3. CB letter to Benton, July 8, 1952, Box 82, Bowles Papers.

4. Author's interview with Galbraith, March 1990. Martin, *Adlai Stevenson and the World,* p. 84.

5. Wofford Oral History interview, Box 398, Bowles Papers.

6. CB, "State of the World in Connecticut, Essex, and the U.S.A., A Comprehensive But Belated Report to Jean and Bernie," undated [probably June 1954], Box 141, Bowles Papers.

7. Hughes Oral History interview.

8. *Promises to Keep,* p. 256.

9. The text of the May 26, 1954, statement is in Box 170, Bowles Papers.

10. In his Columbia University Oral History interview, Bowles recalled: "Friends said, 'If you're really going into foreign affairs you really ought to go into it.' Well it was wrong, terribly wrong. The way to have an effect on foreign policy is to have a strong political base and from that you could use your influence and leverage."

11. Hughes Oral History interview.

12. George W. Ball, who was close to Stevenson and can presumably speak with some authority on the matter, has told the author that he is convinced that Stevenson would not have chosen Bowles as secretary of state had he become president. In Ball's recollection, Stevenson, who had spent much time himself dealing with foreign policy issues, did not regard Bowles as particularly expert on foreign policy and did not take his views seriously (author's interview with former Under Secretary of State Ball, April 1991).

13. CB letter to Stevenson, September 3, 1954, Box 157, Bowles Papers.

14. See draft speeches which Bowles sent to Stevenson on October 3 and October

29, 1954, Box 158, Bowles Papers. CB letter to Stevenson, October 28, 1955, Box 157, Bowles Papers. Martin, *Adlai Stevenson,* p. 191. Walter Johnson, ed., *The Papers of Adlai E. Stevenson: Toward a New America, 1955–1957* (Boston: Little, Brown, 1976), vol. VI, p. 1956.

15. CB letter to Stevenson, October 28, 1955.

16. CB letter to Stevenson, April 27, 1956, Box 157, Bowles Papers.

17. Ibid.

18. CB, "The Foreign Policy Issues and the Democratic Party," December 1, 1955, Box 166, Bowles Papers.

19. CB letter to Thomson, November 8, 1955, Box 159, Bowles Papers.

20. CB letter to Stevenson, October 9, 1956, Box 158, Bowles Papers.

21. The text of the Cincinnati speech is in the *New York Times,* October 20, 1956. Bowles's draft text is in Box 158, Bowles Papers. The day before Stevenson delivered the speech, Bowles wrote to Dean Acheson: "I feel that Adlai has not only neglected a moral responsibility but has missed a political opportunity in failing to deal vigorously with the foreign policy question. Your letter and mine must have had some effect because he called me Saturday night and we talked at some length on this subject" (CB letter to Acheson, October 18, 1956, Box 118, Bowles Papers). CB Oral History interview, Columbia University.

22. CB letter to Joyce, November 10, 1956, Box 141, Bowles Papers.

23. CB Oral History interview, Columbia University.

24. CB letter to Joyce, April 10, 1956, Box 141, Bowles Papers. CB note, January 1962, Box 392, Bowles Papers.

25. CB letter to Rostow, Box 154, Bowles Papers.

26. CB letter to Hoffman, December 31, 1954, Box 138, Bowles Papers.

27. Hughes letter to CB, January 19, 1955, in ibid. CB letter to Benton, February 15, 1955, Box 122, Bowles Papers.

28. CB letter to Humphrey, August 16, 1955, Box 138, Bowles Papers.

29. Bowles and Eisenhower had a particularly interesting exchange of letters in the summer of 1956, when Bowles sent the president a copy of one of his books, probably *American Politics in a Revolutionary World,* a collection of his essays published that year. He got back much more than the courteous note customary on such occasions. In a rambling reply addressed to "Dear Governor," Eisenhower said that he hadn't read the book yet "but a hasty glance through it gives me a feeling of satisfaction that informed individuals are facing up to the fact that our country is confronted with crucial problems in a strange new international world and are striving to establish guideposts leading to reasonable answers." Promising to read the book "earnestly and thoughtfully," the president went on to warn Bowles that "if it suggests an answer that depends on the kind of political argument that presently engages the attention of our press and other publicity media, I shall disagree with you heartily" (Eisenhower letter to CB, July 18, 1956, DDE Diary Series, Box 16, Ann Whitman File, Eisenhower Library). Bowles quickly replied that he hoped that though the book had been written in an election year "you may agree that my central point is valid, i.e. the existence of broad common ground with those of us, regardless of party, who sense the full dimensions of our explosive

interrelated world, and the urgent need to consolidate and expand this ground after the November elections, regardless of who wins." Bowles said it was his personal conviction that "only through such a political coalition cutting across existing party lines can we preserve our free society at home and seize the initiative overseas in behalf of our traditional democratic principles of individual growth and opportunity" (CB letter to Eisenhower, July 30, 1956, Name Series, Box 3, Ann Whitman File, Eisenhower Library).

30. CB letter to Johnson, January 2, 1957, Fulbright Papers, University of Arkansas Library. CB letter to William Benton, July 5, 1957, Box 122, Bowles Papers. CB diary, July 23, 1958, Box 392, Bowles Papers.

31. Dulles memorandum to Sherman Adams, July 6, 1954, Administration File: Sherman Adams, Box 1, Ann Whitman File, Eisenhower Library. Eisenhower-Dulles phone conversation, August 9, 1954, DDE Diary Series, Box 7, Ann Whitman File, Eisenhower Library.

32. A Senate seat would also have improved Bowles's chances of becoming the 1960 Democratic presidential nominee as the candidate of the party's liberal wing. Although the deflation of his presidential prospects would also have been attractive to Ribicoff and Bailey, who were by 1958 strongly behind Kennedy's expected bid, neither Bowles nor others involved have suggested that this was a consideration in their support for Dodd.

33. *Promises to Keep,* p. 263.

34. See in particular Bowles's diary for July 23, 1958 and his letters to Jean Joyce (July 23, 1958, Box 141, Bowles Papers) and Harris Wofford (July 27, 1958, Box 164, Bowles Papers).

35. CB letter to Hughes, July 27, 1958, Box 138, Bowles Papers.

36. CB letter to Joyce, July 23, 1958.

37. *Promises to Keep,* p. 269.

9. Freshman in Name Only

1. With the admission of Alaska, the membership of the House of Representatives rose briefly in 1959 to 436. Following the 1960 census and the subsequent reapportioning of House seats, it reverted to 435. In 1959 the Senate had 98 members, including two newly added from Alaska.

2. Hughes Oral History interview.

3. *Promises to Keep,* p. 274.

4. *Congressional Record: House,* 86th Congress, 1st Session, vol. 105, p. 3054.

5. Ibid., p. 6327.

6. *United States Statutes at Large,* 86th Congress, 1st Session, 1959, vol. 73 (Washington: United States Government Printing Office, 1960), p. 246.

7. *Promises to Keep,* p. 278.

8. The text of the draft concurrent resolution is in *Congressional Record: House,* 86th Congress, 1st Session, vol. 105, p. 2771. CB Oral History interview (1965), JFK Library. For Bowles's efforts to win administration support to develop a consortium of countries providing assistance to India, see his December 28, 1959, letter to President Eisenhower in which he advocated that the United States and Western European nations work up a "realistic and

adequate program to underwrite the capital requirements of India's Third Five Year Plan" (Box 206, Bowles Papers).

9. House of Representatives, Foreign Affairs Committee, *Mutual Security Act of 1959, Hearings, 86th Congress, 1st Session, on draft legislation to amend further the Mutual Security Act of 1954, as amended, and for other purposes,* pt. 1, March 16–25, 1959, p. 114.

10. Ibid., pt. 3, April 13–15, 1959, p. 669. Bowles misdated the British general's alleged remark about Afghanistan. He had quoted it earlier, in a lecture he delivered to the Naval War College on June 7, 1956 (Box 172, Bowles Papers).

11. Bowles was also a member of the HFAC Subcommittee on State Department Organization and Foreign Operations.

12. 86th Congress, 2nd Session, House Report 1226, "Special Study Mission to Europe" (Washington: U.S. Government Printing Office, 1960), p. 35.

13. Stephen E. Ambrose, *Eisenhower: The President* (New York: Simon and Schuster, 1984), pp. 563–64.

14. The text of Bowles's Los Angeles speech is in *Congressional Record: House,* 86th Congress, 2nd Session, vol. 106, pp. 5499–5504. It was inserted by Representative Chet Holifield of California. Bowles's memorandum on defense and disarmament is found in *Congressional Record: Senate,* 86th Congress, 2nd Session, vol. 106, pp. 10241–43, where it was inserted by Senator William Proxmire of Wisconsin.

15. CB, *The Coming Political Breakthrough* (New York: Harper and Brothers, 1959).

16. CB, *Ideas, People, and Peace* (New York: Harper and Brothers, 1958).

10. House Liberal in the Kennedy Camp

1. CB note, "Some observations, personal and otherwise, on the political events of 1960," December 31, 1960, Box 392, Bowles Papers.

2. Hughes Oral History interview.

3. CB note, December 31, 1960. CB letter to Humphrey, August 24, 1956, Box 138, Bowles Papers.

4. CB note, January 27, 1962, Box 392, Bowles Papers.

5. CB note, December 31, 1960.

6. *Promises to Keep,* p. 286.

7. CB note, undated, Box 392, Bowles Papers.

8. Hughes Oral History interview.

9. CB note, undated, Box 392, Bowles Papers.

10. CB note, December 31, 1960.

11. Ibid.

12. Ibid.

13. *Promises to Keep,* p. 288.

14. Ibid., pp. 288–89.

15. Hughes Oral History interview. Author's interview with Hughes, September 1990.

16. Hughes Oral History interview.

17. See John F. Kennedy, *The Strategy of Peace* (New York: Harper and Brothers,

1960), which is a collection of Kennedy's speeches edited by Allan Nevins. The quotation is from a speech Kennedy gave at Riverside, California, November 1, 1959 (p. 142).

18. John Kenneth Galbraith, *A Life in Our Times* (Boston: Houghton Mifflin, 1981), p. 373.

19. Kennedy letter to CB, January 29, 1960, Box 210, Bowles Papers.

20. CB letter to Kennedy, February 12, 1960, in ibid.

21. CB letter to Kennedy, February 11, 1960 (dictated February 10), in ibid.

22. Harris Wofford, *Of Kennedys and Kings* (New York: Farrar Straus Giroux, 1980), p. 42.

23. Wofford letter to CB, March 5, 1960, Box 218, Bowles Papers. Reprinted by his permission.

24. Abram Chayes, Oral History interview, JFK Library.

25. *New Republic,* January 11, 1960.

26. Thomson Oral History interview.

27. Hughes Oral History interview.

28. CB note, December 31, 1960.

29. Ibid.

30. Donald Bruce Johnson, ed., *National Party Platforms: 1960–1976* (Urbana: University of Illinois Press, 1978), vol. II, pp. 574–600.

31. *New York Times,* July 13, 1960.

32. *Promises to Keep,* p. 294.

33. Hughes Oral History interview.

34. Ibid. Robert F. Kennedy Oral History interview, JFK Library.

35. *New York Times,* August 12, 1960.

36. CB Oral History interview (1965), JFK Library.

37. CB note, December 31, 1960.

38. Chayes Oral History interview.

39. CB letter to Kennedy, July 19, 1960, Box 210, Bowles Papers.

40. The memoranda are in Box 208, Bowles Papers.

41. "Memorandum of Conversation with Secretary of State Christian Herter," August 11, 1960, in ibid.

42. CB memorandum to Kennedy, October 15, 1960, Box 210, Bowles Papers. In addition to the briefings, Herter and Bowles had at least one exchange of letters before the election. In late September, Bowles worried that Nikita Khrushchev might use intermediaries to arrange a meeting with Eisenhower when the Soviet leader came to the United Nations, and feared that the administration would draw back because of potential domestic political repercussions as the election neared. In a September 22 letter, he suggested that Herter notify him should such a situation develop, so that he could inform Kennedy and do everything possible to prevent the question from becoming a political football "and jeopardizing whatever opportunity may have existed for fruitful discussions." Herter replied on September 27, stating that nothing had happened to indicate a change in Khrushchev's tough line. He said he was grateful for the purpose which motivated Bowles's offer and would keep it in mind if there was any change in the situation (Papers of Christian A. Herter, Box 19, Eisenhower Library).

11. Number Two at Foggy Bottom

1. Chayes Oral History interview.
2. *Promises to Keep,* p. 299.
3. CB memorandum to Shriver, November 17, 1960, Box 216, Bowles Papers.
4. CB memorandum to Kennedy, December 1, 1960, Box 210, Bowles Papers.
5. CB memorandum to Kennedy, December 5, 1960, in ibid.
6. Thomson Oral History interview and interview with author, March 1990. Robert F. Kennedy memorandum, February 9, 1961, pp. 10–11, Robert F. Kennedy Papers, quoted in Arthur M. Schlesinger, Jr., *Robert Kennedy and His Times* (New York: Ballantine Books, 1978), p. 240. Acheson Oral History interview, JFK Library. Thomas J. Schoenbaum, *Waging Peace & War* (New York: Simon and Schuster, 1988), p. 18. Warren I. Cohen, *Dean Rusk* (Totowa, N.J.: Cooper Square Publishers, 1980), p. 92.
7. Both Bowles and Rusk provide substantially the same account of the Williamsburg incident in their autobiographies.
8. Schoenbaum, *Waging Peace & War,* p. 17. Dean Rusk, *As I Saw It* (New York: W. W. Norton, 1990), p. 202.
9. Cohen, *Dean Rusk,* p. 94.
10. Galbraith, *A Life in Our Times,* p. 404.
11. Rusk, *As I Saw It,* p. 204.
12. Author's interview with Rusk, April 1991.
13. As the Department of State was organized in 1961, the senior under secretary could take responsibility for either political or economic affairs. The decision was usually made on the basis of his own interests and qualifications and the secretary's needs. This confusing arrangement was ended in the Nixon administration, when the position of deputy secretary was established. Since then, the under secretaries (there are now four) have been placed on the third rung of the department ladder.
14. CB Oral History interview (1965), JFK Library.
15. Ibid.
16. Ibid.
17. CB memorandum to Rusk, February 13, 1961, Box 300, Bowles Papers. Rusk memorandum to CB, February 19, 1961, ibid.
18. Samuel W. Lewis, "Random Musings about Chester Bowles and the Department of State," May 26, 1963, reproduced in *Promises to Keep,* pp. 626–30.
19. CB memorandum to Kennedy, July 20, 1960, Box 210, Bowles Papers.
20. CB memorandum to Rusk, December 18, 1960, Box 215, Bowles Papers.
21. Ibid.
22. Kennedy signed off on the letter on May 29, 1961. A copy is in Box 210, Bowles Papers.
23. Some of the lists are available in Papers of James C. Thomson, Jr., POF, Box 2, JFK Library.
24. Bowles wrote a memorandum for the files dated February 6, 1961, detailing the difficulties the Reischauer appointment was encountering (Box 304, Bowles Papers). Reischauer Oral History interview, JFK Library.
25. Macomber had so impressed Bowles that he wanted him to stay on as assistant

secretary for congressional relations. Bowles recalled that he approached Kennedy with the idea. The president thought it unusual and suggested he sound out Senate Foreign Relations Committee Chairman J. William Fulbright. According to Bowles, Fulbright said that Macomber had done a good job as assistant secretary in the Eisenhower administration but a Democrat was now needed (CB Oral History interview [1970], JFK Library).

The Schaetzel Shitlist is in Papers of James C. Thomson, Jr., POF, Box 3, JFK Library.

26. Roger Jones Oral History interview, JFK Library.
27. CB Oral History interview (1965), JFK Library.
28. Lewis, "Random Musings."
29. In the chapter of his autobiography in which he discusses the administration of the State Department, Secretary Rusk recalled: "Some of my colleagues were skeptical of the Foreign Service's ability to meet the challenges thrust upon American diplomacy in the sixties. For example, Chester Bowles instinctively looked outside the Foreign Service when we had slots to fill. I felt that career officers had a leg up on another candidate and battled hard for them. Only when needing special talent was I inclined to reach outside the Foreign Service" (Rusk, *As I Saw It,* p. 527).
30. CB memorandum, September 23, 1961, Box 392, Bowles Papers. Bowles wrote that his purpose in preparing this memorandum was "to record my reactions to the events of the last few months [that is, his difficulties as under secretary] so that I may not be led too far astray as I try to reconstruct them in future years." Hughes Oral History interview. Peter Wyden, *Bay of Pigs* (New York: Simon and Schuster, 1979), p. 96. CB Oral History interview (1965), JFK Library.
31. CB memorandum, September 23, 1961.
32. Ibid.
33. *Promises to Keep,* p. 313.
34. Author's interview with Talbot, June 1990.
35. Author's interview with Galbraith, March 1990.
36. CB memorandum, September 23, 1961. It is noteworthy that in a letter to the president on the State Department's organizational needs, Bowles conceded that the European Bureau was the best administered bureau in the department (CB letter to Kennedy, August 21, 1961, Box 297, Bowles Papers).
37. Author's interview with a retired State Department official who preferred not to be identified.
38. Author's interview with Battle, February 1990.
39. Author's interviews with two former senior State Department officials who preferred not to be identified.
40. Thomson Oral History interview.
41. Grove Oral History interview, Box 398, Bowles Papers.
42. Ball, eight years younger than Bowles, was the third-ranking official in the department. A partner in a leading Washington law firm and specialist in international law and commercial relations, he was professionally close to leading figures in European industry. Active in the national Democratic party, he was an adviser to Adlai Stevenson, with whom he shared a Chicago

background. In the recruiting process Bowles had favored William Foster, a Republican who had headed the Economic Assistance Administration under Truman (and had tried at that time to bring Bowles into the aid operation as a roving representative to South and Southeast Asia). The appointment was dropped when influential Democrats protested that too many senior level jobs were going to GOP people, and Ball got the position. Foster later became the head of the newly created Arms Control and Disarmament Agency. Ball is probably best remembered for his strong opposition, as Bowles's successor, to American involvement in Vietnam. For a recent account which focuses on that aspect of Ball's role at the State Department, see David L. DiLeo, *George Ball, Vietnam, and the Rethinking of Containment* (Chapel Hill: University of North Carolina Press, 1991).

43. Author's interview with Rusk. The compilation, which includes twelve memos on personnel issues, is in Box 301, Bowles Papers.
44. CB letter to Rusk, May 19, 1961, Box 300, Bowles Papers.

12. Running Afoul of the Kennedys

1. Arthur M. Schlesinger, Jr., *A Thousand Days* (Boston: Houghton Mifflin Company, 1965), p. 438.
2. Bowles's comment is taken from Thomas Hughes's diary entry of August 1, 1960.
3. CB, "Notes on the Cuban Crisis," May 1961, Box 392, Bowles Papers.
4. Harris Wofford, whom Bowles consulted on the issue, has written that "it was explained that Bowles was excluded from the inner circle because everyone knew what his position would be, and his long arguments against the operation would be boring" (Wofford, *Of Kennedys and Kings,* p. 343).
5. Stephen Broadhead Heintz, "Frustrations of Foggy Bottom: Chester Bowles as Under Secretary of State, January–November 1961," Yale University, 1974, Miscellaneous Mss., No. 170, Yale University Library.
6. CB memorandum to Rusk, March 31, 1961, Box 300, Bowles Papers.
7. Schoenbaum, *Waging Peace & War,* pp. 294–5. Rusk, *As I Saw It,* p. 209.
8. Rusk, ibid., p. 212.
9. CB letter to Kennedy, April 28, 1961, Box 297, Bowles Papers.
10. Patricia Durand Jacobson Oral History interview, Box 398, Bowles Papers.
11. CB letter to Herbert Brucker, May 12, 1961, Box 271, Bowles Papers.
12. *New York Times,* April 7, 1963.
13. Edwin O. Guthman and Jeffrey Shulman, eds., *Robert Kennedy in His Own Words* (New York: Bantam Books, 1988), p. 11.
14. *Time,* April 28, 1961.
15. Bowles's fondness for the Mekong project became something of a standing joke at the State Department. As under secretary, he gave informal press backgrounders and spoke frequently at them of the advantages of the Mekong concept. The briefings were known as "Up and Down the Mekong River with Gun and Camera." See George Ball, *The Past Has Another Pattern* (New York: W. W. Norton, 1982), p. 170. The passage is part of Ball's unflattering sketch of Bowles's performance as under secretary.

16. CB memorandum to Kennedy, March 25, 1961 (summary in Box 301, Bowles Papers).

17. CB letter to Rusk, April 20, 1961 (summary in ibid.).

18. *Promises to Keep,* p. 343.

19. Ibid., p. 407. There is no record available of a Bowles-Rusk memorandum on Southeast Asia at that time.

20. CB memorandum to Rusk, October 5, 1961, Box 300, Bowles Papers. Soon after, Bowles tried to get Kennedy to enlist Nehru in this effort by suggesting to the president that he raise the neutrality guarantee proposal during the prime minister's visit to the United States in November (CB memorandum to Kennedy, November 3, 1961, Box 297, Bowles Papers. See also *FRUS, 1961–1963,* vol. I, pp. 540–41). When Kennedy subsequently asked Nehru for advice on how best to proceed on the Vietnam problem, he received no useful reply (Dennis Kux, *Estranged Democracies* [Washington: National Defense University Press, 1993], chap. 5).

21. CB memorandum to Kennedy, November 30, 1961, *FRUS, 1961–63,* vol. I, pp. 700–701.

22. *Promises to Keep,* p. 409.

23. CB Oral History interview (1965), JFK Library.

24. *Promises to Keep,* p. 396.

25. "Nomination of Chester Bowles, Under Secretary of State-Designate: Hearing Before the Committee on Foreign Relations, United States Senate, Eighty-Seventh Congress," January 19, 1961 (Washington: U.S. Government Printing Office).

26. Rusk's later account of his views on China policy suggests that the secretary was more sympathetic to change than Bowles was aware. In his autobiography Rusk mentioned that he and the president agreed that ongoing China policy did not reflect Asian realities, but that for domestic political reasons change was not possible. He recalled that after a discussion about China policy with Kennedy, the president warned him to keep this conclusion to himself. See Rusk, *As I Saw It,* pp. 282–84.

27. See CB draft memorandum to Kennedy, "U.S. Courses towards China," March 30, 1961, Box 14, Thomson Papers, JFK Library.

28. CB memorandum to Kennedy, March 29, 1961, Box 297, Bowles Papers.

29. CB memorandum to Kennedy, July 1, 1961, Box 28, POF, JFK Library. CB memorandum to Kennedy, May 31, 1961, Box 297, Bowles Papers.

30. State Department Policy Planning Council, "U.S. Policy Toward China," October 26, 1961, Box 15, Thomson Papers, JFK Library. At the White House, NSC staffer Robert Komer wryly noted that "S/P [the State Department Policy Planning Council] has finally written the overall China paper we requested, but doesn't want to discuss it until it has been haggled out in State. Since it will probably make FE's [the Bureau of Far Eastern Affairs] hair stand on end, this process may be prolonged" (Komer memo to McGeorge Bundy and Walt W. Rostow, November 3, 1961, Box 321A-322, National Security Files [NSF], JFK Library).

31. James C. Thomson, Jr., "On the Making of U.S. China Policy, 1961–1969: A Study in Bureaucratic Politics," *China Quarterly,* vol. L, April/June 1972.

32. Thomson, ibid., and Roger Hilsman, *To Move a Nation* (Garden City, N.Y.: Doubleday, 1967), pp. 305–10, provide good assessments of the way the Mongolian initiative played out.

33. CB memorandum, "The Ominously Changing Balance of Power in Asia," March 22, 1955, Box 166, Bowles Papers.

34. See, for example, State Department Research Memorandum INR [Bureau of Intelligence and Research] 9, September 21, 1961, "Possible Peiping Approaches to Solution of Mainland China Food Deficits," and INR Memorandum of January 5, 1962, "Chinese Communist Food Deficits and U.S. Policy." Both are in Box 15, Thomson Papers, JFK Library.

35. CB memorandum to Kennedy, July 1, 1961.

36. CB memorandum to Rusk, February 8, 1961, Box 15, Thomson Papers, JFK Library.

37. CB memorandum to Kennedy, May 31, 1961.

38. *Promises to Keep*, pp. 401–2. As special representative, Bowles sent the president a series of messages on the "food to China" issue, including memoranda dated February 6, April 4, April 16, May 23, and June 27, 1962. They are all in Box 297, Bowles Papers. See also CB memo to Rusk, April 16, 1962, and CB memorandum to NSC Standing Group, May 25, 1962, Box 15, Thomson Papers, JFK Library.

39. Memorandum from Foy Kohler (assistant secretary for European affairs) to Walt Rostow (National Security Council), March 8, 1962, Box 15, Thomson Papers, JFK Library. Memorandum of Conversation, "Secretary Rusk's Meeting with British Representatives," June 24, 1962, ibid., Thomas G. Paterson, ed., *Kennedy's Quest for Victory* (New York: Oxford University Press, 1989), pp. 190–93.

40. For a useful summary of the issues and contending forces in the battle over African policy during the Kennedy administration, see Thomas J. Noer, "New Frontiers and Old Priorities in Africa," in Thomas G. Paterson, ed., *Kennedy's Quest for Victory*, pp. 253–83. Harris Wofford memorandum to Kennedy, July 17, 1961, Box 28, POF, JFK Library.

41. New Delhi airgram 360, March 1, 1962, Box 62, POF, JFK Library. Bowles was then visiting India following a trip to several African countries.

42. CB memorandum to Kennedy, "The Congo Crisis," December 12, 1962, Box 28A, NSF, JFK Library.

43. In Paterson, ed., *Kennedy's Quest*, p. 266.

44. CB memoranda to Kennedy, November 13, 1962, and January 10, 1963, Box 62, POF, JFK Library.

45. CB memorandum to Kennedy, June 4, 1962, Box 297, Bowles Papers.

46. CB memorandum to Rusk, May 19, 1961, Box 300, Bowles Papers.

47. CB memorandum to Kennedy, August 21, 1961, Box 28, POF, JFK Library. In 1992, following passage of legislation adopted by Congress over State Department objection, India, Pakistan, and other countries in the region were made the responsibility of a newly established Bureau of South Asian Affairs, not linked to East Asia as Bowles had suggested three decades earlier. His 1961 proposal also included placing North Africa with the Middle East (rather than with Sub-Saharan Africa) and giving responsibility for relations with

Greece and Turkey to the European bureau. These recommendations were adopted in 1974 during Secretary Kissinger's tenure.

48. *New York Times,* March 23, 1961.
49. Act for International Development of 1961, *United States Statutes at Large,* 87th Congress, 1st Session, 1961, vol. 75 (U.S. Government Printing Office, 1961).
50. See CB memoranda to Kennedy, August 14 and October 11, 1962, Box 28, POF, JFK Library.

13. The Thanksgiving Massacre

1. CB diary, April 20, 1961, Box 392, Bowles Papers. The passage appears with a slightly different wording in "Notes on the Cuban Crisis."
2. Wofford, *Of Kennedys and Kings,* p. 373. CB memorandum, "Notes on the Crisis Involving the Dominican Republic," June 3, 1961, Box 392, Bowles Papers. CB Oral History interview (1965), JFK Library.
3. *Promises to Keep,* p. 347.
4. CB memorandum to Kennedy, July 1, 1961, and memorandum to Rusk, July 5, 1961, Box 28, POF, JFK Library.
5. James Thomson's July 18, 1961, memorandum to CB, "Press Views of Chester Bowles since December [1960]," Box 304, Bowles Papers, provides a useful summary of the media criticism.
6. *Promises to Keep,* p. 353.
7. Schlesinger memorandum to Kennedy, July 12, 1961, Box 28, POF, JFK Library. Schlesinger, *A Thousand Days,* p. 441.
8. Consulate Florence telegram 5 to Kennedy, July 16, 1961, Box 28, POF, JFK Library.
9. Wofford memorandum to Kennedy, July 17, 1961.
10. Remarks of Senator Joseph Clark, July 18, 1961, *Congressional Record: Senate,* 87th Congress, 1st Session, vol. 107, p. 12876. On the day Clark gave his speech, the morning papers reported that Presidential Press Secretary Pierre Salinger had said the previous afternoon that Bowles would stay on as under secretary. Instead of calling for Bowles's retention, therefore, the senator combined support for him with congratulations to the president for having done the right thing.
11. *Promises to Keep,* pp. 354–55.
12. *New York Times,* July 18, 1961.
13. John Sharon Oral History interview, JFK Library.
14. Hugh Sidey Oral History interview, JFK Library.
15. CB memorandum to Kennedy, July 27, 1961, Box 297, Bowles Papers.
16. *Promises to Keep,* pp. 360–61. CB letter to Adlai Stevenson, July 23, 1961, reproduced in *Promises to Keep,* pp. 619–25.
17. Senator Jackson issued a statement on November 19, 1961, which summarized the main conclusions of his report. The following day it was on the front page of the *New York Times.* Bowles was probably reacting to that account.
18. Many of the changes had been recommended to the president by his national security assistant, McGeorge Bundy, in a memorandum he sent Kennedy on

November 15 about the handling of the Vietnam issue. It is ironic, in light of Bowles's campaign to put Harriman in charge of the Far Eastern Bureau, that Bundy began his discussion of the personnel shifts he believed were called for with the assertion that "if Averell, or any other strong man, is to take McConaughy's place it should be in the context of a general game plan of musical chairs." The list of changes which followed was headed by "Ball for Bowles" and "Bowles for Harriman." Bundy noted that "Secretary [Rusk] won't do this till you tell him to" (*FRUS, 1961–63*, vol. I, pp. 612–14, "Notes for Talk with Secretary Rusk—November 15"). Bundy shared the view that Bowles was in the wrong job at the State Department and was not shy about telling him so. He wrote him on July 18, the day after Kennedy had decided to retain Bowles as under secretary for the time being: "The position you are now in is as wrong for you as it is for the Department—and *not* a good place for the advancement of ideas—your proper role." But in the same letter Bundy also assured Bowles that "your qualities as a man and your ideas of American purpose have been two of the bright spots for me in this Washington tunnel" (Box 297, Bowles Papers, reprinted by permission).

19. Theodore C. Sorensen, *Kennedy* (New York: Harper and Row, 1965), p. 289. Sorensen wrote that Kennedy had been pleased with the way he had handled this latest in his assignments as a missionary to the liberals. He recalled that the president had commented, "Good job, Ted—that was your best work since the Michigan delegation." Sorensen's account of Bowles's ouster stressed the president's concern that the State Department needed a manager.
20. CB notes on the debacle of 1961, January 2, 1962, Box 392, Bowles Papers.
21. *New York Times*, July 20, 1961.
22. Robert F. Kennedy Oral History interview, JFK Library.
23. Wofford, *Of Kennedys and Kings*, p. 372.
24. Author's interview with Rusk, April 1991. CB Oral History interview (1970), JFK Library.
25. *Promises to Keep*, pp. 365–66.
26. CB notes on the debacle of 1961.

14. Inconsequential Interlude

1. Memorandum of understanding and press release, November 27, 1961, Box 297, Bowles Papers.
2. CB note, June 8, 1963, Box 392, Bowles Papers. *Promises to Keep*, p. 369.
3. CB note, May 1, 1962, Box 392, Bowles Papers.
4. Author's interview with Rusk.
5. CB memoranda to Kennedy, June 13 and July 12, 1962, Box 311, Bowles Papers. CB draft memorandum for the president and the secretary of state, "Principles for a Presidential 'Peace Charter for Southeast Asia'," July 18, 1962, in ibid. CB memoranda to Rusk, July 12 and July 18, 1962, Box 28, POF, JFK Library.
6. Harriman memorandum to Rusk, July 30, 1962, *FRUS, 1961–1963*, vol. II, pp. 565–66.
7. Quoted in *Promises to Keep*, p. 414. See also CB memorandum to Rusk,

August 16, 1992, *FRUS, 1961–63,* vol. II, p. 591, in which Bowles cites and seeks to refute the arguments the bureau laid out for the secretary. The bureau's memorandum is not available but it seems reasonable that Bowles's version of it was accurate since he had enclosed it with his own memo.

8. CB memorandum to Rusk, ibid., p. 593.
9. CB memorandum to Kennedy, March 27, 1962, summarized in CB memorandum to Kennedy, December 1, 1962, "My Major Policy Recommendations Sent to You and to the Secretary of State During 1962," Box 28, POF, JFK Library.
10. CB memorandum to Kennedy, December 17, 1962, Box 297, Bowles Papers.
11. CB note, "Impressions: October 1962" (not otherwise dated), Box 392, Bowles Papers.
12. CB letter to Kennedy, December 1, 1962, Box 28, POF, JFK Library.
13. CB draft letter to Kennedy, January 3, 1963, Box 297, Bowles Papers.

15. "Chester Bowls Again"

1. *Promises to Keep,* pp. 435–37.
2. CB note, "Impressions, January 1963," [not otherwise dated], Box 392, Bowles Papers.
3. CB memorandum to Kennedy, February 18, 1963, Box 297, Bowles Papers.
4. CB memorandum to Kennedy, March 12, 1963, in ibid. *Promises to Keep,* pp. 438–39.
5. *New York Times,* April 7, 1963.
6. Ibid., April 30, 1963.
7. Ibid., April 7, 1963.
8. Government of India, Planning Commission, *The Third Five Year Plan,* 1961.
9. See CIA report, "India's Third Five Year Plan Continues to Lag," May 14, 1963, Box 106, NSF, JFK Library.
10. "Memorandum for the record, April 29, 1963, of a meeting chaired by the President [Kennedy] on India, April 25, 1963," Box 24, National Security Files (NSF), LBJ Library. CB Oral History interview (1965), JFK Library. Bowles also gives an account of the meeting in *Promises to Keep,* pp. 439–40.
11. Like other Bowles recruits, many of those he brought with him to New Delhi won considerable success later on. Grove became U.S. ambassador to Zaire, Celeste Peace Corps director and two-term governor of Ohio, and Bennet administrator of the Agency for International Development and head of National Public Radio. Later arrivals to the Bowles New Delhi entourage who achieved prominence afterwards include Phillip Merrill, publisher of the *Washingtonian Magazine,* and Thomas Dine, executive director of the American Israel Political Action Committee. Merrill had been with Bowles at the State Department.
12. Foreign Service officers assigned to New Delhi who later became ambassadors included William Brown (Thailand and Israel), Jane Abell Coon (Bangladesh), Douglas Heck (Niger and Nepal), Roger Kirk (Somalia, Romania, and the UN System organizations in Vienna), Mary Olmstead (Papua New Guinea), Mark Palmer (Hungary), Anthony Quainton (Central African Empire, Nica-

ragua, Kuwait, and Peru, also assistant secretary of state for diplomatic security), John Shirley (Tanzania, also counselor of USIA), Katherine Horberg Shirley (Senegal), Galen Stone (Cyprus), Nicholas Veliotes (Jordan and Egypt, also assistant secretary of state for Near Eastern and South Asian affairs), Richard Viets (Tanzania and Jordan), and the author (Bangladesh). Clair George, who had been a CIA officer in New Delhi during Bowles's time, eventually became the agency's third-ranking official, deputy director for operations.

13. CB diary, July 5, 1964, Box 393, Bowles Papers.
14. CB letter to Bundy, May 26, 1965, Box 384, Name File: "Chester Bowles," White House Central Files (WHCF), LBJ Library. Bowles wrote similar letters to senior White House staffers Douglas Cater and John W. Macy, Jr., at the same time. They are in the same LBJ Library file. See also Brandon Grove Oral History interview. Grove devised the reorganization plan at Bowles's request.

16. Mission Unaccomplished

1. New Delhi telegram 298, July 18, 1963, FOI document. CB Diary, July 18, 1963, Box 392, Bowles Papers.
2. New Delhi telegram 433, July 26, 1963, FOI document. *New York Times,* September 4, 1963.
3. See *New York Times,* April 10, April 13, April 28, and May 9, 1963. A further loan of $379 million at a later date for the second stage of construction was also contemplated.
4. New Delhi telegram 433, July 26, 1963.
5. *New York Times,* September 3, 1963. Nehru letter to Kennedy, August 28, 1963, Box 118a, POF, JFK Library. Kennedy letter to Nehru, September 4, 1963, in ibid. Nehru letter to Kennedy, September 6, 1963, in ibid.
6. New Delhi telegram 474, July 30, 1963, FOI document. Department of State telegram 275 to New Delhi, FOI document. New Delhi telegram 541, August 2, 1963, FOI document. CB letter to Galbraith, August 20, 1963, Box 330, Bowles Papers. Nehru statement to the Lok Sabha, August 13, 1963. Department of State telegram 394 to New Delhi, August 15, 1963, Box 118a, POF, JFK Library, transmitted the text of Kennedy's letter to Nehru. New Delhi telegram 721, August 17, 1963, FOI document.
7. CB letter to Galbraith, September 20, 1963, Box 330, Bowles Papers.
8. New Delhi telegram 972, September 9, 1963, FOI document. New Delhi telegram 1423, October 24, 1963, FOI document.
9. CB memorandum to Kennedy, November 12, 1963, Box 118a, POF, JFK Library.
10. CB diary, November 14, 1963, Box 392, Bowles Papers.
11. Komer memorandum to Kennedy, November 12, 1963, Box 118a, POF, JFK Library.
12. See Kux, *Estranged Democracies,* chap. 5.
13. CB diary, November 22, 1963, Box 392, Bowles Papers.
14. Ibid., November 21, 1963.

15. Rusk memorandum to Johnson, "Next Steps on Military Aid to India and Pakistan," December 11, 1963, Box 30, NSF, LBJ Library.
16. New Delhi telegram 1943, December 19, 1963, Box 30, NSF, LBJ Library.
17. Taylor's report was submitted in Joint Chiefs of Staff document CM-1089–63, dated December 23, 1963, in Box 30, NSF, LBJ Library. Rusk memorandum to the president, January 16, 1964, in ibid. See also New Delhi telegram 1929, December 19, 1963, FOI document.
18. CB letter to Galbraith, January 24, 1964, Box 330, Bowles Papers.
19. CB letter to Humphrey, January 27, 1964, Box 331, Bowles Papers.
20. See New Delhi telegrams 2177, January 18, 1964; 2233, January 23, 1964; and 2423, February 17, 1964. All are FOI documents.
21. NSAM 279, February 8, 1964, Box 24, NSF, LBJ Library. Department of State telegram 1690 to New Delhi, February 21, 1964, Box 128, NSF, LBJ Library.
22. New Delhi telegram 2500, February 25, 1964, Box 128, in ibid. New Delhi telegram 275, September 22, 1964, to Karachi, FOI document, lists five cables the embassy sent the department in the spring of 1964 on the danger of Soviet arms supplies to India. See New Delhi telegrams 2543, February 27, 1964, and 2544, February 28, 1964, reporting separate conversations Bowles had with Minister of Finance T. T. Krishnamachari and Minister of Defense Y. B. Chavan. Bowles said that he told the two ministers that the MIG-21 was not suitable for Indian purposes and would cost much more than they had anticipated. Both messages are in Box 128, NSF, LBJ Library. Department of State telegram 1787 to New Delhi, March 5, 1964, in ibid.
23. New Delhi telegram 2675, March 12, 1964, in ibid. "Memorandum for the Record: Conference between Secretary McNamara and Ambassador Bowles, March 31, 1964,. . . Department of Defense," FOI document.
24. *Promises to Keep,* pp. 482–83.
25. Draft memorandum of understanding, May 27, 1964, Box 128, NSF, LBJ Library.
26. Author's interview with David T. Schneider, November 1990.
27. New Delhi telegram 3577, May 30, 1964, FOI document. Author's interview with David H. Blee, April 1990.
28. New Delhi telegram 3572, May 30, 1964, FOI document.
29. Komer memorandum to Bundy, June 3, 1964, Box 128, NSF, LBJ Library.
30. Author's interview with Komer, September 1990.
31. Department of State telegram 2534 to New Delhi, June 5, 1964, Box 128, NSF, LBJ Library, has the text of the press release.
32. New Delhi telegram 3706, June 10, 1964, in ibid.
33. Department of State telegram 2572 to New Delhi, June 10, 1964, in ibid.
34. New Delhi telegram 143, July 16, 1964, FOI document. See also CB letter to McGeorge Bundy, July 18, 1964, Box 327, Bowles Papers.
35. New Delhi telegram 677, August 27, 1964, FOI document.
36. *New York Times,* September 12, 1964.
37. New Delhi telegram 275 to Karachi, September 22, 1964.
38. CB diary, September 11, 1964, Box 395, Bowles Papers.
39. New Delhi telegram 2867, April 9, 1965, FOI document. More than a quarter

century later, the F-5's manufacturer, Northrop Corporation, was still trying to sell a version of the aircraft to the Indian air force.

40. Box 24, NSF (NSC History, South Asia), LBJ Library.
41. Department of State telegram 2155 to New Delhi, April 14, 1965, Box 129, NSF, LBJ Library.
42. New Delhi telegram 2920, April 15, 1965, in ibid.
43. Department of State telegram, April 15, 1965, referred to in NSC History (Box 24, NSF, LBJ Library) but not identified by number.
44. New Delhi telegram 3430, May 25, 1965, Box 129, NSF, LBJ Library.
45. CB diary, April 18, 1965, Box 395, Bowles Papers.
46. CB letter to Johnson, April 14, 1965, Box 332, Bowles Papers.
47. New Delhi telegram 3037, April 26, 1965, FOI document. New Delhi telegram 3210, May 10, 1965, Box 129, NSF, LBJ Library. The Rann (marsh) of Kutch dispute resulted from the peculiar topography of the region, which is at the western extremity of the border between India and Pakistan. Kutch had been a princely state before Indian independence, when its ruler had acceded to India. It is bounded on the north by Sind, a province of British India which had become part of Pakistan. The region in dispute, a tidal mud flat of some 3,500 square miles, is a desert in the dry season but is almost entirely flooded by the waters of the Arabian Sea during the monsoon. India consistently claimed the entire marsh, maintaining that Pakistani territory did not extend beyond the higher ground that lay to the north, during British times the boundary between Kutch and Sind. Pakistan staked a claim to the territory in 1954, asserting that since the marsh was a body of water part of the year, international law places the boundary in the middle of the territory. Negotiations between the two countries had failed to resolve the dispute, and an armed clash in early April 1965 quickly led to an escalation of fighting. See Barnds, *India, Pakistan, and the Great Powers,* pp. 197–200, and Kux, *Estranged Democracies,* chap. 6, for detailed accounts of the issue.
48. CB memorandum to Rusk, "The Urgent Need for a Review of United States Policy in South Asia," May 20, 1965, Box 336, Bowles Papers.
49. CB letter to Johnson, July 6, 1965, Box 7, Handwriting File, LBJ Library.
50. New Delhi 391, August 27, 1965, FOI document. New Delhi 411, August 28, 1965, Box 129, NSF, LBJ Library.
51. New Delhi telegram 458, September 2, 1965, Box 24, NSF, LBJ Library. Department of State telegram 330 to New Delhi, September 2, 1965, in ibid.
52. New Delhi telegram 478, September 4, 1965, Box 129, NSF, LBJ Library.
53. CB diary, August 29, 1965, Box 395, Bowles Papers.
54. CB letter to Galbraith, September 16, 1965, Box 330, Bowles Papers.
55. CB diary, September 8, 1965, Box 395, Bowles Papers. New Delhi telegram 626, September 15, 1965, Box 129, NSF, LBJ Library.
56. CB diary, September 20, 1965, Box 395, Bowles Papers. There is also a reference to the suggestion in a note Robert Komer sent McGeorge Bundy on September 27 (Box 129, NSF, LBJ Library).
57. New Delhi 813, September 28, 1965, Box 6, Name File, NSF, LBJ Library.
58. Komer memorandum to Bundy, September 28, 1965, in ibid.

59. CB letter to Johnson, October 2, 1965, Box 16, Files of McGeorge Bundy, NSF, LBJ Library.
60. CB letter to Bundy, November 25, 1965, in ibid.
61. CB diary, November 21, 1965, Box 395, Bowles Papers.
62. CB letter to Johnson, March 4, 1966, Box 332, Bowles Papers.
63. Bowles's diary describes how he wrestled with the resignation issue. On July 24, 1966, he wrote that he would have to resign if the provision of lethal weapons to Pakistan were resumed. On December 24, 1966, he noted that Secretary Rusk had stopped in New Delhi for two hours and had told him that the president wanted him to stay on. Bowles went on to record that "if our policies should clarify in an affirmative policy and if I keep my health, I would like to stay until April 1969, assuming that I hold together physically." When Washington decided in April 1967 to allow a case-by-case sale of lethal spare parts and ammunition for equipment previously supplied to Pakistan (as well as to India), a compromise position Bowles had strongly opposed, he listed in an April 16 entry the pros and cons of quitting and concluded that he should stay on unless Washington went even further in allowing the Pakistanis access to American arms.
64. This is the title of chap. 37 of the book.
65. This was in July 1965, soon after Johnson had suggested to his staff that Bowles should probably be reassigned. In a memorandum to the president dated July 19, Robert Komer reported, after a long talk with Bowles, "I think he understands the drill and is [now] determined to be a team player. No one will ever cure Chet of wanting bigger and better programs, but I'm confident he sees they'll have to be earned." (Box 6, Name File, NSF, LBJ Library.)
66. Komer memorandum to Bundy, June 3, 1964, in ibid.
67. Rostow note to Johnson, May 19, 1966, Box 134, NSF, LBJ Library.

17. A New Deal for India

1. Lewis's most important work was *Quiet Crisis in India: Economic Development and American Policy* (Bombay: Asia Publishing House, 1963).
2. Author's interviews with Charles E. Lindblom, December 1989 and February 1991. Professor Lindblom summarized the situation in a personal memorandum of October 22, 1963, which he made available to the author.
3. See Lindblom's memorandum to CB, October 14, 1963, and AID Mission Director C. Tyler Wood's memorandum to CB, October 21, 1963. Both documents were made available to the author by Professor Lindblom.
4. Lindblom memorandum to John Holt, AID New Delhi, October 7, 1963.
5. CB personal memorandum to Nehru, October 30, 1963, Box 160, Bowles Papers.
6. Author's interview with Lindblom, February 1991.
7. *Promises to Keep,* chap. 43.
8. Ibid., p. 552.
9. John P. Lewis's forthcoming book, *Essays in Indian Political Economy,* prepared for the Woodrow Wilson School of Public and International Affairs at Princeton University, has a good account of the forces that brought about the

new agricultural strategy. This and the following paragraphs also draw on the author's interviews with Professor Lewis (July 1990) and former Secretary of Agriculture Orville Freeman (April 1991). Secretary Freeman provided an account of his role in his *World without Hunger* (New York: Praeger, 1968), pp. 145–67.

10. Encouraging private foreign investment in Indian fertilizer production was of major interest to Bowles. In 1965, before the Freeman-Subramaniam agreement was reached, he strenuously championed a Bechtel Corporation project to meet much of India's increased fertilizer needs by building several copies of standard, advanced-design plants. Although Bowles recognized the limitations which historical experience and current political realities placed on the willingness of the Indian government to welcome private foreign investment, he consistently reminded Indian leaders in nonideological terms that such investment could play an important role in economic development. His specific advocacy of Bechtel was ultimately unsuccessful, however, and the project never materialized.

11. An account of the agreement appears in Embassy Rome telegram 1373, November 26, 1965, Box 130, NSF, LBJ Library.

12. Author's interview with Freeman.

13. CB diary, April 6, 1966, Box 395, Bowles Papers.

14. See Peter A. Toma, *The Politics of Food for Peace* (Tucson: University of Arizona Press, 1967); James Warner Bjorkman, "Public Law 480 and the Policies of Self-Help and Short-Tether: Indo-American Relations, 1965–68," in Lloyd I. and Susanne Hoeber Rudolph, eds., *The Regional Imperative* (New Delhi: Concept Publishing Company, 1980); and Shivaji Ganguly, *U.S. Policy toward South Asia* (Boulder: Westview Press, 1990).

15. CB diary, February 6, 1966, Box 395, Bowles Papers. Bowles devoted a chapter to "LBJ and American Wheat" in *Promises to Keep* (pp. 523–36). It includes the February 6 diary comment.

16. CB diary, November 27, 1966, Box 395, Bowles Papers.

17. Lyndon B. Johnson, *The Vantage Point* (New York: Holt, Rinehart and Winston, 1971), pp. 222–31.

18. Rusk memorandum to Johnson, March 26, 1966, Box 133, NSF, LBJ Library.

19. David B. H. Denoon, *Devaluation under Pressure* (Cambridge, Mass.: M.I.T. Press, 1986), pp. 25–53, has a good discussion of the economic package and devaluation. For a somewhat different view, see Francine Frankel, *India's Political Economy, 1947–1977* (Princeton: Princeton University Press, 1978), chap. 7.

20. For a discussion of the political impact of devaluation in India, see Inder Malhotra, *Indira Gandhi* (London: Hodder and Stoughton, 1989), p. 100.

21. "USAID Assistance to India, Obligations for Loans and Grants, U.S. FY 1951–1990," USAID publication, 1990.

22. CB diary, July 18, 1963, Box 392, Bowles Papers.

23. Ibid., December 8, 1963.

24. Ibid., May 27, 1964 (in Box 393).

25. New Delhi telegram 2659, March 11, 1964, FOI document.

26. CB Oral History interview, 1969, LBJ Library. Bowles demonstrated both his

favor for the "Jacksons" and his abiding association with Yale by arranging for the chief minister of the South Indian state of Tamil Nadu, C. N. Annadurai, the leader of a regional political party, to spend a few days in New Haven as a Chubb Fellow in 1968. "Annadurai," Bowles wrote, "typifies the new 'Indianized' leaders in which I place the most hope" (CB diary, September 10, 1967, Box 395, Bowles Papers).

27. CB letter to Shastri, October 17, 1964, Box 336, Bowles Papers. The letter appears as Appendix VI in *Promises to Keep* (pp. 631–37).
28. *The Makings of a Just Society* (Delhi: University of Delhi, 1963).
29. CB letter to Rusk, September 30, 1963, Box 336, Bowles Papers.
30. Author's interview with Celeste, January 1991.
31. *The Makings of a Just Society,* p. 16.
32. Ibid., p. 37.
33. Comment to author of Albert A. Lakeland, Jr., May 1991.
34. Merrill, *Bread and the Ballot,* p. 87.
35. Author's personal recollection.
36. New Delhi telegram 1820, January 17, 1966, FOI document.
37. Author's interview with John W. Shirley, October 1990.
38. CB memorandum to Rusk, "The Political-Economic Situation in India," December 12, 1966, Box 336, Bowles Papers. Bowles accurately predicted the outcome of the 1967 election, correcting the assessment prepared by the embassy political section, which had anticipated a poorer Congress party showing.
39. Richard Celeste Oral History interview, Box 398, Bowles Papers. Bowles's initial concern that Johnson might be more sympathetic to Pakistan stemmed in part from LBJ's sponsorship in 1961 of the visit to the United States of Bashir Ahmed, an illiterate Pakistani camel driver whom the then vice president had seen on a Karachi street and on the spur of the moment invited to come to Washington. Bashir Ahmed's visit had received a highly favorable press in the United States, largely, the author learned at the time, because the sophisticated Pakistani former army officer who acted as his Urdu interpreter used considerable imagination and eloquence in translating his remarks into English. The association of Johnson and the seemingly wise and colorful camel driver stuck in the public mind, not least in India, where a surprising number of people shared Bowles's apprehensions about its influence on the new president's view of the subcontinent.
40. CB diary, November 5, 1964, Box 395, Bowles Papers.
41. Ibid., March 26, 1966.
42. Ibid., December 6, 1964.
43. CB memorandum to Bill Moyers, "A Proposal to Strengthen President Johnson's Hand in World Affairs," August 26, 1965, Box 334, Bowles Papers.
44. CB diary, March 22, 1964, Box 392, Bowles Papers.
45. CB memorandum to Moyers, August 26, 1965.
46. This account is drawn largely from Embassy New Delhi's memorandum for the record, "Defection of Svetlana Allilouyeva," March 15, 1967, Box 326, Bowles Papers. It was prepared by Richard Celeste and approved by Bowles.
47. CB letter to Jha, March 10, 1967, in ibid.

48. Author's interview with David H. Blee, to whom Bowles had passed this story.
49. See *New York Times* of November 24, 1984, and April 19, 1986. Svetlana spelled out her problems and her views of life in the Soviet Union in a long interview which appeared in the *New York Times* on May 18, 1986.

18. Southeast Asia as Seen from New Delhi

1. CB memorandum to Kennedy, "Recommendations for a Fresh Approach to the Vietnam Impasse," March 7, 1963, *FRUS, 1961–1963*, vol. III, pp. 136–40.
2. New Delhi telegram 332, July 19, 1963, FOI document.
3. *Promises to Keep*, p. 416. See also the message Bowles sent to senior Washington officials from Manila on July 10, 1963, following his Saigon visit, *FRUS, 1961–1963*, vol. III, pp. 482–83.
4. CB letter to McGeorge Bundy, July 19, 1963, ibid., p. 519.
5. Bowles apparently used the CIA "back channel" from time to time to send messages to senior Washington officials on Vietnam or to relay his ideas on other sensitive matters. With a few exceptions, these messages are unavailable.
6. CB letter to Humphrey, January 24, 1964, Box 331, Bowles Papers.
7. CB diary, August 11, 1964, Box 395, Bowles Papers.
8. New Delhi telegram 1936, January 9, 1965, Box 129, NSF, LBJ Library.
9. New Delhi telegram 2676, March 24, 1965, in ibid.
10. New Delhi telegrams 2919 and 2922, both April 15, 1965, FOI documents.
11. CB memorandum to Bill Moyers, July 27, 1965, Box 334, Bowles Papers.
12. CB diary, January 29, 1966, Box 395, Bowles Papers.
13. See, for example, New Delhi telegram 1434, November 12, 1964, FOI document.
14. CB diary, December 31, 1964, Box 395, Bowles Papers.
15. "Talking Points for the President's Meeting with Mrs. Indira Gandhi, March 1966," Box 9, Confidential File, LBJ Library.
16. State Department telegram 1649, March 5, 1966, to New Delhi, FOI document. When Vice President Humphrey visited India in February 1966, soon after Indira Gandhi became prime minister, he was told in a personal cable from Secretary Rusk: "The President wants you to be very firm with Mrs. Gandhi about the lukewarm posture the Indians have had concerning Vietnam and also about their failure to carry out their ICC responsibilities with any real forcefulness. He feels that the immense assistance that the U.S. has provided to India over a long period of time, and particularly in our food and other commitments at present, entitles us to considerably more understanding and support than we have received from New Delhi. He sees India as guilty of a double standard whereby they seek U.S. support against Chinese pressure on their own frontiers but fail to react to the same threat in Southeast Asia" (State Department telegram 1498, February 14, 1966, to New Delhi, FOI document).
   Humphrey recalled that at their meeting Mrs. Gandhi told him the American presence in Vietnam was important for India. She was concerned about Chinese support for North Vietnam. She explained to the vice president that he

would have to understand, however, that her public statements would necessarily be more neutral, and indeed critical of U.S. involvement, because of public opinion and political pressure within India. "Later," Humphrey recorded in his autobiography, "when I disclosed that conversation, she denied it, using the traditional dodge that I must have misunderstood what she had said. There had been no misunderstanding." Hubert H. Humphrey, *The Education of a Public Man* (Garden City, N.Y.: Doubleday, 1976), p. 333.

17. "Report of the Johnson-Gandhi meeting of March 28, 1966," Box 131, NSF, LBJ Library.

18. *New York Times,* March 30, 1966.

19. *Foreign Affairs Recorder,* July 1966.

20. Department of State telegram 4535, July 8, 1966, to New Delhi, Box 131, NSF, LBJ Library.

21. *Foreign Affairs Recorder,* August 1966.

22. Author's conversation with Freeman, November 1990.

23. CB diary, July 17, 1966, Box 395, Bowles Papers.

24. CB letter to Gandhi, July 18, 1966, Box 330, Bowles Papers.

25. *Promises to Keep,* p. 526, and CB diary, May 13, 1967, Box 395, Bowles Papers.

26. CB diary, May 28, 1967, in ibid.

27. Bowles's itinerary is drawn from Richard Celeste's account of the visit, Box 360, Bowles Papers, and from the author's interview with Celeste in January 1991.

28. CB letter to Johnson, August 13, 1966, Box 134, NSF, LBJ Library.

29. CB notes on visit to Southeast Asia, August 14, 1966, Box 343, Bowles Papers.

30. USIS New Delhi press release, August 17, 1966.

31. CB telegram to Johnson, December 30, 1966 (unnumbered), Box 131, NSF, LBJ Library. Department of State telegram 118865, January 14, 1967, in ibid. Memorandum from Department of State Executive Secretary Benjamin Reid to National Security Advisor Walt W. Rostow, January 12, 1967, in ibid.

32. CB memorandum to Johnson, February 27, 1967, Box 4, Files of Robert W. Komer, NSF, LBJ Library. New Delhi back-channel message, March 15, 1967, in ibid. CB letters to Johnson, March 15 and May 18, 1967, Box 332, Bowles Papers.

33. Komer message to CB, March 18, 1967, Box 4, Files of Robert W. Komer, NSF, LBJ Library.

34. Komer message to Johnson, March 6, 1967, in ibid.

35. Johnson letter to CB, July 19, 1967, Box 332, Bowles Papers.

36. CB letter to Humphrey, May 25, 1967, in ibid.

37. Johnson, *The Vantage Point,* pp. 408–9. The Bowles proposal was sent in a telegram from New Delhi on March 18, 1968 (Box 132, NSF, LBJ Library).

38. CB letter to Humphrey, July 21, 1968, Box 332, Bowles Papers. For some interesting observations on Bowles's reluctance to disclose publicly his position on Vietnam, see the Oral History interviews of Embassy Deputy Chief of Mission William Weathersby (who succeeded Joseph N. Greene, Jr., in 1967) and Counselor for Cultural Affairs Robert R. R. Brooks, both in Box 398, Bowles Papers.

39. *New York Times,* January 4, 1968.

40. *Promises to Keep,* p. 577.
41. Author's interview with Herbert D. Spivack, October 1990.
42. Press briefing, George Christian, January 4, 1968, Box 84, Name File: "Chester Bowles," WHCF, LBJ Library.
43. *New York Times,* January 4, 1968.
44. The discussion of the meetings which follows is based largely on Embassy New Delhi's May 20, 1968, report of the mission drafted by John W. Shirley (FOI document, also in Box 343, Bowles Papers) and the author's interviews with Shirley and Spivack, both members of Bowles's party.
45. *Washington Post,* December 29, 1967.
46. *Promises to Keep,* p. 578.
47. New Delhi telegram 8395, January 12, 1968, FOI document.
48. *Promises to Keep,* p. 579.
49. See Bernard K. Gordon, "Shadow over Angkor," *Asian Survey,* January 1969, pp. 58ff.
50. *New York Times,* January 18, 1968.
51. CB diary, February 20, 1968, Box 395, Bowles Papers.

19. "Only the Historians Can Determine"

1. Bowles was bemused at the good impression Nixon had made on him. He had never met Nixon before. "To our astonishment," he recorded in his diary after the former vice president's April 1967 visit, "we found him responsible, cooperative, curious. . . . I doubt that he has changed much inside, but I admit that it was a relief to be able to communicate with him. He even asked what he could say that would be helpful to me with the press" (CB diary, May 13, 1967, Box 395, Bowles Papers). Bowles concluded an enthusiastic letter to Rusk about the visit with a postscript: "I am not planning to vote for Nixon" (CB letter to Rusk, April 27, 1967, Box 336, Bowles Papers).
2. CB diary, April 16, 1967, Box 395, Bowles Papers.
3. Ibid., November 21, 1965.
4. CB letter to Reston, September 2, 1966, Box 335, Bowles Papers.
5. CB memorandum to Rogers, March 1969 (not otherwise dated), Box 336, Bowles Papers.
6. Personal recollection of the author, who was present.
7. *Promises to Keep,* p. 367.
8. CB Oral History interview (1970), JFK Library.
9. *Promises to Keep,* p. 587.
10. *New Dimensions,* p. 383. Indian Ambassador to the United States K. Shankar Bajpai, the son of Bowles's old friend and colleague Sir G. S. Bajpai, quoted this passage in his remarks at the memorial service held for Bowles in the Yale chapel in June 1986.
11. CB diary, March 21, 1965.
12. Galbraith made these comments in the eulogy he delivered at Bowles's memorial service.
13. Ball, *The Past Has Another Pattern,* p. 170.

Index

Schaetzel, J. Robert, and Schaetzel Shitlist, 191, 358n25

Schaffer, Howard B., 365n12

Schlesinger, Arthur, Jr., 119, 137, 204, 350n8; and Finletter group, 138, 140; presidential adviser, 203; and Bay of Pigs, 206, 207; on Bowles in State Dept., 222–223

Schoenbaum, Thomas, 183, 184

Second Five Year Plan (1956–61), 132, 134, 169; accomplishments of, 243

Secretary of state: Bowles's ambition for, 137, 151, 182; possible deal with Kennedy, 166–167, 176–177; opposition to Bowles as, 192

Seely-Brown, Horace, 152

Seymour, Charles, 9

Shannon, James, 20

Sharon, John, 224

Shastri, Lal Bahadur, 251, 263, 268; visit to U.S. postponed, 265–266; death of, 251, 271; on agriculture, 280; Bowles on, 288–289; on Vietnam, 304

Sheffield Scientific School (Yale), 8

Shirley, John, 312, 365n12

Shirley, Katherine Horberg, 365n12

Shridharani, Krishanlal, 55

Shriver, Sargent, 172, 183

Shuster, George, 340n34

Sidey, Hugh, 202, 224

Sihanouk, Prince Norodom, 310–311; meetings with Bowles, 312–314

Sind, 367n47

Singh, Swaran, 268

Sino-Indian War (1962), 239, 327; and U.S., 244; and Kashmir, 245. *See also* China, India

Smith, H. Alexander, 39, 40

Smith, Margaret Chase, on Bowles's nomination, 40

Smith, Walter Bedell, 96, 97

Snow, Wilbert, 19

Snyder, John, 17

Son Sann, 312

Sorensen, Theodore, 166, 167, 172, 226–227, 232, 363n19

South Asia, *see* individual countries

Southeast Asia: Bowles's visits to, 91, 235, 306–307; Bowles on security of, 91, 210; Bowles on policy for, 234–236, 302–315; Peace Charter for, 234; Kennedy on, 245. *See also* individual countries

Southeast Asia Treaty Organization (SEATO), 98, 211, 348n10

Soviet Union, 36; in World War II, 30; and India, 49, 72, 109; and China, 81, 128–129, 181, 209, 237; and Korean War, 81, 82, 89; and Pakistan, 111; in Near East, 160; and Third World, 121–122, 132; and Southeast Asia, 210, 237–238; loan for Bokaro mill, 254; military assistance to India, 256; and Vietnam, 305; on ICC, 314

Spivack, Herbert, 310, 311

Stages of Economic Growth, The (Walt Rostow), 285

Stalin, Josef, 49, 143

Stalin, Svetlana (Svetlana Iosifovna), 297–301

State Department, 225, 227; Bowles's refusal of job in, 32; Rusk in, 197–201; appointment of ambassadors, 189–192; Bowles on top-level positions in, 192–196; Bowles on deputy under secretary for political affairs, 193; and Kennedy, 202; organization of, 224, 357n13. *See also* Secretary of state

Stebbins, Dorothy (Mrs. Chester Bowles), 13. *See also* Bowles, Dorothy Stebbins

Stebbins, Henry, 106

Steere, Loyd, 66

Stephansky, Ben, 191

Stevenson, Adlai, 8, 20, 113, 236–237; Bowles's relations with, 137–138, 141–142, 142–143, 164; on foreign policy, 140–145, 197, 217, 353n21; nomination of, 144; disagreement with Bowles, 164–165, 166, 352n12; candidate in 1960, 171, 173; and secretary of state, 175–176, 184; ambassador to U.N., 186; support for Bowles, 223, 225

Stevenson, William, 190

Stilwell, Gen. Joseph W., 182

Stone, Edward Durrell, 247

Stone, Galen, 365n12

Straight, Michael, 116

Stuart, R. Douglas, 28, 29

Subramaniam, C.: on agricultural reform, 279–280, 281; "Rome agreement," 280, 286; and devaluation, 286; and Indira Gandhi, 293